RECOVERY OF THE LOST ATLANTIC CABLE.
SEPT. 1ST., 1866.

(From the painting by Robert Dudley, by permission of Sir Daniel F. Gooch, Bart.)

SOCIAL ENGLAND

A Record of the Progress of the People

IN RELIGION, LAWS, LEARNING, ARTS, INDUSTRY, COMMERCE,
SCIENCE, LITERATURE AND MANNERS, FROM THE EARLIEST
TIMES TO THE PRESENT DAY

EDITED BY

H. D. TRAILL, D.C.L.

SOMETIME FELLOW OF ST. JOHN'S COLLEGE, OXFORD

AND

J. S. MANN, M.A.

SOMETIME FELLOW OF TRINITY COLLEGE, OXFORD

46048.

VOLUME VI.—SECTION II
WITH AN ADDITIONAL CHAPTER BY H. R. WHATES

NEW YORK: G. P. PUTNAM'S SONS

LONDON: CASSELL AND COMPANY, LIMITED

1909

CONTENTS.

vi CONTENTS.

LIST OF PLATES.

———•◇•———

(Brief Notes on some of these will be found with those on the remaining Illustrations.)

NOTES TO ILLUSTRATIONS.

VOLUME VI.—SECTION II.

Punch, April 20, 1867. By Sir John Tenniel. The resolutions were dropped on February 26, after a meeting of Liberal members had decided to vote for an amendment urging the Government to proceed by Bill. The "dual vote," a provision giving a second vote to everyone qualified by two years' residence and the payment of 20s. in direct taxation, was dropped April 1. The safeguard involved in "personal rating" was also eventually lost. The idea was to keep out the small occupiers who "compounded" or paid rates through their landlord, but "compounding" was abolished, and they were let in. The abolition, however, produced such inconvenience that the practice was restored in the following year, though the compounding voters did not lose their votes.

The phrase is Lord Derby's. The Bill received the Royal Assent, August 15, 1867.

Mr. Gladstone prompted by Palmerston's ghost. Appended is an extract from a speech delivered by him while the Conference was sitting: "I have been told that Lord Palmerston always looked on the neutralisation of the Black Sea as an arrangement that might be maintained for a limited number of years, but which it was impossible to maintain permanently."

The Cyprus Convention, signed June 4, but not published till the end of July, provided that Great Britain should hold and administer Cyprus for the Sultan and defend him against attack, he engaging to reform his Government. The island was to be given up to the Porte if Russia retired from Batoum, Ardahan, and Kars. Lord Beaconsfield's return produced an extraordinary demonstration of enthusiasm in London, but the worthlessness of Cyprus was soon discovered.

The *Times*, which kept up the old tradition that it represented the best public opinion of England, had been (like most people) unprepared for the sweeping Liberal victory in 1880. Its articles, just after the result became clear, laid stress on the declared intention of the Liberal leaders to maintain the chief results of their opponent's policy. On April 16 it declared that, after a general election, "the

instinct of the comprehensive changes due to Englishmen, whatever
their party, is to await with impartial judgment the conduct of
the incoming statesmen," and that the changes would be mostly in
domestic politics.

the Commons and the electorate, and Mr. Gladstone was merely using the Royal prerogative to enforce their will against that of the Lords. The system of purchase was an abuse that had grown up at the end of the seventeenth century. and had been declared legal under Queen Anne. For a sketch of its history, *see* the *Annual Register*. 1871.

Captured in the Ashantee Expeditions under Lord Wolseley of 1873–4 and 1895 respectively.

Laing's Nek, just within the Natal border, a ridge connecting Majuba Hill with another hill to the east of it, was crossed by the principal road from Natal to the Transvaal, and was therefore occupied by the Boers (January 27, 1881). Their position gave them shelter, and could not be carried by a frontal attack, so after repulses on January 28 and February 8, Sir George Colley occupied Majuba Hill, commanding the Boer position. Part of the Boers, however, advanced on the hill, under cover of a fire from the rest, made their way to the summit, and drove the British troops into a saucer-like hollow just below it, firing down on them till they broke and fled. The British troops were exposed against the sky-line and offered an easy mark ; the Boers were partly protected by the steepness of the hill, and it was difficult to see them with sufficient distinctness to take aim. Bryce, *Impressions of South Africa*, pp. 365–369.

A twin-screw turret ship of 11,880 tons and 8,010 h.-p. She took part in the bombardment of Alexandria in 1882, and was sold out of the service for breaking up in 1903.

Still retained (1904) at Dartmouth for those cadets who have joined under the old system of naval instruction, of which the abolition was decreed at the end of 1902.

The *Excellent* here shown was a school of gunnery at Portsmouth until about 1888. The name was then transferred to a screw gunboat used for gunnery trials. The *Vernon* here shown was replaced as a torpedo school ship about 1886 by the *Donegal*, an old screw battleship of much larger size, which took her name.

This belongs to the period 1810–1830, but the anchor. compass, davits, boats, and after-skylight are later additions. She carries 14 guns and four swivels. Her length is 85 ft. and her tonnage 130 tons. *Catalogue* of the Naval Museum, South Kensington.

had a peculiar horror of Italian architecture, and of the gaudy quasi-classical decoration affected by many modern Roman Catholics. Ferrey, *Recollections of Pugin*, 1861.

THE GREAT EXHIBITION OF 1851, BY GEORGE WALLIS 625

The scheme was a development, due to the Prince Consort, of the national exhibitions held in France, and copied in England under the auspices of the Society of Arts in 1847–48. It occupied the part of Hyde Park between Prince's Gate and the Serpentine. The building was a parallelogram, 1,851 ft. long by 456 ft. wide in the broadest part, with a transept upwards of 400 ft. long and 72 ft. wide, intersecting it at right angles in the middle. The transept roof was 108 ft. high, to give room for some elms which were enclosed in it. The design, by Mr. (afterwards Sir Joseph) Paxton, was a development of the plan of a conservatory he had built for the Duke of Devonshire at Chatsworth, where he had been gardener, and is said to have been suggested by the structure of the leaf of the great Victoria Regia water-lily. The Exhibition was open from May 1 to Oct. 11, 1851. The total number of visitors was over 6,170,000, the highest number on any one day being 109,760. The Albert Memorial, which commemorates the Exhibition as well as its chief originator, is somewhat to the west of the actual site in Hyde Park. Thornbury, *Old and New London*, V., ch. iii. The building, as is well known, was re-erected, though with considerable alterations, as the Crystal Palace at Sydenham, but part was burnt down on Dec. 30, 1866, and not restored.

OPENING BY QUEEN VICTORIA OF THE EXHIBITION OF 1851 . . 627

By H. C. Selous. In the northern half of the transept and grouped around the throne were the Royal Commissioners, Her Majesty's Ministers, the Executive Committee, the Diplomatic Corps, the Lord Mayor and Aldermen, the Commissioners from foreign Powers, the architect, the contractors, etc. On the north side of the transept were the Archbishop of Canterbury with his chaplains, the Duke of Wellington, the Marquis of Anglesey, Mr. Cobden, and others. The Queen having taken up her position on the throne the report of the Royal Commission was read, she made an appropriate reply, and the Archbishop offered up a special prayer of thanksgiving, with a petition that the Exhibition might promote peace and goodwill among men. The Hallelujah Chorus was then sung by the united choirs of the Chapels Royal, St Paul's, and Westminster Abbey, strengthened by other singers, and a procession was then formed which traversed the Exhibition to the successive strains of an English, a French, and a German organ. The Queen then declared the exhibition open.

DRAWING OF THE CRYSTAL FOUNTAIN AT THE EXHIBITION OF 1851 . 628

The central ornament of the transept, made by Messrs. F. and C. Osler, of Birmingham. They had constructed large glass candelabra a few years previously, but this far surpassed all previous efforts. The principal dish was over 8 ft. in diameter, and weighed, before cutting, nearly a ton. Much difficulty was experienced, and much waste involved, nearly four tons of glass having been used. M. D. Wyatt, *Industrial Arts of the Nineteenth Century*.

CARPET SHOWING FALSE PRINCIPLES OF DESIGN 631

Schools of design had been established in England in 1840 in various provincial towns, and assisted with Government grants to a total amount of £7,000 or £8,000 per annum. After the Great Exhibition of 1851 a number of articles purchased by the Government from it were placed at Marlborough House, then unoccupied, as the nucleus of a Museum of Design. One room was made by Mr. (afterwards Sir Henry) Cole into a "Museum of False Principles" or "Chamber of Horrors," and filled with signal examples of bad taste, of which this carpet, in brilliant colours on a chocolate ground, was one. The Marlborough House collection was transferred to the South Kensington Museum when it was opened in 1857, but the "Chamber of Horrors" had been abolished in deference to the protests of the manufacturers of the objects it contained. Sir Henry Cole, *Fifty Years of Public Life*, I., 185.

SIDEBOARD SHOWN AT THE EXHIBITION OF 1851 631

Carved in oak from Herefordshire : its style is described as a "happy adaptation of the English revival of antique art most generally known under the name of Elizabethan" (M. D. Wyatt, *Industrial Arts of the Nineteenth Century*, II.). It was shown by Messrs. Jackson and Graham of London.

THE INTERIOR OF THE EXHIBITION OF 1862, BY E. WALKER . . 633

Two vast domes of glass 260 ft. high and 160 ft. in diameter—larger than the dome of St. Peter's at Rome—were connected by a nave 800 ft. long, 100 ft. high, and 80 ft. wide, lighted by windows like the clerestory of a cathedral. Laterally, the domes opened into spacious transepts, 692 ft. long and 80 ft. wide, and the nave into side aisles and galleries, roofed with glass. All this structure covered sixteen acres. Besides this there were two annexes of no architectural pretensions containing machinery. The nave was parallel to Cromwell Road ; the transepts ran along Exhibition Road and Queen's Gate. The principal entrance led from Exhibition Road to the eastern dome. The floors under the domes being somewhat raised above those of the nave and transepts, striking views of the interior were afforded. The exhibition was far from attaining the success of its predecessor. The building was designed by Captain Fowke, R.E. Much of its material, rearranged, was used in the construction of the first Alexandra Palace on Muswell Hill, which was opened on May 24, 1873, but burnt down on June 9 of that year, and re-erected in 1875. Thornbury, *Old and New London*, V., chap. iii. and xxxiii. *Annual Register*, 1862.

FLORA : DESIGN FOR TAPESTRY BY SIR E. BURNE-JONES AND WILLIAM MORRIS 637

TAPESTRY REPRESENTING A SCENE FROM THE MORTE D'ARTHUR. . 638

Executed by the Windsor Tapestry Works, after a design by H. A. Bone. It illustrates "Sir Galahad in the Castel of Maydens," Malory, "Morte d'Arthur," Book XIII., c. xiv.-xv. Sir Galahad, "whose strength was as the strength of ten, because his heart was pure," has just driven off, single-handed, a band of seven lawless knights who had held the castle and oppressed its inmates : they are seen escaping in the background. He salutes a lady, who offers him a horn of ivory, that he may blow it and announce their deliverance. An old man offers him the keys ; a sister of some religious order waves the good news to someone in the distance ; the watchdog, recognising Sir Galahad instinctively as a friend, sleeps. Sir Galahad's costume is Frankish, his weapons in part Roman : the architecture Romanesque, with Roman details, such as might be appropriate to the period of the legend (fifth century A.D.), but as the romance is mediæval, some anachronisms are designedly introduced. [Abridged from a description privately printed.] This tapestry is at Aldenham House, Herts. The Windsor Tapestry Works were instituted, not as a commercial enterprise, about 1877, the Duke of Albany being President, but were closed in 1888. The workmen were French from Aubusson ; the tapestries were worked from side to side, like the Arras and Morris

Master of Trinity College, Cambridge, 1866–1886 ; well known for his exceptional powers of sarcasm. When he saw this portrait, he is reported to have said, "Is it possible that I regard all mankind with such contempt ? "

Papyrus cviii. Bought from a dealer in 1847 at Thebes, Egypt ; probably from a tomb. All the fragments of the speeches of Hyperides or Hypereides, the Attic orator, of which others were discovered in 1856, are on papyrus and among the oldest Greek MSS. extant. Their discovery was the first of a series of similar discoveries of other early papyrus MSS., of which the long lost treatise by Aristotle on the Constitution of Athens, the mimes of Herondas, and the poems of Bacchylides, all revealed to the modern world in the last ten years of the nineteenth century, are the most notable. These fragments are probably of the first or second century B.C., and are mounted in glazed frames.

The " Elgin marbles" consist of the frieze and other sculptures from the Parthenon, and of various sculptures and antiquities from Attica and other parts of Hellas. Thomas Bruce, seventh Earl of Elgin (1766–1841), when appointed Ambassador to Turkey in 1800, decided to take Italian artists and modellers to copy the ancient sculptures then within the Turkish dominions. In 1801 he obtained leave not only to erect scaffolding round the Parthenon, but to take away any pieces of stone with inscriptions or figures, and in 1803 he began to exercise this power, seeing that the marbles were running great risk of injury. He was savagely attacked by Byron ("The Curse of Minerva") and others, and the value of his collection questioned. He therefore silenced such criticism by opening it to the public. In 1816, on the recommendation of a House of Commons Committee, it was bought by the nation for £35,000 ; he had spent in all about £74,000.

About 12 ft. high and 12 ft. long, forming, with a companion, a portal to a chamber round which were sculptured figures of deities or priests. Obtained by Sir A. H. Layard in 1849. Assur-nasir-pal reigned 885–860 B.C. The head indicates knowledge, the body strength, the wings ubiquity. Layard, *Nineveh* (ed. 1867), p. 53.

De la Rue's methods were described by him to the British Association in 1859, and also in the "British Journal of Photography" of 1859 and 1860. Proctor, *The Moon*, p. 156.

Described by Mr. Warren de La Rue, its leader, in the Bakerian Lecture, *Philos. Trans.* 1862. The expedition joined others, sent out by the British Government in H.M.S. *Himalaya*. Rivabellosa is seventy miles from Bilbao.

Taken at Sohag, Egypt, May 17, 1882. The results are described in *Philos. Trans.*, Vol. 175 (1884). "The body of the moon appears . . . bordered by a well-defined black line, out of which the prominences are seen to rise." A "luminous streak" was seen during totality, and revealed by the photograph as a comet. In recognition of the hospitality of the then Khedive Tewfik it was called after him, though it was "not expected to be heard of any more." In view of the history of Egypt from 1882 onwards, this is a fine stroke of unconscious humour.

Founded in 1856 ; used for obtaining spectroscopic observations, and photographs of the stellar spectra, the solar corona, etc. An account by the founder is given in the *Nineteenth Century*, June, 1897, and in his *Atlas of Stellar Space*. The observatory was built on pillars to get a freer horizon, and consisted of a 12-ft. dome, replaced in 1870 by an 18-ft. drum.

Described in Sir W. Huggins's *Atlas of Stellar Space*, Plate III. The lines marked H, with a Greek character appended, are hydrogen lines ; that marked 3727 represents an unknown substance, "nebulum" ; that marked 3868 may possibly be helium.

Possibly a star-cluster in process of development from a nebula—a process of which the Pleiades forms a more advanced example. Clerke, *The System of the Stars*, p. 281. This photograph had 37 minutes' exposure in the focus of a 3-ft. silver-on-glass mirror. *Monthly Notices* of the Royal Astronomical Society, xliii., p. 255.

S*

PAGE

THE VRYNWY DAM 742

    1,255 ft. long and 60 ft. high, makes an artificial lake (on the site of a village), whence water is supplied to Liverpool by a two-mile tunnel and an aqueduct 67 miles long.

THE MANCHESTER SHIP CANAL AT EASTHAM 743

    This canal (constructed 1887–1894), from Eastham on the Mersey to Manchester, is 35½ miles long and averages 172 ft. wide on the surface. Besides the locks at Eastham, there are four sets between them and Manchester, overcoming a total rise of 60 ft. 6 in.

BESSEMER STEEL WORKS 746, 747

    An improved plant, saving much labour and dating from about 1891. The molten cast iron is taken up in a truck by a lift and poured into the converter, where air is blown through it (*see* text, p. 749), and thence into a ladle carried by a circular crane, whence again it is emptied into a ladle carried by the central crane of the casting pit. From this it is run into the ingot moulds, but the ingots, as soon as sufficiently set, are lifted by a crane into a soaking pit, or closed firebrick chamber, the invention of Mr. Gjers, introduced about 1882. In this the ingot can cool more equally throughout, so that it can be rolled at once instead of requiring re-working as previously. (*Catalogue ut sup.*)

SIEMENS's STEEL APPARATUS 748

    An apparatus for the "direct" production of steel by heating a mixture of iron ore and fine coal in a chamber containing reducing gases. This chamber, shown on the spectator's left, consists of a lined wrought iron cylinder which can be slowly rotated. Currents of gas and air are passed into this and form a flame in its interior. The ore is thus smelted, and the rotation of the chamber causes the grains of iron to collect into a "bloom." This is carried to the gas reverberatory furnace, seen on the extreme left, and is there converted into steel. According to Mr. Andrew Carnegie, in his paper in the *Nineteenth Century—A Review of Progress* (1901), the Siemens open-hearth process tends to predominate over the Bessemer.

THE *THERMOPYLÆ* 749

    Built in Aberdeen 1869. Made the "record" passage to Australia, and various other "record" trips. Disputes with the *Sir Lancelot* the honour of being the fastest sailing vessel ever built. *See* text, p. 450.

WOMEN AND CHILDREN IN THE COAL MINES 750, 751

    These drawings have official authority, being given in Blue Books of 1842 (reports of Commissions). They created a great sensation in the country. The cases are taken from Lancashire, Yorkshire, and Wales.

DIAGRAM OF HARTLEY COLLIERY 754

    Illustrated London News, February 1, 1862. For ventilating purposes, the single shaft was divided by a partition, as shown. The engine beam missed the cage in its fall, but the timber and *débris* dislodged, killed some of the men and blocked the shaft. The water rose in the pit and forced up the carbonic acid gas. The men, who were working in the "low main" (the third cross-gallery from the top), climbed up a wire rope ladder in the shaft on the extreme left, and were found suffocated in the "yard seam."

MODEL SHOWING METHODS OF GETTING COAL 759

    Showing two forms of the "board and pillar" and two of the "long wall" method. The arrows show air currents. *See* text, p. 757.

accidentally inflicted by his father's gun at the outset of his career ; George Odger (1820–1877) was an active Trade Unionist and Reform Leaguer of 1866, and frequently attempted, but without success, to enter Parliament as a Labour member ; Alexander Macdonald, who began his career as a boy in a coal-pit, was the earliest Labour M.P. (1874). Mr. Burt, M.P., and Mr. George Howell, ex-M.P. and a well-known writer on labour questions, need no further description.

moderate cost, and to train its members in the doctrine and discipline of the Church of England. About £45,000 was spent at the outset on the site, buildings, and in initial expenses, and a superb chapel was subsequently given by Mr. A. Gibbs. Further buildings have since been added. The material is brick, and the buildings were designed by Butterfield. They were opened in October, 1870.

Lord Frederick Cavendish, who was driving on a car to the Vice-regal Lodge. overtook Mr. Burke, dismissed the car and joined him. Near the Phœnix monument they were overtaken by a car with four men, who jumped down, stabbed them, and drove off. The murderers did not know the new Chief Secretary by sight, and killed him merely because he was in company with Mr. Burke, the Under-Secretary, who was the real object of attack. The scuffle was actually seen by a passer-by at some distance and by Earl Spencer, the Viceroy, from a window of the Viceregal Lodge, but they did not recognise the victims, and thought it was merely horseplay among roughs. Five men, members of a secret society, the "Invincibles," were hanged for the murder and fifteen sent to penal servitude. James Carey, who turned Queen's evidence, was smuggled out of the country, but was followed and murdered by an emissary of the society, named O'Donnell, on a Cape mail steamer, July 29, 1883.

A MS. written at the end of the fourteenth century : "a series of disconnected collectanea, the stock-in-trade of some professional shanachy" (*cf.* text, Vol. III., p. 406). It contains various legends, some Irish, others connected with Biblical personages, homilies, moral tales, maxims, etc. The drawing given is a plan of the House of Midchuairt, or banqueting-hall of King Cormac's palace at Tara Hill. In the centre are marked three fireplaces (*Tene*), a vat (*dabach*, of mead ?), a candle and a lamp ; then an open space, with a door (marked) opening into it. The compartments represent seats, the station of the sitters and the portions of meat allotted to them being specified. At the top of the diagram (the back of the hall) are the servants (distributors, cupbearers, herdsmen) ; at the right and left sides of the door respectively are stationed "the king's doorkeepers, and backs (of the animal) for them ; the king's fools, and chines for them." The first four divisions on the outside row to the left, beginning from the top, accommodate "horsemen and stewards, chines for them ; harpers and tympanists, pig's shoulder for them ; Brehons, steaks for them ; professor of literature and Tanist professor, chines for them." Augurs and druids, engravers, shoemakers, trumpeters, and builders are also among the diners A similar diagram, with different details, is preserved in the Book of Glenda-lough. The total number of diners is 116. The description of the king's seat implies that it was placed three-fourths of the way up the hall, *i.e.* between two of the fireplaces. Petrie, *Antiquities of Tara Hill, Dublin*, 1839 ; also in *Proceedings of Royal Irish Academy*, Vol. XVIII. ; Joyce, *Social History of Ancient Ireland*, II., c. xxi.

Lat. 70° 44′ N. ; from a drawing by Captain Sir John Ross. The previous winter had been unusually severe, and many whalers were beset in the ice. The expedition was only absent six months.

Of the relics figured on p. 827, 1 are weapons and implements made by the Eskimo from iron and wood obtained from Franklin's ships ; 2, is a pemmican canister marked E (*Erebus*) ; 3, powder and shot flasks ; 4, goggles, to protect the eyes from the glare caused by the ice ; 5, sextant found at Ross Cairn, Point Victory, in 1859, by Capt. McClintock ; 6, dipping needle ; 7, boat sheet block and hook.

CHAPTER XXIV.

THE SUCCESSION OF THE DEMOCRACY. 1865-1885.

On the death of Lord Palmerston, Earl Russell inevitably became Prime Minister. Just as inevitably he forced upon the Cabinet a Reform Bill that many of its members disliked. It reduced the borough franchise from £10 to £7, the county franchise from £50 to £14, and gave lodgers the vote. The moderate Liberals promptly took alarm, and under the leadership of Lord Grosvenor[1] and Mr. Robert Lowe,[2] formed what Mr. Bright called a new " Cave of Adullam." After carrying the second reading by a majority of five, Ministers, on June 18th, 1866, were beaten on Lord Dunkellin's amendment substituting rating for rental as the basis of the borough franchise. They resigned ; and thus Lord Russell's long official career came to an end.

Once more Lord Derby was called upon to form a Ministry with a minority behind it. Mr. Disraeli was, of course, his Chancellor of the Exchequer ; Lord Stanley[3] went to the Foreign office ; Lord Carnarvon to the Colonial ; and Lord Cranborne[4] became Secretary for India. The leader of the House of Commons saw clearly enough that a measure of Reform could not be avoided. The Radicals were agitating, and before the Government had been many weeks in office the disorderly contingent of a public meeting had pushed down the railings of Hyde Park. Mr. Disraeli next year at first attempted to proceed by way of resolution, but his tactics were vigorously resisted by the Opposition ; and a series of resolutions, proposed by him and explained in debate as foreshadowing the introduction of a £6 franchise Bill, had eventually to be withdrawn, February 25th, 1867. A larger measure of Reform was then submitted to, and adopted by, the Cabinet, with the exception of Lords Carnarvon and Cranborne and General Peel, who retired from the Government.

LLOYD C. SANDERS. Political History. The Second Russell Ministry.

The Third Derby Ministry.

---

[1] Afterwards Duke of Westminster.   [2] Afterwards Viscount Sherbrooke.
[3] The next Earl of Derby.   [4] Afterwards Marquis of Salisbury.

Their resignation led to a hastily concocted compromise, known through the subsequent indiscretion of Sir John Pakington as the "Ten Minutes Bill," which, however, was never introduced into Parliament.   There was nothing for it but to introduce a Household Suffrage Bill, which, after long and bitter debate, **The Second Reform Bill.** was carried.   In the following year (1868) the Irish and Scotch Reform Acts supplemented the English measure.   In their final shape these Acts bestowed the franchise on all male householders paying poor-rate in English and Scotch boroughs; in Ireland there was a rating limit of £4.   In the counties votes were given to occupiers of £10 in England, and £14 in Scotland.   Eleven boroughs were disfranchised, and thirty-five lost a member.   These seats were partly presented to Lancashire and Yorkshire.   Two new London constituencies, Chelsea and Hackney, received two members; Leeds, Liverpool, Manchester, Birmingham, and Glasgow, had a third member; Salford, Merthyr, and Dundee, a second; ten new boroughs, London University and the Scotch Universities, in pairs, one member.   By a rather artificial contrivance, the minorities were given a chance in large boroughs and in some counties, through a provision (abolished in 1885) by which an elector could vote for only two candidates where there were three seats.

The Fenians. The Liberal party was in want of a cry; it was supplied them by an Irish revolutionary organisation known as the Fenians.   Their conspiracy had been suppressed by the Russell Ministry through the timely arrests of Stephens, a "head centre," and O'Donovan Rossa, and the suspension of the Habeas Corpus Act.   They effected, however, isolated risings and outrages, such as a ludicrous invasion of Canada by a disorganised rabble in 1866, and, in the following year, a plot (which came to nothing) for an attack on Chester Castle, the rescue of two Fenian prisoners and murder of Police-sergeant Brett at Manchester, and, finally, the destruction of the wall of Clerkenwell Prison.

The Irish Church Resolutions. The last two crimes, as Mr. Gladstone afterwards explained, brought the disestablishment of the Irish Church "within the region of practical politics."   In April, 1868, he carried against the Government the first of a series of resolutions in favour of that change, and followed it up with a Suspensory Bill, which the House of Lords rejected.   Mr. Disraeli,

THEY'RE SAVED! THEY'RE SAVED!

"DROPPING THE SAFEGUARDS" IN THE REFORM BILL OF 1867.

(Reproduced by special permission of the Proprietors of "Punch.")

(See "Essence," p. 155).

become Prime Minister through Lord Derby's retirement, refused to recommend a dissolution until he had carried his Irish and Scotch Reform Bills. The reckoning came in November, 1868, and the Liberals found themselves with a majority of 120.

Canada. Before his resignation, Lord Carnarvon, with the able assistance of the Canadian statesman, Sir John Macdonald, had laid the foundations of a united Canada. His Enabling Act placed the Dominion under a Governor-General appointed by the Crown, with a Cabinet responsible to Parliament, of which the House of Commons was elected by a low suffrage, while the Senate consisted of life members. The provinces retained their local legislatures and executives. The Union was promptly joined by Ontario, Quebec, Nova Scotia, and New Brunswick, and by 1872 it was completed by the accession of Manitoba, British Columbia, and Prince Edward's Island. The

Abyssinia. Abyssinian War was forced upon the country by King Theodore, who refused to set free some British prisoners. Sir Robert Napier (Lord Napier of Magdala), with 12,000 English and Indian troops, thrust his way through a most difficult country, took Magdala, and drove Theodore to suicide. At the Foreign Office Lord Stanley had kept England neutral during the war between Prussia and Austria, and at its close he averted a serious crisis by arranging the neutrality of Luxemburg.

The First Gladstone Ministry. Mr. Gladstone formed a Ministry extremely strong in ability, though composed of inharmonious elements. Mr. Lowe became Chancellor of the Exchequer; Lord Clarendon, Foreign Secretary; Mr. Cardwell, Secretary for War; the Duke of Argyll, Secretary for India; Mr. Childers, First Lord of the Admiralty. Radicalism was represented by Mr. Bright, as President of the Board of Trade; and Mr. W. E. Forster, as Vice-President of the Council. Even the staunchest friends of

Disestablishment of the Irish Church. the Irish Church perceived it to be doomed. It represented the faith of a minority alien in origin, and it had put off reform until too late. Mr. Gladstone carried his Bill through the Commons by huge majorities. In the Lords, Bishop Magee made a name for himself among Parliamentary orators in defence of a cause that he knew to be lost. The second reading was passed, but the measure was wholly transformed by amendment after amendment. These the Government declined to accept, and a deadlock seemed imminent. Diplomacy and good sense, however, effected a compromise at the last moment possible. The Irish Church received, in the end, quite adequate terms. It was disestablished, its courts abolished, and its bishops deprived of their seats in the House of Lords. But churches, cathedrals, and parsonages were transferred to the Church of Ireland as a corporation, together with all private

THE LEAP IN THE DARK, AUGUST, 1867.
(Reproduced by special permission of the Proprietors of "Punch.")

endowments subsequent to 1660. Altogether the Church received a sum of over ten millions sterling. The clergy obtained full compensation for their life interests, while the surplus was set aside for objects that were not sufficiently defined to be really useful.

With undiminished vigour Mr. Gladstone proceeded, in 1870, to reform the Irish Land Laws. The Government had the reports of numerous Commissions to guide it, while Ministry after Ministry had made half-hearted efforts to readjust the balance between landlord and tenant. It was confronted by an excess of competition which forced rents up to extravagant prices. Contrary

The Irish Land Act.

to the English practice, the tenant, and not the landlord, put up farm buildings and made improvements. The stories of rack-renting and evicting landlords were proved to be flagrantly exaggerated ; some of that class, however, used their powers harshly. In the North, the Ulster custom " permitted " the sale of the goodwill of a farm by the outgoing to an incoming tenant, but it was not recognised by law. The Act, with the accompanying Peace Preservation Act, gave peace to Ireland for some six or seven years. The chief innovations were compensation for " disturbance " and for improvements. Ejectment for non-payment of rent was not reckoned as a disturbance except where the annual charge was under £15, and the court certified that it was exorbitant. Improvements, other than permanent buildings and reclamation made twenty years before claim, did not entitle to compensation. The Ulster tenant-right was legalised, and some purchase clauses authorised the advance of money by the Board of Works for facilitating sales. They proved, however, for the most part inoperative.

The Education Act. In that same session Mr. Forster placed elementary education on a national basis. In the previous year his Endowed Schools Act freed the grammar schools from obsolete conditions, in spite of the clamour raised by vested interests. His Elementary Education Bill met with still more bitter opposition from the Birmingham League, which would be satisfied with nothing less than secular schools under local control. Mr. Forster, however, declined to meddle with the Voluntary schools where they supplied the needs of a district. Where they failed, the rate-payers and burgesses were empowered to start elected school boards, levy a rate, and enforce the attendance of children. After fierce wrangles a conscience-clause was inserted at the instance of Mr. Cowper-Temple by which the Bible should be taught in Board Schools, but no distinctive catechism or religious formularies. The age for compulsory attendance was to be from five to thirteen.

Army Reform. Mr. Cardwell's turn, as Secretary for War, came in 1871. In the course of two years he succeeded in abolishing the purchase of military commissions, in introducing the short-service system of enlistment, in creating territorial regiments, and placing the militia and volunteers directly under the generals commanding districts (p. 557). The abolition of purchase, however, was not

effected without a prodigious amount of turmoil.   Fiercely resisted
in the Commons, it seemed likely to succumb before the hostility
of the House of Lords.   Mr. Gladstone thereupon took the unusual course of employing a royal warrant to effect the change.

By this time the Gladstone Government had about outstayed **The Ballot
Act and
the Licens-
ing Bill.**
its welcome.   Mr. Lowe's budgets were too pedantic to be
popular ; some of the subordinate Ministers, notably Mr. Ayrton,
the First Commissioner of Works, covered themselves with
ridicule.   An appointment or two raised much unnecessary
scandal.   But the chief mistake of the Ministry consisted in an
excess of reforming zeal.   Mr. Bruce's[1] Licensing Bill of 1872 was
furiously opposed by the liquor trade, though it merely placed
some trifling restrictions on the sale of intoxicants.   Again, the
Ballot Bill was nearly wrecked in the Commons by Mr. Vernon
(afterwards Sir William) Harcourt and by Mr. Leatham, and was
freely amended in the Lords.   A quarrel between the two
Houses seemed imminent after the Duke of Richmond had
carried a clause making secret voting optional, but in the end
it was withdrawn.

Lord Granville's management of foreign affairs after the **Foreign
Affairs.**
death of Lord Clarendon could hardly be set down to the
credit side of the account.   The war between France and Germany took him completely by surprise, but he caused it to be
understood that any attempt to violate Belgian neutrality
would bring England into the field.   His attitude was not equally
dignified when Prince Gortschakoff seized the opportunity of a
general embroilment to repudiate the provision of the Treaty
of Paris which closed the Black Sea to ships of war.   The **The
Black Sea
Question.**
Foreign Secretary launched an empty protest, and, in March,
1871, summoned a conference in London, which simply
registered Russia's high-handed action.   The award of the
Geneva Tribunal, which was pronounced in the following year,
turned also to the disrepute of the Ministry.   Little allowance
was made for the circumstance that the envoys who arranged
the Treaty of Washington (May, 1871), whereby the United **The
"Alabama"
Claims.**
States agreed to submit their claims to arbitration, had been
despatched not by Lord Granville but by his predecessor, Lord
Stanley.   Again, the ruling-out of the monstrous indirect claims
did the Government little good.   The decision that Great Britain

[1 Mr. Bruce was afterwards created Lord Aberdare.]

T*

was to pay 15,000,000 dollars for failing to stop some Confederate cruisers was generally regarded as in excess of the offence.

The Irish University Bill, 1873. Mr. Gladstone produced his ill-fated Irish University Bill early in the session of 1873 (p. 882). Its purport was to set up an unsectarian university and to deprive Trinity College of much of its usefulness. Repudiated both by Irish Catholic members and independent Radicals like Mr. Fawcett, it suffered defeat on the second reading by three votes (287 to 284). Mr. Gladstone resigned, but Mr. Disraeli declined to form a Ministry, as he had "no matured policy to present to the country." Mr. Gladstone thereupon resumed the thankless task, and, to a certain extent, strengthened the Ministry by rearranging it.

The Judicature Act. The Lord Chancellor (Lord Selborne) carried out the judicial reforms advocated by Lord Cairns, through an Act which united the courts of law into a High Court of Justice, while retaining the House of Lords as a Court of Appeal, and harmonised the procedure of common law and equity (p. 546 *seqq.*). Despite this excellent innovation, and Mr. Fawcett's Act abolishing religious tests in Dublin University, the constituencies, whenever they had a chance, returned a Conservative. On February 5th, 1874, Mr. Gladstone abruptly announced the dissolution of Parliament, with a promise to abolish the income-tax. He was rewarded by a Conservative majority of fifty.

India. Lord Mayo's death at the hands of a native convict brought his great Viceroyalty of India to an end in February, 1872. He had decentralised finance, and given much impetus to public works. His successor, Lord Northbrook, had to contend with a famine in Lower Bengal, and proved quite equal to the emergency, though a worse visitation awaited the empire in 1876 and 1877. The trial of the Gaikwar of Baroda for an attempt to poison the British Resident ended in an unsatisfactory acquittal, but the Government felt justified in deposing him. **Ashanti.** A war with King Coffee Calcalli, of Ashanti, necessitated by his constant raids into the Gold Coast Colony, resulted in the capture of Coomassie by Sir Garnet Wolseley, and a hastily concluded treaty of peace.

Mr. Disraeli, having attained his own at last, formed a Ministry of experienced men of affairs. Lord Cairns was Lord

Chancellor; Sir S. Northcote, Chancellor of the Exchequer; The
Disraeli
Ministry. Lord Derby (formerly Lord Stanley), Foreign Secretary   Lord Salisbury (Lord Cranborne, p. 519), Secretary for India. Lord Carnarvon went to the Colonial Office again; Mr. Gathorne

THE INJUDICIOUS BOTTLE HOLDER, BY SIR JOHN TENNIEL.

(Reproduced by special permission of the Proprietors of "Punch.")

Hardy (afterwards Lord Cranbrook) became Secretary for War; and Mr. R. A. (afterwards Lord) Cross, Home Secretary.

The beginnings of the new Government were modest The Public
Worship
Act. enough. Much of the session was spent in amending its predecessor's Acts. A Scottish Church Patronage Act removed some of the anomalies of lay patronage, but did not heal the breach of thirty years. The Public Worship Regulation

Bill, on the other hand, engendered much Parliamentary heat. Introduced as a disciplinary measûre by the Archbishop of York, both Lord Shaftesbury and Lord Salisbury received it with unconcealed dislike. Interpreted by Mr. Disraeli as a device for " putting down Ritualism," it irritated the High Churchmanship of Mr. Gladstone, but filled Sir William Harcourt with a Protestant zeal not altogether according to knowledge. The Act was a failure; it merely made martyrdom the reward of eccentricity, and alienated the High Church party (p. 592).

Domestic Legislation.   Early in 1875 Mr. Gladstone abruptly resigned the leadership of the Opposition, that step being dictated " by his personal views as to the best method of passing the closing years of his life." Lord Hartington undertook the dreary duty, and the Government had matters pretty much its own way in Parliament. It passed several useful and unpretentious measures in the course of the next four sessions. Among them were the Agricultural Holdings Act, which made the presumption of law in favour of the tenant; the Merchant Shipping Act, which the energy of Mr. Plimsoll forced on the Ministry; Sir S. Northcote's Friendly Societies Act; and a number of social reforms for which Mr. Cross, a highly efficient Home Secretary, was responsible. They included a Public Health Act, a Labourers' Dwellings Act, and a Factory and Workshops Act. The Universities Act of 1877 was an important piece of legislation, which made provision for University purposes, especially the encouragement of natural science, out of college revenues, through the suppression of " idle Fellowships" (p. 850). The most controversial measure of those years was the Royal Titles Act, permitting the queen to assume the title of Empress of India. It brought up Mr. Lowe in his most bitter mood, but Mr. Disraeli held the advantage.

The Eastern Question.   Foreign politics, in 1875 and onwards, thrust home affairs into the background. The purchase of the Suez Canal shares from the embarrassed Khedive Ismail, though much criticised at the time, proved a most profitable investment. But the general condition of the Turkish Empire was more critical than the finances of the vassal State. The repudiation of half the national debt and the revolt of Herzegovina and Bosnia brought matters to a head. The Sultan, Abdul Aziz, disregarded the Andrassy Note, which had been signed by the Powers, until an outbreak at

Salonica caused the British, French, and German Governments to move their fleets into Turkish waters, and the reforming party, headed by Midhat Pasha, deposed him. Next year (May, 1876) came the Berlin Memorandum, to which Lord Derby declined to be a party, because it implied the right of the Powers to enforce reforms by armed intervention. The rebellion in Herzegovina and Bosnia smouldered on; Servia and Montenegro declared

Photo: Walker & Cockerell.

SIR STAFFORD HENRY NORTHCOTE, FIRST EARL OF
IDDESLEIGH, BY EDWIN LONG, R.A.

(National Portrait Gallery.)

war on Turkey; a movement in Bulgaria was repressed with hideous cruelty by the Turkish irregulars. When the news of the Bulgarian atrocities became known, an agitation swept the country from end to end, and drew Mr. Gladstone from his brief semi-retirement. A Conference met at Constantinople, with Lord Salisbury as our first Plenipotentiary, but, encouraged by some victories over the Servians, the new Sultan, Abdul Hamid, doggedly rejected its terms. In April, 1877, when a Protocol signed by the Powers seemed to have smoothed most difficulties

The Russo-Turkish War.

away, the Russian armies suddenly crossed the Turkish frontier, and carried everything before them, despite the heroic defence of Plevna by Osman Pasha. By the end of the year the way to Constantinople lay open to the Czar's troops. Lord Beaconsfield, however, declared at Guildhall that England was ready, if need were, for a second or third campaign. He sent the fleet to the Dardanelles, asked for a vote of credit of six millions, called out the reserves, and despatched Indian troops to Malta. Lord Carnarvon and Lord Derby resigned, and the latter was replaced by Lord Salisbury.

The Berlin Congress.

The Czar Alexander halted his forces, and concluded the Treaty of San Stefano with the Porte. The British Government insisted on its modification, declaring, in particular, that a " big Bulgaria," extending from the Danube to the Ægean, was inadmissible. After a period of extreme tension, Russia gave way, and the Congress of Berlin met in June, 1878, with Lord Beaconsfield, Lord Salisbury, and Lord Odo Russell as the British Plenipotentiaries. An agreement[1] had already been effected on the main points under dispute by Lord Salisbury and Count Schouvaloff. While the Congress was at work a separate Convention was arranged between England and Turkey, under which the former occupied Cyprus and promised to defend the Turkish dominions in Asia against attack, while the Sultan gave the familiar undertakings about reform. By the Treaty of Berlin the " big Bulgaria " was divided into two, the part north of the Balkans becoming an independent though tributary State, while the southern portion remained Turkish, with a Christian Governor and administrative home-rule.[2] Montenegro, Servia, and Roumania were declared independent, but the last was forced to exchange Bessarabia for the Dobrudscha with Russia. That Power obtained large acquisitions of territory in Asia, including Kars and Batoum, which was to remain a free port. Austria occupied Bosnia and Herzegovina; to Greece there was doled out a prospective rectification of frontier. The Sultan cheerily

[1 The publication of this in the *Globe* (June 14th), through a breach of confidence by a journalist temporarily employed at the Foreign Office, caused much excitement at the time.]

[2 The two were united in 1885. The part popularly known as Macedonia was given back to the Turks. A reformed scheme of administration was devised for it under the authority of the Powers, but was never put into effect.]

expressed his readiness to redress the grievances of his Christian subjects in Crete and Armenia.

Lord Beaconsfield returned home bringing, to use his own

"A BLAZE OF TRIUMPH"—THE CYPRUS CONVENTION, 1878.
(*Reproduced by special permission of the Proprietors of "Punch."*)

words, "peace with honour," but Russia revenged herself by intriguing with Afghanistan, and the Ameer Shere Ali readily received a Russian mission. The Viceroy of India, Lord Lytton, had already causes of complaint against the Ameer, who temporised with the proposal that he should discuss his grievances with a British envoy. At last Shere Ali brought matters to a crisis by turning back Sir Neville Chamberlain's mission on the

The Afghan War.

frontier. War was declared on November 21st, 1878, after Lord Beaconsfield had improved the occasion at the Mansion House by asserting that one of its objects was the acquisition of a "scientific frontier." The ill-armed Afghan levies made a poor resistance to the British forces; Shere Ali fled into Russian territory and died there; his son and successor, Yakoub Khan, signed the Treaty of Gandamak, and received a subsidy from the Indian Government. The British mission under Sir Louis Cavagnari had only been established some six weeks at Cabul, however, when it was massacred (September 3rd, 1879) by the fanatical populace. The war began again, and this time there was a stiff fight at Charasiab before General Roberts occupied Cabul. Forced to retire to Sherpur, he held his own with difficulty against the tribesmen, until relieved by Sir Donald Stewart advancing from Candahar.   An acceptable candidate, Abdur Rahman, a nephew of Shere Ali, presented himself and was installed Ameer.   General [afterwards Earl] Roberts promptly set forth on his famous march to Candahar, and retrieved the crushing defeat of Maiwand which had been inflicted on General Burrows by Ayoub Khan. The Liberal Government directed the new Viceroy, Lord Ripon, to evacuate Candahar, and the Afghans were left to the congenial occupation of settling the succession by civil warfare.

The Zulu War.

In South Africa Lord Carnarvon had failed to set up a confederation, owing to the jealousies of the various States. The annexation of the Transvaal, undertaken with the object of protecting the Dutch population from the Zulus, precipitated a war with their king, Cetewayo. British arms were discredited by the defeat of Isandhlwana; but the heroic defence of Rorke's Drift saved Natal, and Cetewayo's military organisation was finally shattered at Ulundi.

Home Rule and the Land League: Parnell.

In England commercial depression and bad harvests were responsible for not a little discontent towards the close of the Beaconsfield Ministry. In Ireland an agitation, half Parliamentary, half Fenian, had stirred up agrarian war. Irish politics had moved apace since the general election. The control of the Home Rule party, a creation of 1870, slipped from the inert hands of Mr. Isaac Butt seven years later. His place was taken by Mr. Parnell, a man of iron will and unscrupulous tactics, who, in conjunction with Mr. Biggar and a desperate band, determined to render legislation impossible through relentless obstruction. Sir Stafford Northcote's gentle persuasiveness was at a loss how to meet them, and they brought no small confusion on the Government. The Irish Executive was equally powerless when, in October, 1879, the Land League was started by Mr. Michael Davitt with the avowed object of exterminating " landlordism." Funds came from America ; home-grown oratory never failed, and outrages followed on the track of that oratory. The Government did its best to meet the destitution of the peasantry by introducing a Relief of Distress Bill early in the session of 1880. But " a danger, in its ultimate results hardly less disastrous than pestilence or famine," formed the topic of Lord Beaconsfield's letter to the Duke of Marlborough, the Lord Lieutenant, which he published as a political manifesto shortly after the dissolution had been anounced in March.

Mr. Gladstone, fresh from one Midlothian campaign, started, inexhaustible, on a second. His fiery denunciations of the Government's misdeeds hit the popular humour, and, except in London and constituencies bordering on great cities, the revulsion was marked. The election gave the Liberals a majority of nearly fifty over Conservatives and Home Rulers combined. Mr. Gladstone, in accordance with the unanimous desire of the party, became Prime Minister and Chancellor of the Exchequer as well. Of his former colleagues Lord Granville and Lord Selborne were once more Foreign Secretary and Lord Chancellor. Lord Hartington went to the India Office, Lord Kimberley to the Colonial, Mr. Childers to the War Office, and Lord Northbrook to the Admiralty. Sir William Harcourt became Home Secretary, and Mr. Forster undertook the anxious duties of Irish Secretary. Of the old Radicals Mr. Bright was Chancellor of the Duchy of Lancaster ; of the new, Mr. Chamberlain entered the Cabinet as President of the Board of Trade, while Sir Charles Dilke was Under-Secretary for Foreign Affairs.

The Government was much embarrassed by the claim of Mr. Bradlaugh, an avowed Atheist, who had been returned for Northampton, to make an affirmation instead of taking the oath ; and the question, after causing disorderly scenes, remained unsettled. Otherwise Ministers did fairly well during the short session by settling the Burials difficulty, and passing an Employers' Liability Bill and a Ground Game Bill. Mr. Forster's

[marginal notes:] The Election of 1880.

The Second Gladstone Ministry.

English Affairs.

Ireland. Compensation for Disturbance Bill, however, was rejected by the House of Lords by an overwhelming majority, because it covered the obnoxious cases of evictions for non-payment of rent. A most disturbed autumn and winter followed in Ireland. Lord Mountmorres, an Irish landlord, was foully murdered; while Mr. Parnell's advice, that the man who offended against the Land **Boycotting.** League should be shunned "as if he were a leper of old," was crystallised into a system of which Captain Boycott stood for the unwilling godfather. The failure of the prosecution of Mr. Parnell and his fellow-agitators early in the following year rendered the Executive almost impotent.

The Policy of Ministers. Mr. Gladstone prepared to deal with Irish disaffection by what Lord Randolph Churchill, then a brilliant Conservative irregular, called a "mixture of kicks and caresses." Early in the session of 1881 Mr. Forster introduced a stringent Protection of Persons and Property Bill, which the Home Rulers fought line by line and word by word. Sir William Harcourt followed with an Arms Bill. Lord Beaconsfield lived just long enough to see this emphatic fulfilment of his prophecy. He died on **The Irish Land Act.** April 19th, and on the 7th of that month Mr. Gladstone had introduced his second Irish Land Bill. This measure, which took up the whole of the session, and which the House of Lords did not allow to pass without considerable amendment, virtually established as principles the "three F's" — fair rent, free sale, and fixity of tenure. A Land Commission, with sub-commissions forming courts, was established to fix a "judicial rent," which was to remain unchanged for fifteen years, after which it could be revised. During that period the tenant could not be evicted except for non-payment of rent, excessive waste, sub-letting, or certain other specified acts. If evicted the tenant could still sell his interest, and he could claim compensation for improvements. A statutory term could also be created by mutual agreement between landlord and tenant. Future tenants—that is, those taking up their holdings after the passing of the Act—only came under it indirectly, in the event of the landlord raising the rent. The Land Commission was empowered to advance money to tenants for the purchase of their farms to the amount of three-fourths of their value. Contemptuously received by Mr. Parnell, the Act was far from bringing peace immediately to Ireland. On the

THE *TIMES* TACKING: "READY ABOUT," 1880.

(*Reproduced by special permission of the Proprietors of "Punch."*)

contrary, so inflammatory were his speeches that in October Mr. Gladstone, having denounced him and his followers at Leeds as "preachers of the gospel of public plunder," had them
Parnell in Gaol. consigned to Kilmainham Gaol. The Land League thereupon issued a "No-Rent Manifesto," and was suppressed as an illegal and criminal association. Agrarian outrages increased, however,

LORD FREDERICK CAVENDISH, AFTER GEORGE RICHMOND, R.A.

(By permission, from a print by Messrs. Graves, in the possession of his Grace the Duke of Devonshire.)

and the agitation, though worked in secret, showed no signs of abatement.

The Boer War. The annexation of the Transvaal was most unpopular with the Boers, who sent a deputation to England with a demand for the restoration of local independence. This refused, rebellion rapidly gathered head (p. 571). A Provisional Government was formed in December, 1880, and the British garrisons that did not surrender were closely besieged. Hastening up to their relief Sir George Colley suffered two reverses, and on February 29th he met with defeat and death on Majuba Hill, whither he had climbed in the desperate hope

of dislodging the Boers from their position. Nevertheless, Mr. **Majuba.**
Gladstone, recoiling from " blood-guiltiness," directed Sir Evelyn
Wood to conclude an armistice, and eventually a convention
was arranged at Pretoria. Modified in London three years
later, it gave the Boers full self-government, while retaining
for the Crown a rather shadowy suzerainty.

Ireland continued disturbed, and the Government, at the **The Kil-**
cost of Mr. Forster's resignation, determined on an abrupt **mainham**
Treaty.
change of policy. Mr. Parnell and the other Irish members
were released on May 2nd, 1882, after an understanding had
been effected which was popularly known as the Treaty of
Kilmainham. Five days afterwards the new Chief Secretary,
Lord Frederick Cavendish, and the Permanent Under-Secretary
Mr. Burke, were murdered in Phœnix Park, Dublin, by a gang
of conspirators calling themselves the Invincibles. Recourse
was had to coercion again, and a stringent Prevention of Crimes
Act passed, with an Arrears of Rent Act as a sedative.
During the autumn session the Government carried some procedure resolutions to repress deliberate obstruction, and
delegate business to Grand Committees. Irish loquacity was
checked, but not Irish disorder, which found vent for a while
in every kind of agrarian outrage, with an accompaniment of
dynamite explosions in London.

The next two sessions were occupied in legislation for **The**
England. In 1883, the Government carried a Bankruptcy **Franchise**
Act, 1884.
Act, an Agricultural Holdings Act, and a Corrupt Practices Act.
In the following year it undertook once more the reform of the
franchise. Mr. Gladstone's measure extended to the counties
the same voting qualifications as the boroughs enjoyed, namely,
household franchise, lodger franchise, a £10 annual value franchise, and the newly created service franchise. After much
debating in the Commons, the Lords threw out the Bill, because
it was unaccompanied by a scheme for the redistribution of seats.
An agitation of some vehemence then took hold of the country,
and there was talk about " mending " or " ending " the Lords.
Shortly after the House had met for an autumn session, however,
a compromise was effected by the two front benches. The
Government produced its Redistribution Bill, and the Franchise
Bill became law early in December. The companion measure
disfranchised all boroughs with less than 15,000 inhabitants, and

deprived those with less than 50,000 of a member. The country was divided into single-member constituencies, with the exception of the City of London, reduced to two members, and the old boroughs containing a population between 50,000 and 165,000. England obtained eighteen additional members, Scotland twelve, while Ireland and Wales remained unaltered.

Foreign Affairs: Egypt.

Its foreign policy or want of policy proved, in the end, the Government's undoing. Prince Bismarck's colonial projects brought him into sharp collision with Lord Granville, rendered dilatory by advancing years. But Egypt and its Soudanese provinces gave cause for much graver anxieties (pp. 572, 573). The extravagance of the Khedive Ismail had brought about his deposition in 1879, and his son Tewfik had been set up under the Dual Control of France and England. The arrangement never worked smoothly, and in 1882 it collapsed before a native rising under Arabi Pasha. The French Republic declined all responsibility, and it fell to England to suppress Arabi by the bombardment of Alexandria in July, followed by Wolseley's victory at

The Soudan.

Tel-el-Kebir in September. Order had been barely restored, and Lord Dufferin had produced an ingenious scheme of reform, when news arrived that the Soudan was in rebellion under a religious leader known as the Mahdi. In November, 1883, his followers slaughtered an Egyptian army under Hicks Pasha, and a similar fate overtook Baker Pasha, advancing from Suakim. The rescue of the garrisons, more particularly of Khartoum, was clamorously demanded by the Opposition, In utter perplexity,

Gordon.

the Government decided to send up General Gordon on a mission which proved impracticable. He made the startling request that the ex-slave-dealer Zebehr Pasha should come and help him govern, or that he should have troops with which to "smash" the Mahdi. Both ideas were rejected, and Gordon was left to shift for himself. At last popular indignation spurred the Government to action, and in August, 1884, Lord Wolseley was despatched to rescue Gordon. But he started too late; and, though a camel corps under Sir Herbert Stewart pushed across the desert, despite the desperate resistance of the Dervishes, it was all in vain. Sir Charles Wilson—for Sir Herbert Stewart had fallen at Metammeh—reached Khartoum in a steamer only to discover that the Dervishes had taken the town two days before (January 26th, 1885), and that Gordon had been

butchered.   Meanwhile Sir Gerald Graham's operations, with
Suakim for their base, had resulted in much purposeless blood-

Photo: Russell & Sons, Baker Street, W.
CHARLES GEORGE GORDON.
(From the statue by Onslow Ford, R.A., at Chatham.)

shed.   At first the Government was bent on the reconquest of
the Soudan; then it wavered, and determined to retire on the
Egyptian frontier.

As an additional trouble there came in March a collision
between the Russians and Afghans, at Penj-deh.   War between

Penj-deh. England and Russia seemed inevitable. The Indian Government prepared to defend the frontier; Mr. Gladstone asked for a vote of credit of eleven millions. That luckless financier, Mr. Childers, was forced to produce a most disastrous Budget, and on one of his resolutions the Government found itself in a minority of 12 (264 to 252), and resigned.

Lord Salisbury formed a Ministry, with Sir M. Hicks-Beach as Chancellor of the Exchequer and leader of the House, and Lord

THE TURN OF THE TIDE, 1885.

(Reproduced by special permission of the Proprietors of "Punch.")

The First Salisbury Government. R. Churchill as Secretary for India. Sir Stafford Northcote was somewhat ungraciously transferred to the Upper House[1] with the First Lordship of the Treasury. The Cabinet adhered to its predecessor's latest policy in Egypt, while all danger of a collision with Russia was removed by the appointment of a joint commission to determine the Afghan frontier. Before the session closed, the Lord Chancellor for Ireland, Lord Ashbourne, carried a meritorious Act for facilitating land purchase in Ireland. At the general election, however, which began in November, though the English boroughs showed a strong Conservative gain, the

[1 As Earl of Iddesleigh; he died not long afterwards.]

THE RIGHT HON. W. E. GLADSTONE, BY SIR J. E. MILLAIS, BART., P.R.A.

(*National Gallery.*)

counties went against the Government.   The final result was: Liberals 335, Conservatives 249, Home Rulers, 86.   Thus the Irish held the balance of parties—a result which Mr. Gladstone had in anticipation deprecated.   But the events to which it immediately or ultimately led—the advent to power, in January, 1886, of a Liberal Ministry, the introduction of Mr. Gladstone's Home Rule Bill, and the consequent split in the Liberal party—open a new era in English political warfare which lies beyond the chronological limits assigned, for this among other reasons, to the present work.

F. C. MONTAGUE.
Law Reform, 1800-1885.

IN our legal history the nineteenth century is pre-eminently the period of direct legislation.   The development of custom or of a traditional equity by judicial decision is at best a slow and irregular process, and it has its limits.   A time comes when all the important deductions which can be drawn from an accepted principle have been exhausted.   Further growth will then involve a transformation of the principle itself to which judicial authority is inadequate.   The main outlines of our Common Law have been settled for some hundreds of years. The main outlines of Equity were settled before the end of the last century.   The critical spirit of modern times necessarily restricts the latitude of interpretation enjoyed by judges. Yet the circumstances of our age have necessitated immense

Growth of Statute Law.

changes in the law.   The writings of Bentham and his school and the example of foreign nations have called forth the desire for comprehensive and symmetrical legislation.   The reformed Parliaments, at least before the recent unprecedented growth of loquacity, have been eager for work and fairly capable of doing business.   Thus every year has produced a volume of statutes.   Some of these statutes exceed in bulk the whole legislation of a medieval reign.   It would be impossible in our limits to give even a curt analysis of one or two of these statutes, such as the Merchant Shipping Act of 1894, or the Conveyancing Act of 1881.   We can only indicate the subjects with which legislation has been chiefly conversant, and the tendencies which legislation has displayed.

A great part of our modern statutes has been concerned with what it is convenient to call public law.   Not only has the governing authority in the State been remodelled by Reform Acts and Acts for the Redistribution of Seats, but old departments of administration have been reorganised, new departments have been established, and the entire system of local government has been recast. Most of the enactments of this class, such as the New Poor Law (p. 300), the Municipal Corporations Acts (p. 157), the Public Health Acts (p. 267), and so forth, are touched upon in other chapters of the present volume. Here we need consider only those enactments which have altered the constitution of the courts of justice and the forms of procedure. There have been many such enactments in the nineteenth century. The whole administration of justice has been revised more than once; ancient courts have been transformed, new courts have been multiplied, and the rules of procedure have been amended again and again. We may consider first the civil and then the criminal courts, and in each case we may consider the superior courts first. **Public Law and Procedure.**

With regard to the Courts of Common Law the first notable change in this century was the suppression of the separate Welsh judicature. Formerly there had been eight Welsh judges, inferior in dignity to the judges of the courts at Westminster, but discharging similar functions within the Principality. These judgeships were abolished by an Act of 1830, which added one puisne judge to each of the three superior Courts of Common Law. The procedure of the Courts of Common Law was amended and simplified by statutes of 1852, 1854, and 1860, which are known as the Common Law Procedure Acts. In the Court of Chancery, at the beginning of the nineteenth century, justice was dispensed by the Chancellor and the Master of the Rolls acting as judges of first instance, and an appeal lay only to the House of Lords. The increase of business led to the appointment of a Vice-Chancellor in 1813. Two more Vice-Chancellors were appointed in 1841 on the suppression of the equity side of the Common Law Court of Exchequer. In the year 1851 there was interposed between the House of Lords and the Court of Chancery the Court of the Lords Justices of Appeal in Chancery. Down to the passing of the first Judicature Act the procedure of the Courts of Equity had not been much modified by legislation. **Common Law Courts.** **Courts of Equity.**

The jurisdiction in testamentary and matrimonial causes had remained to the Ecclesiastical Courts until the year 1857, when it was transferred to the lay courts, newly estab-

lished. Power to pronounce a total divorce between man and
wife was now first given to a court of justice. The new Court
of Probate and the new Court for Divorce and Matrimonial
Causes inherited much of the substantive law and procedure
in use with their predecessors, and derived from the canon or
the civil law. Although secular, they, with the older Court
of Admiralty, formed a group apart from the Courts of
Common Law and the Courts of Equity.

Thus in spite of many considerable modifications the
superior courts of justice preserved down to the year 1873 the
same general outline which they had received in the thirteenth
and fourteenth centuries. In that year was passed the first and
most important of the Judicature Acts, which have transformed
our courts and our procedure. The Judicature Act of 1873 was
intended to effect three objects. It was to combine in one system
the superior courts already existing; to compound a new
procedure out of all that was best in the old procedure, whether
of the Courts of Common Law or of the Courts of Equity,
and to effect a fusion of the substantive rules of equity with
those of the Common Law.

At the passing of this Act the list of the superior courts
was as follows. There were three superior Courts of Common
Law—the Queen's Bench, the Common Pleas, and the Exchequer.
From each of these courts an appeal lay to the Court of
Exchequer Chamber, composed of all the Common Law judges
except those belonging to the court where the case had been
heard in the first instance. From the Court of Exchequer
Chamber a final appeal lay to the House of Lords. There was,
strictly speaking, but one Court of Chancery, though there were
several Chancery judges. From the Court of Chancery an appeal
lay to the Lords Justices of Appeal, and thence to the House of
Lords. Distinct from the Courts of Common Law and of Chancery, alike in their history, in their jurisdiction, and in their procedure, stood the Court of Admiralty, the Court of Probate, and
the Court for Matrimonial Causes. Appeals from the Court of
Admiralty were carried to the Judicial Committee of the Privy
Council. Appeals from the Courts of Probate and Divorce were
carried to the House of Lords. For judicial purposes the House
of Lords consisted of the Chancellor and the " law 'ords," that is
to say, peers who had held high judicial office. These were men

THE ROYAL PALACE OF JUSTICE.

287

eminent in their profession, but often unfitted by years and infirmities for the task of judges of appeal.

All these courts were concentrated in London. To them we must add the superior courts of the Palatine Counties, the Chancery Court and Court of Common Pleas of Lancaster and the Court of Pleas at Durham.

Courts after the Act.

The Judicature Act of 1873 created a Supreme Court of Judicature, which was to consist of two parts, a High Court of Justice and a Court of Appeal. In the High Court were to be consolidated all the existing superior courts of first instance. Each of the three Courts of Common Law was to become a division of the High Court, and ultimately all were to be merged in the Queen's Bench Division. The Court of Chancery was to form another division; the Courts of Admiralty, Probate, and Divorce were combined to form a third. The London Court of Bankruptcy, the Court of Common Pleas at Lancaster, and the Court of Pleas at Durham, were also merged in the High Court. The Court of Appeal was to take the place of the Court of Exchequer Chamber and of the Lords Justices of Appeal in Chancery, and also (as originally contrived) of the House of Lords and the Judicial Committee of the Privy Council. By the Appellate Jurisdiction Act of 1876, the former jurisdiction of the House of Lords and of the Judicial Committee has been maintained, with the Court of Appeal as an intermediate tribunal between the High Court and the House of Lords.

Now that the Common Pleas Division and the Exchequer Division have ceased to exist, the distribution of judges is as follows. The Queen's Bench Division consists of fourteen puisne judges, with the Lord Chief Justice as President. The Chancery Division consists of the Lord Chancellor, as President, and five puisne judges. The Admiralty, Probate, and Divorce Division contains two judges, of whom one is styled President. The Court of Appeal consists of the Master of the Rolls, who no longer acts as a judge of the first instance, five Lords Justices of Appeal, and the presidents of the several divisions of the High Court.

The House of Lords as a court of appeal was remodelled by the Act of 1876. It now includes, besides the Chancellor and the persons formerly known as the law lords, four Lords of Appeal in Ordinary. These are appointed by the Crown

under the provisions of the Act. They must have practised
at the Bar for fifteen years, or must have been judges in one or
other of the superior courts. They receive a salary of £6,000
a year. They are only life peers, but they have all the rights

THE FUSION OF LAW AND EQUITY.
(Reproduced by special permission of the Proprietors of " Punch.")

of other peers, even after they have retired from their office.
For the purpose of hearing causes three members of the House
form a quorum.

The second object of the Judicature Act of 1873 was the
reform of procedure. Details of procedure were left to the
judges, who were empowered to make rules of court, which if
not called in question in Parliament within a fixed time acquire
the force of law. In the main the new procedure was to be a

combination of all that was best in Common Law procedure and Equity procedure.

In the Courts of Common Law trial by jury was the invariable rule. Trial by jury was not known in the Court of Chancery. The employment of a jury in the Chancery Division or in the Queen's Bench Division is now largely a matter of convenience and the choice of the parties. In the Common Law courts a question of law was decided by all the judges. In the Court of Chancery one judge was competent to decide any point of law, and this rule has been adopted in our modern procedure. In the Courts of Common Law evidence was given orally; in the Court of Chancery it was given on affidavit. The modern procedure in both divisions prefers oral evidence, but admits evidence on affidavit when it is the best that can be obtained. A rule of the Common Law (abrogated, however, long before the Judicature Act) forbade a party to a suit to give evidence. In the Court of Chancery evidence was often extracted from the defendant. At the present day the parties may be witnesses in either Division. Repeated attempts have been made to abridge pleadings and to expedite judgment; but the cost and delay of civil proceedings are still grievous, and the extreme facility of carrying an appeal from court to court is a serious defect in our modern procedure.

Before quitting the subject of the superior courts, something must be said respecting the Judicial Committee of the Privy Council. The jurisdiction of the superior courts hitherto considered did not comprise ecclesiastical causes, appeals from the Court of Admiralty or from prize courts, or appeals from courts in our colonies or foreign possessions. Appeals from the Ecclesiastical Courts were heard by the Court of Delegates. The members of this court were appointed by royal commission under an Act of Henry VIII. Appeals from the Court of Admiralty were made to the same tribunal. The Privy Council heard appeals from the prize courts and from colonial courts. An Act of 1832 transferred to the Privy Council the jurisdiction of the Court of Delegates. But the Privy Council had long been unsuited to discharge the function of a court of justice. It was a large body, chiefly composed of persons without legal knowledge. Its legal members would naturally do its legal business, but no such division of labour had yet been enforced by law. What is known as the Judicial Committee of the Privy Council was first established by an Act of 1833. Under this Act the Judicial Committee was to consist of the Lord Chancellor and other persons holding high judicial office, together with two members specially appointed. Under a later Act the Queen was authorised to appoint four paid members of the Judicial

Photo: Walker & Cockerell.
RT. HON. SIR A. J. E. COCKBURN, BART.,
BY A. D. COOPER.
(*National Portrait Gallery.*)

Committee, who must either at the time of their appointment or at some previous time have been judges of a superior court either in England or in India. As the persons thus appointed die or retire their places will be filled, under the Act of 1876, by the Lords of Appeal in Ordinary. For all practical purposes the Judicial Committee consists of the paid members. The procedure of the committee bears traces of its origin from the Privy Council. Its judgments are couched in the form of advice unanimously given to the Sovereign. The Judicial Committee sits in Downing Street. No other court recorded in history has had so wide a jurisdiction, or has had to administer so many different systems of law.

The inferior courts for civil causes are known as the County Courts. These must be carefully distinguished from the

County
Courts.

county courts of medieval history. Owing to the small size of the kingdom, the early predominance of the central government, and the system of circuits, the ancient local courts throughout England fell early into decay. In the beginning of this century there was practically no provision for the local administration of justice in civil causes. The only exceptions were such courts as the Lord Mayor's Court in the City of London, or the Court of the Hundred of Salford. With the growth of business and population the inconvenience became intolerable. Lord Brougham proposed the establishment of a system of local courts; but it was only in 1846 that the present county courts were established. For this purpose the kingdom has been divided into a number of districts. Each district corresponding with a Poor Law Union has a county court of its own, and the style of County Court is therefore misleading. The districts are grouped into circuits, and all the courts in a circuit are held by the same judge. In all there are fifty-nine circuits, but a few are at present without a judge. The County Court Judge is appointed, and can be removed, by the Lord Chancellor. He must be a barrister of at least seven years' standing. His salary is paid by the State, and he may not sit in the House of Commons. He is assisted by a registrar, who is always a solicitor by profession, and who can act for the judge in undefended causes.

The jurisdiction of the county courts extends to all cases of contract where the sum claimed does not exceed £50, and to most cases of civil injury where the damages claimed do not exceed that amount. A variety of other legal business has gradually been transferred to them, but their chief concern is with the recovery of petty debts. As regards procedure a jury is not necessary unless the sum in dispute exceeds £5, and either party demands one. The jury consists of five persons. A party may appear either in person or by his solicitor, or he may employ a barrister. Upon points of law there is an appeal to the High Court if the judge gives leave, or as a matter of right if the sum claimed exceeds £20. An appeal from a county court is sometimes carried to the House of Lords. But hundreds of thousands of petty causes are rapidly and cheaply decided by the county courts.

The administration of justice in criminal cases is still based upon the ancient system of circuits, and most of the work is done by the Justices of Assize. But the extraordinary growth of London in the present century led to the erection in 1834 of a permanent court for the trial of indictable offences committed in the capital and the adjoining parts of Kent, Middlesex, and Surrey. This is known as the Central Criminal Court. The Lord Mayor, the Lord Chancellor, all the judges of the High Court, the Aldermen of the City, and certain other dignified persons are judges of this court. In practice the more important cases are taken by judges belonging to the King's Bench Division. In extent of jurisdiction and in procedure the Central Criminal Court almost exactly resembles the Assize Courts. **Criminal Procedure: The Central Criminal Court.**

Below the Central Criminal Court and the Courts of Assize come the Courts of Quarter Sessions in the counties and the largest boroughs. In the counties the Court of Quarter Sessions is still composed of all the justices of the peace. To the justices nominated in the traditional way must now be added the chairmen, for the time being, of the County Council and of the district councils within the county. The Quarter Sessions of the large boroughs are held by a Recorder, who must be a barrister of at least five years' standing. In the present century almost all the graver indictable offences have been transferred from the jurisdiction of Quarter Sessions to the jurisdiction of the superior courts. Petty offences are still tried by the justices in town and country. A single justice may not inflict a fine of more than 20s., or imprisonment for more than fourteen days. The summary jurisdiction is therefore exercised in most cases by two or more justices in Petty Sessions. The Crown, however, is authorised by statute to appoint stipendiary magistrates in London, in municipal boroughs, and in any town of more than 25,000 inhabitants; and the stipendiary magistrate, who is always a professional lawyer, has all the powers of the Petty Sessional Court. The summary jurisdiction has been remodelled by the Acts of 1848 and 1879, and under the latter Act the Petty Sessions have certain powers of trying indictable offences. Thus any indictable offence committed by a child under twelve years of age, other than homicide, may be summarily dealt with if the **Quarter Sessions.** **Police Courts.**

parent or guardian consent. Any accusation in the nature of larceny or embezzlement against a person under sixteen years may be summarily dealt with if the accused gives consent. So may an accusation of this kind against an adult if the value of the property in question does not exceed 40s. Lastly, an adult who pleads guilty to a charge of larceny or embezzlement, even where the value exceeds 40s., may be summarily dealt with if he has not previously committed an indictable offence. The heaviest penalty which can be inflicted by a court of summary jurisdiction, is a fine of £25 or six months' imprisonment with hard labour. If an offender is imprisoned without the option of a fine, he has an appeal to Quarter Sessions. If he wishes to raise a point of law he may ask the Petty Sessions to state a case for the High Court, and if the Petty Sessions refuse, he may move the High Court for an order requiring a case to be stated. Owing to the enlargement of the summary jurisdiction a great number of charges for indictable offences never go to the Quarter Sessions or the Assizes. And since the Petty Sessions are narrowly restricted in their power of inflicting punishment, there results an indirect mitigation of the severity of the criminal law.

Changes in Criminal Procedure. Something may here be said regarding the improvement of criminal procedure in the course of this period. In 1836, prisoners who had previously been allowed the help of counsel for other purposes, were allowed to employ counsel to make their defence, and were thus placed upon an equality with their prosecutors. The requirement of an oath on the Gospels to be taken by witnesses has been so modified that persons of any or of no religion may give evidence with a clear conscience, and with full liability to the pains and penalties of perjury. The perverse rules which forbade an accused person, or the husband or wife of an accused person, to give evidence have been broken through in certain cases, and will probably be abrogated altogether. Jurors are no longer denied food or fuel in order to famish them into unanimity. A Director of Public Prosecutions has been created to take care that justice is not defeated for want of a private person to prosecute; but up to the end of this period he had not yet been of much service to the public.

Another improvement in the administration of criminal justice was made by the Act establishing the Court for Crown Cases

Reserved. Subject to certain qualifications, too technical to be Criminal
Appeals. explained here, it may be said that English law does not confer any right of appeal against the sentence of a criminal court. But an Act of 1848 empowers the judge or the justices in Quarter Sessions to reserve any point of law for the opinion of a court consisting of at least five judges now belonging to the Queen's Bench Division, of whom one must be the Lord Chief Justice. The prosecutor or the person convicted may appear and argue his case, either in person or by counsel, and judgment must be given in open court. The court has the amplest power to reverse, amend, or affirm any judgment given in the court below. It is not strictly a Court of Appeal, but rather a court to determine doubts as to the law entertained by the judges who hear criminal causes. So well settled is the criminal law that such doubt is rarely possible, not twenty cases in a year, according to Sir James Stephen, coming before the court. No provision has yet been made for an appeal from the finding of a jury on a question of fact.[1]

The progress of reform in substantive law has especially affected the Law of Property, the Law of Contract, and the Law of Corporations. The law of real property, "the Herculaneum of feudalism," being the most archaic part of the law, has undergone the most extensive alteration.

Many attempts have been made to facilitate the buying and Land Law
Reform. selling of land. Thus the Prescription Act of 1832 has virtually abolished the curious doctrine of time immemorial, and has made it possible to acquire profits and easements (*e.g.* rights of common or rights of way) by peaceable enjoyment for comparatively brief periods. The Statutes of 1833 and 1874 for the limitation of actions relating to realty have not only curtailed the time within which the owner may sue a stranger in possession, but have deprived him of his title altogether unless he sues within that time. The Fines and Recoveries Act of 1833 has substituted a simple disentailing assurance for the clumsy collusive actions formerly necessary to bar an entail (*i.e.* to convert an estate tail into an estate in fee simple). The Acts for the Amendment of the Law of Real Property have simplified the methods of conveying land, and the Conveyancing Acts of 1881 and subsequent years have done much to abridge the necessary legal documents. Another series of Acts culminating in the Settled

[1 But see page 1024.]

Land Act of 1882 has enabled the limited owner, whether tenant in tail or tenant for life, to convey to the purchaser of his land an estate in fee simple, and has annulled by anticipation every contrivance for depriving him of this power. These Acts have rendered useless all the expedients formerly employed to keep land in the possession of one family for an indefinite period. Land is still made the subject of settlements, but a settlement now assures to the posterity of the tenant for life not the land, but only a certain amount of wealth, whether invested in land or in certain securities. In spite of all these reforms, the trouble and expense of proving a title are often considerable, and form an appreciable obstacle to free dealing in land. The complete removal of this obstacle can be effected only by a good system of registration. Two of our greatest lawyers have tried to establish one—Lord Westbury, in 1862, and Lord Cairns, in 1875—but with only partial success.[1]

Other Acts have provided for the enfranchisement of copyholds, for the commutation of tithe, and for the extinction of the troublesome right of dower. Land has been made fully liable for the debts of a deceased owner, and the heir or devisee of a mortgaged estate can no longer claim that the mortgage debt shall be paid out of the personalty of his predecessor. The law of mortmain and charitable uses has been recently revised and consolidated. The Settled Land Act of 1882 has enabled a tenant for life to grant agricultural, building, or mining leases for long terms. It has also enabled him to expend money derived from the sale of part of the settled land in executing certain permanent improvements upon the land which he retains. The Agricultural Holdings Act of 1883 has secured to the tenant of agricultural land the value of permanent improvements which he has executed. The Allotments Act, 1887, and the Small Holdings Act, 1892, have given the labourer facilities for cultivating land on his own account. The enclosure of commons has been regulated not merely in the interest of those who have rights in the common land, but to provide for the healthy recreation of the general public.

The Law of Contract has gained in importance through the

[1 The Land Transfer Act of 1897 carried the process a step further by empowering the Crown to make registration compulsory in any county or part of a county.]

vast increase of business transactions in the present century. **Law of Contract.**
In this field, however, more has been done to codify existing law
than to introduce new principles. Thus the Bills of Exchange
Act, 1882, comprises the entire law of negotiable instruments.
The law of partnership was codified in an Act of 1890, and the
law relating to the sale of goods in an Act of 1893. The Judi-

RICHARD, LORD WESTBURY, LORD HIGH CHANCELLOR OF
ENGLAND, BY SIR F. GRANT, P.R.A.
(By permission of the Treasurers of the Middle Temple.)

cature Act of 1873 has facilitated the transfer of rights arising
under a contract. The Infants' Relief Act of 1874 has rendered
contracts by persons under age for goods supplied other than
necessaries or for money lent absolutely void, whereas at Common
Law they were only voidable. The Married Women's Property
Act of 1882 has vastly enlarged the contractual capacity of
married women. Special forms for particular classes of contracts
have been imposed by various statutes. Exceptional pains have

been taken to render the promoters of companies liable for misrepresentation of fact to persons taking shares. Notwithstanding all these statutes the law of contract remains for the most part case-law.

Company Law.

The Law of Corporations has been enlarged chiefly by the enormous growth of company law. The State has always reserved to itself the power of creating corporate bodies. For a long time this power was exercised either through an Act of Parliament or through royal charter or letters patent, and in either case the instrument creating the corporate body defined its character and organisation. This procedure may have sufficed so long as commerce and industry were carried on chiefly by private individuals, and trading corporations like the East India Company or the Bank of England were exceptional; but when commerce and industry, outgrowing individual resources, came to be more and more carried on by joint-stock companies, it was necessary to devise a simple and uniform procedure for their creation, and to enact full and precise rules for their government. Companies invested with exceptional powers, such as railway companies, still require an Act of Parliament for their creation, though even here certain general provisions have been enacted once for all (*e.g.* in the Lands Clauses Consolidation Acts), and applied by reference in the Acts creating particular companies. The law determining the rights and duties of railway companies alone would already fill many volumes. As regards ordinary trading companies the Companies Acts from 1862 onwards have provided for their easy creation and for the conduct of their business (p. 498). The reported cases which elucidate these Acts may be counted by thousands.

Shipping.

In the principal maritime country of the world shipping has naturally attracted the attention of the legislature (p. 825). The law of ships was consolidated in the Merchant Shipping Act of 1854, now repealed, and again in the Merchant Shipping Act of 1894, the longest and most elaborate Act on the Statute Book.

Labour Laws.

The relations of employer and employed in almost every branch of industry—in mines, in factories, in workshops, and on board ship—have been regulated over and over again in a multitude of Acts, which are noticed in other chapters

of this volume.[1]   The liability of the employer for injuries
sustained by the workman in the course of his service was
not settled till 1897, and then only in certain specific trades
and industries.

WHEN the successive waves of excitement caused by the
Crimean War, the Indian Mutiny, and the threatened French
invasion had subsided, thinking men began to realise that
the want of elasticity in our military system was a serious
danger to the State.   Before the Mutiny, only 30,000 of the
queen's troops had been stationed in India, but after the
outbreak in the native army it was decided to maintain a
garrison of nearly 70,000 Britons in that country.   Thus a
large proportion of the British army was permanently withdrawn from the defence of the United Kingdom and the
colonies.   To replace them adequately in time of war it was
essential that the Government should command a large
reserve of well-trained men, fit at once to take the field;
but though the War Office endeavoured to organise such a
body of old soldiers, its efforts were so unsuccessful that the
militia practically remained the only reserve of troops upon
whom the country could count in case of need.   In 1866 the
"Seven Weeks' War" between Prussia and Austria proved
that it was possible for an army, small in time of peace, to
be capable of immense expansion in case of war; for as soon
as the Prussian army was mobilised tens of thousands of
well-trained reservists rejoined its ranks, and brought up its
numbers to full war strength.

   Anxiety at our own failure to form a reliable reserve,
astonishment at the brilliant success of the Prussian arms,
and embarrassment at our ever-increasing deficiency of recruits,
paved the way for the introduction of the short-service system,
by which Mr. Cardwell, then Secretary of State for War, revolutionised the army.   Had England, like Germany, adopted the
system of compulsory and universal service, and had she, like
Germany, possessed no important colonies, no coaling stations,
no Indian empire, Mr. Cardwell's task would simply have
been that of the copyist.   But he had to devise a system

G. LE M.
GRETTON.
The Army.

Mr.
Cardwell's
Reforms.

---

[1] *Cf.* pp. 298. 300, 312, 528.

based on that of Prussia, yet suitable to an army recruited by voluntary enlistment, and of which half the strength is ever serving beyond the borders of the United Kingdom. He had to provide that the army in India should always be kept up to its full war strength, and the colonies and the coaling stations adequately garrisoned. He had further to arrange that the army at home should be prepared, not

Photo: Walker & Cockerell.

EDWARD, VISCOUNT CARDWELL, BY GEORGE RICHMOND, R.A.

(National Portrait Gallery.)

only to supply the troops for small expeditions abroad, but also to make good the annual waste in the strength of the forces in India and the colonies, whether caused by death, invaliding, or transfer to the reserve. Finally, he had to create in England a strong reserve of thoroughly trained soldiers, ready to rejoin the ranks at a moment's notice. To provide such a reserve short service was essential; and this system, which has now obtained in the British army for a quarter of a century, was definitely adopted by the Govern-

ment in 1870. Young men of ages varying from eighteen to
twenty-four are enlisted for twelve years, of which six years
or more are spent " with the colours " (as service in the army
is termed), and the remainder are passed in the reserve, where
the soldier is free to carry on his civilian avocations, though
liable to be recalled to the colours in time of need. It is
obvious that under this system far more recruits are required
than in the days of long service, and to obtain them the
territorial system was devised, by which infantry regiments,
linked together in pairs, were assigned to the counties with
which they were connected by sentimental or historic ties.
Pitt's system (Vol. V., p. 715) of associating the militia with
the regular army was revived and amplified; the militia and
the volunteers were attached to the line regiments which are
" localised " in (*i.e.* assigned to) their county; and this combination of regular and auxiliary forces was termed a territorial regiment. In each county were built large barracks,
depôts, which serve as recruiting offices and training schools
for the newly-enlisted regulars and militia-men, who side by
side there receive their first lessons in discipline and drill.
Not only did this association with the line greatly improve
the militia from a military point of view, it also so
familiarised them with the service that out of the 34,000 men
who, about 1895, annually enlisted into the regular army about
14,000 were volunteers from the Constitutional force. In 1885
the strength of the army was about 180,000; but in the next
ten years there was a considerable increase in its numbers,
which in 1895, exclusive of the reserve, was about 213,000 men
of all arms. To these must be added 80,000 men in the first-
class reserve and 30,000 of the militia who, for a small annual
bounty, had taken upon themselves the same liabilities as the
first-class reserve.

The Territorial System.

Strength of the Army.

The plan of closely connecting each battalion with a particular part of the country proved successful; local *esprit
de corps* was stimulated, and the interest of the civilian
population in the army sensibly increased. In 1893 it was
ascertained that of the infantry nearly 56,000 had been born
and bred in the districts to which their battalions were
localised.

To insure a regular supply of men for the Indian and

colonial garrisons it was decided that one or other of the battalions of each regular regiment shall always be on foreign service, drawing its reinforcements from the battalion at home. From the depôt the recruits are transferred to the English battalion, where their education is carried on until they are drafted into the battalion abroad, where their military training is continued until their time comes to return to England and pass into the reserve, in which there were in 1895 about 80,000 soldiers, young men in their prime, forming the backbone of the first fighting line of the army at home. On the two occasions in our period that the reserve was called out, 95 per cent. of the men responded to the summons, and showed, by the perfect ease with which they resumed their military duties, that they had forgotten nothing since their return to civil life.

Competition for Commissions.
The short-service system is not the only improvement which the nation owes to Mr. Cardwell. When he took office in 1868, though a certain number of appointments to cavalry and infantry regiments were offered for competition, the large majority of commissions were obtained, not by merit but by favour. Except in the scientific corps (the engineers and the artillery), professional education was at the lowest ebb. Owing to the vicious system by which all responsibility was centred in two or three of the officers of each regiment, the remainder had so little to do that to hold a commission in the cavalry or infantry was not considered to involve serious work, but rather to be a light and agreeable occupation for rich men, to whom the purchase system gave many advantages **Abolition of Purchase.** over their less wealthy comrades. Before 1874, when Mr. Cardwell retired from office, all this had been changed. Thanks to the abolition of purchase (p. 524), officers no longer found themselves compelled to pay large sums of money for almost every step of promotion, under the penalty of seeing their wealthy juniors "purchase over their heads." The complete adoption of the principle of open competition for all commissions rendered it possible for young men with brains, but without interest or money, to force their way into the charmed circle of the British army. The career of arms became a profession in which talent and industry were allowed fair play. These innovations naturally raised a storm of indignation, and

it was loudly asserted that the social status of the officers would completely change. But time proved that the successful candidates were still drawn from the same rank of life as of old.

THE ABOLITION OF PURCHASE, 1871—AJAX DEFYING THE LIGHTNING.

(Reproduced by special permission of the Proprietors of "Punch.")

Officers, moreover, were compelled to study their profession —to pass qualifying examinations in fortification, tactics, military law, and topography, before they obtain promotion to a higher rank. These tests were originally instituted in 1871 for subalterns, and were afterwards extended upwards. Schools of gunnery, of musketry, of engineering were also established, as well as classes on every conceivable military subject, even to shoeing a horse and recognising whether the meat issued for

Military Education.

288

the men's rations is fit for human food. In addition to the brain-work which all these professional studies involved, much work and great responsibility was thrown upon regimental officers in training the men under their immediate command, and instruction was also provided for the sergeants and rank-and-file, as well as for the children of the married non-commissioned officers and men.

Standing Camps. When the British army landed in the Crimea (p. 360) it was found that few of the troops had any practical knowledge of camp-life, and that the different arms were wholly unused to working together. To prevent the recurrence of so disastrous a state of affairs, large permanent camps of exercise were formed, and the troops are taught to manœuvre across country in combination with each other under conditions to some extent resembling those of active service. In 1853, again, shooting was a lost art in our army, and men were hurried to the Crimea who had never fired a round of ball cartridge in their lives (p. 172). By 1885 each infantry-man was carefully and systematically taught the use of his rifle, and fired at least 200 rounds a year in practice at the butts.

The Soldier in Barracks. Among the many admirable changes which have taken place during the last thirty or forty years, the improvement in the condition of the soldier is, perhaps, the most remarkable. The squalor and indecency in barracks (p. 169) had become by 1885 a thing of the past. The barrack rooms were bright, airy, not overcrowded, and well provided with bath rooms and lavatories. The tentlike-screens round the beds of the soldiers' wives had disappeared; and married people had come to be now provided with comfortable quarters, separated from each other, and quite apart from the buildings occupied by the single men. At some stations large dining halls had been built, and throughout the army the greatest care is taken that the rations should be adequate, varied, and well cooked. In every barrack there are rooms set apart for the regimental institute—a soldiers' club and co-operative store combined. In some stations, billiard tables, shooting galleries, fives courts and skittle alleys have also been provided for the men; and regimental football clubs turned out mixed teams of officers and privates, who played for the military challenge cups competed for in every district. The allowance of furloughs and, for recruits at the depôt, occasional visits home at a "week-end," not only keep up family ties, but maintain local connections, invaluable in helping the men to obtain work when they return to civil life on passing into the reserve.

Outside the barracks, in every garrison town, there are 'Soldiers' Homes and Institutes," where men are welcomed and entertained by philanthropic people who wish to keep them out of mischief in their spare time. Thanks to all these efforts to

The Morals of the Soldier.

SOLDIERS' RECREATION ROOM, ALDERSHOT.

civilise the men, to the better class of soldier whom short-service has attracted to the ranks, and above all to the excellent example now set by the officers to the rank-and-file, good conduct and sobriety are increasing every year in the army. The modern English soldier has discovered that there are pleasures in life other than those of inebriety; he looks forward to the future and places money in the regimental savings bank; he is in every way as respectable a member of society as the young civilians of the rank of life from which he springs. In point of material comfort he is far better off than they, and he knows that no strikes, no hard winters, no depression in trade will throw him out of work. His "deferred pay," held back until his transfer to the reserve, enables him to start respectably in civil life. The remuneration of the non-commissioned officers has been increased by one-half to two-thirds since the beginning of the century.

The Militia. During the closing years of the period there was a steady improvement in the efficiency of the militia, especially after the War Office ceased to lodge the men in the public-houses and the slums of country towns during the annual training of the regiments. Though Wellington had decided that each soldier should have a bed to himself, the authorities had considered that this order did not apply to the militia, who were accordingly "doubled up," two in a bed, in quarters where the whole surroundings were thoroughly demoralising. Happily this is now all changed. At the close of our period, however, the troops were trained in standing camps or barracks, where they not only learn drill, shooting, and regimental routine, but they also acquire invaluable habits of discipline, cleanliness, and punctuality. The total of the various bodies of infantry, artillery, fortress engineers, and submarine miners, who assembled for instruction in 1894, was about 100,000; of these about 8,000 were old soldiers, who, on the expiration of their service in the army and reserve, voluntarily enlist in the militia. During the war in the Soudan in 1885 there was a partial embodiment of the infantry and artillery militia, to strengthen the garrison of England, which had fallen much below its usual numbers; about 20,000 men were called up, and for seven months did duty in various parts of the United Kingdom. With so little friction and difficulty was this addition to the strength of the regular army effected that comparatively few people in England were aware that any embodiment had taken place.

Yeomanry and Volunteers. The depression in agriculture acted injuriously upon the Yeomanry Cavalry; farmers became less and less able to afford the expense of serving in this force, which by 1896 dwindled to about 9,000 sabres. The numbers of the volunteers, on the contrary, increased between 1886 and 1896 from 215,000 to 231,000; but the dearth of officers in this branch of the service has seriously militated against its efficiency. There were, in 1896, no less than 1,800 commissions vacant, for which applicants were not forthcoming.

Among the most important alterations in our military Concentration of the Imperial Army. system effected during Mr. Cardwell's tenure of office was the deliberate reversal of the Duke of Wellington's policy of scattering the army in detachments throughout the colonies. The troops were gradually withdrawn from Canada, Australia, and New Zealand, and either concentrated in the United Kingdom, or sent to garrison the over-sea fortresses and coaling stations, which serve as bases of operations for the fleets to which the

[*Photo: Symonds & Co., Portsmouth.*

THE SOLDIERS' INSTITUTE, PORTSMOUTH.

aggressive defence of the empire is entrusted On the great self-governing colonies was thus thrown the burden of providing for their own local protection. The Governments of those smaller colonies in which Imperial garrisons are still stationed, have largely contributed to their defence by raising auxiliary volunteer corps. The total effective strength of the various forces of the colonies, including their local regular soldiers, militia, volunteers, and armed military police, in 1892, amounted to the very respectable total of 91,000 men. Twice in the period covered by this chapter did the colonies offer contingents of their local troops to the Imperial Govern-

Colonial
Troops
Oversea.

ment during a campaign. In 1881, within twenty-four hours of the news of our defeat at Laing's Nek, 2,000 Australian militiamen had volunteered for service against the Boers. Their offer of help was rejected ; but in 1885, 800 stalwart men from New South Wales fought side by side with British and Indian troops at Suakim, on the Red Sea, while a band of Canadian *voyageurs* shared in the perils of the Nile Expedition with their brothers from the "Old Country." [1]

Tactics
and Arms.

The axiom of Napoleon that "tactics change every ten years" has been fully verified during the last quarter of a century. This generation has seen the science of handling men in action, if not wholly revolutionised, at least constantly modified by the improvements which have from time to time been effected in firearms and in explosives. Rapidity of fire has been greatly augmented by the invention of breechloaders and of magazines. Accuracy of shooting has been equally increased by the improvements in the grooving of rifle-barrels. An enormous length of range has been obtained since gun-powder was virtually superseded by cordite, an explosive of remarkable strength and one which produces so little vapour on ignition that it is popularly known as "smokeless powder." To what extent the absence of smoke on a battlefield will influence the disposition of troops is one of the many problems which only the result of the next European war can solve. The most difficult question of all had been to devise a formation in which the infantry of the attack can cross the space swept by the defenders' fire. Before the wars of 1864, when breechloaders were first used in Europe, "the great object of offensive tactics on the Continent was to bring one or more sufficiently imposing infantry columns in good order up to the position of the defenders." [2] In 1870 the Prussians had not experienced on themselves the effects of breechloading fire, though they had used it with overwhelming success in the Danish and the Austrian wars, and they accordingly attacked the French in the small columns so popular in the German army during the last years of their struggle against the great Napoleon. But it was soon found

[1 The far more extensive help given during the South African War lies, of course, outside the scope of this chapter.]

2 Hamley's "Operations of War," 5th ed., p. 424.

that under the hail of bullets which the French breechloaders
poured into them, these columns dissolved into clouds of
skirmishers, and that the attack was delivered, not by men
fighting shoulder to shoulder, but by soldiers acting more or
less independently of each other. To evolve order out of this
disorder, to systematise the attack in extended order, has
been the constant pre-occupation of the generals of every
army since the war of 1870. All nations have now adopted

BRASS CANNON CAPTURED AT TEL EL-KEBIR.
(Royal United Service Institution.)

much the same views. They recognise that to bring up men
in the face of an enemy armed with breechloaders is impossible until the *morale* of the foe has been greatly shaken.
Therefore, the Napoleonic tactics of massing batteries against
the point to be breached have been revived, and a crushing
artillery fire is concentrated upon the troops who occupy
the threatened point in the defenders' position. When they
are considered to be sufficiently demoralised, the infantry
is launched against them, in successive waves of skirmishers,
constantly reinforced from the supporting troops in rear, who
follow them at distances which are gradually diminished as

the enemy is approached. When the final bayonet charge is to be made, the reinforcements hurry up in line, and, carrying with them the survivors of the skirmishers, hurl themselves upon the enemy in overwhelming masses.

This method of fighting throws very great responsibility on the captains and subalterns, as the command virtually passes into their hands during the battle. As the fight grows fiercer, the strain on the men's nerves increases, and the amount of control over their firing and their general conduct which can be exercised by subordinates depends largely on the warlike training and the nationality of the individual combatants. In the latter respect no army has profited more by the extended order-fighting than ours.[1] To quote from a well-known military writer—

> The direction of modern infantry tactics is peculiarly adapted to the genius and temperament of the English people. For years British troops, formed in lines two deep, have met and defeated the best armies in Europe. Extended order is but an extension of the two-deep line. The steadiness of the individual British soldier, his coolness and his proverbial ignorance of the time when he is beaten, tend to make individual fighting simple and natural to him . . . The peculiar genius of a nation invariably comes out on the battlefield, and it is essential that it should be clearly understood that the British army, with its historic training and traditions of advancing and fighting never more than two deep, possesses qualifications for modern fighting that the army of no nation does." [2]

One of the many curious features of our military position is that though, as a European nation, we are compelled to assiduously practise the tactics of modern warfare, as a great colonial power our actual fighting is almost always against partially or wholly uncivilised races. In fact, although the British army was actively engaged in many parts of the world between 1865 and 1885, only twice—in the Transvaal in 1881, and in Egypt in 1882—did we encounter troops armed in European fashion. In each of our little wars our methods have to be adapted to local requirements, under the penalty of disasters such as that of Isandhlwana (p. 571).

At the commencement of the period with which this chapter deals the New Zealand War was not yet over, and

Our Campaigns: Abyssinia.

[[1] Written in 1897. The South African and Russo-Japanese Wars have reopened many questions in tactics, but the text seems to need no alteration.]

[2] Hume's "Précis of Modern Tactics" (revised by Lieut.-Col. Pratt), p. 50.

British and colonial regiments were still engaged in "bush-whacking" against the insurgent Maoris. In 1868 it became necessary to send an army to Abyssinia to rescue a number of Englishmen whom the Emperor Theodore had imprisoned in his rock-fortress of Magdala. The military critics of the Continent, remembering our failures in the Crimea, were openly incredulous as to the possibility of England successfully organising an expedition into the heart of Africa. But this campaign proved that the bitter lessons of the winter of 1854 had not been altogether thrown away upon us. The transport and the commissariat did not break down in Abyssinia as they had done in the Crimea. Forty thousand animals—elephants, camels, and mules—carried the supplies for the troops, who, from their base of operations at Annesley Bay, marched to Magdala—a distance of 400 miles, across a savage and mountainous country, yielding but little food, and without roads worthy of the name.

Equally picturesque and satisfactory in organisation was the Red River expedition in 1870, when to a young colonel on the staff, afterwards Lord Wolseley and Commander-in-Chief, was entrusted the task of quelling a rising of Indian half-breeds on the prairies of Manitoba. At that time the only approach to Manitoba from Quebec or from Toronto was by water, from the north-west extremity of Lake Superior, over a network of lakes and rivers, in the heart of a wilderness which could furnish the troops with nothing but water and fuel. Of these the supplies were inexhaustible, but for this voyage of six hundred miles every other requisite had to be provided. On board the fleet of two hundred open boats, specially constructed for the occasion, were packed stores of every kind, guns and ammunition, camp equipage and food for sixty days. The crews consisted of twelve hundred fighting men, of whom more than half were Canadian militia, and four hundred Indian and French-Canadian *voyageurs*, who took charge of the hndling of the heavily-laden craft when the navigation became dangerous. The labours of both officers and men were incessant. Forty-seven times it became necessary, in order to avoid impassable rapids or cataracts, to unload each boat, to carry by hand all its contents to the spot fixed for re-embarkation, to return to the little vessel and drag her bodily

The Red River Expedition.

over the "portage," and finally re-launch her, and re-pack her. So admirably had all the arrangements been thought out, so carefully had all the calculations been made, that in this expedition—then unique of its kind in the annals of war, though since far surpassed by the Nile campaign of 1885—nothing went wrong, and nothing had been forgotten, down to the tea which for the first time was issued to the men instead of spirit, with most excellent results on their discipline and their health.

Our next little war was in 1873 against the Ashantis, who inhabit a district of the west coast of Africa, in which no pack-animal can live. The natives act as beasts of burden; and all the stores, ammunition, and provisions for the little army were transported upon the heads of stalwart negro porters. Though this method of carriage is most unsatisfactory, as the natives are liable in sudden fits of panic to throw down their loads and to disappear into the

KING KOFFEE'S
UMBRELLA.

Ashanti.

bush, yet so well were they watched, and so judiciously had Lord Wolseley and his staff made all their arrangements, that the British troops wanted for nothing on their march through the fever-stricken forests of Ashanti.

In 1877 Britain had two wars upon her hands. In India the intrigues of Russia had embroiled us with Afghanistan, and involved us in two long and arduous campaigns

KING PREMPEH'S UMBRELLA
(Royal United Service Institution.)

against the Ameer. In South Africa we were fighting hard with the Zulus, a splendid race of savage soldiers who threatened the existence of the colony of Natal. In the earlier part of the Zulu war history repeated itself. As in the eighteenth century (Vol. V., p. 260) a column of British and provincial troops were destroyed in the forests of North America owing to the English general's contempt for the advice of colonial officers, so in the nineteenth century the uplands of South Africa were the scene of a similar disaster. A British force had encamped at Isandhlwana, on the borders of Zululand, and part of the troops were led by their general on a recon-naissance in force, while the remainder were left to guard the camp. The colonists who accompanied the expedition, men experienced in South African warfare, urged the absolute necessity of fortifying the camp by surrounding it with a "laager" of the transport waggons. They pointed out that the Zulus were fearless, and admirably drilled and disciplined in their own tactics. It was in vain; the camp was left "unlaagered"; ten thousand Zulus surrounded it and by sheer weight of numbers crushed the defenders. A few white men escaped with their lives; but the Zulus, besides capturing tents, stores, ammunition, rifles, and colours, slew no less than fifty-two officers and eight hundred and six non-commissioned officers and men of the Anglo-colonial force. The road into Natal lay open to them; there was nothing to prevent their raiding into the colony but a weak detachment of about a hundred and thirty men at Rorke's Drift at the crossing of the River Tugela. This post, which had been roughly fortified with "mealie" bags and biscuit tins, was fiercely assailed; but so splendidly did its little garrison defend it, that after a series of attacks lasting all through the night, the Zulus retired, leaving the plain covered with their dead. A few months later, when reinforcements had arrived from England, the battle of Ulundi broke the Zulus' strength, and in our satisfaction at the con-clusion of the war, the bitter lesson we had learned at Isandhlwana, not to despise our enemy, was speedily forgotten. In 1880 the Transvaal, which had been annexed to Britain four years before, rose in rebellion against the handful of troops who were scattered over its vast area. The English general hastily collected a few hundred men, and without

waiting for reinforcements from England, without reflecting
that his foes were a race of hunters, trained from their earliest
youth to trust to their rifle for their daily food, advanced
against them. In three engagements the Boers signally
defeated us. Probably for the first time in our national history,
England allowed her defeats to remain unavenged (p. 537).
The Ministry hastily made peace with the Boers, and a

Photo: W. H. Pocock & C ., Capetown.

MAJUBA HILL.

Convention was concluded with them, conceding autonomy,
with certain reservations, under the suzerainty of the British
Crown.[1]

There is no space even to mention the other campaigns
which have occurred in the twenty years ending in 1885.
In India, besides the Afghan War, there have been constant
expeditions of varying importance, to maintain order among
the savage races on our frontiers. In Egypt Lord Wolseley's
campaign of 1882 brought into prominence the harmony with

[1 The precise meaning of this Convention, which subsequently was replaced
by another omitting the term " suzerainty," was constantly in dispute until it
was terminated by the war of 1899-1902.]

which the Army and Navy now work together, and the ease
with which England can send a combined force to any part
of the world. Three years later, when Lord Wolseley led an
expedition up the Nile, the British soldier proved that
neither short service nor School Board education have made
him less handy, less gallant, less adaptable to his surroundings,
than were his predecessors.   It is no part of a soldier's
ordinary duty to row boats or to ride camels, yet in 1885
many British regiments embarked in the fleet of 800 whale
boats which covered the waters of the Nile, and picked detachments of all arms, mounted on camels, penetrated into a desert
untrodden by European soldiers since a Roman army perished
in its sandy wastes.

THE peace of 1815 left the " great gun " very nearly where it
had been a hundred years earlier.   There had been no important
increase in weight ; and the only considerable improvements in
naval gunnery had been the introduction of the carronade,
or "smasher," for throwing comparatively heavy shot for short
distances at a low velocity ; and the adoption of the gun-lock in
lieu of the various primitive arrangements for igniting the
priming of the charge by means of red-hot irons, smouldering
rope-ends, etc. The use of shells had also become more general,
and the shell itself had been improved, though it was still
employed almost exclusively in mortars.   But as the century
verged upon its middle age, attention began to be directed to
the problem of the diminution of windage in heavy guns, with
a view to obtaining greater accuracy and velocity by utilising
as much as possible of the elastic force of the explosion, and
allowing as little as possible of it to pass the projectile and
escape without doing its due share of the work.   In certain
small-arms the problem had long before been dealt with by the
adoption of the device of rifling the interior of the barrel, and
giving to the grooves of the rifling a slight turn, which was
found to increase accuracy by imparting a twist to the bullet.
In the old muzzle-loading rifles the bullet was hammered, or
violently forced, down upon the powder; but very little
experiment showed that it would be vain to attempt to do with
an iron projectile, weighing perhaps 68 lb., what could be done,

**Rifled
Cannon**

with comparatively small labour, with a leaden bullet weighing
a few grains.   Whitworth and others therefore devised an
elongated bolt or projectile which, instead of being forced into
the bore, was of size and shape to permit of its being pushed
home with little exertion, but which, nevertheless, acquired a
twisting motion in its flight by reason of some peculiar correspondence between a cross-section of the projectile and a
cross-section of the bore of the gun, the bore being itself
twisted.   Whitworth's section was hexagonal ; the section
chosen by Lancaster was slightly oval.   Yet still, as the projectile could not fit with more than approximate accuracy,
there was much windage ; and at length it became obvious that
if windage was to be reduced to the lowest practicable point, the
gun must be loaded not by the muzzle, but by the breech.

**Breech-
loading
Cannon.**

Sir William Armstrong, about 1858, was the first in England
to turn the conclusion to advantage, by the invention of his
first breech-loader.   This was a tube, cut into near its rear end
so as to admit of the dropping-in of a wedge or breech block,
which then filled the aperture and closed the bore.   A hollow
screw, working in the tube from the rear, pressed the wedge
home and held it fast.   The gun, therefore, soon came to be
known as the Armstrong screw-gun.   But the system, though
embodying great improvements, proved unsatisfactory, owing to
the tendency of the wedge to jump out of its place upon the
firing of the gun ; and for a time there was a reversion to
muzzle-loaders.   Some of these, especially after the introduction
of Armstrong's plan of building them up, instead of constructing
them in one or two heavy pieces, were very large, and, all things
considered, very powerful weapons ; and towards the close of
the muzzle-loading era, guns of this description, weighing as
much as 80 tons, and having a calibre of 16 inches in diameter,
were turned out for the Navy.   Four of them were mounted in
the battleship *Inflexible,* which was launched in 1876, and
which did good work with them at the bombardment of
Alexandria six years later.   Before long, however, the difficulties
in the way of securing a completely satisfactory breech arrangement were solved by Sir William Armstrong ; and, after the
opposition of prejudice and habit had been overcome, the year
1881 witnessed the launch of the *Conqueror,* the first British
battleship armed exclusively with modern breechloaders.   The

largest of these weighed only 45 tons each; yet even they were
much better than any muzzle-loaders; and presently bigger
guns on the same system were constructed, until, at the close
of the epoch under review, guns weighing 111 tons were in
existence, though not actually mounted on board ship, in this
country. They were destined for the *Benbow*, which was begun
in 1882 and launched in 1885. It will be interesting to compare
the best smooth-bore gun of the end of the ante-breechloading

AN EARLY ARMSTRONG BREECH-LOADER.
(*From a photograph supplied by Sir W. G. Armstrong, Whitworth & Co., Ltd.,
Elswick, Newcastle-on-Tyne.*)

days (1859) with the best muzzle-loading gun of days of rifling
(1876) and the best breechloading rifled gun of 1885 :—

Date.	Weight of Gun. cwts.	Calibre of Gun. ins.	Weight of Projectile. lbs.	Weight of Charge. lbs.	Initial Velocity ft. per sec.	Muzzle Penetration. ins. of iron.
1859	95	... 8.12 ..	68	.. 16	... 1,490	... 3
1876	1,600	... 16 ...	1,684	... 450	... 1,590	... 24
1885	2,300	... 16.25 ..	1,800	... 960	... 2,087	... 38

Nor is this all. In the twenty-six years the length of the
biggest gun of the day grew from 10 feet to 43 feet 8 inches;
and the iron spherical projectiles, lying comparatively loosely in
the bore, were exchanged for steel projectiles provided with soft
copper circumferential bands in such a manner that as the
missiles were driven through the gun the copper entered into

the grooving of the rifling so intimately as practically to abolish windage. One particular performance of the great gun of 1885 ought not to go unmentioned here, although the actual penetration of the gun was not determined until a few years later. An armour-piercing projectile was fired from it against a specially built-up target. The material traversed in succession was— compound (iron steel-faced) armour, 20 inches; iron, 8 inches; oak, 20 feet; granite, 5 feet; concrete, 11 feet; or, in all, 38 feet 4 inches. The projectile came to rest in other material just beyond the concrete. The cost of firing that shot was, it may be

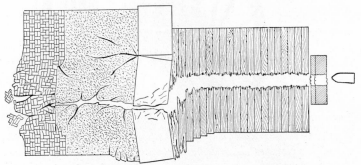

DIAGRAM SHOWING PENETRATIVE POWER OF AN ARMSTRONG GUN.

added—for the projectile, about £125, and for the powder, about £80; total, about £205. A little earlier a gun of similar type, but of much smaller size, had been fired with a high degree of elevation in order to test its extreme range, which was found to be 21,800 yards, or upwards of $12\frac{1}{4}$ miles. It is doubtful whether the best gun of 1859 could have thrown its shot, in the most favourable circumstances, to a distance of two miles and a half.

But all these improvements, striking though they were, were none of them final. Towards the end of 1881 the Government invited designs for a gun which should fulfil the following requirements:—The weight of the gun and its mounting were not to exceed half a ton; the projectile was to weigh six pounds, and to have a muzzle-velocity of not less than 1,800 feet per second; the projectile and powder-charge were to be made up in one cartridge; the gun was to require a crew of not more than three men, and it was to be capable of discharging at least twelve

Photo: W. Symonds & Co., Portsmouth.

H.M.S. INFLEXIBLE IN 1880.

Quick
Firing
Guns.

aimed shots a minute. In reply Mr. Hotchkiss, Mr. Nordenfelt, and others, drew up plans and specifications for what have since been known as quick-firing guns. Time was saved, not merely by having charge and projectile in one cartridge, but also by simplifying and reducing the number of necessary motions in opening and closing the breech-apparatus. The result presently was the introduction to the service of 3-pounder guns that could be loaded and fired 30 times a minute; of 6-pounder guns that could be loaded and fired 25 times a minute: and of 12-pounder

Photo: W. Gregory & Co., Strand, W.C.

THE WHITEHEAD TORPEDO.

guns that could be loaded and fired 20 times a minute. When to this is added the fact that the third quarter of the century also saw the general adoption of machine-guns—weapons which by mechanical arrangement can discharge an almost uninterrupted succession of small bullets—it will be realised what astonishing progress was made in that period in the art and science of killing.

Torpedoes.

A kindred development of the time was the automobile torpedo, of which the Whitehead may be regarded as the leading type. This torpedo is a spindle-shaped steel vessel, furnished with a screw driven by means of compressed air, and with a large charge of gun-cotton, capable of being exploded by concussion. The machine was so arranged that it would automatically maintain itself at a given depth while running through the water, and would preserve its original direction. It was suitable for discharge, by means of tubes, either from ordinary ships, or from torpedo-boats peculiarly adapted for it: and as it was rapidly improved, until it became very accurate, it threatened, towards the close of the period under consideration, to revolutionise all preconceived theories concerning the methods of naval warfare. Large numbers of torpedoes were manufac-

Photo: W. Symonds & Co., Portsmouth.

TORPEDO BOAT IN 1880.

tured; and many torpedo-boats were built, constructors and contractors vying with foreign builders in producing faster vessels of the type than existed elsewhere. This rivalry had, indirectly, an important influence in bringing about enormous improvements in ships' boilers and machinery; and, with the new type of craft, speeds previously undreamt of were quickly attained.

After the commencement of the second quarter of the nineteenth century, improvements in the *matériel* of the fleet were introduced with ever-increasing frequency. The use of iron, presently to be superseded by steel, for the construction of hulls and for armouring; the general adoption of the screw; the accelerated speed of ships; the development of the power and

General
Improve-
ments.

accuracy of the gun; and the invention of the Whitehead torpedo, have been alluded to already; but there were hundreds of minor improvements of a not less significant character, and these affected almost every operation that is performed on board a man-of-war. Steam began to be employed not merely for propelling ships, but also for pumping them; for propelling their boats; for hoisting their boats in and out; for weighing anchor; and, in short, for doing all sorts of subsidiary work. Hydraulic power was next called in for many purposes, notably for loading heavy guns, for turning them in their turrets or barbettes, for elevating and depressing them, for controlling their recoil, and sometimes for hoisting up to them their powder and shell, and for placing these within them. As the period now being dealt with closed, a tendency was exhibited towards the supersession of even steam and hydraulic power, for certain purposes, by electricity. This power had already taken over the lighting of ships, and, to a limited degree, the transmission of orders and signals from one part of them to another. The ancient practice of heaving the log with a view to ascertaining the speed of a vessel, though persisted in, was to a large extent superseded by the introduction of various mechanical self-registering devices, driven for the most part by the automatic revolutions of a screw trailing astern of the moving ship. Improvements in the compass and in deep-sea sounding apparatus were introduced by Sir William Thomson, afterwards Lord Kelvin (p. 711); signalling from ship to ship was facilitated by the adoption of better codes and an increased number of flags for the purpose, as well as by the use of Colomb's system of flashing longs and shorts at night, in accordance with the principles of the Morse alphabet, and by the development of the semaphore: and the whole scheme of naval tactics underwent revision. The effective internal subdivision of ships became one of the chief aims of the naval architect; sails and rigged masts slowly disappeared from vessels of war; double bottoms and cellular methods of construction became the rule rather than the exception, and wire ropes took the place of many of the hempen ones for the support of such masts as remained, while the lower masts themselves were cylinders of iron or steel.

In the earlier days of the Royal Navy there was no regular

scheme for providing the service with officers.   Some were obtained by promotion from the lower deck of ships of war ; others
were taken from the mercantile marine ; yet others were transferred from the land forces ; and not a few seem to have gone
straight from civil life ashore to the novel responsibilities of
the quarter-deck.   But in all ages a custom, which was practically one of apprenticeship, prevailed—at least, to some extent.
Captains took youngsters to sea with them ; made them subordinate officers if they appeared to deserve promotion ; and
ever afterwards, so long as good behaviour warranted it, kept
a friendly eye on their *protégés* with a view to securing their
advancement as opportunity offered.   Yet for a long period
there scarcely existed such a thing as the naval career, for there
was little or no continuity of service, nor was there any half-pay
as a retaining fee.   In war a certain class of people who had had
previous experience naturally returned to a calling which was
alike honourable and profitable ; but in peace the greater
number of these followed other employments.   The first change
of importance was the appointment of gunners, boatswains,
carpenters, and pursers, as standing or permanent officers.   The
superior ranks continued to be filled by the temporary engagement and commissioning of persons who were more or less out-
siders.   Further developments were very gradual, though they
all arose out of the ancient custom of captains taking with
them to sea a retinue of servants and youngsters.   The custom
was officially recognised and sanctioned in Elizabeth's time,
after which the captains drew pay and rations for these followers
of theirs, and were thus enabled to provide some sort of start
in life for the sons of their relatives and friends.   It soon
became usual for a captain to appoint his own lieutenant.   He,
of course, frequently chose one of his followers.   Next, the
status of midshipmen and lieutenants was recognised and regularised, and so a channel of promotion for deserving youngsters
was insensibly established, though for a long time the steady flow
of the current remained liable to interruption by appointments
from outside.   Under Charles II. the practice of admitting
to men-of-war "volunteers by order"—or, as they were more
commonly called, "king's letter boys"—was sanctioned ; and
formal regulations established the qualifications for attainment
of the rank of lieutenant, and prescribed a rudimentary system

of examination for a commission.   In 1728 the "king's letter" was abolished, and a Naval Academy was formed at Portsmouth, youngsters entering from it being granted certain advantages.   But, comparatively speaking, few officers entered through the Naval Academy, so long as they could enter more easily as nominal servants or retainers of some friendly captain.   Joining the Naval Academy involved actual presence and study there; joining as captain's servant did not necessarily involve, for several years at least, any active participation in the work of the service; for the inevitable abuses which grew up permitted a boy's name to be placed and kept on the books of one of the king's ships while he was still in the nursery or at school, and gave him the advantage, when he first went actually to sea, of finding several years of service already standing to his credit, and counting in favour of his eligibility for promotion.   The bogus servant system existed until nearly the close of the eighteenth century.   The Naval Academy at Portsmouth, as a door of entry, existed until 1837. Then succeeded a system by which volunteers, later called Naval Cadets, were entered on board large sea-going ships, which carried naval instructors to attend to their technical education. Special training-ships were next established at Portsmouth and Devonport, and in one of these, after passing a preliminary examination at the Royal Naval College at Portsmouth, the cadet was required to serve and study for three months and to qualify, ere being sent to sea.   Finally, a single training-ship was considered to be sufficient.   The Portsmouth one was chosen, and at the end of 1858 the then existing vessel there, the *Illustrious,* not being considered suitable, and further changes in the direction of improving the course of training being contemplated, the *Britannia* was assigned to do the duty   She was a fine 120-gun ship, that had been built in 1820, and had served as one of the flag-ships in the Black Sea during the Russian War.   She was altered, and was commissioned for her new work on January 1st, 1859, since which date the cadets' training-ship has always borne her name. The original vessel was moved to Portland in 1862, and thence, in the following year, to Dartmouth.   In 1869 the vessel, being worn out, was withdrawn, and the *Prince of Wales,* which took her name, was substituted for her.   Modifications of the earlier regulations were made from time to time, until, in 1885,

they were substantially as follows :—The system of admission
was by limited competition, after nomination.   Candidates were
required to be not more than thirteen and a half, and not less
than twelve years of age on July 15th (if going up in June) or on
January 15th (if going up in November), following the examination.   The course of training was for two years, at the expiration
of which the cadet, his conduct and progress having been satisfactory, was appointed to a sea-going ship.   He then passed for
midshipman, and subsequently for lieutenant, becoming at first

Photo: Smale & Son, Dartmouth.

THE OLD *BRITANNIA*.

an acting, and then a full sub-lieutenant, and remaining one
until the passing of further technical courses and examinations.
His appointment to be lieutenant placed him in the way of promotion by selection, subject to sufficient time having been served,
until his attainment of the rank of captain, after which his
further promotion was by seniority.   The establishment of the
Britannia, or of some corresponding school, was rendered absolutely necessary by the greatly increased technical knowledge
demanded of the naval officer after the introduction of steam
as the general means of propulsion at sea, and after gunnery
had become a really progressive science ; yet the practice of
cutting short a boy's education at the age of thirteen and a
half had the natural but regrettable effect of seriously limiting

Entry and Training of Seamen.

the average naval officer's mental culture ; and before the new system had been in working order for a generation it began to be recognised that the change could not be regarded as final.[1]

Still more radical alterations took place, as the century grew old, in the methods whereby the Navy was provided with seamen. During the old wars men either volunteered or were pressed, and when their services were no longer needed, the poor fellows, with comparatively few exceptions, were cast adrift, and had to find for themselves other employment, or starve. The country took care of those who had been wounded, or who had seen long service, or who had become petty or warrant officers ; but as a rule the young men who, possibly contrary to their inclinations, had served only for one or two commissions, were thrown upon the world ; and these were the majority. During the peace, impressment, though it still remained legal, was not often had recourse to, for only a small number of men were required, and these were generally provided by voluntary enlistment. But such a system, even in peace-time, could not produce satisfactory men. The Navy held out inducements to the improvident, the scampish, and the vicious, far more than to the steady and fore-sighted. So long as casual engagements were the rule, so long was something approaching to savagery necessary for the main-tenance of any kind of discipline throughout the fleet. It was said, with nearly literal truth, of certain commanders in the 'thirties and the 'forties that they had flogged every man who had ever served under them. The habit of allowing large rations of rum (which had superseded the heavier but withal less injurious beer as the nautical beverage) to ships' companies increased the inborn tendencies towards disorder and crime ; and presently it was decided that the only hope for improvement in the morals of the lower-deck lay in the introduction of continuous service. This was effected in 1852, and the happy results of the change have ever since been conspicuous. A further measure tending to promote *esprit de corps* and neatness was the adop-tion, in 1857, of a uniform dress for seamen. When the "new Navy" which had been thus created had been established for a few years, it was found safe and feasible to abolish flogging

---

[1] [The revolutionising of naval education, and the assimilation of officers in the three branches of the service announced in 1902, fall, of course, outside the scope of this chapter.]

as a punishment for ordinary offences among blue-jackets; and although old martinets objected that this leniency would infallibly send the service to the dogs, it is now admitted on all hands that discipline, order, and sobriety have since been at a higher level than ever before. Sobriety, it should be added, was assisted by the cutting down in quantity of the daily ration of rum, the issue of it already mixed with water, and the prohibition of it altogether to those of less than twenty years of age. And the gradual improvement of the food rations was not without a beneficial effect, though it was not carried as far as it should have been, and even in 1885 it remained incomplete.

These and other causes contributed to make the blue-jacket of the third quarter a very different man from the blue-jacket of the first quarter of the nineteenth century. He became clean, neat, orderly, self-respecting, scientific, and, with few exceptions, sober. Rules were made to assist him in remitting home or in saving his wages, and he took full advantage of them. His habitual rowdiness while on shore, and his traditional inclination to take a wife in every port, and to desert all with equal indifference, became characteristics of the past. It was prophesied that whenever any amelioration of the seaman's status was brought about, the class, becoming less rough and hard, would deteriorate as a fighting force; but nothing has ever happened to justify this forecast. On the other hand, events have repeatedly happened to call for the display of cool courage and manly devotion; and the exhibition of these qualities by the seamen of the reformed Navy has been invariably such as would not have shamed the seamen of Nelson's time: so that it may be concluded that the reforms, although they have not perhaps been carried as far as they should be in all directions, have been wholly beneficial. *The Modern Blue-jacket.*

The increasingly scientific character of the naval profession, the improvements in gunnery, and the introduction of the torpedo, necessitated the creation, alike for men and for officers, of special facilities for scientific education, after the preliminary technical knowlege of the profession had been acquired, by the men in the harbour and sea-going training-ships, and by the officers in the *Britannia*, on foreign stations, and in the course of their general preparation for a commission. *Higher Naval Training.*

The first move in the required direction was made as early as 1832, when the *Excellent*, at Portsmouth, was fitted up as a gunnery training-ship, and entrusted to the command of Captain (afterwards Sir) Thomas Hastings. All ships which have since fulfilled the same functions at Portsmouth have, in succession, been given the same name; and although the Portsmouth gunnery establishment was at length transferred to the shore, and housed on Whale Island, the officers and men attached to it continued to be borne on the books of a small craft whose name was changed from *Handy* to *Excellent* for the purpose. The corresponding establishment at Devonport has its headquarters in the *Cambridge*, that having been the name of the vessel first assigned to the duty in 1856. Analogous establishments for training in torpedo, mining, and electrical work were created in 1872 in the *Vernon* at Portsmouth, and later in the *Defiance* at Devonport. In all these, officers and men receive instruction and pass through long or short courses, terminating with examinations. Other forms of technical education of an advanced kind are given to officers of all the ranks above and including that of sub-lieutenant, at the Royal Naval College, which has its home in Greenwich Hospital. But although the termination of the period under review found the British naval officer much better equipped technically than in any former age, the methods of his general education were still almost as unsatisfactory as they had been at the beginning of the century. Looking to the nature of the diplomatic and other special services which he is frequently called upon to perform in all parts of the world, this cannot but be regretted. Yet the system which terminates the methodical portion of his general education as a gentleman and man of the world while he is still a mere child renders the result almost inevitable.[1]

Until the nineteenth century the sole reserves of naval *personnel* existed in the ranks of the miscellaneous seafaring population which was not actually serving in the Navy. This population was almost untrained; but, on the other hand, the amount of knowledge and training necessary to make an expert man-of-war's man was not then half as great as it has since become. Ships could, and did, go to sea, even in war-time, with

[1 The system, however, has been given a new lease of life by the new scheme of education announced at the end of 1902, which makes the age of entry even earlier, in order to give time for the technical education necessary to facilitate the assimilation of ranks in the different branches of the service.]

H.M.S. *EXCELLENT* AND H.M.S. *VERNON* IN THE EIGHTIES.

(From photographs by W. Symonds & Co., Portsmouth.)

Coast-
guard and
Reserves.

many raw landsmen on board, fight one or more successful actions, and return to port, after a not very long cruise, with a crew which had grown entirely efficient. Yet the system was a haphazard and dangerous one then, and it would have been still more dangerous afterwards. The reserves, in addition to the body of Naval Pensioners, successively created to cope, to some

A REVENUE CUTTER. 1810–1830.
(Victoria and Albert Museum.)

extent, with the difficulty, were the Coastguard and the Royal Naval Reserve, with—for the corps deserves mention here, though it did not long exist—the Royal Naval Artillery Volunteers.[1]

The Coastguard grew out of the establishment, necessary in the early years of the century for the prevention of smuggling, of what was known as the Coast Blockade of Kent and Sussex. This was effected by means of a naval force having its head-quarters afloat in the Downs and at Newhaven, and having numerous landed parties housed ashore in the martello towers or in special barracks. These parties and stations were commanded by lieutenants. The arrangement lasted until 1831, when

[1 A Royal Naval Volunteer Force was established in 1902.]

the naval force was supplanted by a body of preventive men with revenue cutters, and by civilians, the whole being then denominated Coastguard.   This in time was again supplanted by a body of seamen who had served in the fleet, and who in 1857 were placed under an officer designated the Admiral Superintendent of Naval Reserves.   They were periodically drilled and inspected both ashore and afloat, a part going to sea every year for a short cruise, and all being immediately available for naval service.   It was always an excellent body of men, but necessarily a small one.   To supplement it, the Royal Naval Reserve was regularised by an Act of 1863, and finally established by an Order-in-Council of 1864, though it had then existed in an embryonic form for two years.   It was composed at first of officers belonging to the mercantile navy, but subsequently men of the merchant service were also enrolled in it; and it rapidly became numerically considerable. A certain degree of efficiency was originally secured by obliging the members to undergo a given number of drills annually, old vessels being stationed at convenient spots around the coast for the purpose; and, finally, further efficiency was attained by allowing a few officers to enter for temporary service on board sea-going ships of war, this service, properly performed for a year, qualifying them for an annual retaining fee.   The Royal Naval Artillery Volunteers were raised under an Act of 1873 from among yachtsmen and landsmen possessed of specified qualifications; but they were disbanded in 1892 (p. 586).

In 1885 the total strength of the *personnel* of the Navy, includ- **Strength** ing the Royal Marines and all the reserves above mentioned, was: **of the Navy, 1885.**

Officers and Seamen, for sea-service ...	34,737
Boys, under training	5,900
Coastguard	4,693
Royal Marines	12,400
Various services ashore	995
Royal Naval Reserve	19,000
Seamen and Marine Pensioner Reserves	1,950
Royal Naval Artillery Volunteers ...	1,600
	——81,275 [1]

The number of vessels in commission on November 1st of the same year was officially returned at:—Ironclads, 30; frigate, 1; corvettes, 26; torpedo-ram, 1; sloops, 16; gun-vessels, 22;

[1 In the Navy Estimates for 1904 the total strength was 131,100.]

gunboats, 48 ; miscellaneous vessels, 25 ; despatch vessels, 2 ; troopships and troop store-ships, 7 ; Indian troopships, 4 ; royal yachts, 4 ; surveying vessels, 5 ; total steam vessels, 191. Sloop, 1 ; schooners, 4 ; training brigs, 6 ; Coastguard tenders, 19 ; total sailing vessels, 30. Stationary and drill ships, 37. Grand total in commission, 258.[1]

W. H. HUTTON. The Church.

THE period from 1865 to 1885 is marked by the growing importance of the small body of Roman Catholics in England, caused not by conversions from members of the English Church, nor by any marked increase of immigration from Ireland or abroad, upon which their numbers chiefly depend, but by the energy and public spirit of Henry Edward Manning, sometime Archdeacon of Chichester, who, next to John Henry Newman, was the most eminent seceder from the Anglican Communion. In 1850, when Wiseman had been created by the Pope Arch-

Roman Catholicism.

bishop of Westminster (p. 346), a beginning had been made in a new and vigorous assertion of the right of members of the Roman Communion to take their part in public affairs ; Manning, with great energy and public spirit, took a still more prominent position than his predecessor. The literature of the day, and notably Disraeli's " Lothair," which is of high value as showing the view taken by one of the greatest statesmen of the period, affords evidence that the Roman policy in England was now regarded as distinctly, and by some as dangerously, aggressive in political as well as religious life. On the other hand, the decrees of the Vatican Council of 1870, which declared the infallibility of the Pope, rendered the severance between the Roman Catholic body and even the most advanced section of those who followed the Tractarians far more deep. It became quite clear to the leaders of the " High Church " party in England that their position had not advanced since the day when Archbishop Laud had written in his diary that approximation was impossible " till Rome is other than she is."

Since 1841 and Tract 90 the Tractarian movement had spread widely, through the influence of laymen and clergy, who, without being partisans, were strongly convinced of the

[1 In April, 1904, the number was :—On active service, 191 ; Coastguard, drill ships, and special service, 45. The Indian troopships had been abolished, and some of the stationary and sailing ships also.]

importance and truth of its teaching, such, for example, as **Ritualism.**
Mr. Gladstone and Richard William Church, from 1871 Dean
of St. Paul's. It led—in the hands of parish priests, who
wished to influence their people by the eye as well as the
ear, and also of ecclesiastical and antiquarian scholars, who
studied with care the text and history of the English Book
of Common Prayer and the ancient Liturgies upon which
it was based—to a revival of the use of the "ornaments of
the Church and of the ministers thereof" which were believed
to be ordered by the explicit rubric at the beginning of the
Prayer Book, revised and emphasised in the face of Puritan
objections by authority of Church and State in 1662. It was
clear that this rubric had never been at all widely obeyed, and
the special "ornaments" had long fallen into disuse. Thus
it was natural that the revival of special vestments for the Holy
Communion, and even the use of the surplice in the pulpit,
where it had been commonly neglected, should arouse great
opposition. It seemed as if those who had been asleep to the
significance of doctrine awoke in alarm at "ritual," which was
believed to express views to which some were anxious to deny
the support of the Anglican formularies. Many cases were
brought before the courts; some, in spite of protest, before the
Privy Council, to which many of the clergy were unable con-
scientiously to give obedience in matters ecclesiastical. A Royal
Commission issued some valuable but inconclusive reports.
Legal decisions, though they were the result of searching investigation and earnest consideration by conscientious judges,
seemed to not a few to be ill-informed and even partial.

Finally, strong Protestant feeling, misunderstood by leaders **The Public**
both in Church and State, led to the passing in 1874 of a Public **Worship**
Worship Regulation Act, which gave power to prosecute clergy **Act.**
who used unusual ritual, before a lay judge now appointed.
The Bill was opposed in both Houses by leaders of lay opinion
favourable to the Church movement of the last period, such
as Mr. Gladstone and Lord Salisbury, but was supported by
the eminent Evangelical and philanthropist, Lord Shaftesbury,
and the Archbishop of Canterbury, Dr. Tait, who had been one
of the four Oxford tutors who protested against Tract 90 (p. 192).
It led to much litigation and to the imprisonment of four
clergymen who were unable to accept the decisions of a lay

court as binding. It satisfied no one. In 1877 one of the wisest thinkers of the day wrote of the state of affairs which it had brought about: " I can only see in the legal decisions, and in the measures which have brought forth their results in the present crisis, a misuse of law such as has before now been known in history, and a policy of injustice towards an unpopular

ARCHBISHOP TAIT, BY GEORGE RICHMOND, R.A.

(*By permission of His Grace the Archbishop of Canterbury.*)

party, which has, I think, as much to say for itself as any other in the Church, which has done good service to the Church, and which, provoking as it has often been, has had more than parties in English controversy usually have to provoke them." As the years went on the Act was seen to cause friction rather than allay it; its mischievous effect became apparent to the rulers of the Church, and Archbishop Tait at last did his best to discourage its operation. His successors, Benson and Temple, were averse to the prosecution for " ritual" offences of earnest and self-denying men.

During this period the Oxford Movement had passed from the academic arena to the world of practical work, and some of the most earnest and successful parish priests in large towns and in London avowed themselves adherents of its principles. It had effected a transformation of the English Church at least as marked as that worked by the Wesleyan movement. It reached, perhaps, its greatest effect in the restoration to dignity and efficiency of the great cathedral church of St. Paul, London, where Milman and Mansel were succeeded by Church and Gregory, men of enthusiasm and power, and a chapter of able and earnest men assisted in making the services, spiritually as well as musically, a pattern of reverence and beauty for all England.

Effects of the Oxford Movement.

But this was by no means the only influence working strongly in the Church during these years. The "Evangelical" School had for a long time, owing to political causes, enjoyed a commanding position among the Anglican hierarchy, and owing to the position won by various bodies of trustees who held the patronage of many benefices, was very largely represented among the parochial incumbents. Scientific discoveries, however, and Biblical criticism, had severely shaken the influence exercised by the theology generally professed by that school. Modifications of doctrine once vehemently preached became necessary; and in this regard the influence of a new school became apparent.

The "Broad Church" School.

The "Broad Church" party may be regarded in some sense as the successors of the "Latitude men" of the later Stuart days (Vol. IV., p. 572); but they had now a wholly new force. Frederick Denison Maurice, a preacher and thinker of unusual power, though he strongly repudiated the name of Broad Churchman, was really a leader in the movement for a wider view of Christian dogma than had been current among the "Low Church" party. With him were men like the brilliant Charles Kingsley, a popular writer, only superficially acquainted with history, but imbued with a magnificent enthusiasm and a manly and tender religious feeling, and the lawyer, Thomas Hughes, filled with a strong sense of social evils and a determination to meet them in the spirit of Christ. Arthur Stanley, first at Oxford and then as Dean of Westminster, was a champion of the most liberal opinions; and, less prominent, but in the end exercising a wider and more durable influence,

290

was Benjamin Jowett, Master of Balliol College, who dwelt little upon the positive teachings of the Christian faith, but much upon its ethical principles. The work done by these men was very widely accepted and valued, but they were assimilative and progressive rather than learned or original.

Thus there was work for another school still. History and Biblical criticism had long been mainly in the hands

FREDERICK DENISON MAURICE, BY S. LAURENCE.
(National Portrait Gallery.)

Learning in the Church: Bishop Stubbs. of German scholars. During the years 1865–1885 it came to be seen that England possessed among her clergy scholars as great, and defenders of the Faith whom no assaults could overthrow. William Stubbs rose from a country cure, through an Oxford professorship, to be Bishop of Chester in 1884. His work during the twenty years before that date had established the constitutional history of England on sure foundations, and had put before the world the historic position and the historic services of the national Church, as they had never been put before. When a Royal Commission was appointed to consider the vexed question of the history, rights, and powers of the

Ecclesiastical Courts, it was his massive learning and strenuous energy which caused the truth, long obscured by common law encroachments and partisan influences, to be clearly set forth. The conclusions of the Commission were ineffectual, and have never been acted upon; but the impressive learning of the appendices contributed by Dr. Stubbs caused the constitutional rights of the clerical estate to be more clearly understood, and

MONUMENT TO BISHOP LIGHTFOOT, BY SIR EDGAR BOEHM, R.A.,
AND ALFRED GILBERT.
(*Durham Cathedral.*)

tended to the withdrawal of all official support from the legislation of 1874. Meanwhile, two eminent Cambridge scholars. Joseph Barber Lightfoot (Bishop of Durham, 1879), and Brooke Foss Westcott (Bishop of Durham, 1889), had vindicated the authenticity, and closely illustrated the text, of many of the New Testament books. It was seen that English learning could hold its own in Europe, and that Englishmen were still able powerfully to vindicate the foundation doctrines of the Christian religion. Never since the time when Bull was thanked by the French bishops for his defence of the Nicene Creed had the Anglican body been so rich in great scholars.

New Testament Criticism.

It was of happy augury for the Church that when Archbishop

Two Primates. Tait, whose goodness had made him as much beloved as his strength of will had made him influential in regard to the political position of the Church, died in 1883, he was succeeded by Edward White Benson, who had already done a noble work as first Bishop of Truro, and who was the bosom friend of the two great Cambridge scholars, Lightfoot and Westcott. He was thoroughly in touch with the modern spirit, while he was an enthusiastic student of the historic past.

Politics and the Church. Irish Disestablishment. A few words must be said of the political history of the Church during these years. The most important event undoubtedly was the disestablishment and disendowment of the Irish Church (p. 523), which since the Reformation had maintained the closest association with the Church in England. The social influence of the measure, which was not opposed by Archbishop Tait, lay chiefly in the tendency to divergence between the English and Irish Churches which almost necessarily followed. The Bill was strongly combated in the House of Lords by the eloquent William Connor Magee (Bishop of Peterborough, 1868, Archbishop of York, 1891), a great preacher whom the English Church had received from Ireland.

The Burials Act. In 1880, against the strenuous opposition of bishops such as Magee and the learned and devoted Christopher Wordsworth, of Lincoln, the burial grounds of the Church were thrown open to all persons who should desire to conduct a "Christian and orderly religious service" therein.

The period witnessed the removal of much that had been regarded as the exclusive privileges of the Church. It showed, no less, both at home and abroad, the great increase of her religious influence and her philanthropic effort.

H. D. TRAILL. Literature. IN this chapter of the work, which brings the history of our Society down to the middle of the year 1885, it has been thought advisable to deal with the subject of Literature in the form of a general review of literary movements and tendencies during the period embraced by the years 1815-85. And this not only because a detailed account of the principal writers who have appeared since 1815 and of their works would, in the majority of cases, involve an attempt to class and determine the position of living men (which, except in the few

instances in which the influence of a writer has passed into A Retro-
history in his lifetime, it is desirable to avoid), but also because spect, 1815-1885.
the nearer the narrative approaches towards the closing date the
more difficult to the point of impossibility does it become to
assign to a writer his proper place in relation either to his
predecessors or to his contemporaries.

Looking back, then, over the seventy years which divide the The
year 1815 from the year 1885, it will be found, we think, without Three Tidal
any too fanciful a search after symmetry, to divide itself roughly Periods.
into three periods, marked successively—though more plainly
no doubt at first in poetry than prose, and afterwards in prose
than poetry—by an alternating flux and reflux of the literary
tide.

In the year 1815 it was undoubtedly nearing, and between The Flow, 1815-1822.
that year and the year 1822 inclusive it touched, high-water
mark. Shelley, Keats, Byron, Coleridge, and Wordsworth in
poetry; Scott, De Quincey, Wilson, Lamb, and Hazlitt in prose,
had all of them reached the maturity of their genius, and some
of them the height of their productive powers. This brief
period witnessed the publication of Shelley's "Alastor,"
"Prometheus Unbound," and "Adonaïs"; Keats's "Endymion"
and the two immortal "Odes"; Byron's Third and Fourth
Cantos of "Childe Harold," the first Two Cantos of "Don Juan,"
and the finest of his dramas; Coleridge's "Christabel"; Wordsworth's "Duddon Sonnets"; De Quincey's "Confessions of an
Opium-Eater"; the first of the "Elia Essays"; some of the
best of Hazlitt's work (p. 42); and no fewer than thirteen of the
Waverley Novels, including among them the masterpieces of
the "Antiquary," the "Heart of Midlothian," "Ivanhoe," and
"The Legend of Montrose." Probably no other period of equal
brevity in the world's history added so much to the imperish-
able treasures of its literature.

But with the death of Keats, followed within three years by
that of Shelley, and with the gradual decline, not indeed in the
fertility of Scott's invention, but in the commanding excellence
of his work, we already become sensible that the tide has
turned; and, on the whole, the third and (until close upon its
end) the fourth decade of the century are years of receding
waters. The diminishing ranks of the poets and the depreciated
standard of poetic achievement during the interval between the

death of Byron and the emergence of Tennyson—a time when
Mrs. Hemans and " L. E. L." were the most popular singers of the
day—tell an unmistakable tale. We know now, of course, that
the spirit of English poetry was not dead, but only sleeping,
and that the broken lyre of Keats was only waiting to be taken
up and re-strung with new and richer chords, and tuned to more

WILLIAM HAZLITT, BY JOHN HAZLITT.
(*By permission of William Carew Hazlitt, Esq.*)

varied melodies by the great poet of the Victorian age. But to
any man who was then old enough to be able to recall the
twenty years of incomparable brilliancy with which the century
opened, the outlook in that day of sugared inanities and elegant
commonplaces and of " Keepsakes " and " Books of Beauty "
must have seemed discouraging enough.

In prose fiction the relapse was less marked, for though
between 1820 and 1830 Scott held the field alone, with the
beginning of the fourth decade it began to be reoccupied by
novelists of high ability and distinction, if not of the first order

of genius, in the persons of Disraeli, Bulwer, and others. Yet **Prose Fiction, 1820-1837.**
even here it is no less true that English literature had to wait
from 1814, the date of the publication of " Waverley," until 1837,
for another master of the novel, though of a widely different
school and temperament, to arise. The authors of " Vivian
Grey" and of " Pelham," with all their genuine merits of
imagination and showy qualities of literary execution, were but
poor substitutes for the " Wizard of the North." When Scott
ceased writing, it became no more possible to regard any living
and working novelist, than any poet or poetess, as among the
foremost representatives of English literature. Its representation
had passed into the hands of critics and essayists, and pre- **The Prose of the Essay.**
eminently into those of Macaulay, who had already enriched
periodical and, as the event proved, permanent literature with
his essays on Milton and Machiavelli, on Moore's " Byron " and
Croker's " Boswell," to mention these alone ; who had indeed
already left an impress upon our critical and biographical prose
which is still visible, and given it an impulse which is not yet
exhausted, and to whose extraordinary influence it is due that
in this branch of it, and perhaps in this alone, the history
of our literature has run a smooth and uniform course,
unbroken by any of those vicissitudes of flux and reflux
which are elsewhere to be recorded. From the point of
view, in fact, of the historian of letters, the formative work
of Macaulay in prose stands side by side with that of
Tennyson in poetry as the two most important phenomena
of the last seventy years. As regards its effect upon expression—upon the form as distinct from the matter of English
literature—the career of Macaulay reduces that of Carlyle
to the proportion of a mere meteoric episode.

The second of the three periods into which the era under **The Flowing Tide 1837-1862.**
consideration divides itself began within a few years of the
close of the 'thirties, and lasted a full quarter of a century.
From the first work which brought Dickens at a bound into
popularity in 1837, to the death of Thackeray in 1863, the
tide of great literary production was coming in in splendid
strength and volume. It is possible, indeed, to find a period
of seven years at about the middle of this quarter of a century
which, except in the single article of poetry, would bear
comparison with that wonderful septennium of the early

century which has been above described. Thus the years
1846–52 witnessed the publication of "David Copperfield";
of "Vanity Fair," "Pendennis," and "Esmond"; of the first
two volumes of Macaulay's "History"; of "The Princess" and
"In Memoriam"; of "The Seven Lamps of Architecture"; of
"The Latter-Day Pamphlets" and "The Life of Sterling"; of
"Christmas Eve and Easter Day"; of Mrs. Browning's first
two volumes of "Poems"; and of "Jane Eyre," "Shirley," and
"Villette." This list, as has been said, is not so rich in poetry
as that with which we have compared it, and, perhaps, even
Dickens and Thackeray combined do not more than suffice to
balance that astonishing mixture of profusion and perfection
which makes Scott victorious over any single competitor save
Shakespeare alone. But though the writers figuring in them
are in each case nine in number, more varieties of genius
are represented in the later than in the earlier catalogue, and
many of the above enumerated works are scarcely less sure
of immortality than the Waverley Novels, and considerably
surer than the rhapsodies of De Quincey and the discoursings
of Hazlitt. In fact, no competent judge of literature could
possibly, we think, ignore the manifold evidences of a turn of
the tide having set in at about the date of Queen Victoria's
accession, and having reached its flood about midway in the
first decade after the completed half century.

When, however, we are about to claim 1837–63 as another
"great period" of literature, and to class it in imagination with
those two other great periods, both also so curiously occurring in the reigns of our two other female sovereigns—the
Elizabethan, and the so-called "Augustan" age of Anne—we
come across certain "stones of stumbling" which were either
absent from the path of the critic in the two eras referred to,
or of which the very memory has disappeared. There is at
least no evidence to show that when Shakespeare and the
other great dramatists and lyrists ruled, in the late sixteenth
and early seventeenth century, or when, as at the beginning
of the eighteenth, Addison and Steele and Pope and Swift were
the admired and honoured leaders of the national literature,
there flourished side by side with them one or more writers
of vast inferiority to these great men, but of quite as wide,
if not of wider, celebrity, and commanding a "paying public"

A Paradox of Popular Taste.

of a numerical magnitude to which the admirers of Shakespeare and Ben Jonson, of Pope and Addison, never at their
most successful moments approached. If any such fortunate
impostors existed in these periods their very names are lost to
us. Poetasters and prose twaddlers no doubt abounded; but
not with money. The " poor devils " worked " for the book-
sellers " at a pittance, and Pope had the satisfaction not only
of lashing their literary in-
competence but of jeering at
their rags. What he would
have thought and felt, and
how he would have given
expression to his feelings, if
one of the tenth-rate scrib-
blers whom he scarified in
the " Dunciad " had written
a book which maintained the
highest vogue for a generation, passed through forty
editions, and brought the
author twenty thousand
pounds, one shrinks from
the mere attempt to con-
jecture.

Photo: Russell & Sons, Baker Street, W.
MARTIN FARQUHAR TUPPER.

Yet it is with almost as strange a portent as this that the
literary history of the century confronts us. For though it
would in many respects be unjust to compare Martin
Farquhar Tupper (1810–89), a man of education, refinement,
and amiability, with the ignorant and disreputable crew
whom Pope pursued with a brutality as shocking as their
own, yet it is hardly an exaggeration to say that his claim
to be regarded as a poet—and it was as a poet that he presented himself to, and was apparently accepted by, a large
body of his countrymen—was little less preposterous than
theirs. Tupper could, and did, occasionally, acquit himself
respectably as a writer of ballads and other kinds of minor
verse, but it was not to these he owed his popularity. This
was due to the extraordinary collection of rhymeless and,
indeed, rhythmless platitudes which he published under the
name of " Proverbial Philosophy," which was eagerly taken up

Proverbial Philosophy.

by the public, and was in immense demand as a "gift-book" for a long series of years. There were those, indeed, who declared, and not wholly in an ironical spirit, that its purely material and external attractions, its conveniences in shape and size, combined with the unimpeachable propriety of its contents—that these and not any popular delusion as to its literary merits were the operative causes of its truly astonishing, and its yet more astonishingly prolonged, vogue. But no such explanation will entirely account for the fact. The public taste in bookbinding and book decoration is liable to all the vicissitudes of fluctuating fashion; and in all ages the supply of platitudes, whether in concealed or in avowed prose, has always been large enough to prevent any single purveyor of them from establishing a monopoly. It seems, therefore, impossible to doubt that Tupper's lasting attraction for so large a body of his countrymen must have been mainly an attraction of form and not of matter, and that they must have read and admired him in such numbers not merely because he uttered correct sentiments, but because his manner of uttering them struck his public as beautiful and distinguished. The vast and steady popularity of the author of " Proverbial Philosophy" during the greater part, if not the whole, of Tennyson's prime, and still more, the unquestionably immense numerical preponderance of the poetaster's public over the poet's, is one of the most singular phenomena of that literary era.

The Second Ebb in Poetry

Its chief significance, as we shall have to point out later on, resides in the fact that the period of its appearance coincided with a flow of the literary tide. It was while Tennyson was adding to his triumphs, while Browning was slowly approaching to that wider recognition which he cannot be said to have achieved until the publication of "The Ring and the Book," that this many-headed prostration before the commonplace was going on: nay, it lasted up to and over the date when the sudden and startling apparition of Mr. Swinburne was to add a new name to the list of great English poets, and at the same time to strike English poetry for the better part of another quarter of a century with sterility in all save imitative production. From the early 'sixties till almost the middle of the last decade but one of the nineteenth century

the influence of Swinburne, waning towards the end of
the period, but still perceptible, dominated all the younger
poets of the later Victorian era; and it is only now, when
it is almost, if not quite, exhausted, that an original note is
beginning to make itself heard. During the 'seventies and
'eighties, however, we have to note another poetic influence,
issuing indeed from the same Romanticist sources of inspira-

Photo: Elliott & Fry, Baker Street, W.
ALGERNON CHARLES SWINBURNE.

tion, but slightly divergent in its course. The poetry of
Dante Gabriel Rossetti (1828-82) had far less widely capti-
vating power than that of Swinburne; probably it affected
but one young writer to five who came under the influence
of the author of "Poems and Ballads." Still it diverted attention from the musical to the pictorial side of poetry, and
so tended to substitute one form of imitative composition
for another. But it would be hardly too much to say that
for full twenty years after the Swinburnian note was first
sounded in the public ear, little else but its echo was to be
heard in the strain of any younger singer. During these two
decades almost all original poetic impulse seems to have disappeared from among the literary youth of England.

Decline of the Novel.

In prose fiction, too, during the self-same period there was a notable, and as it seems to some of those who now look back upon it, almost calamitous decline upon lower ideals.

Thackeray died in 1863; and though Dickens was still alive and went on writing for another seven years, all his best work was done. Of Charles Reade and Charles Kingsley much the same might be said. The two finest romances of

DANTE GABRIEL ROSSETTI.
(*From a photograph by Lewis Carroll.*)

the latter were written in the 'fifties; the former's greatest novel, " The Cloister and the Hearth," in 1861. The last of George Eliot's indisputable successes, " Silas Marner," appeared in the same year, and there remained but one work which is even arguably worthy of her genius, the brilliant but unequal " Middlemarch," to be added to her record. Even Wilkie Collins (1824–89), a novelist usually described as of the school of Dickens, though he possessed few or none of the master's gifts save a certain command of the weird and terrible, had woven the most successful of his mystery plots. When the first of the two decades had run little more than half its course, the next ten or twelve years may be described with substantial accuracy as the period of the unbounded vogue and popularity of Anthony Trollope (1815–82), a writer who followed Thackeray in the systematic confinement of his studies to the "comfortable" classes of society, but who has nowhere displayed the faintest traces of Thackeray's subtle humour, his genuine though restrained pathos, his unrivalled insight into character, or his admirable prose style. Within certain narrow limits—those, for instance, of the cathedral close—Trollope was not without an eye for character, and he has portrayed certain naturally humorous types to be found within these limits with a fidelity which in itself assures for them a humorous effect; but speaking generally, his art, in its mechanical realism, stands related to Thackeray's as that of the cheap photographer to the masterly portrait-painter's. It is the commonplace carried to its highest power; and the fact that for so long a series of years he stood unquestioned at the head of

CHARLES READE.
(From a water colour by Mdlle. Stefanofska, in the possession of C. L. Reade, Esq.)

his branch of the literary profession and commanded a public so large that the amount of his professional earnings was for his day unprecedented, affords a phenomenon almost as discouraging in itself as the reign of Tupper in another field of literature. Indeed, if it would be unjust to the novelist to treat the two instances as precisely parallel, it is only because, vast as may be the interval which divides the third-rate in prose fiction from the first-rate, the difference between the poetaster and the poet is one not in degree but in kind.

It is somewhat unfortunate and not a little unfair to this branch of our social history that we should be compelled

The Literary Revival.

to close this review of it during a period of temporary retrogression, or, at any rate, of temporary pause. But it does so happen that that stir of new forces in our literature, which will be denied by none but those who have been, perhaps, pardonably disgusted by daily exaggerations of it, only began to be felt about 1880. During the fifteen or sixteen years which have since elapsed[1] its effects have been most marked in almost every department of letters. For, if it be true, as no doubt it is, that neither in poetry nor in prose fiction, nor even in history, in biography, or in the essay, can we as yet, with any confidence, indicate the successors of the deceased masters of these various literary forms, it is, at the same time, equally true that the claimants to a place very near the highest have never been so numerous nor their claims anything like so strong as they are to-day. If some critics are slow to recognise this, their hesitation is probably due to one or other of two causes. Either they have been so far irritated out of their own critical impartiality by the extravagant *réclame* of newspaper writers who find a second Shelley or another Keats every alternate week, as to deny the existence of any new poetic genius whatsoever; or else they have been really prevented by the immense elevation which has taken place in the average standard of verse-making during the period in question from being able to discern among the host of new-comers the pre-eminence of a few. Yet they are there, and there of their own right; more than one or two of them with a manner of their own, and no longer, as had been the case for the previous twenty years, mere echoes of Tennyson or Swinburne, mere mimics of Browning or Rossetti. If the great poet of the coming century has not yet appeared, the mere number of genuine poets whom the closing century has produced need not discourage hopes of his appearance.

The New Romance.

The romantic movement in fiction, except in so far as it is a mere reaction from pessimistic realism, is again a sign of reviving strength. And it is a fortunate circumstance for the future of literature that its leader and foremost representative should have possessed the distinguished literary gift of Robert Louis Stevenson (1850–94), a writer whose

[1 This was written in 1896. Mr. Traill died early in 1900.]

exquisitely finished style, while for the reader it suffers somewhat from its evidences of too conscious art, affords for that
very reason an all the more inspiring and serviceable model to
the student. His influence is largely traceable in all the lighter
literature of the imagination at the present day, and, due
allowance being made for the dangers which beset all young

ROBERT LOUIS STEVENSON, BY SIR WILLIAM
BLAKE RICHMOND, R.A.
(*National Portrait Gallery.*)

writers still in the imitative stage, it has been on the whole
an influence for good; while the prose of essay and criticism
which had sought, perhaps, an excess of point, precision, and
emphasis under the long-continuing and only now declining
domination of Macaulay, has—thanks in part to the unparalleled power and fascination of John Ruskin, the successor to the tradition of Landor, De Quincey, and the
other early nineteenth-century masters of the rhetorical and
"impassioned" prose style—acquired a colour and flexibility,
and an adequacy of response to emotional and æsthetic

needs, in which for more than a generation it had been lacking. In every field of literature, in short, the endeavour after literary correctness, literary grace, and, if possible, literary distinction, is conspicuous and increasing. The impulse has extended even to the drama, which for more than half a century had lived in contented divorce from literature, and even before that period had been able to effect no closer or happier union with it than is recorded in the respectable, but absolutely undistinguished, productions of Sheridan Knowles (1784–1862), and the deftly constructed but

Later Victorian Drama. showily rhetorical dramas of Bulwer Lytton. Our leading dramatists of to-day are nothing if not literary, at any rate in aspiration and purpose, and are, some of them, avowedly committed, with what success we have yet to see, to the undertaking of regaining for the English drama a position in English literature of equal consideration with that to which accomplished writers like Augier and Dumas the younger have raised French drama in the literature of France. This, however, is but one among many signs of the universal eagerness for literary acceptance and recognition which is one of the most striking characteristics of the age, and which the immense development of the cheap newspaper press and its largely increased attention to literary things and persons have provided with the means of gratifying itself in far too many spurious, pretentious, and ridiculous ways. But it is the duty —though the difficult duty—of the critic of literature and the student of its history to endeavour to discover, and measure the extent of, the reality which underlies this somewhat rank overgrowth of sham; and our belief is that those who address themselves with patience and without prejudice to this task will find that, on the whole, it yields them not merely satisfactory but highly encouraging results.

F. G. STEPHENS. Later Victorian Artists. In one respect, to which, perhaps, not sufficient attention is usually given, Pre-Raphaelitism was remarkable. It was really the one which in this country tended to the formation of a school in the historical sense of that term, as it is applicable to Roman, Florentine, Low Country, German, and modern French painting. Here, in fact, was a group of men of genius,

JOHN RUSKIN, BY SIR HUBERT VON HERKOMER, R.A.
(By permission, from the portrait at the National Portrait Gallery.)

291

who, however diverse they might be, acted according to a common impulse. Of no other congeries of English artists can this be said. In the course of a few years, too, the group became the centre of a very important company of artists, each of whom was, as the members of the Brotherhood began and continued to be, perfectly independent. In respect to time and his early death, the first to be reckoned in this numerous rank of more or less eminent and original

painters was Walter Howell Deverell, a youth of extraordinary promise, much beloved by the Pre-Raphaelite Brotherhood. Far more developed was Mr. Arthur Hughes, whose delightful " April Love " is one of the few examples fit to be ranked with Millais's " A Huguenot " and " The Order of Release," and is instinct with exquisite sentiment.   Mr. Henry Wallis's " Death of Chatterton," " The Stone-breaker," and a host of pictures in water-colour, proved him to be an artist of very rare accomplishments and sympathies.   The next in the order of time who was a confessor of the same order was G. P. Boyce, whose " The Confessor's Chapel," " Bridewell," and " Where stood Bridewell," delight all eyes, and charm those whose sense of beauty does not need to be aroused by startling effects and gorgeous coloration.   Subtle, delicate, and demure, the art of this painter will endure.   The brilliant, solid, and powerful seascapes of John Brett qualified him to be Neptune's Painter in Ordinary, while Mr. Hook and Henry Moore have shown the world more of the splendour and beauty of the ocean and its shores than was ever known before.   But, however true to nature the latter two great artists may be, they cannot, in the ordinary sense of that designation, be called Pre-Raphaelites.   W. J. Inchbold's art never obtained the recognition its merits, expressiveness, and delicious harmonies of tint and tones demand, and which it will some day receive.   His " Lake of Geneva " might have been painted by the king of Faëry-land.   A more fortunate and resourceful poet-painter was Alfred William Hunt (1830–96). Mr. J. G. Naish, C. P. Knight, and half a dozen less known land- and sea-painters deservedly hold high places in the ranks of naturalistic landscapists, one of whose aims it is to infuse the fidelity and vigour of their works with sentiment of the higher and less obvious sort.   J. W. Oakes depicted Welsh mountains and valleys with a profound sentiment which is not "classical," nor in the manner of John Varley, Turner, or any other master; his work excels in brightness, research, and precision. A confessor, it might be said an early martyr, of Pre-Raphaelitism is Mr. W. S. Burton, who, in 1856, gave the world an austere and original tragedy called "The Puritan," which represented a dying Cavalier after he has been wounded in a duel.

Insomuch as his antetype and model in art was Millais

HOME WITH THE TIDE, BY J. C. HOOK, R.A.
(National Gallery of British Art.)

no less a person than Frederick Walker might be enrolled with the distinguished group of men we are now discussing. Notwithstanding the vulgar notion that Pre-Raphaelitism and high stippling were one, it is impossible not to call Walker's "Boys Bathing," "The Harbour of Refuge," "Fishmonger's Shop," "Philip," and "The Ploughman" most brilliant, happy, powerful works of that order which includes Millais's masterpieces in figure- and landscape-painting. With these, too, must be ranked Mrs. Allingham's for ever charming "A Flat Iron for a Farthing," which either Walker or Millais might have produced, and half a score more of fresh and fair illustrations of rustic life. Mr. W. Gale

Frederick Walker.

had joined the company we speak of with several capital pieces, the best of which is " Mr. F.'s Aunt." One of the most splendid and highly endowed poet-painters of the Victorian Age was Rossetti's analogue, Sir E. Burne-Jones (1833–98), the artist of " The Golden Stair," " King Cophetua," " Love among the Ruins," " The Sleeping Beauty," and a host of lovely and mystical pieces. Mr. Spencer Stanhope's art

THE VAGRANTS, BY FREDERICK WALKER, A.R.A.

(*National Gallery of British Art.*)

allies itself with Rossetti's, and his picture of " The Wine-Press," a parable of Christ, not unworthily occupies a place among the finer achievements of Rossetti, Mr. Holman Hunt, and Sir E. Burne-Jones, with many of which it has something in common, and yet is independent, potent, and original.

Other Groups: Gilbert, Watts, Brett, Hook, Moore

Leaving this original and finely equipped group, most of whose names are already written in capitals upon the rolls of fame, let us recall to the memories of all who delight in art, and are just, catholic, and sympathetic enough to give honour wherever honour is due, a still more numerous and varied, as well as a highly accomplished and able, category of men, who in whatsoever country they had lived and laboured, or in

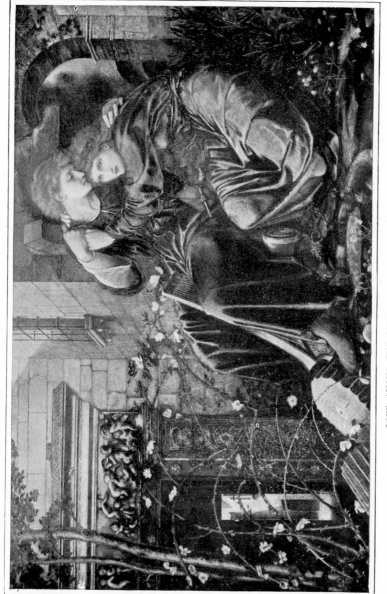

LOVE AMONG THE RUINS, BY SIR E. BURNE-JONES.

(From a photograph by Mr. F. Hollyer of the picture as originally painted.)

whichever age their distinctions had been won, would have deserved our gratitude and the world's applause. His ever-abundant invention, mastery of design, and rare power in painting compel us to give Sir John Gilbert the first place in this splendid company. Of quite another stamp, but worthy to be ranked with the greatest portrait-painters of all time, was G. F. Watts (1817-1904), some at least of whose noble and ambitious allegories are pre-eminent in their way, while, strange to say, the same master excelled in humour when he depicted how the first oyster-eater fared under the eyes of his admiring yet fearful spouse; the pair of aborigines being seated, naked of course, upon the sea-shore. Who shall think of sea-painting and not remember Mr. J. C. Hook, the Titianesque master of our time who immortalised himself with " Luff, Boy ! " and " The Broken Oar " ? To the sea we must return again when we remember that it was John Brett who painted the resplendent " Britannia's Realm." If Henry Moore (1831-96) had produced " The Newhaven Packet " and nothing else, how great would have been our debt to him ! Apart from this we owe to this master of cloud-land and ocean's phases and passions the superb " Loss of a Barque in Yarmouth Roads," " The Last of the Light," " A Winter Gale in the Channel," and " Rough Weather in the Mediterranean," to say nothing of great numbers of almost equally fine examples in oil- and water-colours. The brothers Wyllie, if not Pre-Raphaelites *de facto*, are, each in his line, of the best grade. No one but the elder of the two has attempted to paint the bottom of the sea; no one has depicted summer sunlight on a flowery meadow with so much tenderness and truth as the younger.

Leighton, Burton, Poynter. Among the finest eclectic masters only M. Bouguereau, the French leader in that line, can, technically speaking, take a place near Lord Leighton (1830-96), whose " Syracusan Brides," " Venus Disrobing," " Wedded," two newly married lovers ; " Daphne-phoria," and " David," are but the finest and most complete, the most elegant, animated, and refined, of a long series of examples, which only the ungrateful and half-taught will venture to call academic, or describe as over-laboured and excessively polished. The antithesis of Sir John Gilbert, Mr. Holman Hunt, and other dramatic, and in painted prose moralising, artists, Leighton thought of beauty, and was satisfied with nothing less ; just as

THE BATH OF PSYCHE, BY LORD LEIGHTON, P.R.A.

(National Gallery of British Art.)

Millais thought of nature and life, which, when wholesome, is never
less than beautiful. Sir F. Burton (1816–1900), another eclectic of
a high degree and sparse productiveness, takes a place in line with
Leighton. Not far remote from them, with a dash of austerity
and abundance of learning, energy, and grace, comes Sir Edward
Poynter, whose "Atalanta's Race," "Suppliant to Venus," "Israel
in Egypt," and, best of all, "Venus's Visit to Æsculapius," which
is at the Tate Gallery, are masterpieces to be enjoyed wherever culture and chastened art obtain.

Midway between Poynter and his antitheses, H. S. Marks
and Mr. Frith (whom, of course, no one would care to compare),
the student will group a body of incident and anecdote painters,
some of whom incline to humour, some to pathos, some to sentiment, some to character, some to costume, and some to idyllic
poetry. John Philip (1817–67) was a leader of this sort, good in   Philip,
nearly all the lines here named ; his "La Gloria" is a tragi-comedy,   Calderon,
his "Murillo" an "illustration," his "Free Kirk" and "The   Marks,
Catechism" are, in their designs at least, almost worthy of Wilkie   Faed.
at his best ; and his "Chat Round the Brasero" is a capital
piece. Calderon's finest production of late years was "Ariadne
lorn of Theseus," which was in the Academy in 1895. "Her Most
High, Noble, and Puissant Grace" was a gem of a fine and charming kind ; nor was "On Her Way to the Throne" unworthy of so
excellent a taste as his. As a brilliant painter Calderon (1833–
98) might be compared with Pettie, when Pettie was at his
best, not otherwise, and with Mr. Orchardson, although he is not
nearly so great in the sardonic vein in which the latter triumphs
when he appears as the Michael Angelo of cynical and pathetic
anecdote painting. As a master of humour, Marks (1829–98), when
he does not labour his points too much, is very welcome ; but to
his "Three Jolly Post Boys" his immortality will be due. T. Faed
(1826–1900) will remain eminent as a painter proper apart from
the pathos of his best efforts, which are "From Dawn to Sunset,"
"The First Break in the Family," "His Only Pair," "Baith
Fether and Mither," and some later exercises in the same line.
Renowned among modern painters of anecdote, history, romance,
costume, and beauty, Sir Laurence Alma-Tadema, who, if not
of it, is in the English school, stands on one of the loftiest
pedestals. A hundred pictures call him great, and leave his critic
at a loss in which category to place so resourceful a designer, so

learned and acute an observer, and so admirable a master. Apart from paintings which delighted Continental Europe before he came among us, the superb inventor of the "Danse Pyrrhique," "*Fête Intime*," "Tarquin," and "Death of Prætextatus," has given us "*Un Amateur Roman*," "Phidias at the Parthenon," "An Antique Sculptor," "The Picture Gallery," "The Sculpture Gallery," "Water Pets," "An Audience at Agrippa's," and quite a host of similar specimens, any one of which would go far to win the reputation of an artist.

Fildes, Leslie, Briton Riviere. It is difficult to place Mr. Fildes, whose "The Doctor" is a true *chef-d'œuvre*, as full of purpose and excellent painting as of pathos. Equally difficult it is to decide how the future will find where Mr. G. D. Leslie's statue shall stand; among those of the rustic, pathetic, or anecdotic painters it is sure to hold a high position. The distinction of Mr. Briton Riviere will be decided by "The Magician's Doorway," "Actæon," and "Persepolis," if not by "Phœbus Apollo" and some of his delightful "dog-pictures." He is a friend of the canine race, and, as such, quite as great, though in a very different way, as Landseer himself. In this indeterminate category of artists, to whom the English world owes so much, it is right to put George Mason, who excelled in poetry as well as in designing. A very choice idyllic spirit often rules in the landscapes of Mr. David Murray, who, when he does himself full justice, demands a very rare and noble sort of distinction, while he is a sympathetic observer of nature. Professor Costa and Corbet are twin stars of eclectic landscape painting of the highest class; they are not remote from Mason, and if, like him, they painted English subjects, the likeness of any one of the three to the others would be more obvious than it is. That Mr.

Crane, Linton. Walter Crane is a master of decorative art has not prevented him from giving us some very precious quasi-classical exercises upon romantic and chivalrous themes. Sir James Linton must not be omitted when learning, care, and a fine pictorial sense are under consideration. He is one of the best draughtsmen England has produced.

Whistler. It was Whistler's misfortune rather than his fault that no less a portent than the so-called Impressionism is, artistically speaking, his illegitimate offspring. Not, however, to this fine and original artist—a rare colourist, a delicate master of the etching-needle, and, as a chiaroscurist, not easily to be sur-

A VISIT TO ÆSCULAPIUS, BY SIR EDWARD JOHN POYNTER, P.R.A.

(National Gallery of British Art.)

passed—are due the preposterous fads and vagaries represented at the exhibition of the New English Art Club; not on
Whistler (1834–1903) are to be fathered the crude and audacious
vulgarities of MM. Degas and Manet, and their feeble English
imitators. When Time, the avenger of common-sense, has
brushed away the monstrosities of this new avatar of presumption, ignorance, and incompetence, then will it become apparent
that, though in moods the most diverse and unequalled, every
modern English artist of renown may be grouped with one or
another of three distinguished men, whose names will survive as
Sir John E. Millais, Dante Gabriel Rossetti, and James
McNeill Whistler. The first was an Englishman complete, who
had, practically speaking, never been out of his native country;
the second was an Italian of the sixteenth century, born in England and tempered by English ways; the third, and not the
least original, though far more limited, artist of the trio, is a
Parisian of the later days who happened to be born in one or other
of the States of the North American Union, and can hardly
be said to have come under the influences of ancient art-culture
at all. That he, Lord Leighton, and Sir E. Burne-Jones belong
to the same generation of artistic mankind will sorely puzzle
future historians of painting.

**MAY MORRIS.
Decorative Art,
1800–1885.** At the beginning of the century the decorative arts present a
mixture of pompous pseudo-classicism—a Renaissance of the
Renaissance, a degenerate ghost of a borrowed style with the
superficial and trifling rococo of the eighteenth century; while
there lingered a remnant of spontaneous and almost unconscious
ornament applied to those wares, made rather for domestic use
than for trade, which had escaped as yet the growing machine
industry. Interesting as must be the last vestige of the popular
art which at its best and strongest period covered France,
England, Italy, and Germany with architecture and ornamental work, whose remains are at once our delight and
our shame, this homely side of belated eighteenth-century
decorative design has its own not very characteristic pretti-
ness, its faint odour of romance—the romance of blue china
and faded roses—and, compared with the complete negation of
beauty in ornament of the late Georgian and early Victorian

THE ARTIST IN HIS STUDIO, BY JAMES McNEILL WHISTLER.

(By permission of Douglas W. Freshfield, Esq.)

Lingering Traditional Ornament. periods, it is charming indeed. In such homely decora-tion the less wealthy classes expressed something of their need for beautifying life. We cannot wonder, recalling the events that have built up the century, that every form of ornamental handwork soon began to decay. The use of machinery not only intensified labour, but where for decora-tive purposes it has been substituted for the craftsman, it has lowered the standard of taste until, in the end, the hand-worker himself is driven to copy the work of a machine.

Art and Industry. Early in the century public men were concerned at the growing estrangement between art and industry; only they not unnaturally mistook the effect for the cause: they saw only the deterioration of the art and not the causes which had made intelligent art impossible. Their national pride was hurt: England, first of industrial countries, should also be first in the arts. And they came to the conclusion that the designers and draughtsmen must be looked to, their artistic education enforced; they talked of the "Union of Art and Industry," a common-sense union—Art the handmaiden, Industry the master. At last their doubts and misgivings— voiced now by a politician, now by a manufacturer—crystallised in a Special Committee of the House of Commons (1835) "to inquire into the best means of extending a knowledge of the Arts and of the principles of Design among the people, especially the manufacturing population of the country; also to inquire into the constitution, management, and effects of Institutions connected with the Arts."

Schools of Design. One gathers from the report of the Committee, reappointed in 1836, evidence of the popular attitude towards art. The Committee came to the conclusion that "it was most desirable that the principles of Design should form a portion of National Education." A vote of £1,500 for a normal school of design was passed, its expenditure being placed in the hands of the Board of Trade. In 1837 the first Government School of Design was opened at Somerset House with twelve pupils, the modest forerunner of the present Royal College of Art at South Kensington, as of the quite inestimable historic collec-tions of the Museum itself. The plan of study was in bare outline very much what it is to-day, however much the instruc-tion itself may have altered. To the ordinary drawing-school routine was added instruction in design for branches of industry—(*a*) study of fabrics and of conditions of processes admitting of design, (*b*) study of the history of the arts in manufacture, styles of ornament and "such theoretical knowledge as was calculated to improve the student's taste and add to his acquaintance with art." Local schools were formed in the manufacturing districts, the first at Spitalfields. They soon became unpopular, and, owing to the dissatisfaction they caused, a Committee of the House of Commons was appointed (1849) to inquire into the management of the Government school at Somerset House. In 1852 a Department of Practical Art was formed, all the schools in the country being placed under its management. In 1853 the London school moved to Marlborough House, and thence to South Kensington in 1857. The unpopularity of the system is not surprising; it should have been foreseen that a designer of artistic instincts and artistic training cannot be turned out to order, machine-made, well-calendered and finished, like a bale of Manchester cotton. The disappointment expressed at this obvious negative result is curiously mixed with a dread of change, thrusting back as idealistic and unpractical a new train of ideas not strictly in the line of machine-development No doubt the complaints that the school-instruction was incomplete and unsystematic were well-founded, nor could it well be otherwise. It is always difficult to decide what, in a movement involving anything beyond the material necessities of life, is artificial, and what a spontaneous expression of the need of the time. We have so many centuries of historic art behind us that an indolent or unimaginative brain, merely borrowing from the past, may produce work which a public grown too hurried to criticise accepts as original. When we see, as the result of Special Committees, Schools of Design, and Museums of Historic Art, the enormities of the Exhibition of 1851, the monumental dulness of that of 1862, and even the trivialities displayed in our West-end shops at the close of our period, it cannot, we fear, be said that the effort to unite the arts and manufactures of the country met with any rapid or universal success.

During the first half of the century manufacturers had been contented to copy French designs; the great idea, even

French
Influence.

of those who were endeavouring to create an English school, was at once to emulate French skill and to be independent of it. Some of the manufacturers examined by the Committee of 1836 declared that the figured silks of Spitalfields were copied from French designs, "as they were almost destitute of taste in England." The designers, too, of Paisley shawls were chiefly occupied in arranging and copying from "French" cashmeres.

The questions asked by the Committee show how confused were the notions of decorative art entertained by the average member of Parliament in those days. "Have not the French lately devoted their attention to a style which they call the Renaissance, or the early style which prevailed in Italy when the arts began to dawn?" This is a typical leading question. A Royal Academician read to the Committee a paper on Design (he called it a "Lecture on the Oval"), which introduces the subject in these promising words:—"By a concatenation of ovals . . . an agreeable range of lines is produced." He then proceeded to show that if once a workman had the idea of the oval in his mind he could never make a badly-shaped vase.

"Gothic"
Art.

Early in the century the first signs of the "Gothic revival" (p. 238) sprang up, a movement which, directly and indirectly, has left its mark equally in architecture and in ecclesiastical and domestic decoration. For us whose ideas as to the value of revivals and imitations of dead schools have changed, it is difficult to distinguish what in it was genuine love of Gothic art and what mere grotesque travesty. It was to be expected that a desire should arise for something more vigorous and distinctive than the Louis Quinze and the classical style, with its "five orders," that had so long held their ground; but the expression of this desire—in church-spires soaring above the roofs of a gentleman's country-house, in miniature castles complete even to the dungeons, in shoddy sentiment through which nakedness of invention is apparent—was as naïve and inconsequent as the "Mysteries of Udolpho" in literature, or Horace Walpole's Gothic villa in architecture, and equally unconvincing in its attempt at reproducing old-time romance.

It has often been said that to revive a period of art that has passed away is as impossible as to revive the conditions under which that art was produced. Nor is there any mystery in the want of success in the " Gothic revival " in its earlier or later developments. Medieval art could be caricatured, but not reproduced. It was free, leisurely, individual, wayward, too—arising out of a way of seeing life and out of a belief in the unseen that are quite outside the habit of modern thought. A nation which has to a large extent lost the power or the desire to produce work of great beauty loses therewith the faculty of criticising and appraising such beauty when they meet with it. The strange and varied richness of imagination manifest in Gothic work is to them an exhibition of savagery; it is too far-off, too incomprehensible in its apparent simplicity to touch any chord in their sympathy.

The popular criticism of this revival of medieval art is expressed by James Fergusson the architect :

" The great recommendation of Gothic Art is that it is so rude that any journeyman can succeed in imitating it ; and they have done so till all our grand old buildings are clothed in falsehood, while all our new buildings aim only at deceiving.

" Thirty or forty years ago, if you entered a cathedral in France or England, you could say at once, ' These arches were built in the age of the Conqueror—that capital belonged to the earlier Henrys.' . . . Now all this is changed. You enter a cathedral, and admire some iron-work so rude you are sure it must be old, but which your guide informs you has just been put up by Smith of Coventry. You see . . . some painted glass so badly drawn and so crudely coloured it must be old—Jones of Newcastle. "

Augustus Welby Pugin, the best-known of the second genera- **Pugin.** tion of Gothic revivalists, aimed at reproducing the medieval church in its entirety, with all its mural paintings, hangings, altar-vestments, embroideries, brasses, tiles, etc. To that end he found himself obliged to inspire the manufacturers with whom he came in contact with something of his own enthusiasm, or to establish workshops to carry out his own ideas. His father, A. C. Pugin, had been a pupil of Nash the architect ; in passing, it may be noted that George IV. had sent his *chef* to him for instruction in drawing and design, with a view to the æsthetic adornment of his dinner-table. A. W. Pugin's enthusiasm and admiration for Gothic art were genuine ; he felt the logic and beauty of its construction and ornament, and was interested in all its detail. With his head full of

the work of the thirteenth and fourteenth centuries, he designed
and produced gold, silver, and copper work, embroideries,
stained glass, etc., for ecclesiastical uses, besides wall-papers
and tiles and other things for domestic decoration "in the
medieval style." For all this, he failed to catch the temper of
the period he genuinely loved and admired, and his work is
lacking in grace and distinction. His appreciation of himself

ST. AUGUSTINE'S CHURCH, RAMSGATE.
(Built by Augustus Welby Pugin.)

in 1850—he died a few years later, still young—is strangely
pathetic, reading into it, as one must, the implicit admission
of some weakness to which his failure as an artist was
partly due.

"I believe, as regards architecture, few men have been so unfortunate
as myself. I have passed my life in thinking of fine things, studying fine
things, designing fine things, and realising very poor ones. I have never
had the chance of producing a single fine ecclesiastical building, except
my own church,[1] where I am paymaster and architect; but everything else,
either for want of adequate funds or injudicious interference and control,
or some other contingency, is more or less a failure."[2]

[1] St. Augustine's. Ramsgate.   [2] Remarks on articles in the *Rambler*, p. 11.

To confess that external conditions are too much for him
is an admission of weakness; a
stronger man would have realised his conceptions in the work
he had to do.

If the Great Exhibition of
1851 is to be taken as the
expression of all that is best
in the artistic efforts of the
mid-century, they must be
ranked extremely low. We see
in all the excitement and wonder over the "Palace of Glass"
that curious idealisation of the
commonplace in which people
indulge to whom the æsthetic
side of life is unstudied and
unknown. They rhapsodised
over the crystal fountain, describing the delicate, fairy-like
structure and the sun's glitter
through the falling water-jets.
Chaucer himself is pressed into
service :—

> "I dreamt I was
> Within a temple made of glasse"

is made prophetic of this modern
glimpse of fairyland—a fairyland decorated by Mr. Owen
Jones "in the three primary
colours."

"The Great Exhibition of
the Works of Industry of all
Nations, 1851," was an inspiration of Prince Albert and the
Society of Arts, and the outcome of the yearly exhibitions
begun in 1847 with a view

THE GREAT EXHIBITION OF 1851, BY GEORGE WALLIS.

(*Victoria and Albert Museum.*)

The 1851 Exhibition. to establish a "quinquennial Exhibition of British Industry." In spite of the chorus of praise lavished on it, it was seen that on the artistic side the Great Exhibition was a failure, and that the union of the arts and industries of Great Britain would have to be brought about in some other way. One contemporary writer[1] thus sums up his criticism of it:

> "There is nothing new in the Exhibition in ornamental design, not a scheme, not a detail that has no. been treated over and over again in ages that are gone; the taste of the producers generally is uneducated; and in nearly all cases where this is not so, the influence of France is paramount in the European productions, bearing exclusively on the two most popular traditional styles of that country—the Renaissance and the Louis Quinze."

In short, it is not too much to say that English decorative art had no distinctive style, tradition, or conviction, and in borrowing it went the easiest road by instinct, copying not the spirit of the Renaissance, but the easily caught elegance and finish in it and the ignorant vulgarity of the late French school.

Wall Papers. Perhaps the most useful way of arriving at a true conception of the progressive condition of decorative art in England is to examine in some detail exhibits representative of those arts in the Exhibition of 1851. Of these we may begin with paper-hangings, where the process, of all mechanical processes, most shows the master-hand, and most relentlessly reveals defects and slovenliness. At best, wall-paper is but a substitute for distemper, painting or woven hanging; its surface is poor, and its colour wanting in depth; its whole success therefore depends on the delicacy and characteristic treatment of the design. The æsthetic instinct of the period expressed itself aptly on the one hand in a *chiaroscuro* frieze, copying "the best portions of the Elgin marbles," and on the other in papers with a surface cleverly imitating white silk or satin, on which natural flowers were arranged in vertical sprays or panels, remarkable neither for fidelity as studies nor for ingenuity as adaptations of natural form. The *chiaroscuro* mimicry of antique sculpture was not a new idea; a hundred years before, one Mr. Jackson of Battersea advertised his papers for a wall which represented statues—"lively portraitures of gods and goddesses in *chiaroscuro*." Such productions were a very

---

[1] R. N. Wornum : Essay on the Exhibition as a Lesson of Taste.

OPENING, BY QUEEN VICTORIA, OF THE EXHIBITION OF 1851, BY H. C. SELOUS.

(*Victoria and Albert Museum.*)

caricature of ornament, though they seem to have satisfied the taste of the day. One paper exhibited is spoken of as " particularly elegant and ladylike."

The carpets and woollen hangings of this date were more aggressively ugly than the paper-hangings, more commonplace

DRAWING OF THE CRYSTAL FOUNTAIN.
(*By permission of Messrs. F. & C. Osler, Birmingham.*)

in their attempt to be startling and original. One of the requirements of carpet-designing is that it should be flat and quiet, and the colours—however bright—rich and broken up, and sometimes even set, mosaic-like, in dividing outlines of a contrasting colour. But the draughtsmen of the time had no idea of following this or any other sober principle; the convention of design was meaningless to them, its laws misunderstood, the study of nature a travesty. Black was a favourite background; on it rose-wreaths and arabesques, in crude colours and heavily shaded, started forward, striking the eye with an unpleasant feeling of unrest. The most costly shawls were all copies or "improvements in the French taste" of the Indian pine-pattern, though sometimes the less pretentious webs had rather pretty patterns—plain centres, with a narrow border of traditional Eastern design, pleasant in feeling and colour. We can hardly realise the enormity of these shawls when the design was large and striking.

The figured silks of the time had the advantage of the sheen of a beautiful material. They were usually rich and pure in quality, but their design and colour were poor, and sometimes extremely ugly, especially in those ambitious pieces where manufacturer and designer were on their mettle; the small patterns, however, were often prettily arranged.

CARPET SHOWING FALSE PRINCIPLES.
(Formerly exhibited at Marlborough House.)

That *tour de force*, the "Coventry town ribbon," shown in the Exhibition, was probably the most disastrous piece of wasted labour ever conceived and executed. A committee of the principal manufacturers of the town were busied in its creation, 10,000 cards were used; the

Silks.

outcome of all this labour and expense was a remarkably hideous ribbon, with a black ground, on which are huddled a wreath of roses, petunias, yellow corn, and grasses.

Printed Cottons.

But of patterned textiles in the mid-century it is the printed calicoes that, as a rule, alone show distinct technical skill in design. In many of these the ground is well and evenly covered, the flowers clearly and simply drawn, and, though the design is too uniform and too small in scale to be really remarkable, yet some very pretty things were produced without any straining for effect. In no other industry is this comparative excellence discoverable, though here and there, as it were by chance, a delicate form appears. For instance, one may find on a piece of pottery of this date a vine-pattern so graceful and pure in line that its union with the mechanical so-called Greek form it decorates becomes sheer incongruity and affords no pleasure. The fine porcelain of Messrs. Copeland (p. 770), flower-stands, *tazze* "peculiarly adapted for general purposes of elegant decoration," the portraits in Sèvres china of Queen Victoria and Prince Albert, Minton's majolica ware, the so-called Della-Robbia—which "connoisseurs" declared might be taken for the work of Della Robbia himself—the imitation marble-ware, in short, scarcely a thing in the whole ceramic art, calls for comment or praise from the artist's point of view.

Makeshift Art.

It is difficult to imagine the entire absence of critical feeling in all the arts; a dessert-service presented by the queen to the Emperor of Austria roused veneration for its costliness (£1,000); in an embroidered bed-hanging an admiring critic estimates the actual number of stitches and the variety of colours used. Everything that was a clever invention—this usually means the invention of some cheaper counterfeit of some other process more costly in labour and material—was considered admirable apart from the æsthetic value of the wares produced. The public eye had lost the faculty of distinguishing a good material from the imitation; "statuary porcelain" was of equal value in their eyes with marble from the Italian quarries, and hangings printed on canvas in imitation of a wrought web satisfied their desire for sumptuous Arras tapestry. These unsatisfactory results of modern invention make one consider whether the misapplications of scientific discoveries in relation to the industrial arts have not usually been as ingenious as the discoveries themselves.

In furniture, though we have since returned to the elegant **Furniture.** but thin lines and the sparse surface-decoration of the eighteenth-century designers, inspiration was sought, during the twenty years of triumphant vulgarity between 1840 and 1860, in the never-

SIDEBOARD SHOWN AT THE EXHIBITION OF 1851.
(From "Industrial Arts of the Nineteenth Century," by Sir M. D. Wyatt.)

forgotten late Renaissance and French decadence; while a market was found also for the "Wardour Street Gothic" of the architects of the new school. Some quite amazing drawing-room cabinets and *consoles* were evolved—decorations including star-spangled niches with statues unimpeachable in their decorous marble nakedness, patriotic groups of England's soldiers in cast bronze, gilded griffons, trophies of arms, and cornucopias of peace and plenty. Ebony tables inlaid with silver or costly *marqueterie* were reserved for the wealthy, while paltry imitations of them satisfied the poorer classes. Beds were grandiose and superb—carved and polished, and hung with heavy curtains, with valances round, sometimes embroidered with medallions emblematic of the domestic virtues in tent-stitch.

Stained Glass. The one obvious criticism on the stained glass of this and more recent times is that not only was there no attempt to procure a beautiful quality of colour—a matter of trouble and care, but not an impossibility—but that the fundamental mistake was made of trying to produce a *picture* on glass, with the detail painted up and highly shaded and the leading symmetrically divided, and as little of it as might be. The principal claim to admiration of several very costly windows of the time was that they were painted on one huge sheet of glass and put up, at great trouble and risk of breaking, without any lead at all. All the most beautiful glass has been treated from the earliest times as a mosaic of rich colour, only slightly painted, broad leads breaking the surface and giving extraordinary value to the colour. One window at the Exhibition exemplified this misapprehension of the capabilities of stained glass: some French thirteenth-century glass was copied, with all the characteristic scrolls and branches drawn with a good deal of skill; but the artist bethought him to shade some of the broad stems, leaving others in relief; and transformed into a genteel piece of commonplace the flat silvery effect of the old design.

Goldsmiths' Work. A mixture of naturalism and childish symbolism was specially noticeable in gold- and silver-smiths' work. A cream-ladle must be fashioned out of a buttercup with a wriggling leaf and stalk for a handle; grape-scissors must, of course, have the rugged stem of a vine; a boudoir-clock would scarcely be complete without some banal time-emblem about it, and a silver tea-set must be engraved with scenes of the various stages of tea-cultivation. Could symbolism, the shorthand of story-telling, once fascinating us by its wayward poetry, its retelling of solemn and beautiful stories, have sunk into worse swamps of confused **Jewellery.** twaddle? It was the same with gold and silver jewellery. In the more costly ornaments the great preoccupation of the jewellers was to match their stones as perfectly as possible, and the

THE INTERIOR OF THE EXHIBITION OF 1862, BY E. WALKER.

(*Victoria and Albert Museum.*)

setting of these rarely-matched stones and pearls was heavy and mechanical, little calculated to set off their splendour. Fetters and padlocks of gold, nailheads of diamond, jewelled flowers shining with the glitter of steel—the ornaments of the period are characteristic ; they no longer recall the field-flowers and gar- lands that delight us in their frail brilliance, but suggest the chains and rivets of machinery.

The 1862 Exhibition.
The Exhibition of 1862 showed a slight improvement on the astounding absurdities of 1851, but little that calls for comment. The exhibits are at least varied. The Gobelins tapestry works send a copy of Titian's "Assumption"; an English firm send an Axminster carpet (to be used as a hanging), in which Napoleon III. is depicted, with top-boots and nicely-waxed moustache, presenting a Treaty of Commerce to the Queen, who has a surprised smile and a profile more than Grecian. The artist has exhausted his intellect in representing the shine on the Emperor's boots, which are superb. Morris and Co. (a newly-started firm) show furniture, stained glass, and embroidered hangings; William Burges, a painted cabinet, with panels by E. J. Poynter. John Thomas is grandiose with his steel and marble fireplaces, Copeland magnificent with glittering cut-glass and imitation jewelled Limoges ware. "Art-manufacture" is the trade catch-word, and there is a great deal of talk about "style," with very little knowledge or conviction. In a trade- advertisement of the day we read the following comprehensive enumeration :

"A coffee-service in the Grecian style; a wine-cooler in the Roman ditto; dinner-service in the Flemish ditto; claret-jug in the Louis Quatorze ditto."

A very masquerade procession of art !

New Architec- ture.
But a change was coming over the decorative movement. Pugin was dead, and Gothic architecture, with its attendant arts, was taken up by other hands. Little apparent as it may be among the fooling and trifling which have been described in the last paragraph, a certain feeling for sincerity in art, and for beauty apart from show and splendour, began to manifest itself at last. New ideas had arisen with regard to the building and decoration of houses. The red-brick domestic architecture which has long since begun to enliven many of our streets, as far as the smoke-laden air permits, had its origin in the buildings designed

by Philip Webb—buildings whose simplicity and dignity stand out alike from the stone and stucco of the earlier part of the century and the cheap villadom of later days. All credit must be given to him and to the younger men who have made an effort to bring a new life and interest into our street-architecture.

Difficult as it is to make quite a fair estimate of any move- **Contrasts.** ment near the time in which we ourselves live, one may safely say that out of the experiments and the mistakes of the century some lesson has been learnt, some feeling has arisen for the decorative arts, with some perception of their importance in our daily life. Twenty or thirty years ago, if a woman with educated tastes went into one of the big London silk-mercers', it would have been impossible for her to make a satisfactory choice from among the colours and patterns shown her; she must either have been content with black or white dress-stuffs, or have turned to one of the Oriental houses where fine colours and traditional patterns were still to be found. To-day, she is no longer condemned to be isolated in a desert of ugliness; she can dress well in handsome stuffs and fine colours, and can, by paying highly, have her rooms harmoniously fitted and deco-rated. But only by paying highly; the "popularising of art" is at present one of those abstract phrases dear to the senti-mentalist: art cannot be had cheaply, and is as much out of reach of the poor as if it were non-existent.

While the newspapers were exhausting their flowers of speech **The New** over the Great Exhibition of 1851, a few men here and there, **Decora-** writers and artists, were producing work whose influence has **tion.** coloured, one way or another, the life and surroundings of the later years of the century. The first volume of Ruskin's " Modern Painters" was published in 1847, the " Seven Lamps of Archi-tecture " (of which one critic said that " Mr. Ruskin had left one lamp out of account, and that was the Lamp of Industry ") in 1849. In his writings, and notably the chapter in the " Stones of Venice " on " The Nature of Gothic "--one of the finest pieces of modern writing existing—Ruskin is the first critic of authority and note in England to draw attention to the fundamental characteristics of Gothic architecture and ornament. It is unnecessary to comment on the influence his treatises on this subject have had on modern work, no less than his pregnant and often-repeated comments on the "Lamp of Industry" of the nineteenth century.

Rossetti and the P.-R. B.

The names of artists like Dante Gabriel Rossetti, Ford Madox-Brown, Holman Hunt, Edward Burne-Jones, Walter Crane, to mention no others, are associated not merely with picture-painting, but with a movement embracing every side of creative work in art and literature, finding its first and temporary expression in the Pre-Raphaelite Brotherhood (p. 408 *seq.*). The movement developed some ten years later into one involving all the decorative arts, bringing into modern life something of that beauty of detail in costume, in colour and form of decoration and furniture, whose absence had been so painfully, if indistinctly, felt during the century. The Pre-Raphaelite Brotherhood,[1] as such, had a short life, but the movement that inspired it and the enthusiasm of the young men who formed it gave it much more historical significance than such youthful associations among close friends usually have. The ridicule and somewhat scurrilous abuse that greeted the exhibition of their earliest work have long since given place to admiration and to the serious criticism which is due to serious art.

William Morris's Firm.

In 1860 the firm of Morris, Marshall, Faulkner and Co. began business with the intention of producing everything necessary for house-decoration; materials were to be the best procurable, the work to be done by hand where the process permitted of it, designs to be original and without reference to the prevailing public taste. Furniture, wall-papers, stained glass, painted tiles, woven hangings, tapestry, embroidery, carpets, silk brocades—everything was attempted sooner or later, and with marked success. Both Rossetti and Madox-Brown made at first cartoons for the stained glass, but even then the greater part were designed by Burne-Jones. The furniture in the hands of Philip Webb took the characteristics of his architectural work, in a certain mixture of austerity and elegance which harmonised in all details with the decorative work produced by this group of artists. William Morris's designs for applied ornament (wall-papers, carpets, hangings, etc.) were an entirely new departure. Carefully restrained within the convention prescribed by the different processes for which they were intended, they

_____

[1] The P.-R.B. was formed in 1848 by D. G. Rossetti, Holman Hunt, and J. E. Millais, who joined the names of four other friends to their own.

manifested a keen sense of the beauty of natural forms and a remarkable power of translating that beauty into inventive and characteristic ornament. Perhaps his most remarkable undertaking has been the Arras tapestry made in the high-warp loom by the same simple process as the famous Gothic hangings of

"FLORA"—A DESIGN FOR TAPESTRY, BY SIR E.
BURNE-JONES AND WILLIAM MORRIS.
(By permission of Messrs. Morris & Co.)

four centuries ago. Apart from the fact that this has been the only permanent production of the kind in England (the Windsor Tapestry Works are no longer in existence), it will probably be held the most notable and enduring decorative work of the century.

The decorative movement whose history has here been slightly traced has been the principal influence of the latter part of the century, and nearly every production with any claims

Japanese Influence.

to distinction shows traces of it more or less defined. The most important influence apart from them has been the introduction of Japanese art consequent upon the breaking-up of the feudal empire in 1868, and the dispersal of its treasures of art on the introduction of Western civilisation.[1] Before

TAPESTRY REPRESENTING SCENE FROM THE "MORTE D'ARTHUR," EXECUTED
BY THE WINDSOR TAPESTRY WORKS, AFTER A DESIGN BY H. A. BONE.

(By permission of the Right Hon. Lord Aldenham.)

Japanese work was vulgarised (an outcome at once of the modern craving for novelty and of its comparative cheapness) the beautiful colour of this Oriental china, these silken stuffs and glittering embroideries, and the charm of a strange traditional art hanging about them, made such wares—in moderation —a valuable addition to English home-decoration. But their very cheapness and effectiveness became a snare to the amateur decorator.

[1] Since that date a "young" movement of decorative art has arisen, whose growth, genuine and hopeful, it would be interesting to follow, were it not excluded by the limitation of the period covered by the present volume.

The success of these decorative movements has not been universal. The praiseworthy attempts of the manufacturers to improve the decorative quality of their goods by establishing schools of art in connection with their works have been the means of stereotyping traditions out of touch with the modern movement. The tendency is towards reducing everything to a machine-finish. Thus, in china-ware, for example, the attempt to obtain purity of line and smoothness of material overwhelms the boldness of touch essential to good work; a rough piece of Breton pottery is a more pleasant object of daily use than the carefully-painted and elaborately-finished productions of our celebrated potteries. Briefly, then, at the close of our period the position of decorative art stood thus: important branches of our manufacture, such as pottery and gold and silver work, seemed to be unaffected by the modern movement. In textiles there was a marked improvement in design, and a wide range of often beautiful colour and texture had been achieved. Decorative metal-work had not yet begun to exist. In furniture the influence of the eighteenth century was perhaps paramount, though conditioned largely by the new style of architecture. As a result the representative English house of 1885 differed completely from the dreary and hopeless residence of 1850. Persian rugs, blue china, and fresh chintzes had taken the place of horsehair and mahogany and moreen curtains; some form of decoration had succeeded to a mere blind contempt of anything outside strict utility. If this attempt resulted very often in calamitous failure, that failure was due to an attempt to make out of cheap material and hurried work what can only exist as the result of wealth and leisure.

The Position in 1885.

As regards symphonic music, it would scarcely be too much to say that its history in England for the last seventy or eighty years has been the history of the Philharmonic Society. This body had been established seven years when, in 1820, the conductorship, previously divided, according to the fashion of the time, between the "presiding" pianist and the first violin, was entrusted to Spohr. Cherubini had previously, for the sum of £200, furnished the Society with a new symphony and other

H. SUTHERLAND EDWARDS, Music since the Georgian Era: The Philharmonic.

compositions ; and it now became the custom to invite distinguished composers to visit London, as Cherubini and Spohr had done, and then direct the performance of some of their most celebrated works. It was in response to the invitation of the Philharmonic Society that Beethoven undertook the composition of his Ninth Symphony. The invitation was accompanied by a draft of £50. Afterwards, when the great composer was in his last illness, the Society forwarded to him, through Moscheles, £100, as a mark of sympathy and of homage.

In 1826 one of the Philharmonic Concerts had been conducted by Weber, who was in London with a view to *Oberon*, which he produced at Covent Garden. In 1829 Mendelssohn directed his C Minor symphony at the Philharmonic, and afterwards, writing about the performance, spoke of the "brilliant execution of the orchestra."

In 1842 Mendelssohn again appeared in the double capacity of conductor and pianist. Two years later he directed five of the concerts ; and it was in this memorable year that Joachim made his first appearance at the Philharmonic. After the production of *Elijah* at Birmingham, in 1846—Mendelssohn's culminating triumph in England and in the world of music generally—the composer whose influence on English musicians was so remarkable conducted at the Philharmonic Society his symphony in A Minor, and played the pianoforte part in Beethoven's G Major concerto.

In 1853 Berlioz conducted at the Philharmonic his *Harold in Italy*. In 1855 Wagner directed the concerts, producing the *Tannhäuser* overture at one and a selection from *Lohengrin* at another. In the next ten years Sterndale Bennett was conductor ; and it was during the first year of Bennett's conductorship that Schumann's compositions were introduced at the Philharmonic. Among subsequent conductors may be mentioned Mr. W. G. Cusins, Sir Arthur Sullivan, Mr. F. H. Cowen, and Sir Alexander Mackenzie.

"Since its institution in 1813," wrote the late J. W. Davison in the *Times*, on the occasion of the Society's jubilee, "the Philharmonic has, to use a homely phrase, seen various ups and downs. Nevertheless, even in its darkest and most threatening periods, it has never once departed from the high standard which it set itself from the beginning, never once by lowering that standard endeavoured pusillanimously to minister to a taste less scrupulous and

SIR ARTHUR SULLIVAN, BY SIR J. E. MILLAIS, BART., P.R.A.
(*National Portrait Gallery.*)

refined than that to which it made its first appeal, and to which it is indebted for a world-wide celebrity."

About 1850 the New Philharmonic Society came into

293

existence, founded by the late Dr. Wylde; and, the Ancient Concerts having been brought to an end, the New Philharmonic was for some time, with the exception of the old society of the same name, the only permanent institution in England for the giving of orchestral concerts. In 1852 the New Philharmonic Concerts were conducted by Berlioz, and in 1853 by Spohr. The Crystal Palace Concerts had already been established. But it was not until Mr. (afterwards Sir) August Manns took direction of the orchestra, and engaged special players for its reinforcement on the Saturdays of each week during about six months of the year, that the so-called "Winter Concerts" were founded. They were the best of their kind ever given in England. The orchestra was finely composed; the conductor one of the most powerful and skilful orchestral directors that England has known; and he had under his guidance and control a practised body of players, well accustomed to follow his beat on all points, great and small. But perhaps the greatest of his merits was that he has introduced to the English public a large number of orchestral works by great masters never before heard in this country. Besides familiarising the frequenters of the concerts with Beethoven's symphonies, of which the muse-like nine have been played again and again in regular series, he produced works, previously unheard in England, by Schubert, together with the earliest and latest works of Wagner and Brahms. Extracts and arrangements from the later works of Wagner were presented at the Crystal Palace Concerts long before the *Meistersingers*, *Tristan und Isolde*, or the *Ring der Nibelungen* had been performed at any London Opera House.[1]

For some twenty years or more the New Philharmonic Concerts were carried on; and just about the time of their discontinuance a far better series of orchestral performances

The Richter Concerts

was introduced under the direction of Herr Hans Richter, the famous conductor, first of Pesth and afterwards of Vienna. The Richter Concerts were of a type easy enough to describe. Consisting, as a rule, of orchestral performances exclusively, each concert was divided into two parts, the first of which was

[1 Sir A. Manns announced his retirement in 1904, after fifty years' service. The Permanent Crystal Palace Orchestra was disbanded in 1900, but series of concerts of a no less high class continued to be given during each spring and autumn.]

made up of excerpts, or orchestral arrangements from the operas
of Wagner, while the second was filled almost invariably by
one of Beethoven's symphonies. These concerts, successful from
the first, and better than any that had been heard before in
London (Sydenham is beyond the Metropolitan radius), presented another distinctive feature: they were wonderfully short.
Schumann, in connection with Schubert's C Major symphony,
speaks of " its heavenly length." The Richter Concerts never
lasted, including the interval, for more than two hours.

The original type of the Richter Concert, so long maintained,
was subsequently varied. Many of the Wagnerian excerpts
eventually became too familiar; though it is apparently in the
form of orchestral extracts that English lovers of Wagnerian
music love best to hear it. This applies more particularly to the
later operas of Wagner, and especially the *Ring der Nibelungen*,
which in its original form proved too indigestible a mass for
the artistic stomach of the English public.

A new impetus was given to the growing taste for
orchestral music in England by the arrival of several famous
conductors from the Continent, each with his own manner of
conducting, often with his own new readings, in one case with
his own orchestra: Herr Mottl, of the energetic attitudes and
gestures; Herr Nikisch, so little demonstrative, or demonstrative
only in the neatest and quietest manner; Herr Siegfried Wagner, who without being left-handed conducted, for the sake of
originality, with his left hand; Herr Levy, who now and then
laid down the *bâton* on the desk before him, as if to say, " I
have directed them so well through difficult passages that they
can now be trusted to go on for a time without any direction at
all"; and finally M. Lamoureux, who brought over his own
admirable orchestra of 100 players, and gave several interesting
and finely conducted concerts of German and French, or rather
of French and Wagnerian music.

Symphony Concerts were also founded by Mr. Henschel and
carried on under his conductorship, and the taste for orchestral
music has shown a constant increase. But while these and
similar concerts, such as those at the Crystal Palace directed
by Sir August Manns, were dependent for success on the
continued co-operation of their respective conductors, the
concerts of the Philharmonic Society have stood by them-

selves. The Philharmonic has always maintained a high standard of musical taste, and often as it has been reproached with neglecting new works, and works by new composers, it has generally kept abreast with the artistic movement in the leading musical countries of Europe. Some lesser lights may have been overlooked, but not the unmistakably great ones.

English Composers. There can be little doubt but that the first works by English composers ever performed out of England (with the exception only of the nocturnes and other compositions for pianoforte by John Field, of Moscow) were the orchestral productions of Sterndale Bennett and of Macfarren, given at Leipsic when Mendelssohn was the director of the Leipsic Conservatorium. They were heard by Schumann, who made them the subject of highly appreciative articles (especially the symphonies and pianoforte concertos of Sterndale Bennett) in his famous musical journal. But they left little impression; and no other orchestral works of English origin seem to have been performed on the Continent until Mr. Cowen's Scandinavian Symphony was introduced, some dozen years ago, at Vienna, whence it made its way to various German cities, to Milan, and to St. Petersburg.

Balfe. Meanwhile, apart from the Royal Academy and from academical training generally, there had appeared among us a composer of great natural talent, Michael William Balfe. He had played as violinist at the Dublin Theatre, he had sung light baritone parts with considerable success at various opera-houses in Italy, and he had even composed to Italian *libretti* several operas which were much admired, when he produced at a London theatre (in 1836) an opera called *The Siege of Rochelle*, which was received with enthusiastic applause. The work was in the ordinary operatic form of that day, which remains the only form cultivated with success by English composers and received with favour by an English public: spoken dialogue, that is to say, with solos in ballad form, duets, concerted pieces, and an occasional concerted finale. The next great success achieved by Balfe was *The Maid of Artois*, composed for Malibran, who " created " the principal part at Drury Lane under the management of Alfred Bunn.

After composing several other operas and endeavouring to found at the Lyceum Theatre an English Opera-House, Balfe brought out in 1846, at Drury Lane, his most successful work, *The Bohemian Girl*, which has been played far oftener, both in England and abroad, than any other opera by an English composer. Known by more than one work in Italy, Balfe had also made himself a name in France by two comic operas, *Le Puits d'Amour* and *Les Quatre Fils d'Aymon*, which he brought out with success at the Théâtre de l'Opéra Comique. After being played for hundreds of nights in England, *The Bohemian Girl* made its way to Germany, where it was played at various theatres under the title of *Die Zigeunerin*, and to France, where, as performed at the Théâtre Lyrique of Paris, it was called *La Bohémienne*.

Under Mr. Bunn's management at Drury Lane, Balfe, Wallace, Benedict, Macfarren, and other composers produced a considerable number of original works. Of these *The Bohemian Girl* and Wallace's *Maritana* have survived even to the present day. In *The Bond-*

MICHAEL WILLIAM BALFE.

(*From a lithograph by C. Baugnier*, 1846.)

man, written throughout in music—with accompanied recitative in lieu of the ordinary spoken dialogue, with elaborate finales and plenty of solid work for the orchestra—Balfe made an attempt to secure for a grand opera the same favourable reception which had always been extended to his operas of the familiar *Bohemian Girl* type : ballad opera, that is to say, with the addition of a few concerted pieces. But *The Bondman* was coldly received ; and Balfe soon reverted to the only form in which, even to this day, opera has proved acceptable in England to the general public.

English Opera.

All musico-dramatic experiments made subsequently in the form of grand opera have proved failures ; though not, perhaps, by reason of the form alone. The only two composers in England who, since the time of Balfe, have written with success for the stage are the late Goring Thomas, whose

Esmeralda on its first production made a decided mark; and Professor (afterwards Sir Charles) Villiers Stanford, who in his Irish opera of *Shamus O'Brien*, composed in a style at once popular and artistic, has made an infinitely more favourable impression than was left by his *Savonarola* or by his far more tolerable *Canterbury Pilgrims.*

Oratorio.   The history of operatic and that of symphonic music in England do not march together on parallel lines, or with

SIR CHARLES VILLIERS STANFORD.
(By permission, from the painting by Sir H. von Herkomer, R.A.)

equal step; and the frequenters of oratorio performances form a class apart from *habitués* of the Italian opera and from subscribers to the Philharmonic and other orchestral concerts. Few, however, of our genuine lovers of music can have failed to hear *Elijah*, the finest oratorio of modern times, and the most important work composed, since the time of Handel, for production in England.

The Handel Festival, which since 1857 has been given

triennially at the Crystal Palace, has familiarised thousands and tens of thousands of amateurs with the great oratorios of a composer whose name and fame are for ever associated with England, although he was not an Englishman by birth but only by naturalisation and adoption. Latterly the Crystal Palace directors showed their high appreciation of the *Elijah* by performing it on Handel Festival scale. Mendelssohn's masterpiece is the only work of the kind, apart from *The Messiah* and *Israel in Egypt*, which our musical societies know well enough to be able to do justice to its magnificent choruses.

All things considered, the most popular English composer of the period ending with the year 1885 was beyond doubt Sir Arthur Sullivan. From song to symphony, from opera to oratorio, there was scarcely a form or a style which he had not cultivated. But his most brilliant successes were achieved in association with his unrivalled librettist, Mr. (afterwards Sir) W. S. Gilbert, first at the Opera Comique and afterwards at the Savoy ; and the *Mikado*, one of the happiest efforts of the two collaborators, made Sullivan's music known in all the principal cities of the German and of the Austro-Hungarian empires. For Sir Arthur Sullivan's grand opera of *Ivanhoe* it may fairly be claimed that no more successful work in that particular form has ever been produced in English. Its success, however, was by no means equal to its merit. *[marginal note: Gilbert and Sullivan.]*

IN the history of classical scholarship in England the foremost name in the latter part of the eighteenth century is that of Richard Porson. Born at East Ruston, near North Walsham, in Norfolk, he was sent to Eton by the liberality of the future founder of the Norrisian Professorship. Similarly a subscription started by Sir George Baker, President of the College of Physicians, enabled him to enter Trinity College, Cambridge, in 1778. He won the Craven in 1781, was elected to a Fellowship in the following year, and held it for ten years, vacating it in 1792, solely on the ground of his resolve to remain a layman. His friends once more raised a fund in his honour, and the loss of his Fellowship was thus made good by an income of *[marginal note: J. E. SANDYS. English Scholarship, 1742-1885. Greek Scholars : Cambridge.]*

£100 per annum.   In the same year he was unanimously elected Professor of Greek, the annual stipend being at that time only £40.   In 1806 he was appointed librarian of the London Institution, and in 1808 he died.

Greek-
Scholars:
Porson,
1759-1808.

Porson's literary activity was mainly limited to the twenty years between 1782 and 1803.   The former is the date of his reviews of certain editions of Æschylus and Aristophanes; the latter, that of his restoration of the Greek inscription on the Rosetta Stone.   In his first important work, the " Letters to Travis " (1788–9), he conclusively proved the spuriousness of the text on the three heavenly witnesses (1 John v. 7), thus upholding an opinion which had recently been expressed by Gibbon, and had also been maintained by all the best critics from Erasmus to Bentley.   In 1790 appeared his preface and notes to a new edition of Toup's " Emendations on Suidas."   In 1795 the Foulis Press at Glasgow produced a folio edition of Æschylus with many corrections, which were really due to Porson, though the book saw the light without his name and even without his knowledge.   Twelve years had passed since the syndics of the Cambridge Press had invited Porson to edit Æschylus, and when he offered to visit Florence with a view to collating the Laurentian MS. the offer was rejected, Dr. Torkington, Master of Clare and Vice-Chancellor of the University, speaking strongly against it, and asking " why Mr. Porson could not *collect* his manuscripts at home " ?[1]   The syndics had also insisted on an exact reprint of Stanley's corrupt text, and Porson, not unnaturally, declined the task.   In 1797 his edition of the " Hecuba " of Euripides was published, to be soon followed by the " Orestes " (1798), " Phœnissæ " (1799), and " Medea " (1801), the last alone bearing his name on the title-page.   In the first edition of the " Hecuba " certain points of Greek metre were settled in a sense that was inconsistent with the opinions propounded by Hermann in a youthful work published in the previous year; Hermann retorted with a " Hecuba " of his own in 1800, and was finally answered in Porson's second edition (1802).   The famous supplement to the preface is justly regarded as his finest piece of criticism; he here sets forth and elucidates certain rules of iambic and trochaic verse, and lays

---

[1] Kidd's " Tracts." p. xxxvi; and F. Norgate in the *Athenæum*, May 9, 1896, p. 621.

down the law determining the length of the fourth syllable from
the end of the normal iambic line, tacitly correcting the errors
of Hermann, but never mentioning his name, though he had
named him five times over in a celebrated note on the
" Medea " (l. 675). It is interesting to add that, in 1816, Hermann
did honour to the memory of Porson in the most generous

RICHARD PORSON, BY J. J. KIRKBY.
(Trinity College, Cambridge.)

terms, describing him as *vir magnæ accuratæque doctrinæ*, a
man of great and equal learning.[1] A transcript of an important
MS. of the lexicographer Photius, in the library of Trinity
College, which cost Porson the labour of at least ten months,
was destroyed by fire in 1796; it was transcribed afresh by
Porson, and published by Dobree in 1822, fourteen years after
Porson's death. His transcript of the " Medea " is still to be
seen in the library of his college—a work so marvellous in its

[1] " Elementa Doctrinæ Metricæ," ed. 1817, p. xiii.

caligraphy that it was made the model for the Greek type which was cut under his direction and bore his name, though it was never used during his life.[1]

Porson's services to scholarship were mainly in the department of textual criticism. He advanced the study of Attic Greek in particular, by elucidating many points of idiom and usage, by establishing the laws of tragic metre, and by the emendation of texts. His emendations were the fruit of an innate acumen exercised on an extraordinarily wide range of reading, and aided by the resources of a marvellous memory. Had it not been for the deplorable dipsomania which certainly wasted his time and probably shortened his life, he might have accomplished much more. He might have not only completed his Euripides, but also achieved that edition of Aristophanes for which a publisher vainly offered him £3,000 in 1802; he might also have left behind him a monumental work on Athenæus. The moral quality in which he was most conspicuous was his honesty —honesty in the sacrifice of his Fellowship to his conscience; honesty as a critic as well as a man. As a critic he was wont to say: "Whatever you quote or collate, do it fairly and accurately." It was said of him in his lifetime by Dr. Parr, "He is not only a matchless scholar, but an honest, a very honest man"; while after his death it was confidently affirmed by Bishop Turton that "he had no superior in the most pure and inflexible love of truth." Of himself he modestly confessed, "I am quite satisfied if, three hundred years hence, it shall be said that one Porson lived towards the close of the eighteenth century, who did a good deal for the text of Euripides." Porson counted Heyne, Ruhnken, and Villoison among his correspondents; Thomas Kidd, Martin Davy, Horne Tooke, and Charles Burney among his friends. The last was one of the trustees of the fund founded in his honour, and it is to this fund that we owe the execution of his bust by Chantrey, the engraving of the portrait painted by Hoppner, and the establishment of the Porson Prize and Porson Scholarship in his own university. Nor are these his only memorials. For Cambridge and for England he became in a large measure the creator of that ideal of finished and exact verbal scholarship which prevailed for more than fifty years after his death, and is not unworthy of recognition

[1] Wordsworth's "Scholæ Academicæ," p. 392.

for its disciplinary and educational value even in the present day.[1]

Among the contemporaries of Porson we must mention Twining 1734-1804. Thomas Twining of Sidney, the translator of Aristotle's " Poetics " (1789), and Samuel Parr, of Emmanuel and St. John's. Parr added to the reputation which he affected as a conversationalist

SAMUEL PARR, BY GEORGE ROMNEY.
(Emmanuel College, Cambridge.)

a certain degree of real distinction as a writer of Latin prose Parr, 1747-1825 whether in the form of stately epitaphs (modelled mainly on Morcellus), or in the Ciceronian periods of his famous preface to Bellenden (1787). It was by a sedulous reading of this preface that facility in Latin prose was sometimes acquired at Cambridge in the age immediately succeeding the death of its author.[2] A minor light of the day was Gilbert Wakefield, the author of a Wakefield, 1756-1801. hasty diatribe, prompted by the omission of Wakefield's name in Porson's " Hecuba." Porson " had forborne to mention him

[1] Jebb, "Porson," in "Dict. of National Biography," xlvi. 163*a*.

[2] Pryme's "Reminiscences," p. 136 ; quoted by Wordsworth, "Scholæ Academicæ," p. 100.

from kindness," and, on the eve of the publication of the diatribe, had good-naturedly proposed as a toast, "My friend, Gilbert Wakefield," adding the apposite quotation, "What's Hecuba to him, or he to Hecuba?" Wakefield's best work was his Lucretius (1796-7), and even this was disfigured by his rage for needless conjecture, and by his intemperate railing at the eminent French scholar, Lambinus.[1] In 1799 his treasonable expression of a hope that France would invade and conquer England compelled the Ministry to prosecute him. He was consequently imprisoned for two years (1799–1801) in Dorchester gaol; during his imprisonment he continued to correspond with Fox on points of scholarship, and shortly after his release he died. Both as a politician and as a scholar he was wanting in judgment and self-control.

**Elmsley,
1773-1825.**

Peter Elmsley, who was educated at Westminster and Oxford, was one of the first to recognise in the *Edinburgh Review* the great value of Porson's "Hecuba"; and he enjoyed the esteem of that great scholar until the latter "found him too ready to make use of other men's emendations without acknowledgement."[2] After staying for some years in Edinburgh, he went abroad to collate MSS. in Italy from 1816 to 1820, returning to spend the last five years of his life as Professor of Ancient History at Oxford. He edited the "Acharnians" of Aristophanes, and several plays of Sophocles and Euripides. He was the first to point out the importance of the Laurentian MS. of Sophocles; that of Æschylus was first appreciated at its proper value by a theological opponent of Porson, Thomas Burgess (1756–1837), Bishop of Salisbury.

**Dobree,
1782-1825.**

The year of the death of Elmsley was also that of the death of Peter Paul Dobree, Fellow of Trinity College, Cambridge, who died at the early age of 43. As a native of Guernsey, he had a perfect mastery of French, which made him most acceptable abroad. He travelled in Spain; visited France in 1814, when he was among the first to recognise the importance of the Paris MS. of Demosthenes;[3] in the following year he was a welcome guest at the Dutch University of

---

[1] For an estimate, *see* Munro's ed. of Lucretius, i., p. 19.

[2] Wa⁺son's "Life of Porson," p. 310.

[3] Dawes, "Misc. Crit." (ed. 2, Kidd), p. 221; quoted by Voemel, Dem *Cont.* p. 223.

Leyden.[1] He was a devoted admirer of Porson, and edited his "Aristophanica" in 1820 and his "Photius" in 1822. His own studies as a textual critic were mainly devoted to Greek prose, especially to the Attic Orators. He was Professor of Greek from 1823 to 1825. His "Adversaria" were published in 1831–3 by his successor, Scholefield.

The Porsonian tradition was no less ably maintained at Cambridge by Porson's immediate successor, James Henry Monk, Fellow of Trinity, afterwards Bishop of Gloucester, the biographer of Bentley, and editor of the "Alcestis," "Hippolytus," and both the "Iphigenias" of Euripides ; and also by another Fellow of Trinity, Charles James Blomfield, who published valuable notes and glossaries to five of the plays of Æschylus, and was afterwards Bishop of London from 1828 to 1856. His able brother, Edward Valentine Blomfield (1788–1816) of Gonville and Caius, and Fellow of Emmanuel, the author of a Greek ode "In Desiderium Porsoni" (1809), showed the highest promise as a Greek scholar. He translated Matthiæ's "Greek Grammar," and was embarking on the preparation of a comprehensive Greek and English Lexicon, when his life was cut short at the early age of twenty-eight. A far longer life was allotted to another able grammarian, who was born only six years later than the birth, and died nearly seventy years after the death, of E. V. Blomfield, and proved himself a worthy countryman of Ruddiman—William Veitch, of Edinburgh, whose "Greek Verbs, Irregular and Defective," was first published in 1848, and has long been recognised as a standard authority on the subject. The task of editing Æschylus for the Cambridge Press, declined by Porson in 1782, was accepted about fifteen years later by Samuel Butler, of Rugby and St. John's, Cambridge, afterwards Bishop of Lichfield, whose edition was published in 1809–16. Verbal scholarship was not Butler's forte, but he devoted unsparing labour to the accomplishment of the work.[2] His fame, however, must rest mainly on his great services to the cause of education as Headmaster of Shrewsbury for thirty-

Monk, 1784–1856. Blomfield, 1786–1857.

Veitch, 1794–1885.

Butler, 1774–1840.

---

[1] Bake's "Scholica Hypomnemata," II (1839), pp. iii–v, xiv. Dobree's friend, George Burges (1786–1864), a far too eager emender of tragic texts, is briefly characterised, *ibid.*, pp. viii.–xii. For Gaisford's visit, *cf.* pp. v–viii.

[2] Mayor's "History of St. John's College," pp. 908–922 ; also Butler's "Life and Letters," i., pp. 23, 53 ; ii., p. 368.

eight years, from 1798 to 1836. The same remark may be applied to his distinguished pupil and immediate successor, **Kennedy, 1804-1889.** Benjamin Hall Kennedy, Fellow of St. John's, a most able and vigorous teacher who was Headmaster for thirty years (1836–66), and ended his days as Professor of Greek at Cambridge. Besides several school-books, he edited the "Agamemnon" of Æschylus, the "Œdipus Tyrannus" of Sophocles, and the whole of Virgil; he also translated the "Birds" of Aristophanes and the "Theætetus" of Plato. A volume of verse entitled "Between Whiles," together with numerous contributions to the "Sabrinæ Corolla," gave evidence of his remarkable mastery of classical composition. One of his many distinguished pupils, Richard **Shilleto, 1809-1876.** Shilleto, began at Repton and completed at Shrewsbury, under Butler and Kennedy, the training that placed him in the front rank as a classical scholar at Cambridge. He will be best remembered as the editor of the Speech of Demosthenes, "De Falsa Legatione"; of his long-promised edition of Thucydides, only the first two books saw the light. His acquaintance with the facts of the Greek language was unrivalled, and his skill as a teacher was widely appreciated at a time when private tuition in classics was more usual, and indeed more necessary, in Cambridge than it is now. Wider interests than those of pure scholarship are represented by the name of Joseph Williams **Blakesley, 1808-1885.** Blakesley, of St. Paul's School and Trinity, Cambridge, the editor of Herodotus (1854), and the writer of a Life of Aristotle (1839). In 1872 he became Dean of Lincoln. William **Thompson 1810-1886.** Hepworth Thompson, Master of Trinity from 1867, was a year or two younger than Blakesley and Shilleto, and was Kennedy's predecessor as Professor of Greek. In that position he was singularly successful as a lecturer on Euripides, Plato, and Aristotle; but he unfortunately published little besides his excellent edition of Archer Butler's "Lectures on the History of Greek Philosophy," and his admirable commentaries on the "Gorgias" and "Phædrus" of Plato. His dry humour is exemplified in many memorable sayings, but his sensitiveness and kindliness of feeling were certainly far greater than the world in general was aware; and one of his friends, the late Dean Merivale, was right in holding that too much had been made of "his pungent sayings, which acquired their fame as much from the prominence of his position as from their own saliency."[1] The serene dignity of his noble presence still survives in the portrait by Herkomer in the hall of his college. When the Greek Professorship was vacated by Thompson in 1867, one of the foremost candidates for the office was Edward Meredith Cope, best known for his elaborate introduction to the " Rhetoric " of Aristotle, the precursor of a comprehensive edition of that work (1877), published posthumously together with a translation

BENJAMIN HALL KENNEDY, BY W. W. OULESS, R.A.
(St. John's College, Cambridge.)

of the " Phædo." One of Thompson's ablest contemporaries was John William Donaldson, author of the " New Cratylus " and " Varronianus," and editor of Pindar. His name is also associated with the " Theatre of the Greeks," and with the completion of K. O. Müller's " History of Greek Literature." Donaldson, 1811-1861.

A strikingly original and independent type of scholarship was represented by Charles Badham, in early life a pupil

[1] *Journal of Philology,* **xv.**, 307.

Badham,
1813-1884.

of Pestalozzi, and afterwards educated at Eton, who entered Wadham College, Oxford, and, after spending seven years in Germany, France, and Italy, proved his affinity for the Cambridge school of scholarship by becoming a member of Peterhouse. He edited the " Iphigenia in Tauris," the " Helena" and the " Ion " of Euripides, and the " Philebus," the " Euthydemus " and " Laches," and the " Symposium " of Plato. In 1867, at the age of fifty-four, he became Professor of Classics and Logic at Sydney, a position which he held with distinction until his death in 1884.

Paley,
1816-1888.

A still greater variety of interests was exemplified by Frederick Apthorp Paley, of Shrewsbury and St. John's. Besides being a keen botanist, he was an enthusiastic student of ecclesiastical architecture, and an active member of the Camden Society, which flourished at Cambridge between 1838 and 1843. He joined the Church of Rome in 1846, returned to Cambridge in 1860, and finally left it in 1874. His best work was his Æschylus, begun in 1844, and published, with Latin notes, in 1847-51, and English notes in 1850 and in several later editions. He also edited Euripides (1858–60), Hesiod (1861), Theocritus (1863), and the " Iliad " (1867), besides several plays of Sophocles (1880). As he was unfamiliar with German, his scholarship owed little or nothing to foreign sources of erudition, and his learning, though not profound, was certainly wide, and distinctively his own. A certain facility of execution tempted him to undue rapidity of production, and there is little doubt that, had he written less, he would have enjoyed a more durable reputation. Some of his best work is to be found in his prefaces.

Paley, like other able scholars of his time in Cambridge, was prevented from even competing for honours in classics by his failure to obtain honours in mathematics. The same misfortune befell his accomplished schoolfellow, who was a member of the

T. S
Evans,
1816-1889.

same college, Thomas Sanders Evans. His edition of the " First Epistle to the Corinthians" (1881) won him the recognition of an honorary degree at Edinburgh; and, after his death, a volume of " Latin and Greek Verse " was published " as a memorial of an original and highly gifted man, considered by many to have few rivals in his special department of scholarship."

A scholar of similar but more varied gifts, and sprung from the same school, was William George Clark, Fellow of Trinity, who from 1857 to 1869 adorned the office of Public Orator at Cambridge. He visited Spain, Italy, Greece, and Poland, and, among other works of travel, published his "Peloponnesus" in 1858, the results of his Greek tour in the company of Thompson.

W. G.
Clark,
1821-1878.

WILLIAM HEPWORTH THOMPSON, BY SIR H. VON HERKOMER, R.A.
(Trinity College, Cambridge.)

In 1860 he designed a critical edition of Shakespeare, which, with the aid of an able colleague, was happily brought to a successful conclusion in 1866. Earlier in his career he had also formed the plan of editing Aristophanes, an author for whose interpretation much had been done by T. Mitchell, Fellow of Sidney, in his translations of 1820–23, and his editions of several plays in 1836–39; while John Hookham Frere (1769–1846), Fellow of Gonville and Caius, had produced at Malta a remarkably fine rendering of five of the plays between 1830 and 1840 On the completion of the Cambridge Shakespeare, Clark spent part of 1867 in examining the MSS. of Aristophanes at Ravenna and elsewhere, and began preparing a commentary on the "Acharnians," which he was unfortunately compelled by failing health to leave unfinished. Munro, his friend for nearly forty years, thought that "his was the most accomplished and versatile mind he had ever encountered." His work was marked by a "surprising tact and readiness," a "consummate ease and mastery." "As a charming companion and brilliant, yet gentle, talker, he had no superior"; and the late Lord Clarendon, who had spent his life in the choicest social circles at home and abroad, declared that "Clark was the most agreeable man in society he had ever met."[1]

Babington, 1821-1889. The year of Clark's birth was also that of the birth of Churchill Babington, Fellow of St. John's, and Disney Professor of Archæology from 1865 to 1880, who produced the *editio princeps* of four of the speeches of Hyperides, which had been recovered from the tombs of Egypt, beginning with the "Speech against Demosthenes" in 1851, and ending with the "Funeral Oration" in 1858. **Holden, 182?-1896.** Hubert Ashton Holden, Fellow of Trinity, and Headmaster of Ipswich School from 1858 to 1883, was born a year later than Clark and Babington. He was widely known for his "Foliorum Silvula," a collection of English poetry for translation into Greek and Latin, and also for the versions of the same by various scholars published in his "Folia Silvulæ." He edited a text of Aristophanes, with an onomasticon, besides many elaborately annotated editions of classical authors, including the Seventh Book of Thucydides, the "Cyropædeia," the "Hieron," and the "Œconomicus" of Xenophon, eight of Plutarch's "Lives," and the "Pro Plancio," "Pro Sestio," and "De Officiis" of Cicero.

Oxford. Among the representatives of scholarship at Oxford during this period, the first place in order of time belongs to Thomas Tyrwhitt, the editor of Aristotle's "Poetics" (1794: Vol. V., p. 91). The next to be named is the Nestor of his University, Martin Joseph Routh, who died in the hundredth year of his age. He edited the "Euthydemus" and "Gorgias" of Plato in 1784, published in 1832 the "Scriptorum Ecclesiasticorum Opuscula," and lived to produce the fifth volume of his "Reliquiæ Sacræ" in 1848. In the previous year, when asked, at the age of

[1] *Journal of Philology*, viii., 173-5.

FIRST FRAGMENT OF THE HYPERIDES MS.

(Papyrus CVIII., British Museum.)

Greek
Scholars
at Oxford:
Tyrwhitt,
1730-1786;
Routh,
1755-1854.

ninety-two, whether in the course of a long and thoughtful life he had had occasion to experience the special value of some one axiom or precept, after some reflection, he brightened up and said, "I think, sir, since you care for the advice of an old man, sir, you will find it a very good practice *always to verify your references.*" [1]   Though without originality of genius or power of imagination, "his marvellous memory, his quick perception, his tenacity of purpose, his indomitable industry and calm judgment—these stood to him in the place of genius." [2]

Gaisford,
1779-1855.

The editorial labours of Elmsley (already mentioned in connexion with Porson), and of William Linwood (1816–78), were limited to the Greek drama.   A far wider field was covered by Thomas Gaisford, Dean of Christ Church and Regius Professor of Greek, who, after examining a large number of classical MSS. in the libraries of Europe, edited, among many other works, the "Poetæ Græci Minores" (1814–20), Herodotus (1824), and Stobæus (1822 and 1850), as well as the great lexicons of Suidas (1834) and the "Etymologicum Magnum" (1848).   As the editor of the metrical writer Hephæstion (1810), he is praised by Hermann as *dignus qui multa cum laude*

Scott,
1811-1887.

commemoretur.   Robert Scott, Master of Balliol, and afterwards Dean of Rochester, has a permanent place in the history of scholarship in England as the joint editor of a monumental lexicon of the Greek language (first published in 1843).   As

Jowett,
1817-1894.

Master he was succeeded in 1870 by Benjamin Jowett, who had already succeeded Gaisford as Professor of Greek in 1855. Jowett's translations of Plato (1871), Thucydides (1881), and the "Politics" of Aristotle (1885), are masterpieces of English, which have extended a knowledge of Greek literature among many who are unfamiliar with Greek.   His Plato was welcomed with enthusiasm by no less a judge of good English than John

Pattison,
1813-1886.

Bright.   His contemporary, Mark Pattison, rector of Lincoln, was deeply read in the history of scholarship, especially that of the late Renaissance, as is proved in part by his "Life of Casaubon" (1875), and his "Essays on Scaliger" (reprinted

Chandler,
1828-1889.

1889).   Henry William Chandler, Fellow of Pembroke, produced in 1862 a standard work on Greek accents.   As Professor of Moral Philosophy he gave lectures on Aristotle which were highly appreciated.   He had a remarkable knowledge of bibliography,

[1] Burgon's "Twelve Good Men," i., 73.   [2] *Ibid.*, p. 109.

in particular of that of the "Ethics," and his extensive collection of Aristotelian literature has happily found a permanent home in the library of his own college.

In Latin scholarship the first name in order of time is that **Latin** of John Martyn, Professor of Botany at Cambridge, whose useful **Scholars:** work on the "Bucolics" and "Georgics" of Virgil began to **Martyn, 1699-1768**

THOMAS GAISFORD, DEAN OF CHRIST CHURCH.
(*By permission of the Dean and Governing Body, Christ Church, Oxford.*)

appear in 1741, and passed through several editions in the next generation. The enduring influence of Bentley is apparent in the "Horatius Restitutus" of James Tate, of Richmond, in whose edition (1832, 1837) the works of the poet are printed in chronological order according to Bentley's views. The "Æneid" was the theme of the unwearied labours of James Henry, the Dublin physician **Henry,** who began to study Virgil seriously when over forty years of **1798-1876.** age, and published in 1853 his "Notes of a Twelve Years' Voyage of Discovery in the First Six Books of the Æneis." His larger work, the "Æneidea," founded on a personal knowledge of all the best MSS. and editions of the poet, and containing many original and valuable contributions to the interpretation of the text, was printed in four volumes in 1873–89.

Munro, 1819-1885.

Hugh Andrew Johnstone Munro, educated at Shrewsbury, Fellow of Trinity, and first Professor of Latin in the University of Cambridge, produced in 1864 his masterly edition of Lucretius. His other works include an edition of the "Ætna" of an unknown poet (1867), a revised text of Horace, with illustrations from ancient gems, selected by the learned archæologist, C. W. King (1869), and, lastly, his "Criticisms and Elucidations of Catullus." He was hardly less masterly as a Greek critic; as early as 1855 he was the first to maintain the Eudemian origin of the fifth book of the "Ethics," and towards the close of his life he paid special attention to the text of Euripides. His translations into Greek and Latin verse are held in great repute; though not, like Kennedy, "an original Latin poet,"[1] he won the admiration of another master of the craft by

Conington, 1825-1869.
Sellar. 1825-1890.

his vigorous version of Gray's "Elegy."[2] John Conington, educated at Rugby, became, in 1854, the first Oxford Professor of Latin, edited Virgil (1863-71) and Persius (ed. Nettleship, 1872), and translated into English the whole of Horace and the "Æneid," besides completing Worsley's rendering of the "Iliad," and editing, in the early part of his career, the "Agamemnon" (1848) and "Choëphoræ" (1857) of Æschylus. William Young Sellar. Fellow ot Balliol, born in the same year as Conington, was Professor of Humanity at Edinburgh from 1863 to his death. In the former year he produced his "Roman Poets of the Republic," a masterpiece of literary criticism, not unworthily followed by his valuable works on Virgil (1877) and on "Horace and the Elegiac Poets" (1892). Conington's edition of the "Æneid"

Nettleship, 1839-1893.

was completed by his successor in the Chair of Latin, Henry Nettleship, who was mainly responsible for the second half of the work. In 1875 Nettleship embarked on the preparation of a great Latin dictionary, but was prevented from completing more than a tenth part, published in 1889 under the title of "Contributions to Latin Lexicography." Much of his time was devoted to the study of the ancient Latin grammarians, and one

---

[1] Thompson in *Journal of Philology*, xiv., 109.

[2] *Qui stant quasi marmore versus et similes solido structis adamante columnis.* T. S. Evans, *ibid.*, v. 307-8.

of his latest tasks was the revision of the edition of Nonius, left unfinished by his friend and former pupil, J. H. Onions (1852–89). Many of Nettleship's most valuable papers have been collected in two volumes, entitled " Lectures and Essays " (1885 and 1895).

English scholars in general may be said to have paid more attention to Greek than to Latin, and to verse than to prose. Among commentaries on Latin prose authors there are few that call for mention besides the edition of Cicero's "Pro Cluentio," by William Ramsay, formerly Professor of Humanity at Glasgow, editor of the "Mostellaria" of Plautus, and author of an excellent "Manual of Roman Antiquities"; and the series of editions of Cicero's philosophical works published between 1836 and 1856 by Henry Ellis Allen ("Henricus Alanus"). The only other editions of prose authors that need here be noticed are by editors whose main reputation rests on their work as historians, Cicero's "Speeches" and Cæsar's "Gallic War" having been edited by Long, Sallust by Merivale, and the first book of Livy by Seeley.

Ramsay, 1806-1885.

In Ancient History our earliest and most notable name in this period is that of Edward Gibbon (Vol. V., p. 610). A friend of Gibbon, William Mitford, wrote a "History of Greece," in which the author allowed himself to be unduly biassed by a dislike of democracy in general. The publication of this work extended over more than thirty years (1784–1818). Though written in a spirited and lively style, it was destined to be superseded by the works of George Grote and Connop Thirlwall (p. 386). Both of these great historians of Greece were educated at the same school (Charterhouse), both attained the age of seventy-seven, and both are buried in Westminster Abbey. Thirlwall, Fellow of Trinity, and afterwards Bishop of St. David's (1840–74), produced his first volume in 1835 and his last in 1844. Grote, who had planned and begun his history as early as 1823, published his first volume in 1846, and his last ten years afterwards. His history was followed by a great work in three volumes on "Plato" (1865), and an unfinished work on "Aristotle" (1871). As a historian, Thirlwall is undoubtedly a sounder scholar and a better writer than Grote; he has also a more judicial temper and a finer sense of proportion. Grote, on the other hand, is obviously inspired with all the zeal of a partisan in his devotion not

Historians: Gibbon, 1737-1794. Mitford, 1744-1827.

Grote, 1794-1871.

Thirlwall, 1797-1875.

merely to Athenian democracy, but even to the Athenian demagogue; yet, as an intelligent and sympathetic interpreter of the ancient historians of Greece, he has great merits, while his judgment on the political and economic condition of Athens derives fresh weight from his experience as a banker and as a member of the first Reformed Parliament down to the year

WILLIAM MITFORD, AFTER H. EDRIDGE.

Mure,
1799-1860

1841. William Mure, who, like Grote, was a Member of Parliament, and, unlike Grote, actually visited Greece, published in 1850-7 five volumes of a "Critical History of the Literature of Ancient Greece," a work which is still useful in relation to Xenophon in particular. Modern historians of Greece and Rome are deeply indebted to the chronological researches of that most methodical scholar, Henry Fynes Clinton, whose "Fasti Hellenici" were published in 1824-32, to be followed by his "Fasti Romani" in 1845-50. Thomas Arnold, Headmaster of Rugby and Professor of History at Oxford, besides producing his memorable edition of Thucy-

Clinton,
1781-1852.

dides (1830–5), left behind him a splendid fragment of a Arnold, 1795–1842. "History of Rome" (1838–43), closing with the end of the Second Punic War. In Arnold's history the influence of Niebuhr is apparent. The historical structure raised by Niebuhr's genius was attacked by an accomplished English statesman, Sir George Cornewall Lewis, who, besides translating G. C. Lewis, 1806–1865. Boeckh's "Public Economy of Athens," editing Babrius, and

BISHOP CONNOP THIRLWALL.
(*Westminster Abbey.*)

writing on the "Astronomy of the Ancients," produced in 1855 his "Inquiry into the Credibility of Early Roman History." George Long, of Trinity, Cambridge (who won the Long, 1800–1879. Craven with Macaulay and Malden, and was elected Fellow over the heads of both), after holding Professorships in Virginia and in London, and contributing to Smith's Dictionaries many articles on Ancient Geography and Roman Law, produced translations of Marcus Aurelius and Epictetus, and illustrated the Civil Wars of Rome in an annotated rendering of select "Lives from Plutarch." But his best work was undoubtedly his "History of the Decline of the Roman

Republic" (1864–74), the value of which is enhanced by the care bestowed on setting forth the evidence of the ancient authorities.   Charles Merivale, of Harrow and St. John's, Cambridge, appointed Dean of Ely in 1869, produced in the seclusion of a college living his able "History of the Romans under the Empire" (1850–62), closing at the point where the narrative of his great predecessor, Gibbon, begins.   The comparative method was successfully applied to the study of early institutions by Henry James Sumner Maine, of Pembroke College, Professor of Civil Law at Cambridge (1847–54), who, after seven years of noble work as legal member of the Supreme Government of India, became Professor of Jurisprudence at Oxford (1870–78), and was Master of Trinity Hall from the end of 1877 to his death.   His best known books are "Ancient Law" (1861), "Village Communities" (1871), and "Dissertations on Early Law and Custom" (1883).   Other work on the constitution of primitive society will be dealt with in the section of the next chapter devoted to Philosophy.

There are few departments of classical research in which the reputation won by Englishmen has been higher than in the field of classical topography and the archæological studies connected therewith.   The foundation of the Society of Dilettantti at the close of 1733 (Vol. V., p. 360) led to the production of a splendid series of works on Greek and Roman Antiquities, including Stuart and Revett's "Antiquities of Athens" (1762–1816), Richard Chandler's "Travels" (1775–6) and "Inscriptiones Antiquæ" (1774), Sir William Gell's "Rome and its Vicinity" (1846), Penrose's "Principles of Athenian Architecture" (1851, 1889), and Cockerell's "Temples of Ægina and Bassæ" (1860). The same Society has also promoted excavations conducted by Richard Popplewell Pullan at Teos and Priene and also in the Troad (1862–70).   Edmund Chishull's "Travels in Turkey" (1698–1702) were not published until 1747.   Robert Wood, a member of the Dilettantti Society, travelled in Greece and Palestine in 1751 and published his works on Palmyra and Baalbec in 1753 and 1757 respectively.   The ruins of Pæstum were visited and described by Major in 1768 and Swinburne in 1779.   The sculptures of the Parthenon, removed to England by the Earl of Elgin in 1801–3, were purchased by the Government for £35,000 and placed in the British Museum in 1816 (p. 400).

Merivale, 1808–1894.

Maine, 1822–1888.

Classical Topo- graphy.

THE ELGIN MARBLES—PORTION OF THE FRIEZE OF THE PARTHENON.

(British Museum.)

Dodwell,
1767-1832.

The accomplished traveller, Edward Dodwell, spent the greater part of his life in Greece and Italy ; his " Tour in Greece " (with a volume of " Views ") appeared in 1819, his " Cyclopean Remains " in 1834. The foremost of Greek topographers was

Leake,
1777-1860.

William Martin Leake, the author of " Researches in Greece " (1812), " The Topography of Athens " (1821), " Travels in Northern Greece " (1835), " The Morea " (1830), "Peloponnesiaca " (1846), and " Numismata Hellenica." His library and his collection of coins now belong to the University of Cambridge.

Fellows,
1799-1860.

Sir Charles Fellows became famous as the explorer of Lycia and the discoverer of the Xanthian marbles (1840), and his example was followed, with no small success, by Spratt and Forbes, who visited Lycia in 1842. The former of these published in 1865 the " Travels and Researches in Crete," which he had undertaken in 1851–3. Cyrene was successfully explored by R. Murdoch Smith and E. A. Porcher in 1860–1, and the necropolis of Cameiros in Rhodes was excavated by Salzmann and Biliotti in 1858 and 1865, to the great advantage of the collection of Greek vases in the British Museum. Among the many public services

Layard,
1817-1884.
Newton.
1816-1894.

of Sir Austen Henry Layard was his exploration of Nineveh (1845). The latest name of note is that of Sir Charles Newton, the discoverer of the mausoleum of Halicarnassus (1857). During the latter part of the nineteenth century, and subsequently, Greek archæological studies have been fostered in England by the foundation of the Society for the Promotion of Hellenic Studies (1879) and by the institution of the British School of Archæology at Athens (1886).

Greek
Testament.

The study of classical archæology and topography was happily united with that of the criticism of the Greek Testament in the person of Christopher Wordsworth, Bishop of Lincoln, who edited Theocritus (1844) and wrote on the *graffiti* (or wall-scribblings) of Pompeii, and also on Athens and Attica and the " Topography of Greece," divining in the course of this last work the long-lost site of the oracle of Dodona. In 1856 he published a commentary on the Greek Testament, rich in citations from patristic literature. Fuller reference is made to the German commentators in the edition of Henry Alford, Dean of Canterbury. Several of the Pauline Epistles in particular were admirably edited by Joseph Barber Lightfoot, Bishop of Durham (p. 595), who was also the editor of Clement

of Rome, and Ignatius and Polycarp. In connection with
textual criticism must be mentioned, besides the names of

WINGED AND MAN-HEADED LION FROM THE PALACE
OF ASSUR-NASIR-PAL, KING OF ASSYRIA; EXCAVATED
BY SIR A. H. LAYARD.
(*British Museum.*)

Tregelles (d. 1870), Scrivener, and Hort (d. 1892), the Revision
by the joint labours of English and American scholars of the
Authorised Version of the New Testament, a work which occupied ten and a half years, from June, 1870, to November, 1880.

Hebrew.

In the study of Hebrew almost the only notable names of Cambridge scholars in the present century have been those of Samuel Lee (1783–1852), Professor of Hebrew and Arabic at Cambridge; W. H. Mill, his successor in the Chair of Hebrew, who died in 1853, and was better known as a learned theologian and scholar; and Frederic Field (1801–85), honorary Fellow of Trinity, whose edition of Origen's " Hexapla " placed him in the first rank of Hebrew and Syriac scholars. Meanwhile, at Oxford the chair of Hebrew was filled for fifty-four years by Edward Bouverie Pusey (1800–82), who published a " Commentary on the Minor Prophets " and " Lectures on the Prophet Daniel " (1862–4). The Revision of the Authorised Version of the Old Testament, the joint work of many competent Hebraists, begun in 1870, was not completed until 1884. The Revised Version of the Old Testament has met with a more favourable reception than that of the New, partly because it did not disturb the text of the original, partly because it was confined to the correction of errors without attempting a rigid uniformity of rendering.

Syriac.

The study of Syriac was successfully pursued by William Cureton (1808–64), of Christ Church, Oxford, Canon of Westminster, who published a Syriac MS. of the " Epistles of St. Ignatius " in 1845 and 1849, the text of the Syriac version of the " Festal Letters of St. Athanasius," and the remains of an ancient recension of the Syriac Gospels from a MS. of the fifth century (1858); by Robert Payne Smith (1818–95), Dean of Canterbury, who, besides many other labours in the field of Oriental learning, began, in 1868, the publication of an important Syriac Lexicon; and by Robert Lubbock Bensly (1831–93), Fellow of Gonville and Caius College, who was the first to publish, in 1875, from an Amiens MS. of the ninth century, the missing fragment of the Latin translation of the Fourth Book of Ezra, discovered by him in the previous year, and who spent part of the last year of his life in deciphering an important Syriac MS. of the Gospels, discovered in 1892 in the Convent of St. Catharine, on Mount Sinai.

Arabic.

Bensly's discovery of the missing fragment of the Fourth Book of Ezra was anticipated by John Palmer (1787–1840), Fellow of St. John's, Professor of Arabic from 1804 to 1840, a master of many languages, who was so singularly reticent that it was said of him that he could be silent in more languages than any man in Europe. During his travels in Spain in 1826 he discovered the missing fragment in a Complutensian MS. of the eighth century, but he buried all knowledge of this fact in his papers, and his discovery was not published until thirty-seven years after his death.[1]   The most eminent representatives of Arabic during the present century have been Edward William Lane (1801–76), the author of the great Arabic Lexicon, and translator of the "Arabian Nights"; William Wright (1830–89), Fellow of Queens', Professor of Arabic in Cambridge from 1870 to 1889, the author of the best Arabic grammar now in existence, and distinguished as a Syriac scholar; and Edward Henry Palmer (1840–82), Lord Almoner's Reader in Cambridge, a man of singular versatility, who showed the highest genius for the acquisition of Oriental languages, travelled in the "Desert of the Exodus" in 1868–9, produced, among many other works, an excellent Arabic grammar (1874), and died in Arabia in the service of his country during the rebellion of Arabi in 1882. His successor in the readership, William Robertson Smith[2] (1846–94), after studying physics with distinction, devoted himself to Oriental languages, and became famous for his encyclopædic learning. He was librarian of the University of Cambridge, and afterwards Professor of Arabic. Thomas Chenery[3] (1826–84), of Gonville and Caius College, Lord Almoner's Reader at Oxford, was mainly an Arabic scholar, but he was also a good Hebraist, and wrote Hebrew with elegance.

In Turkish one of the leading authorities in England was Sir James William Redhouse, the author of a grammar and dictionary of the Ottoman language, and other works, and the translator of a mystical Persian poet. It was Redhouse's pocket manual of Turkish conversation that was used by our officers during the Crimean War. To the distinguished diplomatist, Sir John Malcolm (1769–1833), we owe the "History of Persia," which is still the standard work on the subject   The Persian

Turkish

---

[1] J. S. Wood, *Journal of Philology*, vii. (1877), 264.

[2 Eventually one of the Editors of the *Encyclopædia Britannica*, and the occasion, by his advanced views on Old Testament criticism, of a prolonged controversy in the Free Church of Scotland, 1875–1881.]

[3 Editor of the *Times* after the famous Delane.]

Persian. language was successfully studied by Sir William Ouseley and his younger brother, Sir Gore Ouseley (1770–1844). The former was the greater scholar, though less conspicuous in public life; the latter, apart from his public distinctions, was author of **Cuneiform Inscriptions.** "Lives of the Persian Poets." The cuneiform inscriptions of Persia, Assyria, and Babylonia were deciphered by Sir Henry Creswicke Rawlinson (1810–95), and by Edward Hincks (1792–1888), Fellow of Trinity College, Dublin.[1] Lastly, the **Chinese.** Chair of Chinese was founded at Oxford in 1875; while, at Cambridge, an honorary professorship of that language was held by the eminent diplomatist, Sir Thomas Francis Wade (1820–95), who presented to the University his valuable library of Chinese literature.

Sanskrit.   The first Englishman who obtained any mastery of Sanskrit was Charles Wilkins (1749–1836). Beginning his study of that language in India in 1778, under the encouragement of Warren Hastings, he translated the " Bhagavadgītā " (1785) and the " Hitopadeça " (1787); he also produced a Sanskrit grammar (1808), and a work on " Sanskrit Radicals " (1815). Sir William Jones (1746–94), of University College, Oxford, the translator of the legal speeches of the Attic orator, Isæus, was first attracted to Sanskrit (in 1784) by its bearing on Indian law; he soon detected its philological importance, pointing out in 1786 its affinity with Greek, Latin, Gothic, and Celtic, and in 1789 its connection with Zend. He translated Kālidāsa's drama, " Sakuntalā," and also the " Institutes " of Manu; his commentaries on Eastern poetry, and his history of Nadir Shah are still classical works. Burnouf and F. Schlegel both learnt their Sanskrit from an Indian civilian, Alexander Hamilton, who was captured by Napoleon in 1802 and detained until 1807, and was thereby enabled to excite the first interest in the language in France and Germany. William Carey (1761–1834), the Baptist Missionary, published a Sanskrit grammar (1806), and edited and translated the " Rāmāyana " (1806–10); he also translated the Bible into Sanskrit, as well as into Bengali and Mahrathi. But the greatest of English Sanskritists was Henry Thomas Colebrooke (1765–1837), whose " Essays on Sanskrit Literature," published in a collected form in the year of his death, are recognised

---

[1] " Royal Irish Academy," vol. xxi ; W. G. Vaux in " Annual Report of Royal Society of Literature," 1867.

as masterpieces of insight and research. He had previously produced elaborate translations of the two standard Sanskrit treatises on the law of inheritance (1810), and also of certain mathematical and philosophical works (1817). Even more was done for the actual spread of the study by a man of less genius,

SIR WILLIAM JONES, BY SIR JOSHUA REYNOLDS, P.R.A.

(By permission of the Right Hon. Earl Spencer.)

Horace Hayman Wilson (1786–1860), the first Professor of Sanskrit at Oxford (1833), whose dictionary (1819, 1832) made the further study of the language possible in Europe. B. H. Hodgson discovered the remains of Northern Buddhist literature in Nepal; and J. Muir, the founder of the Sanskrit Chair in Edinburgh, was to the close of his life an enthusiastic student of the Veda; while R. C. Childers was the first to publish, in 1875, a dictionary of Pāli, the sacred language of the Buddhists. The discovery of the affinity of Sanskrit with other languages led to the foundation of the Comparative Philology of the Indo-European languages, which has become a recognised branch of study in the universities of England.

Anglo-Saxon and English. The study of Anglo-Saxon received a new impulse in 1772 by the publication of Lye and Manning's dictionary; 1823 is the date of Sharon Turner's "History of the Anglo-Saxons," described by Kemble as a "learned and laborious work, yet, in all that relates to the language and poetry of our forefathers,

J. M. KEMBLE, BY T. WOOLNER, R.A.
(*Trinity College, Cambridge.*)

often deficient, often mistaken." Thorpe produced an edition of Cædmon in 1832, the "Analecta Anglo-Saxonica" in 1834, and "Ancient Law" in 1840; while John Mitchell Kemble (1807–57), of Trinity, Cambridge, a friend and pupil of Jacob Grimm, edited Beowulf in 1833–7, and the "Codex Diplomaticus Ævi Saxonici" in six volumes in 1839–48, founding on this great collection of charters his important "History of the Saxons in England" (1849). Edwin Guest, Master of Gonville and Caius from 1852 to 1880, was the author of a "History of English Rhythms" (ed. Skeat, 1882) and of "Origines Celticæ" (ed. Stubbs, 1883), containing important papers on the Anglo-Saxon conquest. Among those who did excellent work for the Philological Society, and the Early English Text Society (started in 1864), was Richard Morris, who, in his "Specimens of Early English" (1867) clearly made out the chief characteristics of the three main dialects of Middle English, the Northern, Midland, and Southern. Some of the most successful researches into pronunciation of English in bygone times were those of Alexander John Ellis (1814–90), of Trinity, Cambridge, whose "Early English Pronunciation, with special reference to

Chaucer and Shakespeare," was published in several parts between 1869 and 1875. Our list of Anglo-Saxon scholars may here close with the honoured name of Joseph Bosworth (1790–1876), a member of the same college, whose elementary grammar appeared in 1823, and his larger dictionary in 1838. He filled the Chair of Anglo-Saxon at Oxford from 1858 to 1876, and, by a gift dating from 1867, led to the foundation of the Elrington and Bosworth Professorship at Cambridge eleven years later. [1]

THE English philosophical tradition is continued in our present period first of all by Alexander Bain (1818–1904). Professor Bain's two greatest works, which form together a complete treatise on psychology, with philosophical applications, belong chronologically to the preceding period. The first, "The Senses and the Intellect," appeared in 1855; the second, "The Emotions and the Will," in 1859. In his statement of Associationism, Professor Bain modified the position of Hartley and James Mill; recognising "association by similarity" as equally fundamental with "association by contiguity." One of his most conspicuous merits was that he had taken up and developed the doctrine of the "muscular sense." His theory of the growth of volition was an original achievement in psychology. Assuming the infant to start with a tendency to spontaneous activity, in addition to the passive susceptibilities constituting special sense, he traced developed will to association of other psychical states, by links of feeling, with spontaneous movement as its germ. "Mental and Moral Science" (1868) is a compendium of psychology together with a short treatise on ethics and a historical account of systems. Professor Bain's "Logic" followed the lines of Mill; but a sharper demarcation was made between the provinces of formal and material logic, and in the latter more

Marginal notes: T. WHITTAKER. Philosophy and Anthropology. Bain.

---

[1] The above outline of the history of English scholarship for the century and a half which closes with 1885 does not pretend to be anything more than a brief retrospect of the careers of its leading representatives in the past. We can hardly presume on the present occasion either to estimate the eminence or to forecast the fame of scholars who are, happily, still living. *Olim nominabuntur, nunc intelleguntur.* (They will be named hereafter: they are appreciated now.)

account is taken of contemporary physical ideas. "Mind and Body" (1873) gave a concise statement of the doctrine that mental and physiological processes (more particularly those in the nervous system) are uniformly concomitant, but are not to be regarded as causes of one another.

PROFESSOR ALEXANDER BAIN, BY SIR GEORGE REID, P.R.S.A.

(By permission of the Principal and University Court of Aberdeen.)

Spencer.   Herbert Spencer (1820–1904), whose influence begins to become marked early in this period, was both a great psychologist and a great systematic philosopher. His first published book was "Social Statics" (1851). Here he laid down positions which led to the minimising of State action, a political doctrine which he held to the last, though on somewhat different grounds. This first work comes nearer to the assertion of "abstract rights" known prior to experience than was really consistent with the principles of Spencer's philosophy; for he was, like the greatest among his English predecessors, an experientialist.

Where Spencer made a new departure in modern thought was in introducing the doctrine of evolution into psychology and philosophy. This step had already been taken in the "Principles of Psychology" (1855), four years before the appearance of the "Origin of Species." Here biological

Evolution in Mental Science.

Photo: Elliott & Fry, Baker Street, W.
HERBERT SPENCER.

evolution is expressly accepted as an incomparably more scientific doctrine than special creation, though the imperfection of the evidence for it is fully recognised. In the "Principles of Biology" (1864–7) the Darwinian doctrine of natural selection is incorporated; but for Spencer this is only one of the factors of organic evolution, the others being direct action of the environment on the organism, and inherited effects of the use and disuse of organs. "First Principles" (1862) set forth Spencer's general philosophy. It contains in its first part a metaphysical doctrine, and in its second a scheme of cosmical evolution embracing both the

physical phenomena of the universe and the phenomena of
life, mind, and society. Spencer put forward his metaphysical doctrine as a consistent development of Hamilton's
and Mansel's philosophy of the Conditioned. The Uncondi-
tioned, or Absolute, is positively known to exist, but is in itself
for ever unknowable. Mental and material phenomena are
its manifestations. These are knowable, and are the objects
of science. The Unknowable is the object of the religious
sentiment. Remaining always a mystery, insoluble by human
thought, it is yet ever presenting itself anew at the bounds
of science. Science and religion are reconciled by acquiescence
in the mystery, without any attempt to evade it by assertions
which are necessarily groundless or meaningless.

The formula of evolution, stated and illustrated in the
second part of "First Principles," is applied in the succeeding
volumes of Spencer's "System of Synthetic Philosophy"
to Biology, Psychology, Sociology, and Ethics; the detailed
application to inorganic nature being omitted. The "Biology"
and "Psychology" (second edition, 1870–2) have already been
referred to. The "Sociology" was not finished till 1896, and
the completion of the "Ethics" also lies beyond our period.
The very important first volume of the "Principles of
Sociology," however, appeared in 1876, and the "Data of
Ethics" in 1879; so that a word may be said of them here.

In the "Psychology" the doctrine of evolution is applied
to explain those cognitions that seem intuitive, in a manner
consistent with the philosophy that derives all knowledge
from experience. The results of experience, Spencer holds,
are passed on from one individual to another by heredity;
hence in explaining knowledge we are not confined to the
experience of each individual. There is an inherited experience of the race, on which that of the individual is
superimposed. This same conception can be applied to
ethical theory. By inherited experience, along with other
factors, we get what are practically moral intuitions. Also, in
the attempt to arrive at moral rules for new cases, the doctrine
of evolution gives us an immense advantage over the older
utilitarianism. We are able to take for our basis certain
biological and sociological laws in order to arrive at rational
precepts such as could never be arrived at by mere empirical

summation of pleasures and pains. We have thus for our morality a rational instead of an empirical utilitarianism.

The first volume of the "Sociology" contains what is known as Spencer's "ghost-theory" of religion. Generalising from accumulated facts about savage tribes, and then reconstructing subjectively the mental processes of primitive man, Spencer traces the idea of invisible personal agents with powers over man's destiny to the idea of a second and invisible self accompanying the body. This idea is suggested naturally by various normal and abnormal phenomena, such as shadows, reflexions, sleep, dreams, trances, etc. In its application to explain some of these phenomena, the second self, or soul, has to be supposed capable of an existence separate from the body. Pursuing the same train of thought, the savage thinks of his invisible self as still existing after death, with powers intermittently active in the visible world. A world of ghosts is imagined, having more or less fitful or constant relations with the world of living men. The ghosts of ancestors are propitiated by offering to them—in some way that to the savage mind seems efficacious—such things as they were pleased with during life. The most potent of the imagined ghosts—the ghosts, for example, of kings—are from the first objects of a special worship, and this may come to predominate more and more. Here we have the beginnings of a pantheon, and of the whole subsequent evolution of religion.

This is only one of the topics dealt with in the "Sociology." Other topics are marriage customs, modes of ceremonial observance, political and ecclesiastical institutions. It is noteworthy that in their actual treatment of the science they both call "Sociology," Comte and Spencer lay stress on different parts of the subject. Comte deals mainly with the historical evolution of Europe; Spencer dwells especially upon the prehistoric and archaic preparation for all historical evolution. Both alike treat their subject as philosophers; that is, in subordination to a scheme meant to include the whole of scientific knowledge in a synthetic or unified form. Simultaneously with this philosophic development, a number of investigators have arisen who aim at dealing with the origins of society in the spirit of purely special and positive science.

[margin note: Spencer's "Sociology."]

Treated in this way, the science has come to be called Anthropology. Chief among its cultivators are John Ferguson McLennan (1827–81) and Dr. E. B. Tylor. McLennan's "Primitive Marriage," which in England marks the beginning of one class of anthropological inquiries, appeared in 1865. In the same year appeared Dr. Tylor's "Researches into the Early History of Mankind." Since about that time there has been practically continuous work on the subject (*cf.* p. 666).

Anthropology: McLennan and Tylor.

From various symbolical forms which remain in the marriages of peoples that have attained the highest monogamic stage, taken along with what can be learnt of savage and archaic customs, McLennan reconstructed the history of the marriage relation. The system of tracing kinship through males, he found, is preceded by a stage in which it is traced exclusively through females. This was the kind of blood-relationship that first became obvious when men emerged from a stage of promiscuity within the tribe. The "patriarchal" family, instead of coming at the beginning of social development, comes at the end. McLennan himself carried the subject further in essays on "Kinship in Ancient Greece" (finding there traces of "female kinship"), "Totemism," *i.e.* the relation between certain tribes and animals or plants held sacred by them, etc. Many of his particular conclusions are still matter of dispute, but he must always be regarded as a pioneer in the subject. Dr. Tylor also has worked at this branch of inquiry. His name, however, is more particularly associated with investigations into the history of religion. In his theory of a primitive "Animism" he attacks the problem which Spencer tries to solve by the "ghost-theory." Ideas of the soul, according to Dr. Tylor's view, arise as a kind of primitive philosophy to explain the connexion between mind and body. The notion of the soul or invisible self is naturally suggested by the phenomena of reflexions, shadows, etc., as in Spencer's view. When definitely formed, it is used as a perfectly general means of explanation; souls of all objects being assumed, as well as of men, animals, and plants. This primitive Animism contains the germ of religion. The most important difference between Dr. Tylor's theory and Spencer's seems to be that while Spencer traces all gods to ancestral ghosts, Dr. Tylor leaves

open the possibility of explaining some deities as direct imper-
sonations of natural phenomena, after the idea that all things
have souls has once been formed.

Of those who have dealt with Anthropology as a special
science, Dr. Tylor has done most to define its exact scope
and to develop its method. He places it, as the "science of
culture," between the inquiries of prehistoric archæology, on
the one side, and of
history proper on the
other. Geological con-
clusions with regard to
the antiquity of man
give scientific ground
for assuming a long
interval between the
earliest beginnings of
arts, of religions, of
political institutions,
and so forth, and their
developed state in
civilisations such as
those of Asia and
Europe. It is this in-
terval that the special
inquiries of anthro-
pologists aim at filling
up. As confirmatory
evidence of the recon-

Photo: Gillman & Co., Ltd., Oxford.

DR. E. B. TYLOR.

structed process of development, they point especially to the
phenomena known as "survivals in culture"; that is, traces
in the most highly civilised societies of what are held to be
primitive institutions. These correspond exactly to function-
less "rudiments" of organs in biology. We readily see that
an evolution such as the anthropologists suppose is in perfect
harmony with the doctrine of biological evolution, being both
confirmatory of it and confirmed by it.

The influence of Comte on English thought was especially Lewes
promoted by the writings of George Henry Lewes (1817–78), and
whose exposition of "Comte's Philosophy of the Sciences" Comte.
appeared in the same year (1853) as Miss Martineau's abridged

translation of the " Philosophie Positive." In Lewes's "Problems of Life and Mind " (1874–9) a profound idea of Comte that was not taken up by Mill, and for which Spencer has no precise equivalent, was introduced into English psychology. Comte, indeed, repudiates the notion of psychology as a subjective science with introspection for its method ; nevertheless, he brought out more effectively than anyone before him the dependence of the individual for his mental life as a personality on the existence of the " social medium." This idea Lewes worked out so as to give psychologists the benefit of Comte's insight.

Photo ; Elliott & Fry, Baker Street, W.
GEORGE HENRY LEWES.

Lewes, though distinctively a psychologist and philosopher, occupied himself also with physiological research, and, in his " Problems," sought to define the relations between physiology and psychology. Others who are more distinctively cultivators of special science worked in the same direction. Drs. Maudsley and Hughlings Jackson brought the study of mind into relation with pathology as well as with physiology. Dr. D. Ferrier, in " The Functions of the Brain " (1876), tried to found on experiment a theory of the localisation of particular sensory impressions and motor powers in defined cerebral areas. Among men of special science Professor Huxley perhaps did most service to general philosophy. Mr. (afterwards Sir) Francis Galton, besides his important biological work, contributed to the theory of psychological heredity, and, in papers on " mental imagery," threw new light on what takes place in the mind when we form conceptions. The suggestive metaphysical speculations of W. K. Clifford may also be referred to.

Psychology itself began in this period to be treated more

**Physio-
logical
Psychol
ogy.**

as a special science. The work of Professor Sully, for example, was mainly positive psychology, to the exclusion of the metaphysical inquiries mixed with it in older English treatises on the mind. The necessity for this clear demarcation was urged by George Croom Robertson (1842–92), who also best represents the English tradition face to face with the reaction of what is known as the Hegelian school.

The leader of this reaction was Thomas Hill Green (1836–82), whose celebrated Introductions to a new edition **The Hegelian Reaction** of Hume in 1874 were meant to overthrow English Experientialism as represented especially by J. S. Mill. The later English thinkers, Green insisted, were wrong in trying to retain the principles which Hume had shown to result in scepticism. Hume's scepticism was the starting-point for the genuine reconstruction begun by Kant on different lines, and carried higher by Hegel; but to maintain anything like Hume's or Locke's own positions is no longer possible. With the purpose of proving this in detail, Green undertook a close examination of Locke, Berkeley, and Hume. The self-contradictory character of their positions being shown, nothing really remained, in his opinion, for the assailant of Experientialism to dispose of; all its later representatives being less thorough-going than Hume, and having avoided scepticism only by not pushing their arguments, as Hume did, to the end.

Photo: Walker & Cockerell.

PROF. W. K. CLIFFORD.

(By permission, from the Portrait by the Hon. John Collier, in the National Portrait Gallery.)

Green's more original works, in which he states his doctrine on its positive side, have appeared posthumously, beginning with the "Prolegomena to Ethics" (1883).

In other contemporary philosophic writers as well as in

Green the German influence goes deeper than in those who, like Whewell and Hamilton, came at an earlier period more or less under the influence of Kant. To the intervening period belongs Dr. Hutchison Stirling's "Secret of Hegel" (1865), in which Hegel was definitely put forward as the author of a true philosophy for this and succeeding ages. Mr. Shadworth Hodgson's works, the most important of which is "The Philosophy of Reflection" (1878), have been deeply influenced by the thought both of Kant and Hegel, though Mr. Hodgson attaches himself not to the German but to the English tradition. Within the Hegelian school an independent position is taken by Mr. F. H. Bradley, from whom has proceeded important logical work. Professor W. Wallace, of Oxford (1844–1897), translated Hegel's "Logic," and furnished it with valuable prolegomena.

Croom Robertson.

On the lines of Mill, the logical works of Dr. Venn take a chief place. Others, in general philosophy, have continued to follow the experiential tradition without directly considering the objections of its new opponents. The most direct attempt to meet the Hegelian school on general philosophic ground was made by Croom Robertson (1842–1892), who, while recognising the force in Green's criticisms, questioned his assumption that later English thinkers have made no advance on Hume. Even as against Hume and Berkeley, if we make explicit that distinction between psychological questions about the origin of knowledge and philosophical questions about its validity which they did not themselves formulate, many of Green's arguments lose their point. It is true, Robertson allowed, that English experientialists of the present century would have done better to meet Kant in detail; but their failure to do this has had its compensation, since, by working on their own lines, they have arrived at principles that furnish a real reply to the new objections against their traditional mode of philosophising. What is essential in the English tradition from Locke onwards is simply this, that philosophical questions, though not identical with psychological questions, are to be approached through psychology. Robertson himself sought to make good a defect in Mill's "Logic" by his theory of mathematical axioms (1875), which may be regarded either as a translation of Kant into psychological terms or as a solution of Kant's problem from the experiential point of view.

To our present period belong several important ethical **Ethics.** treatises. Dr. Martineau's "Types of Ethical Theory," coming at the end of the period, was a classical expression of the doctrine known as Intuitionalism. Professor Sidgwick's "Methods of Ethics" was on utilitarian lines, but seeks to arrive at principles common to Utilitarians and Intuitionalists. Leslie Stephen's

DR. JAMES MARTINEAU, BY A. E. EMSLIE, A.R.W.S.
(By permission of the Artist.)

"Science of Ethics," written from the evolutionary point of view, makes great use of the revived conception that man is fundamentally a social being. This conception, which belongs both to Hegel and Comte, is implied all through Green's "Prolegomena to Ethics." Green's lectures on political philosophy, published in the collected edition of his works, depended on the same conception; which may, perhaps, be regarded as the one incontestable acquisition of English thought during the latter part of the nineteenth century without respect to the distinction between rival schools.

ON September 19th, 1848, an eighth member of Saturn's family of moons was discovered simultaneously by Lassell at Starfield, and by Bond at Cambridge, U.S.A. It received the name of Hyperion. The recognition of Saturn's dusky ring was likewise a duplicate event, although Dawes, the English observer, on November 25th, 1850, had been slightly anticipated by Bond. The meteoric constitution of the entire ring-system was theoretically proved by Clerk Maxwell (1831–79) in 1857, and, after the lapse of thirty-seven years, was experimentally verified with the spectroscope by J. E. Keeler, at Allegheny, in Pennsylvania.

An important contribution to lunar theory was made by Adams's demonstration, in 1853, that the cause assigned by Laplace for the secular acceleration of our satellite was insufficient, although, in its measure, true. This raised the question of a possible lengthening of the day by tidal friction, and brought into view the part played by that agency in modifying the relations of mutually revolving bodies. Professor G. H. Darwin showed, in 1879, that it had been exceptionally effective in the earth-moon system ; and his researches pointed to the origin of the secondary body by " fission " from a fluid, or plastic primary. He extended them, in 1881, to the whole solar system, but obtained no such definite results. This effort to apply rigorous methods to cosmogony has been imitated for binary stars by Dr. See, of Chicago. Of far wider import was the introduction of the great principle of the Conservation of Energy, due, in large measure, to Joule's determinations, in 1843 and 1849, of the mechanical equivalent of heat (p. 258). One of its effects was to set a limit to the age of the sun. Since its heat· emissions involve contraction in bulk, it must—according to Lord Kelvin's calculations—have been, some twelve million years ago, eight times less dense than now—in other words, its specific gravity was about one-sixth that of water ; while, after the lapse of five to ten million future years, it will be as heavy as lead. We cannot, indeed, say for certain that a body six times more tenuous than water might not have been brilliantly luminous, but there can be no doubt that extinction will long anticipate condensation even to the average massiveness of the earth. Estimates of this kind, however, should be accepted with due allowance for complications of which we are ignorant.

The announcement made by Sir Edward Sabine, May 6th, 1852, of a strict coincidence between the terrestrial-magnetic and sun-spot periods, drew increased attention to solar physics; and the observations of spots made by Richard Christopher Carrington (1826–75) during the years 1853–61, led him to the significant conclusions that the rate of the sun's rotation slackens

Solar Physics.

THE MOON, PHOTOGRAPHED BY WARREN DE LA RUE.
(*By permission of the Royal Astronomical Society.*)

progressively from the equator towards the poles, and that the spot-zones close downwards in latitude with the exhaustion of each cycle of disturbance.

Warren de la Rue (1815–89) was a pioneer in celestial photography. He obtained pictures of the moon by the collodion process in 1853; and the systematic self-registration of sun-spots was begun at Kew, in 1858, with his "photo-heliograph." His photographs of the eclipsed sun, July 18th, 1860, taken with the same instrument at Rivabellosa, in Spain, proved decisively the

Photography in Astronomy.

solar status of the "red prominences" by exhibiting their independence of the moon's motion.   The high value of the camera
for the delineation of the solar corona was accentuated by the
fine photographs taken by Brothers during the Mediterranean
eclipse of December 22nd, 1870, and by artists attached to Lord
Lindsay's party at Baikul, and to General Tennant's party at
Dodabetta, during the totality visible in Southern India, December
12th, 1871.   Their discussion by A. Cowper Ranyard in 1879

THE RIVABELLOSA EXPEDITION, 1860.

(From an old photograph in the possession of the Royal Astronomical Society.)

brought out the "synclinal" arrangement of coronal streamers;
while their comparison with photographs of the American eclipse
of July 29th, 1878, suggested to him a variation of coronal type
in correlation with the variation of spotted surface, since amply
verified.   Plates exposed by Dr. Schuster to the eclipsed sun,
May 17th, 1882, at Sohag, in Egypt, disclosed a beautiful comet
hurrying past perihelion while half enmeshed in coronal rays;
and the brilliant radiated solar halo, characteristic of spot-maxima,
was imprinted upon them, as well as in photographs taken by
Messrs. Lawrance and Woods, May 6th, 1883, on Caroline Island,
in the Southern Pacific.

During the period now under consideration, a far-reaching change has taken place in the methods and aims of astronomy. The telescope has found auxiliaries in the spectroscope and the camera, and auxiliaries of such versatile powers that their performance continually outstrips their promise. The new science

DR. SCHUSTER'S PHOTO. OF THE ECLIPSED SUN, 1882.
(By permission, from the Philosophical Transactions of the Royal Society, 1883.)

of astrophysics deals with the nature of the heavenly bodies, while the elder gravitational astronomy is concerned with their movements; but a meeting-place has been provided by spectroscopic determinations of motion in the line of sight; and signs are not wanting that celestial mechanicians will fully respond to the novel demands upon their resources.

The principle that the qualities of prismatic light emitted or

296

Spectro-
scopy.

absorbed by glowing vapours are unfailingly distinctive, was, by Kirchhoff, in 1859–60, made the basis of solar chemistry. In England the subject was energetically prosecuted by Mr. (now Sir) Norman Lockyer, who devised the "analysing spectroscope," and, on March 4th, 1866, applied it to the examination of a sun-spot. The spectroscopic method of viewing prominences in full sunshine was also arrived at by him, independently of Janssen, in October, 1868, after their light had been proved, by observations during the Indian eclipse of August 19th, 1868, to be of gaseous origin.

Photo: Elliott & Fry, Baker Street, W.
SIR NORMAN LOCKYER.

Bright lines due to hydrogen were conspicuous in it; and with them appeared a yellow ray emitted, as Lockyer and Frankland quickly perceived, by a then unknown substance to which they gave the name of "helium." Lockyer's and Respighi's examination with the "slitless spectroscope" of the corona seen, by favour of the interposing moon, at Baikul in 1871, had an experimental value; but the first definite and complete record of the nature of the coronal spectrum inscribed itself on Dr. Schuster's negatives in 1882. Their study inspired Dr. (now Sir William) Huggins with the idea of photographing the corona itself without the aid of an eclipse, by means of its strong ultra-violet emanations, and he obtained some apparently genuine pictures; but their promise has remained unfulfilled.

In conjunction with William Allen Miller (1817–70), he entered, in 1862, upon an investigation of stellar spectra; and communicated to the Royal Society, May 26th, 1864, the earliest definite particulars regarding the chemistry of stars. In the spectrum of Aldebaran, lines characteristic of hydrogen, iron, sodium, calcium, magnesium, and other substances were identified; and the composition of Betelgeux was shown to be similar, though not identical. The outburst of "T Coronæ," detected May 12th, 1866, by John Birmingham, of Tuam in Ireland, afforded the first opportunity of analysing the light of a temporary star. It was proved at Tulse Hill to be enveloped in a blaze of hydrogen and other gases. Nova Cygni, which leaped into visibility November 24th, 1876, showed itself to be similarly circumstanced; but a strange development of light at

OBSERVATORY OF SIR WILLIAM HUGGINS, K.C.B., TULSE HILL

the core of the great Andromeda nebula in August, 1885, was of a different and dubious nature.

On August 29th, 1864, Dr. Huggins made the capital discovery of gaseous nebulæ. The subject of his initial experiment was a "planetary" in Draco. He found nearly the whole of its light concentrated in a single green line, as yet unidentified with any terrestrial substance. And the case was typical. In all gaseous nebulæ (with perhaps one exception), comprising, besides planetaries, the irregular kind exemplified by the vast structure in Orion, the same ray predominates, although associated, as Dr. Huggins at once perceived, with hydrogen-emissions. He stated at the same time that the majority of undistinguished nebulæ, besides all star-clusters, give an unbroken spectrum, indicating notable progress in condensation.

The first photograph of a star-spectrum was taken by Dr. Huggins in 1863; but it was his adoption, in 1876, of the "dry-plate" method, permitting long exposures, that determined his success in this branch. On December 18th, 1879, he exhibited to the Royal Society seven very perfect "spectrograms," six of which were derived from "white stars" like Vega. And in all of these a rhythmical series of dark lines was strongly impressed, evidently representing the ultra-violet continuation of the hydrogen-spectrum, the essential character of which was thus brought to view through the analysis of rays emitted many years previously in the depths of space. The spectrum of the Orion nebula was photographed with the same apparatus March 7th, 1882. At Tulse Hill, also, the momentous step was taken in 1868 of introducing into astronomical researches the spectroscopic method of determining motion in the line of sight. Its importance can scarcely be exaggerated. It is true that stellar radial velocities, thus visually estimated, are subject to large uncertainties; from which, however, measures on photographic plates are for the most part exempt. On this principle, a couple of years later, the tremendous agitations of the solar chromosphere were studied by Lockyer, with the result of showing the prevalence there of tornadoes whirling at rates up to 120 miles a second.

Variable Stars. John Russell Hind (1823–95) was the first English discoverer of asteroids. As an observer at Mr. Bishop's establishment in the Regent's Park, he captured Iris and Flora, August 13th and October 13th, 1847, and added later six more members to the same family. On April 28th, 1848, a "new star" was detected by him in the constellation Ophiuchus. It rose in four days from the seventh to the fifth magnitude, then rapidly faded into obscurity. But his most remarkable discovery, made October 11th, 1852, was that of a small nebula in Taurus, which has since frequently disappeared and re-appeared. Confirmatory instances are not wanting. The phenomenon of variability in these objects adds vastly to the importance of their photographic portrayal, the complete success of which was assured by Dr. Common's exquisite picture of the Orion nebula, taken with his three-foot silver-on-glass reflector January 30th, 1883.

From an examination of the spectrum of Winnecke's comet in 1868, Dr. Huggins concluded its chief material to be a hydrocarbon gas; and the inference has proved true of most, if not all, comets. The two bright apparitions of May and September, 1882, blazed, however, with sodium as they closely approached

Comets and the Spectroscope.

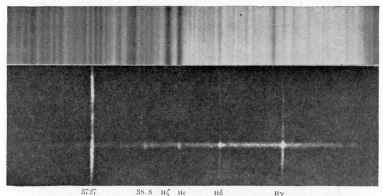

3727   38.8 Hζ Hε   Hδ   Hγ

SPECTRUM OF THE SUN AND GREAT NEBULA IN ORION.

(By permission, from Sir William and Lady Huggins' "Atlas of Stellar Spectra," 1899.)

the sun, and the latter with iron besides. Both were observed by Dr. Copeland at Dunecht. The transit of the September comet across the sun, watched by Mr. Finlay and Dr. Elkin at the Cape, was an unique event. Photographs of this fine object, taken under the supervision of Dr. (afterwards Sir David) Gill showed the unexpected advantages of common portrait-lenses for getting impressions of nebulous masses; and the multitude of stars on the plates not only suggested to Dr. Gill the plan of his photographic "Durchmusterung" (review), giving the places of 350,000 southern stars, but started a grand international star-charting enterprise.

English astronomers have led the attack upon the arduous problem of the sun's distance. The necessity for a large reduction in the accepted value of ninety-five million miles was recognised by the Royal Astronomical Society in 1864, and the transits

The Sun's Distance.

of Venus in 1874 and 1882 were anticipated as opportunities for settling the matter definitively. Expeditions, admirably organised by Sir George Airy and Mr. Stone, the late Radcliffe Observer at Oxford, were despatched, on both occasions, to

THE ORION NEBULA, PHOTOGRAPHED BY DR. COMMON, JANUARY 30TH, 1883.
(*By permission of T. A. Common, Esq.*)

various parts of the globe; yet with little effect in diminishing the uncertainty. More confidence was inspired by Dr. Gill's single-handed operations upon Mars at Ascension in 1877, giving ninety-three million miles as the value of the great unit.

Stellar Distance. The parallaxes of several stars were reliably measured by Dr. Brünnow (1821–91), astronomer royal for Ireland, and by his successor, Sir Robert Ball, between 1867 and 1881. The determinations of nine southern stars by Gill and Elkin, in 1882–3, showed the heliometer to be the instrument best adapted for this class of work. They fixed the distance of *a* Centauri—still our nearest known sidereal neighbour—at twenty-five billions of miles; showed Sirius to be about twice as remote; and the brilliant Canopus to lie altogether beyond the reach of their soundings. Dr. Gill succeeded Mr. Stone as

PHOTOGRAPH OF COMET OF SEPTEMBER, 1882, SHOWING NUMEROUS STARS.
(*By permission of Sir David Gill, K.C.B.*)

H.M. Astronomer at the Cape in 1879, Mr. Stone having occupied the post from the retirement of Sir Thomas Maclear in 1870. At Greenwich Sir George Airy was succeeded in 1881 by Mr. (afterwards Sir) W. H. M. Christie.

A profound alteration has, since 1846, affected ideas regarding the structure of the universe. Sir John Herschel's description of the Magellanic Clouds as aggregations of sidereal matter in all stages of condensation proved, as Whewell insisted in 1853, and Herbert Spencer in 1858, that star-clusters and nebulæ differ generically; and the fact was rendered patent by Huggins's application to them of the spectroscope. The distribution of nebulæ, too, in obvious correspondence with the

The Nebular Problem.

lines of the Milky Way (shown in Mr. Sidney Waters's chart of 1869), effectually reduces them from the status of independent starry realms to the less pretentious rank of members of the galactic system. This truth was enforced in many of R. H. Proctor's writings. Thus, the investigation of the nature, distance, and architecture of the Milky Way has come to be the prime object of cosmical inquirers.

T. G.
BONNEY.
Geology
and Palæ-
ontology,
1846-1895.

Using 1833, the year when the publication of Lyell's " Principles " was completed, as a new point of departure, we may trace the progress of the science down to the present day. Soon after this date a separation into subordinate branches becomes more easily recognised. The palæontologist found an ample field in studying fossils, not only as the stratigraphist had already done, for chronological purposes, but also for the significance of their zoological (or botanical) affinities and diversities. In this matter, during the earlier part of the century, Brongniart, Deshayes, and Lamarck, in France, were ahead of any English workers in their knowledge of fossil conchology, and Cuvier may justly claim to be the father of vertebrate palæontology. But soon after his death (in 1832) Richard Owen began to rise into repute as a British successor to the distinguished Frenchman, and a little later—early in the fourth decade—Edward Forbes became distinguished for work among the invertebrates, which was ended by his death, while still in his prime, in 1854.

In 1847 the Palæontographical Society was established, with the avowed intention of figuring all the British fossils. Among the contributors to the splendid volumes which are annually issued will be found most of the palæontologists who have attained eminence in Britain. It must suffice to name only a few memoirs from those members whose work is done, such as that of T. Davidson, on the Brachiopods ; J. W. Salter, on the Trilobites ; Milne Edwards, Haime, and P. M. Duncan, on the Corals ; T. Wright, on the Sea-urchins and Starfish ; Searles Wood (aided by his son), on the Crag Mollusca ; and R. Owen, on extinct Reptiles and Turtles. The work also of W. B. Carpenter, on the Foraminifers ; of his son, P. H. Carpenter, on the Crinoids ; of Hugh Falconer and T. H. Huxley, the one in certain, the other in many departments of vertebrate palæonto-

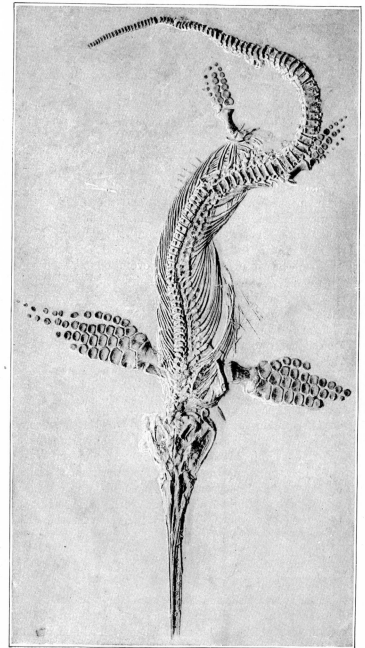

ICHTHYOSAURUS TENUIROSTRIS (CONYBEARE).

(From the Lower Lias of Street, Somerset, Natural History Museum.)

Reproduced by permission from the "Geological Magazine," Vol. VIII., 1891.

logy, and that of W. C. Williamson, in fossil botany, though published elsewhere, must not be forgotten. Many still living have followed in their steps, but an enumeration of these, in the limits to which this notice must be restricted, would be a mere catalogue of names ; a selection would be an invidious task.

Natural Selection and the Geological Record.

In 1859 Charles Darwin published his famous book " On the Origin of Species by Means of Natural Selection " (p. 434). This idea, which had occurred independently to A. R. Wallace while he was at work in the Malayan Archipelago, though mainly an induction from the study of living animals and plants, obviously depended also on the evidence of fossil forms. At first sight this seemed, on the whole, unfavourable, and the independence of species was maintained by not a few eminent palæontologists, although Darwin in his famous chapter on " the imperfection of the geological record " had indicated the need of caution in dealing with negative evidence. But evolution, as the new doctrine was called, found from the first an advocate in T. H. Huxley ; and more recent discoveries in palæontology have not only removed many difficulties, but also supplied much additional evidence, so that the old idea of separate centres of creation now finds but few supporters among philosophic naturalists.

The Glacial Theory.

One immediate result of the publication of the " Principles " was to give greater prominence to the study of physical geology, a subject hardly separable from physical geography. The older geologists had seen in mountain-peaks and valleys the records of mighty movements of the earth's crust, and W. Hopkins, of Cambridge, had attempted to explain the valleys of the Weald as a result of strains in the upheaval of the region ; but as " convulsionist " views lost ground, a more and more confident appeal was made to the forces still at work. The credit of indicating clearly that the rivers make the valleys, rather than the valleys the rivers, is due, more than to any other man, to J. B. Jukes, Director of the Geological Survey in Ireland. His views were published about the year 1862, and are now generally accepted among geologists.

But before this another great forward step was made. In many parts not only of Britain but also of Northern Europe superficial deposits of gravel, often coarse as well as fine, of sand and of clay, commonly full of stones, occur at various elevations, lying like a mantle over the ordinary Tertiary and older rocks. Some of these stones attain a large size, and isolated boulders are scattered here and there over the country. These were formerly claimed as proofs of the tumultuous action of an universal deluge, but careful study began to show the difficulties in this hypothesis, and appeal before long was made to another means of transport. About 1835 De Charpentier, a Swiss geologist, maintained that the erratics and boulder clays of his country had been deposited by glaciers at a time when they had extended far beyond their present limits in the Alps; and in 1840 Agassiz, of Neuchâtel, devoted himself to a careful study of the Alpine glaciers. He was visited, while thus occupied, by J. D. Forbes, noted for his researches into the physics of glacier ice, and by W. Buckland, with whom he afterwards

ERRATIC BLOCK AT SEAMER STATION, YORKSHIRE.

investigated the north of Britain. Here they found signs of ice action similar to those in Switzerland; the discovery, announced by Buckland, though too startling to be at once accepted, gradually obtained credit, and further examination showed that all the mountainous districts of Britain had been similarly occupied by glaciers. But as to the extent of the ice considerable difference of opinion still prevails. By one school a very large part of the English lowlands, the bed of the Irish Sea and most of Ireland as well as Northern Europe to the south of Berlin, are asserted to have been enveloped in a great ice sheet, which is even believed by some to have invaded the country from Polar regions. Another school restricts the ice within narrower limits, and attributes most of the lowland deposits, with certain shell-bearing gravels found even in the hill regions, to the action of shore-ice and floating ice while the land was submerged.

But in 1862 A. Ramsay, who had already done excellent work on the track of ice in Britain, aroused a controversy by claiming a new effect for glaciers. In a paper read to the London Geological Society he attributed the basins of the greater Alpine lakes to the erosive action of ice, and *a fortiori* the lakes of the various mountainous regions of Britain. This produced a controversy. His opponents maintained the effect of ice to be abrasive rather than erosive, and thus to be incompetent, under the most favourable circumstances, to produce more than a shallow tarn, and they attributed the larger lakes to unequal movements in the beds of valleys at a very late period in their history. The controversy is not ended, but it is perhaps not unfair to say that Ramsay's views have not found their most ardent supporters among those geologists who are most familiar with mountains and glaciers.

Slaty Cleavage.

No unimportant step was made in physical geology when the structure called slaty cleavage was understood. The phenomena were observed and correlated by Sedgwick in a masterly communication to the Geological Society in 1835. The true explanation, that this structure was a consequence of pressure, was gradually established by Sharpe and others. The

The Ocean Depths.

knowledge of the form, deposits, and fauna of the deeper parts of the ocean has been enormously augmented since the middle of the present century, especially by the voyage of the *Challenger*, which, after three or four tentative expeditions, was sent out by the Government from 1873 to 1876. The results of this extended investigation of the great ocean basin have been embodied in a long series of memoirs, the publication of which is only just completed (1896 ; p. 927).

The Antiquity of Man.

Closely connected with the last epoch in the earth's history is the question of the Antiquity of Man. Buckland so early as 1822 had described the contents of Kirkdale Cave in Yorkshire, in which bones of hyænas and other animals foreign to this country had been found, but had appealed to them in his "Reliquiæ Diluvianæ" as proofs of an universal deluge. Lyell in 1833 had examined a collection made by Dr. Schmerling from caves in the Meuse valley, where the bones of man were associated with those of extinct mammals, and had formed his own conclusions. In 1847 Boucher de Perthes had announced the discovery of flint implements of human workmanship in

gravel on the flanks of the Somme valley, but this announcement did not obtain general credence among English geologists
till about twelve years later, when it was confirmed by John
Evans, Falconer, and Prestwich. The river gravels in southern
and eastern England were then examined, as well as the caves

WILLIAM PENGELLY, F.R.S., BY A. S. COPE, A.R.A.
(*By permission of the Torquay Natural History Society.*)

in various hill districts, notably that called Kent's Hole, near
Torquay, which was systematically searched by W. Pengelly,
with the aid of the British Association. The result was to
demonstrate, by overwhelming evidence, that England, not to
mention other parts of Europe, had been occupied by men of a
very low civilisation at an age when many animals now extinct
were abundant—an age sufficiently remote to allow time enough
for the occurrence of important physical changes. These con-

clusions, like others previously arrived at by geologists, came in for much censure on the part of would-be champions of Christianity; but they have now passed into the category of questions merely scientific, and it is generally admitted that the human race must have appeared in this part of Europe immediately after, if not before, the Glacial Epoch.

Petrology. One branch of geology still remains to be noticed, that whereby the science is connected with mineralogy—namely, the department called petrology or the study of rocks, especially of those which have either solidified from a state of fusion (igneous), or subsequently undergone marked changes (metamorphic). Many of the geologists at work during the earlier years of the century had studied mineralogy, and thus were as good petrologists as was possible with the instruments at their disposal. But with the increasing interest in palæontology and stratigraphy, petrology became temporarily neglected; neither Murchison, who succeeded De la Beche at Jermyn Street in 1855, nor Ramsay seemed to apprehend that it was a subject which demanded careful study. Thus the maps of the Geological Survey often embodied very grave mistakes, and hypotheses which time has proved to be misleading were supported by its authority. Among the latter, one which proved a most serious impediment to progress was mainly due to Murchison himself. In 1858 he recognised, as the result of a personal examination, that the coarse gneissose rocks underlying the Torridon Sandstone of the North-West Highlands were more ancient than any system which had as yet been identified in Britain, but at the same time he claimed the schists and flaggy gneisses south of the area just named (including the Central Highlands) as metamorphosed Silurian rocks. These, however, were maintained by James Nicol, of Aberdeen, to be also parts of a very ancient series; but this view was scouted by Murchison and the Survey, and for nearly twenty years Nicol seemed to be the sole champion of a lost cause. Doubts then began to be raised; the district was again examined; and in 1884 the Director-General of the Survey announced that his predecessor had been wrong, and Nicol right in his main contention. The apparent sequence of the rocks and the modifications which gave a more modern aspect to the seemingly upper mass were due to a remarkable displacement and its mechanical effects. The credit of this discovery is largely due to Professor Lapworth.

Petrology once more came to the front, after H. C. Sorby, in 1856, had applied the microscope to the examination of thin sections of rocks. Though there is yet much to learn, great progress has been made towards a rational classification of the igneous rocks and a proper understanding of the processes by which the rocks called metamorphic have been produced. Since then rapid progress has been made, and important results had been obtained even prior to 1884.

The science of mineralogy—the parent, as some consider it, Mineralogy. of geology—has also made not a little progress in the epoch under consideration, but mostly in directions which cannot be easily described without the use of technical language. Here also, as might be expected, Sorby's method of investigation has proved of great value, especially in tracing the history of mineral changes; while the use of the spectroscope and other appliances of modern chemistry has led to important results, including the discovery of new but rare elements. Great progress also has been made with crystallography, not only by the employment of more perfect instruments, such as the goniometer, but also by the use of a system of crystallography, beautifully adapted for mathematical treatment, which was developed by William Hallowes Miller from the cruder methods of his predecessors. It was published about the year 1838, in a decade which, as we have seen, was remarkably characterised by important advances in science.

The year 1815 found geology in a most rudimentary condition; 1885 left it fully developed. Though as yet an illusion which has always hampered its real progress has not been wholly dispelled—viz. that it is a science in which anyone, however ignorant, may speculate, and on which he may write—there is perhaps at present a little danger from the opposite extreme. It is that of over-estimating the importance of minute details, of missing real resemblances in the study of superficial differences, of dwelling too much on questions of nomenclature and matters which pertain to literature rather than to science; and, above all, of forgetting that hypotheses conceived in the laboratory or the museum are of little value till they have been tested in the open air and compared with the evidence which Nature herself supplies.

W. G. RHODES. Physics, 1846-1885.

WHILST Joule's work (p. 258) was as yet scarcely appreciated in England, Helmholtz in 1847 published an essay, entitled " Ueber die Erhaltung der Kraft," in which, as its title indicates, the principle of conservation of energy was developed. Helmholtz was at the time a military surgeon, and knew but little of Joule's work. The essay was a very powerful one, and, taken together with Joule's experimental evidence, placed the principle on a firm basis. Although for a long time doubted, this law came to be received on the same footing as Newton's laws of motion; and some of the greatest discoveries in thermodynamics, and other branches of physical science, have been deduced from it. To reduce any result now to a contradiction of this principle is to reduce it to an absurdity. Quoting Clerk Maxwell, the principle in its most general form is that " the total energy of any body, or system of bodies, is a quantity which can neither be increased nor diminished by any mutual action of these bodies, though it may be transformed into any of the forms of which energy is susceptible."

Helmholtz, in 1871, gave up his medical work, and was appointed Professor of Physics in the University of Berlin, where he spent the remainder of his life. In his treatises on " Physiological Optics " and " Sensations of Tone," he presented to the scientific world works of rare value. No one was better fitted than he to undertake works like these, for he combined with his extensive knowledge of physics a paramount acquaintance with physiology and psychology. There is scarcely any branch of physics which does not testify to his profound thought and striking originality. Problems which had puzzled the greatest mathematicians were successfully attacked by him, and those students who were so fortunate as to be under his guidance testify by their own works to the greatness of him whose intellect they in part reflect.

Tyndall.   The man who did the most to popularise natural science in England was John Tyndall. From his earliest childhood he had been taught the art of expressing his ideas in a clear and simple manner. He left school in 1839, and joined a division

INTERIOR OF THE GEOLOGICAL MUSEUM, JERMYN STREET.

297

of the Ordnance Survey. In 1847 he accepted a teaching appointment at Queenwood College, Hampshire. Here he stayed till the following year, and applied himself chiefly to the study of chemistry, along with Dr. Frankland, one of his colleagues. In 1848, Tyndall and Frankland went together to Marburg, in Hesse-Cassel. In those days Germany was ahead of England in the teaching of science, so the two determined to add a German training to their English education. Tyndall's attention was called to the new property of magnetism, which Faraday had lately announced, and it was suggested to him by Dr. Knoblauch that the two should repeat Faraday's experiments, and inquire more closely into the true nature of diamagnetism. Professor Plücker, of Bonn, found that some crystals, made of diamagnetic substances, did not exhibit diamagnetic properties. To account for this he attributed to crystals an optical axis, which he supposed to be influenced in a peculiar manner when placed in a magnetic field.

After long and careful investigation Tyndall and Knoblauch came to the conclusion that the action of magnetism on bodies depended upon their molecular structure, or as Tyndall expressed it, upon their peculiarities of material aggregation. In 1851 Tyndall announced that the same laws govern both magnetic and diamagnetic phenomena. In 1853 he was appointed to the chair of Natural Philosophy at the Royal Institution.

The subject which owes most to Tyndall is that of radiant heat. Before he commenced his investigations but little was known about it. The quantities to be measured were so small, and existing apparatus so crude, that physicists had never attempted any accurate measurements of radiant heat. Tyndall, however, overcame the experimental difficulties, and, in 1864, published a paper " On the radiation and absorption of heat by gases and liquid matter," in which he showed that the absorption of non-luminous heat by vapours is the same as that of the liquids from which they are produced.

On January 21st, 1870, Tyndall delivered a lecture, at the Royal Institution, on " Dust and Disease," and gave the results of some investigations of his own on floating organic matter in the air. Examination of air before and after being subjected to a very high temperature showed that a large proportion of the dust it contained was organic matter, since it disappeared on being burnt. In the course of the lecture Tyndall propounded a germ theory of diseases, saying that as surely as a pig comes from a pig, or a grape from a grape, so surely does the typhoid virus, or seed, when scattered about among people, give rise to typhoid fever, scarlatina virus to scarlatina, and small-pox virus to small-pox; and that the virus was carried about by the

Photo: Bassano, Old Bond Street, W.
PROFESSOR JOHN TYNDALL.

floating organic matter in the air. Many eminent men were present at the lecture, and those of the medical profession received his views with disfavour, going so far as to ridicule the germ theory. The accuracy of that theory has since, however, been proved over and over again, and the discovery of the way in which diseases are spread has been of incalculable benefit to mankind.

It was as a popular lecturer that Tyndall excelled. The reason of his success in lecturing to the "unscientific" may be found in his aptitude for imparting his knowledge in the simplest language, and in exciting the interest of an audience by homely illustrations. He probably did more than any other man of science to raise the standard of education amongst the uneducated classes.

Faraday's "Tubes of Force." When Faraday propounded his theory of electromagnetism, in which he explained the various phenomena by means of hypothetical "tubes of force" in a hypothetical medium, his views met with distrust on all sides. His methods were not evident to the mathematical physicists, who had been accustomed to base their calculations simply on the laws of force, without concerning themselves with any medium to act as a vehicle of energy. They believed in the idea of action at a distance. Energy disappeared from one place and reappeared at another. They could form their equations without assuming the existence of any transmitting medium, and the solutions were in accord with observed phenomena. Fortunately Faraday had no such preconceived mathematical notions. He was not a mathematician, and was driven to invent a logic of his own; his tube of force took the place of the mathematicians' differential equation. These tubes of force were mathematical quantities, and his whole theory admitted of mathematical representation; but to bring his theory completely within the comprehension of the mathematical physicist needed an interpreter, who should express his ideas in their own familiar language.

Clerk Maxwell. In 1831, when Faraday was just beginning his work on electromagnetic induction, James Clerk Maxwell was born in Edinburgh. Educated at Edinburgh, and afterwards at Cambridge, Maxwell graduated in 1854, taking the position of Second Wrangler. His original investigations began whilst he was still in his teens, when he contributed papers to the Royal Society of Edinburgh on "Rolling Curves," and on "The Equilibrium of Elastic Solids." Whilst an undergraduate at Cambridge he devoted himself more to research than to working for the tripos. It was during this period that he carefully studied Faraday's original papers. His inclination was always to study mathematics as a means whereby to express his ideas on physical subjects rather than as an end in itself. His private tutor, William Hopkins, said of him: "It is not possible for that man to think incorrectly on physical subjects."

In **1855** Maxwell wrote a mathematical paper on " Lines of Force," expressing the Faraday line of force in mathematical language, and still further developing the idea. In 1856 he was appointed to the chair of Natural Philosophy at the Marischal

PROFESSOR JAMES CLERK MAXWELL.

(From the painting by Lowes Dickinson in the Hall of Trinity College, Cambridge.)

College, Aberdeen. The same year he gained the Adams Essay Prize with a thesis on " The Rings of Saturn," in which he showed that Saturn's rings could not, consistently with stability of structure, be either solid or liquid, but must be of the nature of streams of meteorites revolving round the planet. About the same time he invented the " dynamical top" to illustrate certain problems in dynamics. In 1860 he read a paper at a meeting of the British Association on " The Kinetic Theory of Gases," which supposes a gas to consist of myriads of particles jostling against each other. The theory is consistent with the experimental laws of gases, and gives an insight into their behaviour when subjected to various physical conditions. The first to treat the theory with exactitude was Clausius. He was followed by Maxwell, and by Boltzmann. The three contemporaneously rapidly developed it. Although the theory is on a firm basis it fails to account for the diversity of values of the ratio of the two specific heats in various groups of gases.

An important addition was made to our knowledge of the constitution of bodies when Andrews published his classical researches in 1869, showing the existence of a critical point in gases. He showed that at any temperature there is a pressure at which a gaseous body is in a state of transition, being neither liquid nor gas, but in an intermediate state, such that any increase of pressure will cause some liquefaction, and any diminution of pressure will be followed by a return to the gaseous state.

Much of Maxwell's time was given up to the study of composition of colours. He invented the colour-box for analysing and combining the different colours of the spectrum. Prior to this time, the three primary colours were thought to be red, blue, and yellow. With his colour-box Maxwell showed that this is not the case, but that the three primary colours are red, green, and blue. He showed also that a mixture of blue and yellow produces pink, and not green as is commonly supposed. For these researches on light the Royal Society awarded him the Rumford Medal in 1860. The same year Maxwell was appointed Professor of Physics at King's College, London. In 1866 he retired to his estate at Glenlair. In 1870 he published his "Theory of Heat," an elementary text-book without a parallel. The following year he accepted the Cavendish Professorship of Physics at Cambridge, and shortly afterwards he published his treatise on "Magnetism and Electricity," which is a mathematical treatment of Faraday's method. All electrical phenomena are explained by reference to energy stored up in the surrounding medium.

Maxwell called himself the interpreter of Faraday's views; but he was more than this; he built up a mathematical theory of magnetism and electricity which will be a lasting monument to his genius. He also propounded his electromagnetic theory of light, in which he supposes that electrical energy is propagated by vibrations of the same æther which is supposed to transmit energy in the form of light. His theory supposes, in fact, that electricity and light are simply different aspects of the same phenomenon—a vibrating æther. In recent years Hertz, a pupil of Helmholtz, has, in a series of brilliant experiments, gone far towards verifying the results of Maxwell's theory of light. Electric waves have been obtained, and have been shown to be capable of reflection and refraction in exactly the same way as waves of light.

Maxwell died in 1879, and the scientific world lost its most brilliant genius.

One of the first to appreciate Joule's researches was Professor **Lord Kelvin.** William Thomson (afterwards Sir William Thomson, and, still later, Lord Kelvin). He was educated at Glasgow and Cambridge, and was Second Wrangler in 1845. In 1846 Thomson brought out his theory of " Electric Images," and in the same year was appointed to the chair of Natural Philosophy in the University of Glasgow. Like Maxwell, his original contributions to physical science began when he was still a boy in his teens. As a theorist he has done more than anyone to develop the principle of conservation of energy. In 1849 he published a dynamical theory of heat, based upon the researches of Joule. Three years later he deduced the principle of " Dissipation of Energy," or the tendency of the available energy of a system to diminish while the total energy remains unaltered.

It is as an inventor of electrical instruments that Lord Kelvin stands pre-eminent. Many of the most delicate instruments for the measurement of electrical quantities owe their origin to his inventive genius. In 1858 he brought out his mirror galvanometer, which is capable of detecting excessively small electric currents. Among his more important inventions are a mariners' compass, protected so as to be unaffected by the presence of iron in the body of the ship; his siphon recorder, an instrument for recording telegraphic messages; the electric balance, in which the strength of an electric current is measured by balancing the force of attraction of two coils through which it flows against the weight of a given mass; the absolute electrometer, by means of which the difference of potential of two discs is found in absolute measure; the quadrant electrometer, for comparative measure of differences of potential, and other instruments, too numerous to mention.

The discoveries of Volta, Ohm, Young, Oersted, Ampère, Faraday, Joule, Helmholtz, and Maxwell opened out wide fields

LORD KELVIN, G.C.V.O., F.R.S., BY W. W. OULESS, R.A.
(By permission of the Artist and the Worshipful Company of Clothworkers.)

for scientific research, and almost all subsequent researches have been merely extensions and developments of the principles which these philosophers brought to light. Accurate measurements of the various physical qualities have been made, and refined instruments for delicate observations invented. In all branches of physical science measuring instruments have been brought to a wonderful degree of delicacy and perfection. The galvanometers now in use are a billion times as sensitive as the old detectors of Ampère and Schweigger. Tyndall found it difficult to find instruments sufficiently sensitive to measure radiant heat in large quantities. Instruments are now in use by which the heat radiating even from the moon can be detected.

There are many scientific problems still unsolved, waiting for another Faraday or Joule to come with heaven-born genius, and still further unravel Nature's mysteries. Will such problems as " What is æther, and in what way is it related to matter ? " or, " What is the true nature of gravitation ? " ever be solved ? Problems like these are now occupying the minds of our greatest men of science. They may be solved in the near future ; they may be beyond the powers of human understanding. *The Outlook.*

THE opening of the College of Chemistry in October, 1845, under A. W. Hofmann, marks in some respect an era in English chemistry, and is remarkable as an illustration of the way in which scientific researches which seem to be without any practical bearing often develop into the most important practical consequences. Since the discovery of benzene by Faraday in 1826 a number of allied substances had been discovered by various workers. Indigo, coal-tar oil, and other substances had been distilled, and under various names a substance ultimately called aniline had been obtained from them. Before coming to England Hofmann had proved the identity of these products, and other chemists had shown that aniline could be prepared from benzene. In this country Hofmann continued his researches on aniline, and discovered a number of bodies which, like it, could be considered as substitution derivatives of ammonia, and the methods he used have been of the greatest value in the development of the coal-tar industry. Among Hofmann's earliest pupils and assistants was W. H. Perkin. Under the direction of Hofmann, Perkin set to work on some bodies, anthracene and naphthalene, which have since become the starting-point for the production of very important colouring matters; but it was in attempting to carry out the artificial formation of quinine that Perkin discovered the colouring matter since so well known as mauve : this was in 1856. In 1857 it was first used commercially, and in 1862 a large **ROBER STEELE. Chemistry and its Applications, 1846-1885.**

Chemical Manufacture.

proportion of the colouring matters in use were aniline dyes. Yet in 1858 the following words could be used in an important text-book :—" The compounds of aniline are to be reckoned by hundreds, but they are not the subjects of manufacture : they are not articles of commerce; they are of no use in the arts; they are applied to no purpose in domestic economy." It would be long to trace out in detail the progress of this industry. The next important step was taken in 1868. Two German chemists in that year succeeded in producing for the first time the colouring matter alizarin (the dyeing matter of madder) from anthracene. Aware of the importance of this discovery, Perkin at once set to work, and, by the aid of his former knowledge of anthracene and its derivatives, discovered another method of producing the substance. Before the end of 1869 he had produced one ton of artificial alizarin; in 1870, 40 tons ; in 1871, 220 tons, and so on. Twenty years after the birth of the industry the annual value of the colours produced amounted to over £3,000,000 sterling (1878).

The Constitution of Chemical Compounds. Up to this point little was known of the constitution of chemical compounds. The type theory had proved of considerable assistance, but science was as far as ever from understanding what part organic radicals took. The next advance in theory was due to Frankland (1825–1899), afterwards Sir Edward Frankland, and Kolbe (1818–84). Bunsen had discovered a remarkable compound in which arsenic entered into the composition of an organic body. Extending these researches, Frankland described a series of compounds in which tin took part in the formation of an organic body, and was led to deduce the doctrine of valency—*i.e.* that the combining powers of any element were fixed or satisfied always by the same number of atoms. Kolbe's work after this principally lay in the discovery of the constitution of organic compounds. In 1858 Cannizzaro, an Italian chemist, published a paper which finally formulated the opinions of chemists on the methods employed for obtaining the atomic weights of the elements. The greatest achievement of the doctrine of valency was the explanation of the structure of benzene and the so-called aromatic compounds by Kekulé (b. 1829) in 1865. From his formula Kekulé was able to predict the number of isomeric compounds that could be produced from benzene and its derivatives, and threw great light not only on these derivatives, but on substances like naphthalene and anthracene, which were now beginning to be important commercially.

Soon after the benefits derived from the classification of organic compounds were observed, numerous chemists set about the task of finding some principle of classification of inorganic substances. It was readily seen that many of these substances fell into groups the members of which greatly resembled one another, while the differences between their atomic weights approached multiples of some constant. Schemes for the classification of the elements began to appear. In 1864 Newlands in England and Lothar Meyer in Germany independently arranged a number of the elements according to their atomic weights, and observed a certain periodicity in the behaviour of the elements. In 1869 Mendelejeff made an attempt to classify all the elements according to their atomic weight and bring them together into a natural system. The periodic law thus formulated has received many confirmations. Gaps in the system have been filled up by the discovery of elements whose atomic weights and physical properties were accurately predicted, and of those elements which did not fit into the system the atomic weights have been re-examined and found inaccurate. The law that lies underneath this dependence of chemical bodies on their atomic weights has yet to be discovered, but it is not to be wondered at that many chemists have turned to the ancient theory of one primary matter as an explanation.

Classification of the Elements.

Of late years the development of chemistry has been so rapid that even a mere catalogue of its branches would occupy much of our space, but one of these developments, resulting as it has in photography, is of general interest. Boyle had noticed the blackening of silver chloride when exposed to light, though he attributed it to the air, and Scheele (1742–86) studied the action of the spectrum on paper soaked in chloride of soda. The discoveries of Daguerre and Talbot about 1838 led to the foundation of photography: Daguerre, in his process, received the image produced by the lens on a silver plate, and made it visible by means of mercury; Talbot replaced the silver plate by paper. In 1847 glass negatives coated with albumen were introduced. In 1851 collodion was introduced, and in

Photography.

1871 bromo-gelatine plates were introduced and practically revolutionised photography. From that time to the end of our period the improvements were mainly optical and mechanical. Another important use of light in chemistry has been the development of the process of spectrum analysis, which, in the

A VERY EARLY PHOTOGRAPH.
(*Fox Talbot:* "*Pencil of Nature,*" 1844; *Plate XIV.*)

hands of Bunsen, Roscoe, and Crookes, has led to the discovery of new elements and has rendered important service to astronomy.

Chemical Industry. The growth of chemical industry during the century has kept pace with chemical theory. Metallurgy was the first to benefit; the analysis of furnace gases by Bunsen and Playfair, and the determination of the composition of pig-iron, explained the theory of the blast furnace, and made possible such improvements in the manufacture of steel as the Bessemer process (1856 ; p. 745), and towards the close of our period, the Thomas-Gilchrist process, by which large amounts of practically useless ore have been rendered available, and its very impurities made into a substance of the highest value (p. 747).

The manufactures of sulphuric acid and soda may be looked upon as the basis of all others from their extensive use and the

MODEL OF SULPHURIC ACID PLANT.
(*Victoria and Albert Museum.*)

bye-products formed in the course of their production. The manufacture of sulphuric acid in this country dates from 1746, when the first lead chamber was erected at Prestonpans ; the manufacture of soda from common salt dates from 1823, and that of bleaching-powder from 1779. The improvements of this century are principally in the direction of more economical and scientific working of the processes ; the only other has been that of the introduction of iron pyrites as a source of the sulphur required instead of using native sulphur ; an improvement forced upon British manufacturers in 1838 by the King of Naples, who had granted a monopoly in sulphur. The manufacture of soda from common salt was first discovered by Leblanc at the close of the eighteenth century, but it was not until the salt duty (£30 per ton) was repealed in 1823 that alkali works were set up in Liverpool by Muspratt. The chief important improvement in this process is due to Hargreaves (1877); by it sulphate of soda is prepared directly without the use of sulphuric acid. The chief drawback of the Leblanc process is the loss of sulphur in the unpleasant alkali waste, and of late years an entirely different method of manufacture has been adopted, by which ammonia obtained from gas liquor is injected into the brine solution. Carbonate of soda is at once formed, and from the bye-product ammonia can be recovered and again used. The principal drawback to this process is that the chlorine of the common salt is set free in a form in which it cannot be used for the manufacture of bleaching powder, and thus the Leblanc process continues to be worked.

D'ARCY POWER. Medicine and Public Health. CONTEMPORARY writers too often consider that the advances made in their own day are of superlative importance. The contemporaries of Phidias at Athens, of Lorenzo the Magnificent in Florence, and of Shakespeare in London, might justly boast that their ages were exceptional in the history of the world; but we cannot yet say whether, in spite of steam and electricity, our own times will prove to be equally important in the eyes of our successors. In medicine, as in science generally, this is an age of detail and of criticism. Countless facts are being daily observed and carefully recorded by numerous observers in every branch of medicine. Experiment, too, has afforded results of the greatest value, for it has enabled our science to be built upon the surest foundations; but a master mind is still needed to correlate our facts and to deduce from them hypotheses as far-reaching and as fruitful as those which Darwin gave to biology.

Medical Education. Many great advances were made by the medical profession during the twenty years under review, but the education of its students remained almost as chaotic as in 1858, when the first Medical Bill became law. Apprenticeship and practical teaching were then replaced by an elaborate series of lectures. Medicine, surgery, and midwifery were taught piecemeal, and it was possible for a student to become legally qualified to practise his profession after he had been found proficient in only one of these subjects. Such an abuse was of long standing, for as early as 1588 John Read, a liberal-minded surgeon, had complained that

" Chirurgery is maymed and vtterlie unperfect without those other partes which consisteth in prescribing of inward medicines and conuenient diet, and is so neare linked with these in alyance that no man deserueth to be called a chirurgion that is ignorant in phisicke . . so . . . . that . . I doe withall affirme that all chirurgians ought to bee seene in physicke; and that the barbor's crafte ought to be a distinct mistery from chirurgery."

The latter suggestion was adopted in England as early as 1745, but it was not till 1886 that it became compulsory for everyone to be examined in each of the main branches of his profession before he was permitted to practise upon the public. This wholesome regulation had been foreshadowed in the Medical Act of 1858, which permitted corporate bodies possessed of the power of licensing in a single subject to combine with other bodies to give a complete licence after a joint examination, but it did not become an accomplished fact for many years afterwards. Such an amalgamation, however, had been adopted temporarily by the physicians and surgeons of London in 1421.

The fundamental defect still (1904) exists that no uniform standard of education is required of a medical student. High degrees conferring social distinction may be obtained after a fair examination of no great severity, whilst a much more searching test may be applied to candidates for a mere licence. The medical student, too, is harassed by constant changes in his curriculum, and so much detail is now required of him that he is more inclined to accept the *ipse dixit* of his teacher than to think for himself. Dogmatic teaching is, therefore, in high favour even with the best students, and there is some danger of authority again assuming a position in medicine, though it is hardly conceivable that it will ever exercise its former benumbing influence. It seems probable that we are passing through that phase in medicine which has already been traversed successfully by botanists, zoologists, and anatomists, to whom classification, form, and the relation of parts once appeared to be the sole outcome of a vast amount of labour. Classification, indeed, still forms the basis of all these sciences, but a superstructure has been grafted upon it which enables students to be taught with a minimum of detail. The teaching of the sciences ancillary to medicine will in all probability follow the same lines, as they will be taught by types, but the healing art must always be taught from individual cases, for each body is peculiar to itself.

Medical education has shown a constant tendency to become more thorough and more complete, whilst the duration of its curriculum has been gradually lengthened from three to five years. The advance of education amongst women has led a certain number to enrol themselves in the medical profession. The movement was at first bitterly opposed, and a severe battle had to be fought by the female medical students before they could obtain a licence to practise. They overcame successfully the various obstacles thrown in their way, and in 1874 the London School of Medicine for Women was opened, whilst two years later a short Act of Parliament was passed enabling the names of properly qualified women to be placed upon the register.

The Royal Colleges of Physicians and of Surgeons have moved steadily with the times, though their progress has not been so rapid as some of their more democratic supporters would desire, for the corporate bodies of England are, and always have been, oligarchies.

Medicine and the Applied Sciences. Medicine has become more prophylactic. Improved knowledge of personal and general hygiene has led to a marked increase in the average longevity, as well as in the number of people who survive the diseases and accidents of childhood. The growth of physiology into an experimental science has greatly aided the advance of medicine from its former empirical position, whilst the more careful study of morbid anatomy with improved methods of physical examination have led to the greatest accuracy in diagnosis.

Therapeutics have hardly advanced in the same proportion, though pharmacology is now a branch of experimental physiology. The improvement in chemical processes has enabled the physician to lay aside the old and cumbersome method of administering drugs by infusions, decoctions, and powders, for the crude drug is now replaced by its active principle. The first result of this improvement has been to diminish the doses of medicines and to allow them to be administered in more agreeable forms, whilst it has been found possible to inject many drugs beneath the skin, thereby avoiding the evil effects produced when they are taken by the mouth.

Pathology, too, has become a branch of experimental physiology, and of late years has been advanced in a very remarkable manner by the highly-suggestive work of Lister, of Pasteur, and of Koch. The labours of these three great investigators have shown that an intimate knowledge of pathology is as important and useful to the physician and to the surgeon as a thorough acquaintance with morbid anatomy.

Antiseptic surgery owes its origin to Sir Joseph (afterwards Lord) Lister, who showed that decomposition did not take place in wounds kept absolutely clean, if the air coming to them was filtered from all living germs. As soon as he had converted

Photo: Elliott & Fry, Baker Street, W.

THE RIGHT HON. LORD LISTER, O.M.

this theory into an established fact, it spread rapidly from the pathological laboratory to the operating theatre, where it enabled the surgeon to revolutionise his practice and to extend his domain. It revolutionised his practice by reducing the gravity of all surgical procedures, thereby allowing him to operate at a much earlier period than was thought formerly to be advisable. It extended his domain by enabling him to operate upon those parts of the body which had hitherto remained untouched on account of the violent and fatal inflammation which had usually followed upon any surgical procedure by the older methods. While Lister's work benefits the individual, the labours of Pasteur have proved serviceable to the community, for they have yielded results of great prophylactic value, and have afforded a clue to the prevention of some of those diseases which spread in epidemic form. One—amongst many—of Koch's results has yielded a rational knowledge of tuberculosis, and has shown that consumption in all its protean forms is constantly associated with the presence of a single variety of micro-organism. This discovery proved to be of the utmost importance, for it was the foundation of the science of Bacteriology.

State Medicine.

Hygiene has progressed steadily, for the State has shown an increasing tendency to concern itself with the public health. The Royal Sanitary Commission of 1869–71 established the principle that members of the medical profession should be made serviceable in administering the health laws. The Local Government Board, with Mr. Stansfeld as its President, was established in 1872 as a direct outcome of this Commission. Medical officers of health were then appointed throughout the country. They are empowered to deal with all matters likely to affect the health of the community, and they are paid partly by a rate, partly by grants from the Exchequer. The ignorance and apathy of the local authorities at first went far to neutralise the benefit of the skilled assistance thus rendered available, but better counsels have since prevailed, and the law is now in fair working order. Many members of the medical profession have taken advantage of the new opening thus provided for them, and have accepted the somewhat onerous duties of health officers, for the faithful discharge of which they have endeavoured to fit themselves by a special course of instruction.

Public Health.

The steady decline of typhus even to a vanishing point is one of the most satisfactory results which has to be recorded in connection with the public health of the last twenty years. The diminution of this disease appears to be the direct outcome of the improved sanitary conditions under which the poorer classes are living, and to the higher standard of comfort which they now demand. Smallpox, like typhus, also appears to be a waning disease. It is, indeed, still endemic, and from time to time it becomes epidemic, but the number of deaths is no longer a striking feature in the returns of the Registrar-General. The practice of vaccination was rendered compulsory in 1853, and it became uniform after 1865, when an organised inspection was established throughout the country, and was conducted by officers placed first under the control of the Privy Council and afterwards of the Local Government Board. The operation was further controlled, and was rendered more complete, in 1868, when the public vaccinators began to be paid by results.[1] Typhus fever, typhoid, and smallpox have diminished, but other diseases have increased, and foremost amongst these are diphtheria and cancer. Pathology has recently found a means of minimising the fatal effects of diphtheria, but we are, as yet, wholly ignorant of the true nature and the best treatment for cancer.

Lunatics have shared in the more moderate and rational Lunacy. treatment which has marked the professional work of the present century. The scourgings and chains which from time immemorial had fallen to the lot of these unfortunate individuals in Western Europe began to attract the attention of the Quakers at York at the end of the last century, a few years before Pinel had begun his reforms in Paris. Little, however, could be done even by such men as the Tukes, for the force of public opinion was still in favour of harsh treatment. Mechanical restraint continued, and it was not until Dr. Conolly was appointed resident physician to the Middlesex County Asylum at Hanwell, in 1839, that a public asylum existed without any form of mechanical restraint for its patients. The Hanwell Asylum, justly considered one of the best-managed in the kingdom, contained about 800 patients, for whose use, as Dr. Conolly found on his appointment, no less than 600 instruments of discipline had been provided, about one-half being handcuffs and leg-locks. These, with the strait-waistcoats and coercion-chairs, he abolished in favour of kind treatment upon the part of the physicians and attendants, coupled with a sufficient staff properly trained to carry out their duties in a humane manner. His system soon became world-wide, and its beneficial results are everywhere to be seen in the quiet and routine which pervade the wards of all our asylums, in strange contrast with the accounts of Bedlam and St. Luke's which have been

[1 The exemption of "conscientious objectors" or their families was, however, legalised in 1898 (61 and 62 Vict., c. 49), after a long period of that "passive resistance" which was called out more conspicuously by the Education Act of 1902. At the same time provision was made for vaccination by calf-lymph in all cases, and one of the gravest objections to the operation—the danger of the transmission of disease from patient to patient by its means—was thereby removed.]

transmitted to us from the middle of last century. Medical men are now specially trained in the subject of mental diseases, with the result that a much better system of classification is in use, and that asylums have been founded for the reception of idiots of the middle-class, whilst quite recently a colony of epileptics has been established to enable these unhappy people to work under the most advantageous conditions. Increased knowledge of mental disease has led to the necessity for increased protection both upon the part of the patient and of the practitioner who certifies to his insanity. The law in connection with lunacy has long been in a most unsatisfactory condition, for it was full of contrary precedents, and it appeared to press with undue harshness upon the medical man who certified to a patient's insanity. A new Act, however, was passed in 1890, which enabled him to sign certificates in such cases with less danger of being afterwards cast in damages.

A LUNATIC EARLY IN THE NINETEENTH
CENTURY.

(From a sketch by G. Arnold A.R.A.)

The practice of dentistry in 1841 was in much the

Dentistry. same condition as that of surgery in 1565, when John Halle confesses that—

"Where as there is one chirurgien that was apprentise to his arte, or one physicien that hath travayled in the true studie and exercise of phisique, there are tenne that are presumptious swearers, smatterers, or abusers of the same: yea, smythes, cutlers, carters, coblars, copars, coriars of leather, carpenters, and a great rable of women."

An attempt was made in 1841 to obtain public recognition for dentistry as a branch of surgery, and negotiations were opened with the Royal College of Surgeons to obtain an enactment that no one should practise as a dentist until he had been duly examined by one or more members of that body. The negotiations failed, although the support of the Government had been obtained in the person of the Home Secretary, Sir James Graham. A second and more successful attempt was made in 1855, and in the following year the College was

EARLSWOOD ASYLUM, REIGATE—COBBLING.

memorialised upon the subject, the Odontological Society was founded, and the *British Journal of Dental Science* was published. The College of Dentists of England was established about the same time. It was an independent organisation, whose promoters desired that dentistry should be free from any association with the Royal College of Surgeons, and it proceeded to examine candidates and grant licences in dentistry. It existed for seven years, and amalgamated in 1863 with the Odontological Society. As an institution it is now defunct, and the Royal College of Surgeons of England fills its place. The Odontological Society is a society of qualified dentists established for purely scientific purposes. The dentists gradually obtained a course of sound technical instruction verified by examination, for in 1858 the Dental Hospital of London was founded, and in 1860 the Royal College of Surgeons began to examine candidates for a licence in dental surgery. This course of instruction was purely voluntary at first, nor was it rendered compulsory until 1878, when a special Act of Parliament placed dentists upon the same footing as other members of the medical profession. It established a register of those qualified to practise their art, and it prohibited unlicensed persons from assuming any title implying that they were qualified to practise dentistry. In 1880 the British Dental Association was incorporated. The Association consists of the qualified dentists of the United Kingdom, and the objects for which it is established are the promotion of dental and the allied sciences and the maintenance of the honour and interests of the dental profession.

Nursing.   The great improvement in nursing is, perhaps, one of the most remarkable developments in connection with the history of medicine in our own times. Taking its rise in the Crimean War, with the laudable object of mitigating the horrors of a campaign, nursing rapidly became a profession. Confined for a time to the military hospitals, it spread to the civil institutions of the country, which then became the training schools from which private individuals and the poor in their own homes might obtain the services of highly-qualified and often of socially-gifted women to perform the various duties of the sick-room.

The decay of hatred is as marked in the medical profession as it is in the political world. Medical men used to entertain the most violent animosity, not only for each other, but even for those who endeavoured to make their views known to the rest of the profession. Teaching was almost entirely oral at the beginning of this century, and medical journalism was then **Medical** at a very low ebb. The College of Physicians, the Provincial **Journal-** Medical Association, and a few societies, tried to diffuse know-**ism.** ledge by the publication of " Transactions," and as early as 1781 a Society of Physicians who met together occasionally to converse on medical subjects agreed to set on foot a monthly publication, which should contain an account of new medical books and useful discourses in physic, whilst it was at the

A WARD IN GUY'S HOSPITAL.

same time a repository for original essays. This venture was continued quarterly until 1790, and it was known as the *London Medical Journal.* The new era of medical journalism began on Sunday, 5th October, 1823, when Thomas Wakley published the first number of the *Lancet.* Its beginnings were by no means creditable. There were doubtless plenty of abuses to combat, for the large hospitals were practically close boroughs as regards the staff appointments. The medical officers in each were recruited from apprentices who had paid fees of £500 to £1,000 to the physicians and surgeons on the tacit understanding that they should have the reversion of their places; but the means adopted by the *Lancet* to correct abuses were most unjustifiable. Personal attacks, nicknames, and gross abuse were so often employed that the journal was tabooed for a time even by those members of the profession who were sufficiently enlightened to understand the true value of this new means of diffusing knowledge. Quarterly journals then appeared, but, with a few useful exceptions, all the quarterlies are now extinct. The weekly journals have continued, and, by a slow process of evolution, have become transformed into their present highly respectable shape. Monthly journals, too, have arisen in great numbers, for their growth has been stimulated by the increasing tendency towards specialisation which has marked the progress of medicine.

We thus bring to the year 1885 the history of medicine in this country. The ranks of the medical profession contain, as they always have done, men of the very highest scientific attainments, who devote their lives to the assistance of their fellows irrespective of creed or of nationality; empirics, or men who neglect and disclaim science; tradesmen, for whom the profession is a more or less lucrative business; and quacks, who dishonestly make physic a means of preying upon the credulity and fears of their fellow-men. Quacks, indeed, become fewer as time progresses and knowledge increases, but with keener competition the number of the tradesmen is augmented. Education has a constant tendency to exterminate, or rather to hinder the development of, the empiric or mere pretender to physic; but the scientific physicians daily increase in number, though the best minds in the profession are too often seduced to the study of pure science.

THEORY and practice in real life actually work in parallel courses, the one rarely far in advance of the other, each unable to expand its limits without encroaching on those of its neighbour. Their correlation is well marked in the history of engineering. Electrical engineering is dealt with elsewhere (p. 783 *seq.*), but the causes and general direction of the advance in mechanical and civil engineering may be suitably discussed here.

O. G. JONES. Engineering, 1815-1885.

Mechanical engineering is more than a branch of the subject. It is essentially the application of mechanical principles to the construction of engines for the transmutation of energy, or of machines for its transmission. We may apply electricity, heat, water-power, or any other source of energy, and find ourselves continually requiring the training of the mechanician before we can realise our aims.

The great advances in constructional processes in this country may well be studied with the development in our knowledge of the physical sciences. We may illustrate this first in the case of the principle of the conservation of energy (pp. 258, 704). Its recognition has been but gradual. At the beginning of the century some few leading physicists had begun to realise that a disappearance of energy in one form was simultaneous with its appearance in another. Rumford formulated the doctrine with reference to heat as a form of energy. Davy upheld it, and successfully combated the caloric theory then generally accepted. Joule, Helmholtz, and Lord Kelvin have since completed the work (p. 711), and placed the dynamical theory of heat so that succeeding experiments never fail to strengthen its position. The energy stored up in coal is converted to heat energy in the process of combustion, and transferred, with various losses, to steam. This is made by suitable engines to yield up some proportion of its heat energy for conversion into mechanical motion. More energy than the coal supplies it is impossible by any device to obtain as energy of motion, and engineers, with a clear realisation of this principle, have abandoned all schemes for the solution of the perpetual motion problem. A physicist, therefore, criticises all steam-engines or other sources of power in the light of their physical efficiency. So much energy is supplied to them in one form; what percentage is given out in another desired

The Conservation of Energy.

form, and how may improvement be effected? In different classes of motors the designer has to consider mechanical efficiency. He aims at the elimination of friction in the working parts; he employs methods of construction that will give great power for a small total weight, and equal but not unnecessary strength in each portion of the structure, great durability in those parts that cannot easily be renewed, and facility of access for those that need frequent examination or renewal. In special cases one or the other of these considerations becomes of paramount importance; the rest are often negligible.

The Compound Engine. It was pointed out by Sadi Carnot in 1824 that the efficiency of any heat-engine has its maximum limit fixed by the range of temperatures employed with the working substance. Thus of two otherwise similar engines, working with the same temperature of full-pressure steam, that is the more efficient which can run to a lower exhaust temperature; it utilises a greater percentage of the heat supplied. Likewise a raising of the temperature of full-pressure steam is accompanied by an increased efficiency.

Here, then, we have the ultimate reason for the movement among steam engineers in favour of steam at very high temperatures, with prolonged expansion in low-pressure cylinders till considerations of space economy forbid further abstraction of the energy yet remaining in the steam. Double-expansion was first introduced in stationary engines; triple and quadruple expansions are now exceedingly general, and are applied with great success in marine engineering (pp. 460, 464).

Boilers. There thus enters another question of grave importance, that of the strength of boiler, cylinders,[1] and accessory connections capable of withstanding the enormous internal pressure of the steam at so high a temperature. Were it not for the improvement in quality and adaptability of steel and iron, engines working with steam at 180° Centigrade could not be built of sufficient strength and durability. Until quite recently the strength problem has been attacked directly. Steam boilers have been developed step by step to their present form; methods of strengthening and of accelerating the generation of

[1 The application of the turbine to marine engineering belongs to the beginning of the twentieth century.]

steam have made parallel advances, and no links are missing in the connection between the old waggon boiler for stationary engines and that of a modern locomotive.

Until 1885 steam boilers were built almost exclusively of wrought-iron plates, riveted by hand. With the introduction

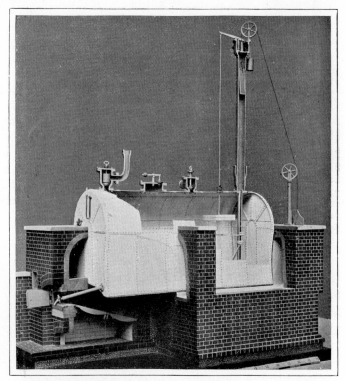

MODEL OF A WAGGON BOILER.
(Victoria and Albert Museum.)

of steel came the employment of mild steel boiler-plates, fairly reliable when the plates are not too large. Nevertheless, to this day it is impossible to ensure perfect homogeneity throughout the plate, and in all important work there are Board of Trade regulations for the testing of samples from each plate supplied. The old hand-riveting was better than any kind of modern machine-work, but very much slower. It is resorted to nowadays in large works only when the rivet is inaccessible to

MODEL OF RICHARDSON'S
VERTICAL BOILER.
(Victoria and Albert Museum.)
*By permission of Messrs.
Robey & Co.*

the machine, or when particular care is needed. Also the old-fashioned method of drilling the rivet-holes was much less injurious to the boiler-plate than is the hydraulic punch now used. An extensive modern practice consists in punching a hole through the plate, and then rymering it out to a slightly larger diameter; this, for the most part, obviates injury to the plate.

Without strengthening stays of any kind a cylindrical boiler is weakest at its flat ends. Its curved surface needs no staying, for the boiler plates are made of sufficient thickness to withstand the internal pressure, which, moreover, has no tendency to distort the plates. The principle of strengthening the ends, while at the same time rendering the boiler more effective by the use of a number of small flue-tubes, is due to M. Seguin in France, and to Booth in England (1829). George Stephenson appropriated the idea and adapted it to his "Rocket," the success of which in the Rainhill competition (p. 276) was partially the cause of the association of multitubular boilers with his name. He should only get credit for his rapid perception of their efficacy. Such a boiler, with perhaps two hundred copper tubes running from end to end, is enormously strength-

MODEL OF COCHRAN'S BOILER.
(Victoria and Albert Museum.)
By permission of Messrs. Cochran & Co.

ened by them and rendered far more efficient thermally by reason of the increased heating surface and diminished thickness of the metal used. It was no new idea to have the flue passing through the boiler, but it marked an acute realisation of principle to have many small flues instead. With the same resistance to collapse, they can be made of much thinner material than the single flue; they are readily cleaned and easily renewed when worn out.

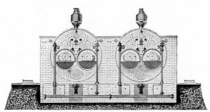

LANCASHIRE BOILER: FRONT VIEW.

Consider for a short space the so-called Cornish and Lancashire boilers. They have one or two large flues leading through from end to end, the furnace being practically an enlargement of one end of a flue. Such large flues subjected to great external pressure from the contents of the boiler are liable to sudden collapse when any portion is thinned down by gradual burning. It is undesirable to have them of thick metal, inasmuch as the burning is more vigorous and the conductivity less. The introduction of Galloway tubes in 1867, which stretch across the flues, and through which the boiler-water can circulate, admirably illustrates the double object of strengthening against collapse and of increasing the heating efficiency.

During the last few years[1] another plan of steam-generation at high

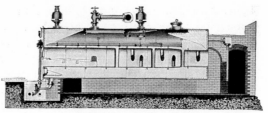

LANCASHIRE BOILER: SECTION.
(Victoria and Albert Museum.)
By permission of Messrs. D. Adamson & Co.

pressure has been introduced, the theoretical consideration of which may be approached with advantage, though it is out of place here to discuss the subject at any great length. Given two copper tubes of the same thickness of material, the diameter of one being half that of the other, then the one can

[1 Written in 1896.]

sustain an internal fluid pressure twice as great as the other. The generalisation is correct that further diminution in the internal diameter will be associated with a corresponding increase in the strength. So for the smaller pipe to possess the same strength in resisting an internal fluid pressure it needs but a proportionately diminished thickness. If the two tubes of different diameters be surrounded by furnace-gases, and be of equal strength, the contents of the smaller tube will be heated more rapidly because of its relatively slight thickness. Or, looking at the fact from a different point of view, if they be made of the same thickness of copper, the smaller can safely contain steam at a greater pressure. It is true that the smaller pipe has a smaller capacity, but this is remedied without loss of the previous advantages by using a greater length of tube.

Considered alike from the strength or heat-efficiency point of view, a steam-generator constructed on a tubulous principle, with no large internal space, has obvious advantages. Such a tubulous boiler with heat supplied to it at a steady rate, can be used for high steam temperatures, so offering a means of approaching the theoretical ideal of a heat-engine (p. 730). It is likely enough that the problem of flying will soon be solved by its aid.[1] In locomotive engineering it has been necessary to consider economy of power in relation to weight of the engine. An old Watts stationary engine with a bricked-up Cornish or Lancashire boiler was more efficient in poundage of fuel per horse-power per hour than a modern locomotive, but offered the locomotive engineer little help in his designing. He has been tied down to conditions of extremely rapid generation of steam by forced draught, to a uniform gauge of rails throughout the country, and a limiting weight of engine per foot length. It may here be remarked that the boilers of torpedo-boats are built on the locomotive pattern. In the earlier history of railways in the country, the " Battle of the Gauges " (p. 280) demonstrated the testing of theory by experiment on a gigantic scale. The questions of initial outlay in permanent way, stability of oscillations of the engine, effect of wind-pressure on an enlarged engine-front, balancing of stresses in the framework, together with the greater comfort of passengers with wider railway carriages—all these were subjected to examination, with the

[1 Petrol and electric motors have been developed since this was written.]

MODEL OF A GALLOWAY BOILER (IN SECTION).

MODEL OF A TUBULOUS BOILER.

(*Victoria and Albert Museum.*)

ultimate result that the ordinary gauge of 4 feet $8\frac{1}{2}$ inches was adopted. The last of the Great Western Railway broad-gauge system was seen in 1895, and, except for lines with excessive gradients and sharp curves, there is now complete uniformity of gauge throughout the country.

Compound Locomotives. The most daring advance in locomotive practice is due to Webb, who in 1881 applied double-expansion to London and North-Western railway locomotives (p. 289). The exhaust steam from the high-pressure cylinders passes into a larger low-pressure cylinder symmetrically placed between them, and there undergoes further expansion in actuating the piston. The engine is somewhat heavier; its centre of gravity is raised; but the difficulties of arranging the mechanism in the smaller available space below the boiler without impairing the stability of the structure have been overcome satisfactorily, and there is a saving of 15 to 20 per cent. in fuel.

Gas and Oil Engines. In internal combustion engines the working substance is heated by its own combustion in the motor cylinder. No furnace is therefore required. The efficiency of the engine itself is much higher than that of the steam-engine, mainly on account of the greater range of temperature employed. The best known types are the gas- and petroleum-engines. The first practical engine of this kind was invented by Street in 1794. It was worked by the combustion of vaporised petroleum oil and turpentine. In 1823 Brown introduced the water-jacket to keep the cylinder cool and prevent its rapid degradation due to heat. The Lenoir engine of 1860 showed a marked advance. Otto introduced in 1863 a very efficient, but noisy and mechanically defective gas-engine, which he superseded in 1876 by his famous "Otto Silent" engine, since that date a powerful rival to small steam-engines. It uses ordinary gas mixed with sufficient air for complete combustion. When working at full power the mixture is exploded every two revolutions of the fly-wheel. The gas reaches a temperature of about 1,600° Centigrade, and a pressure of over 100 lb. per square inch. It uses only 24 cubic feet of ordinary gas per horse-power per hour. If a specially prepared cheap gas be used—the Dawson gas—the consumption works out at 1·3 lb. of coal per horse-power per hour. In large marine engines for ocean-going vessels, where economy of fuel is specially considered, a result of $1\frac{1}{2}$ lb. of coal per horse-power per hour is regarded as satisfactory. Small steam-engines are never so economical.

Reviewing the advances made in civil engineering, we see how much has been due to improvement in materials of construction, facility of transport and manipulation of heavy masses, the adoption of special tools and labour-saving machines for abrogating manual labour. Every piece of work becomes a

Civil Engineering.

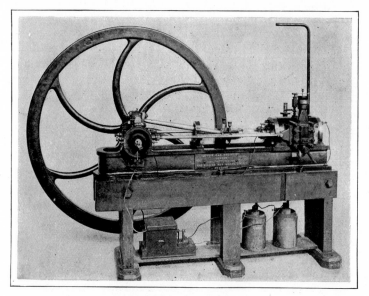

LENOIR'S GAS ENGINE.
(*Victoria and Albert Museum.*)

reference for subsequent engineers engaged on similar operations, who often reduce their average design to a close copy of an earlier one that has survived the test of time and usage. Epoch-making constructions are those that initiate on a large scale the application of special engineering principles. There was no previous history to assist the engineers of the Kilsby tunnel on the North-Western railway, in 1833; no suspension bridge to act as a model for Telford in his design for spanning the Menai Straits; no box-girder like the Britannia tubular bridge (1850) for Robert Stephenson, excepting, indeed, his own smaller structure over the Conway river. Masonry dams were practically new to England when the Vyrnwy reservoir was

299

constructed for the Liverpool water-supply. The Forth Bridge was the sole representative of the cantilever system, when finished in 1890 by Messrs. Fowler and Baker; and the Tower Bridge over the River Thames yet remains the largest bascule (or drawbridge) in the world.

Tunnelling.   Tunnelling and excavation are not so extensively employed in this country as abroad, for the obvious reason that its surface offers fewer inequalities that cannot be surmounted. But vested interests have often compelled direct routes for railways or for roads, when slight *détours* would have vastly diminished the duration and expense of the undertaking. The graver difficulties are due to the obstruction of hard rock, or of subterranean springs and quicksands. The former have been for generations attacked with gunpowder. The most usual explosives employed are gunpowder, nitro-glycerine, and gun-cotton. Nitro-glycerine in the form of dynamite is now effective and safe. The blast-holes in the rock are made by rock-boring machines, of which the prototype was introduced by Sommeiller in the Mont Cenis tunnel. The earliest form of diamond-drill, in which the crown of the borer is edged with a series of black diamonds, was described at the British Association Meeting of 1846.

Great risk is incurred when water floods the work. The Kilsby tunnel was cut through a sandbed, from which it was necessary to pump continually some 2,000 gallons of water per minute to prevent flooding of the tunnel.— The Stephensons had charge of the works, and all their ingenuity and enterprise were called into action to construct the tunnel walls water-tight. In the construction of the Severn Tunnel (1873–85), which passes under the river near Chepstow, and which has a length of $4\frac{1}{3}$ miles, a large spring was tapped that necessitated the erection of permanent pumping engines to keep the tunnel clear. The diving operations during the undertaking were by far the most venturesome and extensive of their kind.

Bridges.   The modern engineer has found it necessary to cultivate an eye for beauty. Even a high-speed vertical engine is open to derision if it takes on the semblance of a coffee-pot, and in the important matter of bridge-design the public taste should be considered seriously. Robert Stephenson's realisation of the strength of the box-girder should not have prompted him to

The Tower Bridge

Telford's Bridge across the Menai Straits.

Robert Stephenson's Tubular Bridge across the Menai Straits.

FAMOUS BRIDGES OF THE NINETEENTH CENTURY.

design the Britannia tubular bridge over the Menai Straits upon that ugly though sound principle, though in justice it must be admitted that his original suggestion for a cantilever bridge was not accepted.

The tubular bridge was the first attempt to use wrought-iron exclusively for long spans. Stephenson and Harrison had finished in 1849 the high-level bridge at Newcastle-upon-Tyne, with its masonry piers, cast-iron arched ribs, and wrought-iron ties—a bridge that remains as the link between the old cast-iron and the modern wrought-iron types. The smaller wrought-iron tubular bridge over the Conway river, of 400 feet span, was successfully opened for traffic in 1848, and the larger bridge was in course of erection. There are two central spans of 460 feet, and two side spans of 230 feet, at a height of 100 feet above high water. There are two separate wrought-iron tubes side by side, each 1,510 feet long, resting on three towers of masonry and the end abutments, so as to give the required spans. The tubes are rectangular in section; the top and bottom booms are cellular; the whole is built up of wrought-iron plates riveted together, supported solidly on the central tower, and on rollers on the side-towers and abutments. The design was closely copied in the Victoria bridge over the St. Lawrence at Montreal, finished in 1859.

The webbing connecting the top and bottom flanges of a girder need not be plain plate-iron, as in the 1850 Torksey bridge in Lincolnshire. It may well be made in lattice form, and, in fact, the open-work type was tried by Sir John MacNeill, as long ago as 1843, over a short 84-feet span near Dublin. The type is now very general, by reason equally of its strength, neatness, and simplicity of construction. A good example is given by the Charing Cross railway bridge in London. The completion of the Forth Bridge in 1889 marked a great advance in the history of girder bridges, as it introduced cantilevers for long spans, and was immediately copied for bridges in various parts of the globe. Imagine two enormous steel brackets back to back, forming together a beam or lattice girder 1,700 feet long, tapering each way from the middle, where the whole is supported on a substantial pier. Such is the double cantilever. Its two parts, built up simultaneously, balance each other. Another similar cantilever is at a distance of 1,700 feet, and the short space between their near ends is bridged by ordinary lattice girders, also built outwards from each end. The Forth Bridge is designed with a taper in plan—that is, it is widest at the piers, narrowest at the centre of each large span. This is mainly to withstand lateral wind pressure safely, a lesson learnt from the

THE FORTH BRIDGE.

sad catastrophe to the original Tay Bridge, overthrown by a storm in December, 1879 (p. 877).

The operations of building the piers in deep water were unique at the time, and offer the best example of the direction of development of this part of the subject. Hollow wrought-iron caissons, or water-tight cylinders, 70 feet in diameter, were sunk to the rock-bed 72 feet below the water-level. The rock was cut away to receive each caisson, by operations carried on in a chamber at its base, supplied with compressed air at 33 lbs. per square inch to resist the encroachment of the water. Where the bed was of mud, the weight of the caisson carried through to the stiff boulder-clay below. In each case the caisson and mining-chamber were filled with concrete, so that, when set, each caisson constituted a firm stone pillar 70 feet in diameter.

The main improvement in suspension bridges has been in the process of stiffening by some form of lattice-work. The suspension principle may well be combined with others, as with the Tower Bridge, where the side spans are half suspension, and the centre span has two permanent lattice-girders and the lower drawbridge. The Telford bridge over the Menai Straits still remains our finest example of the simple type. It was

Photo: C. Vaughan, Acton, W.

THE VYRNWY DAM.

opened in 1825; it has a span of 579 feet, and the roadway is 100 feet above the water-level.

Canals and Water Supply.   The growth of railways has been attended with a decline in canal traffic in this country. Yet it is very possible that this generation will see the advantage of rescuing our extensive waterways from desuetude. The only great canal scheme of this century has been that of the Ship Canal connecting Manchester with the Mersey estuary. It is 35 miles in length, 26 feet deep, and with a bottom width of 120 feet. There are four reaches, separated by sets of three locks. Steamers can effect the whole distance in eight hours, including all delays at the locks.

In the matter of water-supply, the growing interest in problems of public health, and the municipalisation of water - supply, has caused attention to be paid to the purity and sufficiency of the water for large towns, and important alterations have been proposed for Liverpool, Manchester, Birmingham, and London. The Liverpool supply from the River Vyrnwy, in Montgomeryshire, is now an accomplished fact. Manchester now derives its water from Thirlmere, in the Lake district. Birmingham draws its water from South Wales, and London still (in 1904) supplements its former supplies by storing Thames water and drawing from wells in Kent and Herts. From the 'thirties the Metropolitan supply was in the hands of eight different companies till they were replaced in 1904 by a Water Board. A scheme has long been advocated for an aqueduct from Mid-Wales.

The chief engineering difficulties are associated with the formation of the storage reservoir near the source of supply, though the choice of route and construction of easy gradients for the conduit are matters

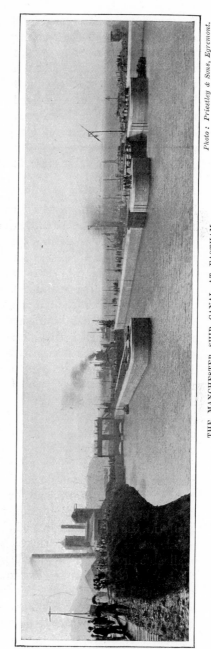

Photo : *Priestley & Sons, Egremont.*

THE MANCHESTER SHIP CANAL AT EASTHAM.

of importance. The main interest in the Liverpool supply scheme attaches to the masonry dam built across the Vyrnwy valley, on a bed of solid rock, forming a basin for the upland waters to accumulate. The lake thus formed is five miles long, and averages three-quarters of a mile in width. The dam is 1,200 feet long, rising 100 feet above the ground, with 60 feet of foundation below. Along the top is a carriage-road, supported on 33 arches, which give the structure a fine appearance. The aqueduct to Liverpool is 67 miles long, whereas that leading from Thirlmere to Manchester is 96 miles long.

H. C. JENKINS. Metallurgy and Mining, 1846-1885.

THE British trade in pig iron continuously, sometimes rapidly, increased, and several new districts have assumed a position of great importance. Chief amongst them is that of Cleveland, with which Sir Lowthian Bell has long been identified, and where his important work in connection with the theory of iron smelting has been done. The maximum output was in 1883 (8,490,000 tons), but since then the American demand has been met locally and our own output diminished in consequence. The annual output per furnace had increased from the 1,500 tons in the early part of the century to from 20,000 to 25,000 tons, a result due to the increased size of the furnaces and improved appliances used with them. Competition has become much more severe in later years, and the phenomenal fortunes made in early days have ceased to be easily obtained by new comers into the field. Much of the growth of the pig iron industry has been for the purpose of supplying raw material for the production of finished wrought iron and steel. In 1815, steel for the

Iron and Steel.

purpose of making tools and cutlery could be obtained of the highest quality. It was, and for these purposes still is, produced by the process of cementation from wrought iron, and it was costly in the extreme. But of cheap steel, or steel suitable for constructive purposes, there was none. The wrought or malleable iron was produced by Cort's process of puddling (Vol. V., p. 632), with the improvements made by Hall, but the rolling-mill with grooved rolls introduced by Cort had made it an easy matter to supply bars of any desired section. It was thus possible to produce the wrought iron rails necessary for the early railways, a requirement that of itself led to a rapid increase in the number of puddling mills. How great that requirement may be, will be realised when it is remembered that a mile of double railway track, even of the light character used in early days, required 100 tons of rails, and these, when of wrought iron, have to be renewed every few years. About the year 1850 the activity in the industry was astonishing. In the great centres, such as the one on the Staffordshire coal-field, the traveller by night seemed to be passing through a pandemonium on earth. He saw the huge flaming blast furnaces, and hundreds of puddling ones, the glowing of the heated masses of metal as they were being moved from place to place in the darkness, with weird human figures seen dimly in outline near them; and although this picture was, on account of better modes of working, soon only a matter of history, the production of puddled bars was not seriously checked until as late as 1882. But in 1856 an invention was made by Sir Henry Bessemer that has had a most important and lasting effect upon the finished iron and steel industries. He was requiring a material for ordnance purposes, resembling steel in its character, but not so costly; and he endeavoured to obtain it by blowing air into molten cast iron in order to oxidise the excess of carbon. Somewhat to his surprise, he found that the temperature rose so much that it was not only needless to employ an external source of heat in order to keep the purified metal fluid, but the latter was so hot that it could be poured into ingots. The process took some little time to perfect, but after that was done, the new steel soon became an article of commerce, over 160,000 tons being made in 1869, for it could be made of many grades of carbonisation at will, and at a fraction of the cost of the "cemented" steel. The cost, moreover, was rapidly lessened, and by 1874 it was possible to obtain Bessemer steel rails at a lower price than that charged for wrought-iron ones. The latter were, therefore, displaced as fast as they were worn out, steel rails being from five to ten times more durable. Indeed, the heavy traffic of modern trunk lines could scarcely be carried on with the old rails. In 1881 the production of Bessemer steel amounted to 1,440,000 tons in Great Britain as compared with 2,680,000 tons of puddled iron produced in that year; but since then the puddled iron trade has undergone a steady decline.

The Bessemer Process.

Other persons had, however, been working in the same

direction as Sir H. Bessemer at the time he made his invention, though they adopted different means.   Sir William
Siemens and his brother Frederick had been experimenting
since 1846 with a view to economise fuel in manufactures, which
was then being wasted in a most alarming way.   These experi-
menters perfected the methods, now very generally adopted, by
which fuel is converted, as far as possible, into the gaseous form
before being finally burnt, for it was only by so doing that it was
found possible to bring about perfect combustion.   They were
also the first successfully to introduce a method—indicated by
Stirling in 1815—by which heat could be accumulated in a
furnace by the so-called regenerative chambers, and they applied
the method in the first place to the furnaces used in the
manufacture of glass.   The application to furnaces used in the
metallurgy of iron was, on account of difficulties and of
prejudices, more tedious, but in the new furnaces they were able
to melt the finished product, which was, in all other respects,
the same as that from the puddling furnace, and obtain, as in
the case of Bessemer's steel, a homogeneous ingot which could
be subsequently rolled.   The process was brought into practical
use during the years 1861–67, and at one time was viewed as a
rival to Bessemer's, but by 1875 the two processes had taken
their proper places in the industry—Bessemer's as unrivalled for
the manufacture of the medium and harder varieties of steel,
such as for rails, and Siemens's, or the open-hearth process, as

BESSEMER

(By permission, from the Model lent by Messrs. Gjers,

being the more suitable one to use for the production of ductile varieties, such as boiler plating, some of which is nearly pure iron. In the year 1882, open-hearth ingots to the extent of 400,000 tons were made, whilst in recent years this variety has, with Bessemer steel and with puddled iron, been made in about equal amounts for each.

During the period of 1874–79 three metallurgists of the London Royal School of Mines, named Snelus, Thomas, and Gilchrist, developed a modification of these processes, by which phosphoric ores could not only be used in making the best steel, but the phosphorus could be incidentally extracted and returned to the land as a valuable manurial agent. This improvement, whilst it enabled the metallurgists of this country to use ores hitherto useless for the purpose of steel-making, has enabled our Continental rivals to do likewise, and has probably been of far greater value to them than to us. *The Gilchrist Process.*

Iron and steel shipbuilding is rather one of the other branches of engineering itself than belonging to metallurgy and mining, but mention is necessary on account of its intimate connection, and also on account of the enormous relative interest this nation possesses in it, and the large amount of employment given to skilled labour by its means. The development of ocean steam traffic—though sailing-ships long maintained their position of supremacy as freight carriers (p. 464)—had of course a considerable effect eventually on the demand for coal. It was in *Ship-building.*

STEEL WORKS.

Mills & Co., to the Victoria and Albert Museum.)

1850 that the industry began to assume importance, when 12,000 tons of iron shipping were built. Iron is so much better as a structural material than wood that its use extended from year to year, some ships being built wholly of iron, others with iron framework and wooden planking, but these latter diminished in number as improvements in the manufacture of iron plates were made. In 1883 the annual production of iron shipping in this country had increased to 732,000 tons (by measurement), and the use of wood had been for some years almost entirely

SIEMENS'S "DIRECT PRODUCTION" STEEL APPARATUS.
(*Victoria and Albert Museum.*)

abandoned for the structural part of British-built ships. In the course of the year 1888 only 54,000 tons were built of iron, a result due partly to bad trade, but chiefly to the extended use of mild or open-hearth steel, the use of which had commenced in 1879. In the subsequent recovery of trade, mild steel has been employed, to the practical exclusion of all other material; wood is, indeed, reserved almost entirely for the purpose of the interior fittings, or as the material for small boats. On account of the use of the new material—mild steel—great improvements have been made both in the forms of ships and in their machinery, and it is now possible to carry goods at very low rates; so that by fitting ships with refrigerating chambers and means for producing artificial cold, even perishable goods can be cheaply brought to this country from the Antipodes. The general economic consequences of this must be dealt with elsewhere (pp. 806–814), but it may here be noted that many ores that were formerly brought to our centres to be smelted can now be more cheaply treated at the mines from whence they are obtained, with coke brought from some other neighbouring country. Again, ores that are of slightly better quality than our own can profitably be imported and smelted instead of it, *e.g.* the Bilbao hematite.

THE *THERMOPYLÆ.*
(From a print supplied by Messrs. G. Thompson & Co.)

At the beginning of the century about 15½ million tons of coal were raised annually, but the output increased very rapidly. It was 64½ million tons in 1854, when the number of work-people employed was about 200,000. It is only since this date that accurate and continuous records have been kept. In 1885 it was 159 millions of tons, a quantity more easily realised by comparison to a cylinder a mile in diameter and 230 feet high; and in that year the industry gave occupation to 478,000 men and boys. Most of this coal is used in this country, about one-eighth of the total being exported. The conditions of the persons employed in coal-mining has been subject to much change. For very many years there was practically no legislation by which to control the conditions under which work was

Coal Mining. The Output.

carried on, and the cheapest way to a given end tended to be the one adopted. Indeed, as regards some Scotch miners, actual and legal slavery existed to as late a date as 1799. The intro-

First Coal Mines Act, 1842. duction of the safety lamps of

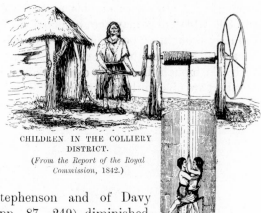

CHILDREN IN THE COLLIERY DISTRICT.

(*From the Report of the Royal Commission, 1842.*)

Stephenson and of Davy (pp. 87, 249) diminished, for a time, the loss of life and the injury to the coal-pits from gas explosions, but other accidents were frequent and of appalling fatality, the workmen themselves, as well as their leaders, being too ignorant to render improvement either in their practice or condition of life an easy matter. The employment of children of tender years, as well as of women, under-ground, although giving occupation to cheap forms of labour, tended greatly to aggravate this evil.

WOMEN CARRYING COAL.

(*From the Report of the Royal Commission, 1842.*)

Some revelations as to the terrible state of things that existed in many parts of the country led, in 1842, to the introduction of a Bill in the House of Commons by Lord Ashley (p. 314). It prohibited the employ-ment underground of girls or women alto-gether, and of boys till the age of ten. Such employment, from the age of seven, appears to have been one regular way by which the Guardians of the Poor provided for their pauper charges. The Act, more-over, limited apprenticeship to a period not exceeding eight years; it prohibited the payment of wages in public-houses, and

WOMEN AND CHILDREN IN THE COAL MINES.
(*From the Report of the Royal Commission, 1842.*)

empowered the Secretary of State to appoint inspectors. One such inspector was appointed; his duties, however, did not at all correspond with those of the inspectors to whom reference will subsequently be made. The Bill did not touch the question of education, although it was quite common for those superintending the miners underground to be themselves unable either to read or to write.

The view was generally held at this time, and, indeed, seems to have been accepted even by Lord Ashley, that underground inspection of the mines would be resented by the miners. But within a few years of this date large petitions were presented to Parliament from the men themselves, asking for means of education, for efficient inspection of the mines by competent Government inspectors who understood the art of mining, that efficient ventilation should be compulsory, and that permanent and accurate plans of all mines be kept for future reference.

Act of 1850.   These conditions were finally embodied in the Coal Mines Inspection Act of 1850. It introduced the principle of State supervision of the work itself in order to prevent accident; the entire responsibility, however, of the proper conduct of operations resting with the proprietors and mine managers. Notice had to be given of all fatal accidents, and the first trustworthy record of these is for the year 1851, when 984 persons lost their lives in coal mines in the United Kingdom. It was soon seen that not one-half of these deaths were due to the explosions of gas, and though such accidents come more prominently before the public, yet the greater part of the loss of life is to the present day by ones and twos at a time from falls of the roof, defective plant, and similar causes. Difficulty was found in obtaining the highly-trained men suitable for inspectors, and no institution existed in the country at which students could get the requisite training in the mining profession, until, by the efforts of Sir H. de la Beche (p. 84), and under the patronage of the Prince Consort, the Royal School of Mines, London,[1] was founded in 1851. Six suitable inspectors were, however, found **Act of 1855.** and appointed; this number was increased to twelve in 1855, when a further Act was passed enforcing the adoption of special rules adapted to the requirements of different collieries.

[1] This, the earliest technical institution in the country (p. 86), has since been incorporated with the Royal College of Science.

Breaches of these Acts were penal, and the proprietors could be fined and workmen imprisoned for committing them. Evasions, for some time far from rare, were less in number after the Cymmer explosion in 1856, when 114 persons lost their lives, and the responsible officials of the mine—namely, the manager, overman, and fireman—were indicted for manslaughter in consequence. Technical grounds prevented an actual conviction, but the deterrent effect remained. In 1860 a further Act raised Act of 1860. the minimum age of engine-men from fifteen to eighteen years, very much increased the powers of the inspectorate, ordered that coal should be truly weighed, and secured that boys should have some education. It also compelled the use of boreholes in advance of new work, whenever old workings were being approached; for these latter are generally full of water very liable to break through without warning. The importance of this precaution, as well as that of keeping accurate plans of all old workings in some easily accessible place, was emphasised in an appalling way in the following year at the Clay Cross Colliery, where some old workings were unexpectedly pierced and twenty-three men and boys lost their lives in the irruption of water that followed. Subsequent investigation showed that at the spot where the irruption occurred, the old workings extended forty-two yards beyond the line at which they were supposed to end.

The importance of duplicate and independent exits for each The mine had for years been recognised by experts, but the provision Hartley had never been made compulsory. In January, 1862, however, Accident. an accident occurred to the pumps in the Hartley Colliery, a pit only provided with one shaft, divided, for the purposes of working, into two parts by a partition. The accident led to the immediate fracture of the large overhanging cast-iron beam of the pumping-engine, and the broken half fell down the shaft, killing the men in the cage and choking the shaft with *débris.* By untiring effort, and in circumstances of great personal danger to the relief parties, a passage was made down to the upper workings of the mine in the space of six days, when it was found that everyone in the pit had perished by foul air, after escaping from the water that accumulated in the lower of the two seams which were worked in the mine. These two seams had not long before been connected by a ladder placed in a

300

Act of 1862. short ventilating-shaft, that did not, unfortunately, extend to the surface, and the connection had been made at the suggestion of the Government inspector as a second means of escape from the lower seam in case that were flooded, of which there seemed to be some danger.   No less than 204 lives were lost, but in June of the same year a short Act was passed compelling all coal-pits employing more than twenty men to have two shafts extending to the surface, and not less than ten feet apart.

DIAGRAM OF HARTLEY COLLIERY, 1862.
(By permission of the proprietors of the "Illustrated London News.")

The next important Act, that of 1872, required all collieries to be in personal charge of competent and certificated managers. More rules for general work were inserted, so that safety-lamps had to be locked wherever their employment was necessary for safety; a daily examination for inflammable gas had to be made with the safety-lamp in all mines before the men commenced to work; and in most cases the lamp used by the fireman for testing had to be locked. These stringent provisions were to

Coal Mines Act, 1872. protect the men against their own wilful carelessness. The Act rendered it penal for any but authorised persons to open safety-lamps underground, and only then under certain well-defined conditions. Blasting of the coal was permitted only under very stringent regulations. It has always been recognised as a source of danger, and many attempts were made to substitute steel wedges, hydraulic presses, and even the expansion of quicklime cartridges when slaked, but the use of explosives has still been found to be necessary in many mines. The Act of 1872 gave to the miners the privilege of maintaining at their own expense a man at the surface to watch the weighing of the coal on their behalf, their work, if by contract, having to be paid for by weight, and it gave them the further right to appoint some of their own number to make a complete inspection of their mine at their own cost—a useful privilege, but one very rarely exercised. Certain breaches of this Act rendered the owners and managers as well as their men liable to imprisonment. In 1887 a new Act recognised a higher grade of managers; so that certificates are now granted in two classes, first and second, the former being for the more responsible leaders, who require high qualifications. Boys were not allowed to be employed under the age of twelve, nor engine-men under the age of twenty-one—a condition that was sought to be inserted in the first Coal Mine Acts; and it was further enacted that the latter, when engaged in hoisting men, should not on any account be interfered with, and should, indeed, be authorised to require any other person to leave the engine-room.[1] The powers of the inspectors and of the Secretary of State were enlarged, and the latter could sanction the payment of a fine to parties injured in an accident, or to their relatives if the accident were fatal. Magistrates could inflict penalties up to three months' imprisonment with hard labour for the graver breaches of this Act.[2]

As the result of such careful and progressive legislation, the annual death-rate from accidents in mines in the United Kingdom has been gradually reduced from 4·5 per 1,000 to 1·5 per 1,000; and although, as will have been seen, inspectors have large powers, and managers many rigid requirements to keep, yet the industry has not been economically prejudiced on that account.

It was for many years an enigma that disastrous explosions **Explosions.** were continually occurring, notwithstanding all the care given to mining problems by trained and scientific men, and the stringent regulations laid down by Act of Parliament. Some of these were traced to sudden liberation of large volumes of gas from the "goafs," or exhausted parts of the mine, usually occurring at periods when the barometer was abnormally low; others were traced to deficient ventilation, and to culpable behaviour of

[1] Prior to 1850 winding had often been entrusted to boys, and shaft accidents were common in consequence.

[2] The age of employment for boys underground was raised from 12 to 13 in 1900.]

someone in the pit, as, for instance, the opening of a safety-lamp ; but in many instances the explosions were in well-conducted mines, and no adequate cause for a long time could be found. Thus in 1866 an explosion occurred at the Oaks Colliery, and 361 persons lost their lives ; another occurred at Blantyre in 1877, and 207 were killed ; whilst in 1878 as many as 268 were killed in an explosion at Abercarn. It was ultimately surmised that the Oaks explosion was due to the sound-wave from blasting, that reached a safety-lamp in an explosive atmosphere with sufficient violence to momentarily drive the flame through the protecting gauze and thus to fire the mine. Experiments showed this to be possible, whilst survivors from the explosion remembered hearing the sound of a blast immediately before the accident. The Acts of Parliament of 1872 and 1887 have therefore contained special conditions in order to provide against the recurrence of explosions from such a cause.

There yet remained the problem why some explosions appeared to extend over all the mine in which they occurred, and were accompanied by great violence, and oy brilliant flames from the shafts as from the mouths of cannon, since ordinary fire-damp burns slowly ; indeed, in olden days the " fireman " intentionally fired the gas to get rid of it in small quantity, dangerous though the practice might be. The hypothesis at length gained ground that these cases mainly owed their violence to the fine coal-dust suspended in dry air that might otherwise be scarcely explosive at all. Notable amongst the investigators who submitted the matter to experiment was Mr. Galloway, one of the Government inspectors for coal mines, who, during the period 1875–80 secured the co-operation of mine-owners, so as to be able to experiment with the actual dusty gases of the mines themselves. His experiments, communicated to the Royal Society of London, show the hypothesis to be true beyond doubt. The obvious remedy was to water all dusty mines. The Act of 1887 did not render this obligatory, yet it has been practised with most satisfactory results. The necessity for good safety-lamps is undiminished, but should explosions of gas occur they remain comparatively local in character, and do not involve the whole mine unless it be full of fire-damp, which is rarely the case. One accident that occurred in 1877 at the Troedyrhiw Colliery attracted much public attention and sympathy, and is mentioned as illustrating a class of accident common to all mining operations, namely, that due to irruption of water. The subsequent rescue, however, could scarcely have been effected in any but a coal mine. Fortunately, only fourteen men were in the pit at the time of the irruption, and the workings were not completely filled with water. Exploring parties in the dry portions of the pit heard signals through the solid coal, and cut their way down towards their comrades, whose position was, of course, known. Four men were rescued during the next day, but it occupied ten days to reach five others who were shut off, by the water, in the top end of an inclined heading, the whole of which was much below the water-level. By the exercise of much skill, the men were rescued by means of the tunnel made by their rescuers, and they recovered, although for eleven days they had been entirely without food. The remaining five men were killed by the accident. Troe-dyrhiw Rescue, 1877.

The mode of working the coal mines has varied during the century rather in detail than in principle. The older method was, after reaching the strata to be removed, to take out as much of the material in "stalls" as was thought to be safe, leaving sufficient "pillar" to support the roof of the workings, and only a portion of the material was thus available. There are still many kinds of "pillar" and "stall" work, differing only in detail, but the introduction of the safety-lamp (p. 87), first used at the Hetton Colliery in 1816, rendered it practicable to work in what were very dangerous circumstances as regards fire-damp, and to remove the "pillars" also. The practice was soon followed by leaving more and more of the coal in the form of pillars, and thus a transition took place to what is known as "long-wall" working, where roadways only are first formed, and almost the whole of the coal subsequently removed, leaving the superincumbent strata to sink down on the top of the "wastes" left behind by the workers. Some form of long-wall working is now usually adopted wherever practicable. Improvements in Mining.

The ventilation of mines has long attracted the attention both of engineers and of the Legislature. About the year 1820, it became the practice to divide the mines, some of which were already large, into distinct portions or "panels," each of which was complete in itself as regards its roadways and ventilation, in Ventilation.

order to ensure that the air from the downcast shaft should not have too long or tortuous a path to travel to the upcast one. The "panels" were frequently divided from one another by a wide band of unworked coal. When the earlier Coal Mine Acts were discussed, it was sought by some to make the use of rather small "panels" compulsory, but the matter was finally left to the judgment of owners and managers. Indeed, there is some difficulty in framing so sweeping an enactment, owing to the widely differing condition of mines even when near one another. Moreover, it was found that the "panels" did not give immunity from explosion involving the whole mine, the danger of the coal-dust itself not being at that time fully understood. For very many years the ventilation was always secured by the use of a large furnace placed at the foot of the upcast shaft but fed by a little fresh air, whilst the foul air was admitted at some distance higher up. This method was so efficient as to necessitate the use of better forms of safety-lamps—such as that of Mueseler—to withstand the faster currents of air that were produced in the workings, and for many years the method was supposed to be without a rival, although jets of steam or of compressed air were occasionally used under special circumstances. But about the year 1849, a Mr Powell had a large centrifugal fan, designed by Brunton, in successful use at the Gelligaer Colliery near Newport. It had a vertical axis and was placed at the surface on the ground. The use of the fan made its way only slowly. It was used in South Wales, and finally in Durham in 1860. But it received a great impetus after the year 1862, when Guibal exhibited another large fan at the London Exhibition. The many advantages accruing from the use of mechanical means at the surface were then more fully recognised, and fans running at various speeds according to their size have since become the usual means of ventilation for coal mines.

Pumping.   The pumping-engine is an invention that belongs to the eighteenth century (Vol. V., pp. 424, 427). It has rendered possible the mining operations of the present time. Many improvements have since been made, with a view to pump the water more economically or conveniently, but these are rather in details that belong more strictly to technical treatises.

The haulage of the coal from the place where it is obtained

MODEL SHOWING FOUR METHODS OF GETTING COAL.

(Victoria and Albert Museum.)

Mechanical Haulage. to the foot of the mine-shaft has, on the other hand, been greatly improved in important particulars. The use of cast-iron tramways in collieries appears to date from 1767, when they were put in the one at Coalbrookdale. The material was adopted on account of its temporary cheapness, but it was soon seen that the outlay was insignificant when compared with the advantages to be gained by its use, which rapidly spread. About 1820 George Stephenson introduced mechanical haulage underground, but not generally, and its ultimate success was only due to the use of steel wire ropes, which belong to a later period; but it should be noted that the coal mines of the Newcastle district were for many years in a much better developed condition than existed elsewhere. The Act of 1842, and the consequent withdrawal of women from the coal-pits, where they had been employed literally as beasts of burden, compelled the proprietors of the Scotch and Welsh mines to use ponies and horses underground; this they soon found to be highly advantageous from the economical as well as from the social point of view. It must be remembered, however, that much hauling has still, and probably always will have to be, done by men and boys.

For many years mechanical hauling and winding had to be performed either by the aid of chains or by hempen ropes. The use, however, of the former means was found to be attended by so much danger, owing to the progressive damage done to the iron itself by the continual vibration inseparable from the passage of chains over wheels, that it had to be abandoned. Flat hempen ropes, many of them of great size, were used for winding until about the year 1862, when Newall carried the **Wire Rope.** manufacture of metallic wire ropes to such a degree of perfection as to justify their substitution in the place of hempen ones; at the present day steel wire ropes are exclusively used, and with their advent mechanical means of haulage underground became both possible and general. The rope is sometimes driven by an engine at the surface, as Stephenson suggested, at others by engines placed underground and driven **Winding.** by steam or compressed air. The speed of hoisting or winding, as it is termed, has, during the latter half of the period of this volume, become uniformly very high, and in this particular the Newcastle district was long in advance of the others. At many pits the load is lifted from the depth of half a mile in the space of a minute, and, if the mine be not so deep, at correspondingly rapid rates. This compares very favourably indeed with the speed of fast railway trains on short journeys; but owing to greatly improved appliances, and the efficient state in which they are maintained by close inspection, as well as the high sense of duty of the present class of responsible engine-men, shaft-accidents are, unlike the case in earlier years,

MODEL OF A SOUTH WALES COLLIERY VENTILATING FURNACE, WITH LEFT WALL THROWN BACK.

(Victoria and Albert Museum.)

very rare. In the best collieries, self-acting appliances are provided in case of need, as, for instance, the self-detaching hooks that liberate the cage from the rope, and prevent it from falling down the shaft again in cases of overwinding. These hooks, the independent inventions of Ormerod and of King, have, since their introduction in 1865, been the means of saving many lives.

The great and increasing activity in the coal and iron trades brought forward the question of the duration of our coal supply. A Royal Commission, appointed in 1866, after

**Our Coal
Supply.**

collecting much evidence and carefully investigating the whole
of our resources as then known, presented its report in 1871,
showing that with the existing rate of consumption, and the
population stationary, there was a visible supply of coal for
1,273 years, but that on the supposition that the rate of
consumption and the population both increased at the rate
observed in the past, there would only be a supply for 276
years.[1] Although more pessimistic views have not been wanting,
yet for many years these figures have been generally accepted
as approximating very closely to the truth. More recently,
however, some discoveries of coal at Dover have led to the hope
that there are still considerable deposits in this country within
reach, but as yet untouched.

It is important to notice that there has been a tendency
in quite recent years for the annual output from each miner
to decrease, notwithstanding the improvement in machinery
and appliances that is always going on. The decrease in useful
output per head has been accompanied by a corresponding
increase in cost per ton—a result due, apart from any difference
in the rate of wages, to the fact that many of the more easily
worked seams are becoming exhausted, and in some degree to
the cost of the means taken for increased protection of life and
limb, as well as to the decreased number of hours worked
during the year by the miners owing to united trade action.

**The
Workers.**

The workers in other industries have been somewhat
differently placed from the miners, whose work is still largely
done by manual labour. The uniform tendency has been to
greatly increase the annual amount of work done per head,
owing to the introduction of labour-saving appliances, and to
thus cheapen the product. But in nearly every branch of trade
this has not led to any ultimate decrease in the number of
workers, but rather to so great an increase in the industry by
the greater consumption of the cheaper and often more convenient product, that the number of employees has increased.
This can be seen in the pig iron industry, where much of the
severe work is done by purely mechanical means, as well as
in the iron and steel manufacture, where even the handling of
the material is performed by machinery; and operations such

[1 Another Royal Commission to inquire into the subject was appointed at
the end of 1901.]

as the production of "Bessemer" or "open hearth" steel have,
to a very great extent, replaced the brutal manual one ot
puddling. The workers, having rather to direct operations
than to labour at them, tend thereby to produce a finer or
more uniform product; at the same time the management
both of mining and of metallurgical concerns has passed into
fewer and fewer hands, on account of the enormous amount of
capital necessary for so complete an organisation as is required
under the new conditions. Individual enterprise has therefore
merged into corporate, and much of such sympathy as formerly
existed between master and workman disappeared in the
change.

What has been true in this respect of the iron industries
has, though to a less degree, been true of those of the metallurgy, of lead, of copper, of tin, and of zinc. Small industrial
concerns have mostly disappeared, being absorbed into larger
ones at a few centres, but where they have survived it has been,
as in the case of iron works, to share in increased trade until
the diminished imports of ores (p. 749) adversely affected them.
But British mining industries, other than those connected with
the coal and iron trades, have generally declined during recent
years. Lead, for instance, has greatly declined as regards the
amount of output, which was about 79,000 tons in 1848, and
only 59,300 tons in 1882. The British tin industry has
occupied an almost stationary position throughout the whole
of the period under review, although the production of
enormous quantities of tin-plate, an industry giving much
employment to labour, has been met by imports of foreign and
colonial tin. The British tin deposits have been worked for
two thousand years, and are at many places at such depths
that the output is only maintained with great difficulty at the
low prices obtained for the metal during recent years, and this
with very low rates of wages. The annual supply of British
copper, another of the metals worked here in Roman times,
increased from 1815, when it was 6,800 tons, to the year 1856,
when it was 13,200 tons, after which it has declined to 2,700
tons in 1885. This has been accompanied by an almost
continuous decrease in the average richness of the ores, a sure
sign of exhaustion of the deposits. Our increased demands
for these metals have been, it is needless to add, necessarily

Minor Metallurgical Industries.

supplied from foreign sources, and the prices have varied very much from time to time, the comparatively small stocks in the world rendering speculation possible on a large scale. In the case of copper the demand has varied, owing, amongst other things, to the substitution of iron and mild steel for its use for many purposes, and to its diminished requirement for the sheathing of wooden ships. It appeared, indeed, at one time

MODEL OF CORNISH TIN STAMPS.
(Victoria and Albert Museum.)

that copper would soon cease to be of its former importance in the industrial arts, but a new and increasing use of the metal for electrical purposes has not only removed that fear, but led to the extensive adoption of electrolytic means for refining. On the other hand, the zinc industry must be said to have become firmly established since 1823, and the metals, aluminium (discovered in 1827), manganese, nickel, and chromium, removed from the list of costly cabinet curiosities to form useful articles of commerce.

J. C. L. SPARKES. Pottery and Porcelain, 1815-1885. THE subject is vast, as it practically covers every grade of manufacture, from a brick or a roofing-tile to the most exquisite example of eggshell porcelain. It will therefore be necessary to deal with certain large sectional divisions in the briefest possible way. The difference in the material, decoration, and use of the modern ware from that which it has succeeded renders it needful to make a general statement in the nature of a retrospect.

The art of the potter had, in the eighteenth century, become not only very important commercially, but very interesting from the artist's point of view. But the industrial depression resulting from the French Revolution and the war with France caused the disappearance of many of the most celebrated potteries that had added charm to the households of the period, and done great credit to those who founded them and those who worked in them.

The importation of Chinese porcelain articles had already severely shaken the more homely pottery of the sixteenth and seventeenth centuries from its hold on the affections of the housekeeper, inasmuch as that and all similar ware—*e.g.* that of Delft—was made of an inferior body, which was porous and of a dark colour, and its artistic beauty—for it was covered with an opaque enamel, on which the lavish decorations of Gubbio, Faenza, or the Delft artists were painted—could not protect it against the claims of the more perfect and cleanly porcelain of China. Nevertheless, until the discovery of the China clay, **Kaolin.** or Kaolin, the imported ware was too expensive to interfere materially with the demand for ordinary pottery. When, however, that discovery was made and applied practically at Meissen, it had stimulated all the potters of England to making similar ware, until the same process was independently discovered by Cookworthy and patented by him in 1768 (Vol. V., p. 428). Then the more beautiful and painter-like ware of the Majolica artists languished until it disappeared altogether. Delft, a ware named from the place of its first origination, continued to be made in Lambeth as late as 1840, though no longer in the form of dinner and domestic ware, but in that of articles of commercial use.

The aim of the potter was first to imitate the porcelain of **China and** China, and this had already been done by Cookworthy; but the **Earthen-** difficulty attending the manufacture of china, as it was called, **ware.** led the makers to produce a cheaper ware than porcelain, which ended in the manufacture of earthenware, the name for the ordinary dinner and tea services, and the innumerable other forms to which the material is applied. In this ware it is believed that the English clay, tempered, wrought, and worked by the English potters, is the best of its kind in Europe. In mere quality of material it stands at the head of all the various French and German or Scandinavian manufactures.

Still, in outlying districts abroad—*e.g.* Brittany, Italy, and some districts in Germany—Delft is still made to supply the local demands for articles of everyday use. Much as in England, there are many potters still making the ordinary red clay pots and pans with a soft lead glaze ; but these are survivals, and, except in special cases, where the old ware is absolutely more suited for its purposes than earthenware would be, it is certainly being slowly but surely ousted from the markets even of country places by the ordinary earthenware, which is cleaner, more durable, cheaper, lighter, and always purchasable. Already in the last century in Staffordshire a better ware than these lead glaze wares for domestic use had been made by a salt glaze process, but this, too, though interesting to collectors of the present day, had to give way to the cheaper and more easily produced material.

Progress in the Trade. The improvements in this material, more than any new methods of manufacture, are, in the main, what the chronicler has to deal with in the period under review, since from the making of a brick to that of a porcelain cup of the finest texture, the principles involved are the same to-day as they were in all previous time. No doubt numberless improvements in machinery have brought about a greater speed of production, and consequently a greater output, but, with trifling exceptions, no new methods can be recorded as helping forward the gradual increase of the productions of this manufacture. Brick- and tile-making machinery has been improved until, probably, finality has been reached in this section of work. Potters' wheels, lathes, and jiggers are driven by steam power instead of by hand ; dies are used more frequently, methods have been quickened and production doubled by these and the introduction of piecework. Great improvements have been made in general arrangements : the workpeople are better housed in better factories, where ventilation and heating are properly applied on scientific principles ; the old stoves for drying the ware are now superseded by steam-pipes, which are less exhausting to the workmen. Steam also heats the printers' presses and prepares the clay. The consumption of coal has been saved by a third by better methods of firing. With all this better lighting and more healthy surroundings it is not surprising that a corresponding improvement in taste and decoration has been possible. Nevertheless, no new principle of manufacture has been

PIERCED WORCESTER WARE.

(By permission, from " A History and Description of English Porcelain," by W. Burton, F.C.S.)

introduced. The eighteenth century saw the discovery of china clay (Vol. V., p. 430) and the numerous establishments for the manufacture of porcelain from it. All other bodies and glazes were known, and to some extent practised, so that it is possible to say that in the time under review, probably only two new inventions, if they may be so called, have been made. One is

Parian Ware

the use of what is called " Parian " as a material for statues and statuettes, and figures of novelties. It is a body of somewhat soft yielding texture, which shrinks very much in the kiln, and, it is feared, shrinks unevenly. This prohibits its use in the reproduction of serious sculpture, or of works of high importance, but it is very useful, and adapts itself prettily to ornamental figures where an uncertain surface and slight disproportion are

A POTTER'S WHEEL.
(*Victoria and Albert Museum, by permission of Messrs. W. Boulton.*)

no great detriment. This material enjoyed great repute through the thirty years from 1851, but is now mainly used for the building up of floral groups, which are very skilfully done, busts, and smaller objects of decoration, which do not form any very important branch of manufacture. It has been used as a material for ornamental and useful ware when fired with a metallic glaze, as at Belleek, county Fermanagh, in Ireland. It has a pleasing mother-of-pearl lustre, and its manufacture is so far a new application of an old method, first introduced by Josiah

Lustre Ware.

Wedgwood. Copper and platinum lustre ware is still made in certain patterns in Staffordshire, in Longton, for foreign markets, especially Spain and Mexico, and Spanish-speaking countries,

VIEWS AT THE ROYAL PORCELAIN WORKS, WORCESTER.

301

but in diminishing quantities. The artistic points in this ware call for no remark; the potter supplies what the buyer demands.

Pressing Clay. Tiles. The other invention is based on the discovery of the power that the particles of quite dry clay possess of adhering together when subjected to strong pressure in a steel die. It is manifest that this obviates the distortion in the kiln that usually results from the evaporation of the water with which the clay is mixed, and has the further advantage that there is less shrinkage than in a clay object pressed in the usual way from clay and water. It is largely applicable to the production of tiles, lids of jars, and innumerable other objects, and was at first and for many years after its discovery applied solely to the manufacture of buttons. Still, few could have foreseen what an important branch of business would ultimately grow out of Prosser's patent, which Herbert Minton perfected and applied to so many uses. Perhaps the most original and characteristic growth is that of the tile industry, which is practically built on the use of this patent. Tiles can be made with various layers of coloured clays in powder, the result being the encaustic tiles of the modern church architect and decorator, which have had an enormous demand for every country in the world, and have taken the place of the old slip-made encaustic tile, a survival of the tiles and method of the Middle Ages.

Advances, 1801-1851. The first twenty years of the present century can scarcely be called examples of business activity; though it was in 1805 that Spode's opaque china drove the French faience from the market. He introduced printed patterns in direct imitation of the china patterns—*e.g.* the willow pattern, which became the rage and brought the firm a fortune. Spode died in 1827, and his firm became Copelands in 1833. The firm was second only to Mintons, founded in 1791. The ware was decorated similarly to Salopian ware, but was wanting in character. In 1836, however, Herbert Minton succeeded to the business, and among other things revived the making of encaustic tiles, which consist of a moulded base containing the pattern with raised edges; into this the coloured slips are poured. This method was superseded by the discovery of the dry clay process for tiles, mentioned above. Later also this firm introduced hard bodied porcelain, dry pressed tiles, pâte sur pâte decoration, and many other processes, before the Exhibition of 1851 gave us a means of

comparing our products with those of other nations. Among
the stimulants which served to improve our art work were the
revival of Gothic principles by Pugin, and the revival of a truer
art feeling in this country, which critics absurdly call Pre-
Raphaelitism (p. 636), and wrongly strove to smother by making
it ridiculous. This singular latter-day Renaissance preceded by
a few years the introduction of an art element into our potteries,
where it had long been absent. France and Italy had also

A TILE PRESS.
(*Victoria and Albert Museum.*)

advanced, but the traditions of Sèvres and of medieval Italy were
too strong for them, and led and kept them in the wrong path.
England, unlike most Continental nations, has never had a State
manufacture for the development of the ceramic art, and the
trade is thus left to the exertions that private enterprise can
make. Hence it is that the merit of having advanced the
potter's art further than it has been carried in Europe since the
days of the Renaissance is due to our own countrymen. They
are at this moment pre-eminent among European potters, not in
the making of artistic ware only, but also in the manufacture of

cheap useful crockery. Our common English earthenware undersells the produce of every country where it is allowed to gain admittance, while our decorative pottery is quite as indisputably the best in Europe. The one thing wanting with us has been invention. This has led our people to apply their technical knowledge and capacity to imitations. The Majolica and Palissy wares have been travestied rather than copied, and English potters have not even feared to attempt to imitate the quite inimitable faience of Henry II.; but our great potters have done worthier things than these, and much admirable, and even original, art work is annually turned out from their kilns.

In 1851, the contributions of the English potters showed an immense improvement on the taste of the three decades that immediately preceded it. The very long unrivalled pre-eminence of the Wedgwood classical taste seemed to show how completely the domain of taste had been abandoned, until, indeed, it seemed impossible to impress the master potters with the idea that there was such a thing as taste. They had not grasped the fact that artistic taste alone could lead to commercial prosperity. The old idea that first-rate artists were to work at some vast product of a State-subsidised manufactory, such as Sèvres, was seen to be futile; and now it is first seen that the first-rate artist can be profitably employed in producing the decorations in form and detail, the ordinary ware of the potter. Hence the movement made from this period. No doubt the production of capable men by the educational power of various schools of design, which had been at work since 1839, enabled the manufacturers to apply this simple principle and make it a practice. This period saw a return to better form, which in pottery is the first great element of beauty. Whatever may be the decoration of an object, it should be applied to a form that gives pleasure to

the cultivated eye. The Wedgwood ware had, all through the dead ages of the first three decades of the century, been a standing protest against the neglect of this simple proposition, but we may date the infusion of a better spirit into the designs of our potters from the 1851 Exhibition, where Sèvres at least gave evidence of taste in form, even if the decoration of that form was not in the highest sense tasteful. It was remarked that the Copeland and Minton ware led the show in taste of colour and decoration; although the forms, as of those of

MINTON VASE: "THE SIREN," BY M. L. SOLON.

(From "A History and Description of English Porcelain," by William Burton, F.C.S.)

other Staffordshire and Worcester manufacturers, were steeped in the French decadent treatment of Louis XIV. and Louis XV.

In 1855, the Paris Exhibition of Art Industries gave the critic another opportunity of comparing the various art products of France and England; and the result seems to have been that although Sèvres had advanced enormously, its productions could not sustain competition with those of ordinary trade sources from the fact that a Government subsidy takes the place of the stimulus to exertion that successful competition in trade inevitably supplies. But the common ware in France had gone on, and the first note of possible competition with our home production is now heard. In the years since 1851 the English potters had no doubt advanced; and although Copelands seemed resting on their well-earned fame, Mintons, and especially Binns of Worcester, had made distinct strides onward.

The threat of French competition had a very notable result, which led to the introduction of French modellers, and above all a French pottery chemist into Minton's works at Stoke-on-Trent, and from that time to this the influence of M. Arnoux as a scientific potter is found in the works of the firm to which he allied himself, and the modelling of Jeanest, Carrier-Beleuse, and others tended to give a forceful French style, which no doubt served to stimulate the manufacturers of Staffordshire to competition with those most able artists, and this tended to the general rise in the character of the productions of the entire district.

In 1855, the English faience gave the French potters the idea of using what is called Majolica in the trade as a decoration, and to Messrs. Minton the credit is due of having sent such a representative exhibition of works of the description as to have been the means of awaking in the French potters the desire to outdo their guests. It can, however, scarcely be said that the English potter has not held his own in subsequent exhibitions in which the two rival nations have competed against one another on this particular ground. From this time the modelling of the ware has more character, the range of colour is more free, and the traditions of the somewhat narrow forms of the old trade were boldly departed from.

The advance of the art schools under the Board of Trade further gave the means to the advanced potters to educate their

Majolica.

young modellers and painters to the standard they wished to reach, and this was done at their doors, and ready to their hand. Therefore, as might be expected, the result of the whole sequence of circumstances was found to be the advance of the work of Staffordshire and Worcester. From this time onward, although Sèvres with its vast resources kept its pre-eminence in large works, yet in smaller products they were rivalled on their own ground by the Englishmen, who had struck out a new line or had so modified their old ones as to postpone the probable French competition to some far distant time ; and the lesson had been learnt that it was unwise to substitute labour for art, and that the pursuit of ends that when attained were but curiosities was futile.

The Exhibition of 1862.

These points of progress were brought into prominence in the Exhibition of 1862, when with the exception of a few foreign pieces—notably Copenhagen ware, produced under the influence of Thorwaldsen, and one or two works from Paris and Austria—the English goods were commendably superior in manufacture and in refinement of taste to their foreign rivals, and it became apparent to critics that English taste will be as attractive, on the score of its refined beauty, as the more learned but less spontaneous art of France. In fact, in the eleven years since the 1851 Exhibition, our manufacturers and our purchasers had learnt the lesson that English taste had an affinity with English perceptions of what was beautiful; and the art of the potter from that time must now have been free from any largely perceptible foreign influence, although the French influence of the modellers named above still lingers in the Minton productions.

Improvements in 1871.

In 1871, the advance was felt to be a remarkable one in every way. The old heresies and false taste had practically disappeared. The handles of ewers imitating rope or reeds or flower-stalks had gone, and many most artistic and beautiful things had been introduced. An example of Minton's pâte sur pâte in the hands of a great artist like Solon became a work of art, to be counted by the collector as the best of its kind then painted. The process is simplicity itself ; a coloured body is painted with the same material as the body, but is uncoloured, the thinner parts being semi-transparent. When fired at porcelain heat, it allows the darker body to show through and take the place of shadow, while those parts which have more impasto become half-tones and lights.

"AUTUMN": A FIGURE IN PARIAN, MODELLED BY
CARRIER-BELEUSE, MINTON.
(*By permission, from "A History and Description of
English Porcelain," by W. Burton, F.C.S.*)

Mintons also introduced a curious application of the property that is possessed by certain pigments of seeming to change their colour when viewed by artificial light. A celadon body appears to change to a pink when lighted artificially, and similarly a dove colour changes to crimson under the same conditions. They also exhibited an ingenious method of using hexagonal tesseræ as a means of giving a ground for wall paintings; the adaptability of the small pieces to any winding surface being a distinct gain. When fitted, these were painted with a device in ordinary enamel colours and fired and glazed in the usual way.

Earthen-ware.

As to the earthenware produced in England, persistent effort has produced wonderful lightness, finish, elegance, and cheapness. The substitution of harmless glazes for those made of poisonous ingredients is very satisfactory and a distinct advance. And, not least, the improvement in design and execution of the superior articles now produced is due to the mutual and individual efforts of some of the leading manufacturers, and to the instruction that has been afforded by the schools of art to the operatives and artists in the manufacturing districts. The chief centres of production remain the same as at the beginning of the period under review, but a notable change is coming over the methods

"Process" Decora-tion.

of decoration; the increased use of "process" in this as in the other decorative arts is a recent peculiarity. It threatens to impair the distinctive type and style left us by the great men who have formed the English pottery-trade and name—the classic feeling in Wedgwood ware, the French influence in Mintons, the Oriental sentiment in the Derby work. Worcester alone has abandoned her traditions and gone to Japan for a new inspiration. Doulton ware is distinctive and full of character. But the tendency, at least in Staffordshire, has been to use various German processes for cheapness' sake, a downward step that at the close of our period threatened the loss of all originality and distinctive character.

Stoneware.

The history of stoneware begins with the first fire-burnt pottery, in all probability. Until recently, in England, it was used mainly for the manufacture of drainage pipes, chemical ware, and other useful things. The variations of tint, colour, and texture, due to the accidental firing in the salt-glaze kilns, were an objection to its use as a table or domestic ware. Hence the discovery of what is called Bristol ware—so named from the place of its first introduction. It is a stoneware dipped into a hard glaze; this equalises the various tones and tints of the ordinary ware, and makes a smooth uniform ware that filled a demand made by the public taste, and at one time threatened the existence of ordinary salt-glaze ware.

Up to the year 1870 stoneware had only been used in its common forms, such as those just mentioned, and for the thousand-and-one things to which this most durable ware could be applied.   The utmost accuracy of manufacture had been attained by the energy, outlay, and practical skill of Sir Henry Doulton; but since the sixteenth and seventeenth centuries no stoneware had been used as a decorative material of use except the "Toby" jug, which found, and still finds, a continuous demand.   There was small scope for the display of fine art—the use of stoneware vessels was confined to the humbler classes, among whom the least appreciation of a beautiful thing is to be expected.   But after a few tentative experiments, in 1870–1 Sir Henry Doulton made the most original and interesting restoration of an old and lost art by the introduction of coloured stoneware produced under the difficult conditions attendant on the use of coal instead of wood, which was the German fuel of the fifteenth, sixteenth, and seventeenth centuries.   The difficulties attending the colouring of this extremely hard semi-vitreous ware are mainly owing to the very high and long fire to which it is exposed, and even more to the method of glazing, which consists in throwing salt into the white-hot kiln and on to the ware.   This is decomposed, and the soda attaches itself to the silicious ware, and a perfect glass glaze is formed in the very texture of the body itself.   Needless to say, this is a very trying and destructive process to all colours; hence the small choice of pigments that will withstand the ordeal.   Few as they are, they were fewer still in the sixteenth and seventeenth centuries, when old German stoneware was brought to its highest point.   As an art product the new Doulton ware surpassed the old in greater freedom of design and greater variety and choice of pigments; in addition to these, many methods of adding to the surface of the ware were adopted by the use of moulds and moulded medallions, applied by the fingers of the artists.   The result was a remarkable ware that made its way in the appreciation of connoisseurs and collectors, and, further, had very considerable ordinary sale as the product of a new and attractive art.   The highest recognition in the more recent Continental exhibitions

Doulton Ware.

gave evidence of the thorough success this beautiful ware has had with the greatest critics of France and Austria. Originality, taste, and modern adaptations of old principles mark the characters of this fine manufacture. The flexibility with which the ware has been applied to objects of architectural decoration, such as drinking-fountains, also string mouldings for buildings, and sometimes for the ashlar work of vast erections, is a proof of the modern spirit of enterprise which it illustrates. In this particular manufacture no competition exists, for the product is

TWISTED THROWN PIECES IN COLOURED SALT GLAZE STONEWARE.
(From a photograph supplied by Messrs. Doulton.)

solely made at Lambeth by the talented discoverer of the possibilities of the ware in its new applications. But it is necessary to point out the competition that threatens, especially in Germany,[1] where the stoneware forms and colours are copied in a soft lead glaze on a Majolica body, and can be sold for a quarter of the cost of the original ware. In this department of trade the gravest sins against consistency are enacted, to the great harm and damage of the national product.

Bricks.   As regards brick-making, no doubt certain patents in the last century indicate that an attempt was made to form bricks by the pressure on the clay as it came from the pug-mill; but any real improvement in the matter must be sought in the first third

[1 Written in 1896.]

of the century, especially from 1830 to 1840, when machinery was applied to almost every branch of manufacturing industry, and the various patents of those years, and later, show great

THE REREDOS, ST. MARY'S CHURCH, LAMBETH, MODELLED BY
GEORGE TINWORTH.
(From a photograph supplied by Messrs. Doulton.)

activity in this handicraft; so that the output of the brickmaker with his three or four attendants, making 7,000 bricks a day, has been exceeded tenfold. In 1851 a pierced brick was introduced that was a distinct improvement for many kinds of work, and moulded bricks were extensively made and used for the second class of builders' work.

As a natural extension of the brick-making industry terra-cotta claims notice. It is no doubt the natural form and material for the decoration of brick buildings, and has been employed as an architectural material from the times of ancient Greek art almost continuously to our own times: it was especially developed in the north of Italy and the north of Germany in the time of the later Gothic and early Renaissance

BRICKMAKING MACHINE.
(*Victoria and Albert Museum.*)

periods. The problems that were solved by the manufacturers of those days remain the same to-day.

In the 1862 Exhibition were first seen architectural details in terra-cotta—*i.e.* cornices, string courses, capitals, and panels, pressed in moulds of excellent sharpness, and rivalling in their definition similar architectural features in stone. No doubt terra-cotta, in a sense, has been always used, and terra-cotta figures, as an economy from the cost of carved stone or marble figures, were not uncommon. For generations artists had perceived the advantages of clay modelled or moulded and burnt,

with every touch fixed for ever as the clay left the artist's hand
and this character should be kept in mind.   But, unfortunately
it is comparatively rare to find architects who have risen to a
thorough appreciation of the peculiar character of the treatment
necessary to take full advantage of the limitations of the
material.   Of some modern designs it might be said that they
would have been far better if worked out in stone.   The
buildings in this country that are thoroughly consistent stand as
examples of what may be done in this durable and beautiful
material.

The manufacture is now one of large importance in the
Midlands, and in Leeds and London, where work is done that
has been hitherto unattainable for texture, colour, and accuracy.
Very large buildings have been built and decorated, two of
which may be mentioned: the Albert Hall, and the Natural
History Museum—both at South Kensington.   Various shop
buildings and private houses have been admirably decorated
by the designs and original modelling of men of note.   Among
the best are the remarkable works by the firm of Doulton's
of Lambeth, a noted instance being the Birkbeck Bank,[1] designed by Mr. T. E. Knightley, a building probably unique in
the history of the potter's art.

A very large trade has sprung up in fire-clay goods made
from the clay found in the iron-measures of Staffordshire and
Yorkshire.   Very large quantities of what are called Stourbridge
clay goods are made for crucibles, gas-retorts, fire-bricks, and
other purposes, and especially for seggars, which are the cases
in which the finer wares are enclosed to protect them from the
direct impact of the flame in firing.   Somewhat old traditions
prevail in this branch of the trade, and it is certain that
American and other potters are becoming aware of the need of a
quicker and better way of making seggars.   Asbestos has been
substituted for ground shards at Messrs. Doulton's with
promising results, and no one can quite say what the future of

[1] The portion first erected (1894–95) in Southampton Buildings, Chancery
Lane, is rich in terra-cotta statuary, the architectural work itself being in
Doulton's " Carrara " stoneware of various tones of colour.   The front in
Holborn, erected 1899–1900 (here illustrated), is entirely in white stoneware.
A more recent erection (1904) in Doulton's " Carrara " Stoneware is the immense
frontage in the Strand of the Savoy Hotel, London, made to the designs of
Mr. T. E. Collcutt.]

the large and subsidiary industry will be, but advance in
methods is certainly to be reckoned on.

Thus the progress in manufacturing skill and resource, as

HOLBORN FRONT OF THE BIRKBECK BANK.
(*From a photograph supplied by Messrs. Doulton.*)

well as the advance in taste, were continuous from 1851 to
the end of our period, and an industry has been established
by the energy of our master potters on a scale hitherto unequalled. The export trade had increased gradually until
1885, but at that time evidence was not wanting to show that
in this industry as in others our former customers had become

our rivals, and that the outlook for continued prosperity in the pottery trades was not so bright as it had been.[1]

THE idea of an electric telegraph dates back into the eighteenth century. In 1774 Lesage constructed a telegraph consisting of twenty-four wires with pith-balls at their extremities. In 1816 Ronalds simplified Lesage's arrangement by using one wire only; and in 1828 Dyar, of New York, invented a method of recording messages. In all these attempts frictional electricity was used, and none attained success. After Volta's introduction of current electricity the idea was revived. Attempts were made to apply Davy's discovery, that an electric current could decompose chemical compounds, to systems of telegraphy. It was not until Oersted discovered that a suspended, or pivoted, compass-needle is deflected by a suitably-placed electric current that telegraphy gave any promise of practical success.

Ampère (p. 252), who did so much towards the development of electro-magnetism, first suggested the application of Oersted's experiment to telegraphy. His idea was to have a number of wires carrying electric currents, and to each electric current two magnetic needles—one at the beginning of the line, and the other at the end. It was found, however, that when the line was long the ability of the current to deflect a magnetic needle was diminished to such an extent that for a time telegraphy remained at a standstill.

In 1832 Schilling, a Russian, devised a system of telegraphy in which thirty-six needles were used. In 1833 Gauss and Weber, two German physicists, established a telegraph line about three miles long at Göttingen. This line was used mainly for experimental purposes. The practical development was left to Steinheil, who constructed several telegraph lines radiating from Munich, and who was the first to make use of the earth as a return circuit.

The placing of the electric telegraph on a firm financial basis in England is due to Professor Wheatstone, of King's

W. G. RHODES. Applications of Electricity, 1815–1885.

[1 It may here be mentioned that the writer of this section was the teacher of Mr. George Tinworth, and started the art section of Messrs. Doulton's works in 1870–71 with his own students from the Lambeth School of Art, which supplied the workers exclusively for a considerable time.]

**Wheat
stone's
Telegraph.**

College, London, and to his partner, Mr. W. F. Cooke. They
took out their first patent in 1837. Wheatstone was chiefly
responsible for the scientific part of the work, while Cooke
undertook the business arrangements. As described in their
first patent specification, their system required five needles and
six wires, one of the wires being used as a common return for the
other five. By various combinations of the five needles all the
letters of the alphabet and the numerals could be represented.
Soon, however, Wheatstone found that five needles were unnecessary, as a code could be devised for representing letters
and numerals and as many words as one pleased by means of
a single needle. In 1840 he invented a dial instrument, on
the face of which were the letters of the alphabet.

In all applications of electricity to commerce the questions
of simplicity of arrangement and cost determine whether or
not the venture will be a practical success. These considerations
induced Wheatstone to abandon his five-needle telegraph for a
two-needle or a single-needle telegraph. Where the needle
system has survived other improved forms, the single-needle
instrument is almost universally employed. If the current
traverses the line in one direction the needle swings to the
right, and on reversing the direction of the current by a suitable
key, or contact-maker, the needle swings to the left. The
letters of the alphabet and the numerals are represented by
combinations of swings of the needle to the right and to
the left.

The first public telegraph in England was established in 1844
between Paddington and Slough, a distance of twenty miles.
The wires were suspended from posts along the Great Western
Railway. The needle telegraph was for some years almost
exclusively used in England. In other countries, however, it was
soon supplanted by a system due to an American named Morse,
which has now almost universally superseded all other systems,
except in submarine telegraphy, in which the needle system is

**The
Morse
System.**

still used. The basis of the Morse system (1838) is the electro-
magnet, as constructed by Sturgeon and improved by Henry.
Its advantage lies in the ease with which a permanent record of
telegraphic messages is obtained. The "key," or sending apparatus, is such that in one position the circuit through the
receiving apparatus is complete, while in another position signals

are transmitted.   The receiving instrument or indicator consists of an electro-magnet, one end of the magnetising coil being connected to the line-wire and the other to earth.   As the key is pressed down at the sending end, the current sent through the line to the receiving end magnetises the soft iron of the electromagnet, attracting a soft-iron " armature " carried at one end of

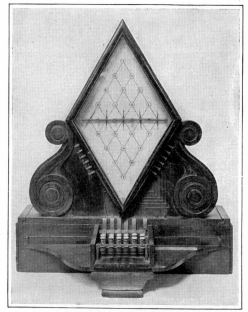

FIVE-NEEDLE INSTRUMENT PATENTED BY MESSRS.
COOKE AND WHEATSTONE IN 1837.
(*By permission of H.M. Postmaster-General.*)

a lever, which is pulled back by an opposing spring when the current ceases.   At the other end of the lever there is a point which presses on a strip of paper, marking it whilst the current is passing.   The intervals between these marks represent the interruptions of the current.   A clockwork, put in motion by a spring, drives a pair of rollers, which draw the strip of paper past the pen so that it receives the series of marks which make up the message.   If the current is momentary a " dot " is made on the paper, but if the current flows for a longer time a " dash " is produced of about three times the length.   At first a pencil was

302

used as the tracing-point, but the point soon became blunt, so that a metal point was substituted. This method demanded a force which the battery-current from the line was generally too feeble to produce. To remedy this defect a " relay " was introduced. This sends a strong local current through the receiving instrument when actuated itself by a feeble line-current, and consists simply of an electro-magnet having many turns of wire, so that the feeble line-current magnetises it sufficiently to attract a soft-iron " armature," which, when attracted, closes a local circuit containing a battery and the receiving apparatus.

In the Morse code letters, numerals, and signs are represented by combinations of dots and dashes. The first Morse line was laid between Washington and Baltimore in 1844. The wires were placed underground, but this was soon abandoned, and afterwards they were mounted on poles.

Between the years 1840–50 the growth of the electric telegraph was very rapid. The rapidity of its growth necessitated either laying many more lines or the adaptation of those already laid to cope with the large number of messages to be transmitted. It was this need which caused various electricians to devise **Multiplex Telegraphy.** systems of multiplex telegraphy, by which the same line could transmit two or more messages simultaneously. In 1852 Farmer, an American, brought out such a system, though not a very good one. The method at present in use for multiple transmission was first suggested by Gintl, of Vienna, in 1853. It was not, however, until 1872 that a successful system of duplex telegraphy was introduced by one Stearns, of Boston. In duplex telegraphy signals may be simultaneously transmitted at both ends of the line, each end simultaneously receiving what the other transmits. An improvement on Stearns' system was brought out in 1874 by Mr. T. A. Edison. There are two methods of duplex telegraphy: the differential method and the bridge method. In 1874–5 Elisha Gray, an American, designed a system of multiplex telegraphy for the simultaneous transmission of several signals. In principle the system depends on the synchronism of sonorous vibrations propagated by electric currents. The name " harmonic telegraph " has consequently been given to the system. All these multiplex systems are modifications and extensions of the Morse system. Amongst other systems of telegraphy may be mentioned Professor Hughes's printing telegraph, and the autographic telegraphs of Meyer and Caselli, which were brought out in 1881.

As early as 1839 Mr. O'Shaughnessy connected the two banks of the Hooghly river in India by an insulated wire plunged into the stream. In 1840 Wheatstone proposed to connect Dover and Calais by a submarine telegraph cable, but the project was not realised until 1850. After transmitting a few signals this cable broke. A new cable was laid in 1851. The difficulty in submarine telegraphy was in obtaining a covering for the wire both as a protection and as a good insulator. The difficulty of insulation was overcome by the use of gutta-percha,

Submarine Telegraphy.

SECTIONS OF THE SECOND AND THIRD ATLANTIC CABLES.
(*Victoria and Albert Museum.*)

whilst the cables were strengthened by surrounding the gutta-percha covering by a thick layer of tarred hemp, which, in its turn, is covered and protected by galvanised iron wires twisted round the core. The first cable insulated by means of gutta-percha was laid in 1848, across the Hudson river, from Jersey City to New York. During the next few years many submarine cables of increasing lengths were laid, and in 1857 an unsuccessful attempt was made to connect the New World with the Old by an Atlantic cable (p. 182). The next year the cable was laid, but only about four hundred messages were transmitted before it ceased to act. Another trial was made in 1865, when the ship used was the *Great Eastern* (p. 454). After about two-thirds of the distance was run the cable broke. The following year a complete cable was successfully laid, and that of 1865 was picked up, joined, and finished.

The weight of an Atlantic cable is something enormous: that connecting Valentia and America weighs 4,300 tons.

Ordinary telegraphic instruments are not sufficiently sensitive for the feeble currents transmitted to the end of a long submarine cable. In place of the ordinary needle-receiver a Thomson mirror-galvanometer is used. Thomson's galvanometer has, however, the disadvantage that no trace of the message transmitted is left. To remedy this defect Sir William Thomson (Lord Kelvin, pp. 580, 711) invented his siphon recorder, which converts the signals of the mirror-galvanometer into curves drawn on a slip of paper. No one man has done more than Lord Kelvin towards making submarine telegraphy a practical success.

Telephony.   The idea of transmitting sounds by means of electricity dates back to the year 1837, when an American physicist, named Page, observed that when substances are magnetised they emit a sound. De la Rive, Gassiot, and Marrian observed the same phenomenon. Philip Reis was the first to notice that electric currents could impose upon a mass of iron vibrations other than that of the bar itself. In 1860 he invented a telephone based on this principle, by which he managed to transmit both words and music, though in an imperfect manner.

In 1876 Graham Bell, a native of Edinburgh, invented the magneto-electric method of transmitting sounds. In Bell's telephone the voice itself generates the electric currents by causing a diaphragm in the transmitter to vibrate and operate a magneto-electric induction apparatus; these induced currents operate on a similar apparatus in the receiver, which causes a diaphragm in the receiver to vibrate in a similar manner to that in the transmitter. On the same day that Bell patented his telephone Elisha Gray, an American, applied for a patent for a similar instrument. Since Bell invented his instrument the arrangements of the receiver and transmitter have been improved by various physicists, with a view to intensifying the effect in the receiver. Of these improvements the most important is due to Professor Hughes, and is the result of a discovery made by him in 1878, that if a piece of carbon be allowed to rest upon another, and an electric current be passed from one to the other in a circuit containing a Bell telephone receiver, the latter will respond to very minute sounds in the vicinity of the carbons. The arrangement, as invented by Hughes, is called a "microphone." The transmitters generally in use at present contain microphonic arrangements.

The cell which Volta discovered in 1800, and which consisted of plates of zinc and copper dipped into dilute sulphuric acid, was far from being perfect. After sending a current for a short time the strength of the cell diminished owing to the collection of bubbles forming on the plates. To remedy this defect was the aim of physicists for a long time. In 1836 Professor Daniell brought out a battery of constant strength, in which two fluids are used. Many other forms of constant batteries have been devised by using different liquids and different metals. **Generating Electricity.**

In Volta's original form of cell the bubbles of gas forming on the plates not only diminish the effective surface of the plates, but also act as the seat of an opposing electro-motive force, which has been called the electro-motive force of polarisation. In 1803 Ritter suggested that this effect of polarisation should itself be used to drive an electric current. In 1843 Grove constructed a gas-battery to illustrate the operation of polarisation. In 1859 Gaston Planté experimented on many metals to see whether polarisation could be made use of in the storage of electrical energy. He discovered that plates of lead immersed in dilute sulphuric acid produced strong polarisation effects. After passing a current for some time through such a cell, he was able to take large currents from it for a considerable time. This discovery is now extensively used for the storage of electrical energy. Cells formed thus are called "storage cells," or "secondary cells." As compared with primary batteries, they have both a higher electro-motive force and a less internal resistance, so that very large currents can be taken from them. **Secondary Batteries.**

Electricity is now generated in large quantities by means of the "dynamo," the origin of which dates back to Faraday's experiment (p. 225), with a disc rotating between the poles of a permanent horseshoe magnet. In 1832 Pixii, of Paris, replaced the copper disc by an electro-magnet of the horseshoe form, and rotated a permanent magnet opposite it, so that induced currents could be obtained from the coils of the electro-magnet. In this form the induced currents would be "alternating," that is, they would flow first in one direction **Dynamo-Electric Machines.**

through the coils and then in the other. To make the current retain the same direction in the external circuit Pixii devised a "commutator," an arrangement which rectifies an alternating current. Many inventors brought various improvements in these induction machines, but no considerable advance was made till Dr. Werner Siemens, of Berlin, invented in 1856 a particular form for the rotating coils, known as the "Siemens Armature." The magnetic field was still produced by means of a permanent magnet. The next step of importance was due to Wilde, of Manchester, who replaced the permanent field magnet by an electro-magnet which was separately excited by a small permanent magnet machine. The idea of making use of the machine's own currents to magnetise its own field-magnets occurred first to Brett, then to Hjörth, and then to Varley, who patented a machine on this principle in December, 1866. The same idea occurred simultaneously to Wheatstone and Siemens early in the year 1867. In 1870 Gramme, of Paris, developed a method of winding the "armature," which was in the first instance due to an Italian, named Pacinotti. The method consists in winding the armature conductors round an anchor ring of soft iron. This type of armature and one known as the "drum" armature are those now principally made. Many inventors have been at work on the production of dynamo-electric machines, which have been brought to a high state of perfection. Whereas the old type of machine with permanent steel magnets might have an efficiency of 25 or 30 per cent., the most modern dynamos can be built to give efficiencies of over 90 per cent.

Electric Motors. Perhaps one of the most interesting, as well as one which promises to be among the most useful, discoveries of modern times is the capability of reversal of a dynamo-electric machine. Faraday had shown that rotation could be produced by an electric current. A dynamo converts mechanical energy into the energy of an electric current. If a current is sent round the armature of a dynamo at rest, it will cause it to rotate and give out mechanical work, or the dynamo will run as a motor. Where there is a plentiful supply of electricity machines are run as motors for workshop purposes.

It has already been stated that the first to discover the Voltaic arc was Davy (p. 249). Until the year 1844 nothing further was done towards raising this discovery above the experimental stage. In 1844, however, Foucault effected an improvement by substituting for charcoal pencils sawn from the hard carbon which is found encrusting gas-retorts, and in recent years still better forms of pencil have been produced. In 1846 Staite devised an arc-lamp. This lamp, however, was a failure, owing to there being no arrangement for keeping the carbon points at a proper distance apart during the process of combustion. The necessary addition

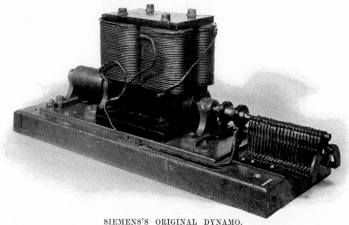

SIEMENS'S ORIGINAL DYNAMO.
(Victoria and Albert Museum, by permission of Messrs. Siemens Bros. & Co.)

was made by the same inventor in 1847, and still further improved by him in 1848. This regulating apparatus was still further improved by Foucault in 1849. As it is difficult to construct arc-lamps of illuminating power less than 400 or 500 candles, their use is confined mostly to the illumination of large open spaces or for lighthouses. Their introduction for purposes of illumination led to the development of dynamo-electric machines. The first occasion when electric light was used for illuminating lighthouses was on December 8th, 1858, when the High Light at the South Foreland was lit by electric currents. In 1863 the electric light was applied to the lighthouses of La Hève, where an illuminating power equal to 475,000 candles is obtained, and the light is seen at the distance of twenty-seven nautical miles.

Electric lighting by incandescence dates from 1841, when

a lamp was constructed by De Moleyns, an Englishman, the light of which was due to the incandescence of a platinum wire. In 1857 De Changy tried thin slips of bone charcoal, enclosed in a vacuum of glass globes. Charcoal was found to be a great improvement on platinum. Edison used a filament

Photo: *J. Thompson, Ventnor.*

ST. CATHERINE'S LIGHTHOUSE, ISLE OF WIGHT.

made of bamboo fibres, carbonised by a special method, and placed in a glass bulb, in which there is a nearly perfect vacuum. These lamps were exhibited with success at the Paris Exhibition of Electricity in 1881, and again at the Crystal Palace Electrical Exhibition of 1882. It now became evident that electric lighting was obtaining a firm footing on a commercial basis, and in consequence Parliament passed, in 1882, the "Act for Facilitating Electric Lighting."

Electro-plating.   Davy's discovery, that an electric current could be used to decompose chemical compounds and deposit metallic elements, led to the large industry of electro-plating and electrotyping. The pioneers of these processes in England on commercial lines are the house of Elkingtons.

THE cotton trade of Great Britain had reached a condition of great prosperity and vast magnitude at the time of the Great Exhibition of 1851. Nevertheless, a want had been felt in preparing for the finer spinning, and this want was supplied by an important machine exhibited at the great show.

H. RIDDELL. The Textile Industries, 1851–1885.

For fine spinnings it is always necessary to select fine, long-fibred cottons, but prior to 1851 English spinners were confined to the very highest grade of material, long, silky, and with fibres particularly even in length. The introduction of the combing machine changed this to a very considerable extent. The machine now selected the fibres, rejecting those of unsuitable length, and laying the remainder parallel to an extent never approached by the card. It is no wonder, therefore, that the new process was eagerly adopted by leading firms in the cotton trade.

This machine was the invention of Joshua Heilmann, and was probably a development of the wool-combing machine of the same inventor. It was exhibited for the first time in England in 1851, and a syndicate of English spinners at once purchased the patent rights for this country, and most wisely entrusted the manufacture to a firm already famed for their cotton-spinning machinery. The price paid for the patent is said to have been £30,000, and there is no doubt it was found a most remunerative speculation. For a time its use was confined to members of the syndicate, but after their wants were supplied it was sold to the trade generally under a heavy royalty. The machine is very ingenious and complicated, though now much simplified and improved by alterations suggested from experience in working. It is not easy to over-estimate the effect of this combing process upon the trade in fine spinnings. In spite of the very great delicacy and perfection of the mechanism of the modern carding engine, and the corresponding improvement in the resulting sliver, the combing process is still indispensable to the production of very fine numbers.

Cotton: The Combing Machine.

There are not many more improvements in spinning machinery to note between 1851 and 1885, but there is one of them which is of such revolutionary importance that it is worthy of a more detailed treatment than it can receive in this page. No modern improvement has had results of

Ring Spinning.

greater magnitude or more wide-reaching importance than the introduction of ring spinning. This beautiful invention, which removes the flier from the spindle and links it directly to the yarn in the form of a small loop of wire, also relieves the thread from the duty of dragging round the bobbin. Thus it becomes possible to drive the spindle at speeds at which fliers could not safely be used, and to limit the drag upon the yarn to that actually needed to wind the thread upon the bobbin. It would have been impossible to take advantage to the fullest extent of these added powers but for the patience, ingenuity, and skill with which different inventors have worked for the improvement of the spindle. Their efforts have been directed towards obtaining a self-contained spindle, which could be driven at the highest speeds with a minimum of vibration, and possessing the power of self-balancing to a considerable extent if loaded unevenly when running. The success which has attended such efforts has been so great that spindles may be seen spinning fine yarns and running at a speed of 13,000 revolutions a minute. Such high speeds of course brought difficulties of different kinds, but these were overcome by a constant succession of improvements, until the process became, at least for warps, a complete and unqualified success.

Ring spinning was invented as early as 1830, was first adopted in America, and there brought to a state of comparative efficiency, but it was not until the year 1866 that it was introduced into the English trade as a practical factor in the production of warps.

Growth of the Cotton Trade. There have been many causes at work cheapening the manufacture of textiles altogether unconnected with improvements in the processes and machinery employed in spinning and weaving. The great improvement in the means of communication with foreign countries has brought large supplies of raw materials to England, and the great increase in demand for such raw material has stimulated production until prices have reached a comparatively low level. The discovery of the aniline colours and the great improvements in dyeing and printing have had much effect. It is impossible to estimate separately the power of each improvement in detail, but it is easy to follow the figures showing the actual increase in the cotton

RING SPINNING MACHINE.

COMBING MACHINE.

(From photographs supplied by Messrs. Dobson & Barlow, Bolton.)

trade. Thus, in 1851 there was consumed in Great Britain a quantity of cotton weighing 659,000,000 lbs. This had increased by 1855 to 840,000,000 lbs., and in 1860 reached 1,084,000,000 lbs. Then came the terrible years of the American Civil War, during which consumption fell to little more than one-third of the figures of 1860. After the conclusion of peace in 1865 the importation of cotton at once began again to increase, reaching in that year to 723,000,000 lbs., and showing in 1870 a consumption of 1,078,000,000 lbs., in 1875 of 1,228,000,000 lbs., while in 1885 the consumption was about 3,500,000 bales, or 1,400,000,000 lbs.

Of course England has not been alone in thus advancing. France, Germany, Russia, the United States, and even far-off Eastern lands, such as India, China, and Japan, have eagerly joined in the race. But in spite of the continued efforts of foreign nations, this country has retained the leading position. The average value of British cotton manufactures exported was, for the five years 1880–84, more than £75,000,000 per annum.

Linen, 1815-1885. There is not the same story of rapid progress to be told regarding the linen trade. The changes have been many and striking, but the trade has not increased with the extraordinary rapidity shown by its competitor. There are many reasons why this should be so. The production of the raw material is much more expensive, and at the same time much more variable both as to quantity, quality, and price. Therefore linen has become rather a luxury than a necessity for the greater part of purchasing humanity. There is also much greater difficulty in working the hard, inelastic linen yarn in the power-loom, and more trouble met with in spinning than in the case of cotton. Considering, then, the disadvantages under which the manufacture is conducted, it is not to be wondered at that it has not progressed " in leaps and bounds."

The process of flax spinning by machinery was already old in 1815, the first introduction dating apparently from 1787, when a mill was erected in Darlington. While this is true, it was but slowly developed; and in 1815 almost all the yarns employed in the manufacture of anything but the coarsest fabrics were hand spun. Hand spinning is not yet quite extinct, and yarns have been spun by female workers in this way which have surpassed in fineness anything which the spinning mill has been able to produce.

The power-loom was very slowly introduced into the linen weaving trade. The advantages were not nearly so obvious as in the case of cotton, and even at the present time hand-looms compete successfully with power-looms in some branches of the trade. It was not until 1821 that power-looms were adopted in the ordinary linen manufacture, while their use in Ireland came very much later. As that country is now the main seat of the linen manufacture, the few figures given later will refer chiefly to the Irish trade.

In 1815 the value of linen cloth sold in the markets of Ulster amounted to about £2,400,000, a statement which shows at once that the trade even then was a large one. Although flax spinning by machinery was introduced into Ireland on a small scale early in the century, it was not until 1829 that the first step was taken in the modern development of the Irish trade. The old York Street cotton mill in Belfast was burned in 1828, and the Messrs. Mulholland at once proceeded to re-erect the building. While the structure was steadily rising the owners had their attention directed to the fact that flax was leaving the port for Leeds, where it was spun into yarn and returned to Ireland to be woven into linen. With true enterprise the opportunity was seized, and the new York Street mill was filled with flax-spinning machinery, and the foundation was laid of a business which has grown to gigantic dimensions in the hands of Messrs. Mulholland's successors. Almost at the same time a mill was built in Castlewellan by Messrs. Murland, who thus share with the Mulholland family the honour of being pioneers in the trade which is now most distinctively Irish. The progress of the spinning industry was so rapid that in 1841 there were in Ireland 250,000 spindles, while in 1851 they reached a total of 390,000. The trade in those early days was exceedingly prosperous and lucrative. The prices of mill-spun yarns at the time of the first Irish mills ran very high. For 40's 13s. 3d. per bundle was paid, and for 60's the price was 11s. 3d. In spite of the inferior skill of the workers and the lower class of the machinery, the trade was profitable. So far, however, was Ireland from possessing the preponderating interest which she now does, that Scotland

Irish
Linen.

in 1850 had already 303,000 spindles, and England actually owned 365,000.

The weaving trade showed a still greater proportion against Ireland in the early days of the industry. In 1850 Ireland only possessed 58 power-looms on linen, while in Scotland there were working 2,529, and in England 1,083.

Up till the year 1851, then, Ireland had taken only a respectable position in the development of the treatment of flax by power, but it must not be forgotten that the great bulk of the fine linens in use were Irish hand-made, and that the trade in such goods was then of exceedingly large proportions, and that the value of the linen manufactures exported from the United Kingdom in 1851 was more than £4,100,000. Many causes combined to bring about this comparatively slow advance. As has already been said, the inelasticity of the flax fibre made it much more troublesome than cotton, so that many difficulties peculiar to the fibre were met with, and required to be overcome. It cannot even yet be said that the methods and machinery of flax spinning have reached the same perfection as in the cotton manufacture, but the advance since 1851 has been very considerable.

The preparing machinery had been generally remodelled, very great attention having been paid, especially to the hackling and roving. In the former of these processes all real development has been from Irish inventors, while in the roving machinery Leeds and Belfast have been constant rivals in construction.

It was in working out his invention of the expanding pulley in the flax roving frame that Combe originated the modern system of rope driving for mill purposes, this exceedingly useful idea dating from 1856.

The general adoption of the hot water process in spinning and the constant call for finer numbers have led to all the modern mills being fitted with machinery of a class suitable for such work, and thus to the comparative disuse in Ireland of dry spinning. Spindles and bobbins are smaller, and speeds are much higher than formerly. The use of ring spinning is, perhaps, the great improvement to which the trade is inclining, but its success has been very partial, and confined to a very few mills.

COTTON PREPARATION IN INDIA.

(From photographs by permission of Messrs. Dobson & Barlow, Bolton.)

Bleaching.   Bleaching and finishing have been greatly cheapened, and
as far as appearance goes, have been brought to a high state
of perfection. It is questionable, however, if any of the
modern methods give a cloth of as natural and durable a
texture as the old process of grass bleaching. Ireland has
more than held her own since 1851 in both spinning and
weaving, increasing rapidly, indeed, the number of the power-
looms in use.

In 1885 the numbers of spindles and power-looms in Great
Britain and Ireland were—

	Spindles.		Looms.
England and Wales	117,000	...	4,061
Scotland	221,000	...	21,626
Ireland	817,000	...	24,300

Thus the linen manufacture was declining in Great Britain,
while it still maintained its strength in Ireland.

Jute.   Jute is not one of the fibres well known to the early textile
workers, but is a very modern importation. The first parcels
were introduced into Dundee in the year 1822, but found no
manufacturer able or willing to make any attempt to work them,
and this particular lot was afterwards sold for mat-making. In
the following year, however, Messrs. Baker and Meldrum received
another consignment, which they succeeded in spinning, and thus
became the pioneers of the great Dundee jute trade.

To the Dundee spinners the difficulty in handling the fibre
was less than to most of the manufacturers in other districts.
They had been trained in working with coarse linen yarns, and
at first adopted with some success similar methods in their treatment of jute. They began by spinning it in the same way as
coarse linen line ; that is, with fibres either in their full length
of six or seven feet, or cut somewhat shorter, and worked upon
the same machines as were used for the production of the coarse
linen yarns. To a very small extent this method is still in use
for special yarns, but it was soon found that, for the fabrics for
which jute was most suitable, it was better to use rather the tow
methods of spinning, and to break all the fibres upon cards,
instead of hackling and spreading as for flax. A rapid advance
upon the machines in use for carding, roving, and spinning was
made by the great machine makers, prompted by the practical
experience of the manufacturers, and the different cards and

roving and spinning frames now employed in the trade are very perfectly adapted for their work, both in design and construction. Of course the experience gained in the flax trade was of immense advantage, and every machine employed has its counterpart, more or less resembling it, in that manufacture. Nevertheless, great changes were necessary, and such firms as Lawson or Fairbairn of Leeds, Combe of Belfast, or Low of Monifieth, among others, did immense service in this respect.

As there was no startling innovation to chronicle, it is sufficient to note results. The trade progressed slowly at first, but afterwards very quickly. Thus in 1829 the import of jute from Calcutta was 364 cwts., in 1830 it amounted to 1,776 cwts., and by 1832 reached 23,852 cwts. In 1833 the import was nearly 26,000 cwts., making a total for the five years of 59,000 cwts., or about 3,000 tons. During the next five years, ending in 1838, the import was nearly 17,000 tons; and twenty-five years later, for the five years ending 1863, the import reached the large figure of 242,000 tons. The progress steadily increased, so that the consumption in Dundee, which during the five years just mentioned had averaged 40,000 tons a year, was in the one year 1883 about 200,000 tons. The trade has thus been the growth of comparatively a short period.

This great achievement may be viewed from another point, as regards the employment given, and the money-value of the production. Thus, in 1862, to go back only to the year of the second great English Exhibition, there were in Scotland twenty-seven factories, with 30,538 spindles and 554 power-looms. These factories employed 5,418 persons. As a means of employment the trade was even then of considerable use, but how much more so in 1885 can be estimated from the fact that in this year there were in Scotland alone 105 factories, with 235,429 spinning-spindles and 10,856 power-looms. The number of persons employed was then 36,269.

Turning now to the money-value of the manufacture, the increase is quite as remarkable. In 1862 the total value of jute manufactures of all kinds exported was about £231,000. In 1870 the value was nearly £2,000,000, in 1885 it was about £3,000,000. While it is not easy to trace the influence of any one cause upon this great addition to Scottish trade, it is still certain that a very large measure is due to the continuous

303

improvement in the machinery and processes employed. Without this improvement the new material could not have been made sufficiently cheap and good to create for it such a market. It must, therefore, be largely credited to such causes, and for this reason the results have been dealt with in some detail.

Worsted and Woollens.   It is not necessary to say much concerning the progress of the worsted and woollen manufactures; not because of any want of importance in the subject, but because it followed, to a large extent, the same course as other manufactures already treated. It is the case, however, that new or changed methods and processes have had rather a large share in the history of these trades, and deserve mention. The woollen trade is a very ancient English possession (Vol. II., p. 742), and had attained a condition of considerable prosperity long before 1815. About this year was introduced the practice of recovering the wool from old rags and waste and reworking it. This "shoddy" trade is often mentioned with contempt, yet it is a source of considerable national wealth, and the material is very valuable when used properly and for suitable cloths. Its extent is very great, about 125,000,000 lbs. of shoddy being made into cloth every year in England alone. This is so large a proportion of the total manufacture of wool, that it is really difficult to imagine the condition of trade if it were withdrawn. An immediate and startling advance in prices would be certain; and such an additional source of supply for raw material is almost indispensable.

There are not many inventions peculiar to the machinery used in the manufacture of wool, but the modifications to suit the fibre are of great importance. The "gills" or travelling bars of comb teeth are common also to the linen trade, while the combing machine is shared with the cotton-spinning in particular. The invention and perfection of this machine marked a great advance, and there are three inventors to whom it is specially due : Lister of Bradford,[1] Donisthorpe of Leicester, and Heilmann of Alsace. Of these, Heilmann seems to have secured priority, but all three have done much to advance the combing process into favour. In spinning, the one machine peculiar to the wool trade is the cap frame, resembling the ring frame in the absence of a flier, but providing no substitute. This machine has been tried in the cotton trade, but abandoned for reasons which have

[1 Created Baron Masham in 1891.]

not the same force in the case of wool. The mule is employed in a modified form, and has proved a most valuable machine for certain yarns, while the ring frame is also very widely adopted.

A very great part of the advance in this trade must be credited to the greatly improved methods of finishing the cloth. The machinery now in use for this purpose is the product of many inventors, and does its work in a manner leaving little to be desired. The dangers and diseases arising from wool sorting and opening have been greatly reduced, although it is, unfortunately, the case that more than necessary suffering is often due to the adoption of imperfect methods and defective arrangements. It is to be hoped that by scientific arrangements and improved methods such suffering and disease may soon become a thing of the past.

The figures exhibiting the modern development of the trade need not be intricate. Going only back to 1860, the consumption of wool in the United Kingdom was about 250,000,000 lb. By 1885 this had risen to about 370,000,000 lb. If the figures relating to employment are considered, they appear equally striking. Fifty years before 1885 there were employed in wool manufactures of Great Britain about 80,000 persons, while in the latter year the number so employed was about 265,000.[1] In the two years thus contrasted the power-looms in use in the trade in woollen and worsted fabric amounted to nearly 5,000 in 1835, and about 140,000 in 1885.

[1 The total number of persons—men, women, and children—employed in the textile trades in the census years is given as follows in the Fiscal Blue Book (Cd. 1761, pp. 363–364), published in 1903, and embodying the results of the inquiry into our fiscal system in consequence of Mr. Chamberlain's advocacy of tariff reform :—

	Cotton.	Lace.	Woollen and Worsted.	Linen.	Silk.
1861	492,196	54,617	230,029	22,718	116,320
1871	508,715	49,370	246,645	18,680	82,963
1881	551,746	44,144	240,006	12,871	64,835
1891	605,755	34,948	258,356	8,531	52,027
1901	582,119	36,439	236,106	4,956	39,035

In the cotton and woollen trades the decline between 1891 and 1901 appears to be chiefly due to the increased saving of labour by machinery, as the cotton used does not show a corresponding decline, and the wool increases (*ibid.* p. 367, *seq.*).

	Cotton. (million cwt.)	Wool. (million lb.)
Estimated quantity used 1891	14·9	487
,, ,, ,, 1901	14·7	541].

Silk.   It is unfortunately the fact that the silk trade of this country has not shown the expansion marking the other textile industries. To whatever reason this may be due, it is, surely, a matter for

SILK-THROWING MACHINE.
(*Victoria and Albert Museum.*)

regret.   There seems to be no doubt that fashion runs more to fabrics produced by French looms, and that the Continental manufacturers have really attained better results from their trading than have been reached in England.   There also seems to be much reason to believe that better art education and more perfect technical training may place this country abreast of its Continental rivals.   At the same time, it must be admitted that the backward condition of the silk trade in Great Britain is partly due to the very success of the other textile industries attracting energy and capital which would otherwise have tended to develop the manufacture.

RINDERPEST, which had made its first appearance in 1865 (p. 488), was raging throughout the United Kingdom in 1866. The Royal Commission appointed to consider the subject reported in May, and the "stamping-out" policy was recommended. This was adopted, and before the end of 1867 the disease was exterminated. At the same time pleuro-pneumonia and foot-and-mouth disease, which had been prevalent and unchecked—the former since 1840, and the latter since 1839—were nearly got rid of for a time by the cattle-plague regulations. In 1869 an Act was passed in relation to all the principal infectious diseases of farm stock regulating imports to some extent; but it was many years before sufficiently stringent measures were passed to rid the country of foot-and-mouth disease and pleuro-pneumonia. Cattle plague again visited the country in 1872, and a third time in 1877; but on both occasions the prudent regulations adopted suppressed the malady in a few months. At the opening of the period now under review there was a partial recovery in the prices of corn, wheat in 1866 averaging 49s. 11d. a quarter, barley 37s. 5d., and oats 24s. 7d. A somewhat deficient harvest, and war on the continent of Europe, conduced to this recovery, which made the prices of wheat and barley about 8s. higher than they were in the preceding year. A very bad harvest in 1867 sent wheat up to 64s. 5d. a quarter, barley to 40s., and oats to 26s.; but after 1868, which was one of the best corn years ever known, prices were lower again, an excellent harvest being gathered in 1870. The Franco-German War sent prices up in the latter part of 1870 and in 1871, and for the four years ending with 1874 wheat was nearer 60s. than 50s. a quarter. From this time, except for a recovery in 1877, due to the Russo-Turkish War, the prices of corn, and of wheat especially, were lower than they had been except on very rare occasions in the times of Protection. Up to 1874 the period of prosperity referred to in a preceding section may be said to have prevailed, with only one considerable interruption. Meat, wool, and dairy produce, as

W. E. BEAR. Agriculture.

Foreign Competition.

well as corn, sold well as a rule, the animal products having kept up in price when corn declined temporarily in value.

By this time foreign competition had begun to tell somewhat severely. Previous to the cereal year 1873–4, the net imports of wheat (including flour) had only once been as much as ten million quarters; but in that year they were over twelve millions, and with some fluctuations they continued to advance. Imports of other kinds of corn together also increased greatly; the total of 1874 being nearly 50 per cent. greater than that of 1866, while a few years later it was 100 per cent. greater than it had been in the 'sixties. No serious advance in the receipts of foreign live stock took place until after 1874; but the total quantity of dead meat of all kinds, never much over 1,000,000 cwt. in the 'sixties, was over 3,500,000 cwt. in 1874, rising steadily till it approached 7,000,000 cwt. in 1879, and reached the maximum for the period under review in 1880, when it was 7,566,681 cwt. After that year there was a decline, not fully recovered till after 1885. Imports of butter and cheese, too, began to increase considerably in 1873, and both were doubled between 1866 and 1885. During the same period the imports of wool were doubled, and the price was reduced 60 per cent. These statements will partially explain the decline in agricultural prosperity which set in after 1874. It is necessary to explain, however, that as live stock imports did not increase out of proportion to the demands of consumers, and much of the dead meat was such as was consumed almost exclusively by people who could not afford to buy home produce, the price of British meat kept up well until nearly the end of the period; also, that the receipts of foreign butter were not in excess of the demands of a growing population, so that prices were maintained at a fairly high level. Indeed, it was not till 1885 that the values of meat and butter showed a decline from the average prices of a long series of preceding years. Cheese dropped in price after 1874, but only once to a decidedly low level before 1885.

Agricultural Depression.

From the preceding remarks it will be understood that, so far as the depression, which began mildly in 1875 and afterwards became severe, was due to low prices, it was, up to 1884, mainly the prices of corn and wool which were accountable. But there was a series of bad seasons in the 'seventies, the yield of wheat having been below the average in seven

years out of the ten. The acute stage was reached in 1879,
known as the "black year," when the harvest was the worst of
any in the second half of the century, if not in the whole of
it. The yield of wheat was estimated at only 15½ bushels an
acre, or not much over half an average, and other corn was
correspondingly deficient. Moreover, the grain was half spoilt
by a wet harvest. Instead of advancing, prices fell, in consequence of heavy imports. America had a great crop, and
shipped to us a much greater quantity of wheat than in any
previous year. Altogether in 1879–80 we imported in wheat
and flour the equivalent of nearly 16,500,000 quarters of
wheat, or 2,000,000 more than we had ever before received
in twelve months. In 1879, too, our markets were glutted with
American cheese, which brought the value down to a price
low beyond record for one season. Again, a disastrous attack
of sheep-rot carried off large numbers of animals, while
pleuro-pneumonia and foot-and-mouth disease caused further
losses. Thus all classes of agriculturists suffered severely,
and thousands of farmers were nearly ruined. Rents, which
had been constantly rising since 1855, had reached their
maximum, and many tenants were unable to pay their
landlords, some of whom granted temporary remissions. The
annual value of "lands" (including tithes) had risen from
£41,117,626 in England and £5,872,714 in Scotland in 1855–6
to £51,798,950 in the former country and £7,769,303 in the
latter for 1879–80. For Great Britain the advance was over
£12,500,000 sterling, or nearly 27 per cent. As the depression
lasted, rents, though not at first commonly, fell. In too many
cases they were kept up, only temporary remissions being
allowed in specially bad years, until many old tenants were
ruined, and then necessarily reduced to new tenants; while
in some cases, where leases were current, no reduction at all
was made. But, when convinced that the depression was
permanent, the great majority of landlords met their tenants
fairly, and the annual value of agricultural land in Great Britain,
including tithes, fell from £59,568,253 in 1879–80 to £53,314,144
in 1884–5. Out of this decline of about £6,250,000 sterling,
less than half a million was due to reductions of rent in
Scotland. The decline did not end with the period under
notice, but has gone on until the present time. As indicated

by the figures just given, depression was much less severely felt in Scotland than in England, the farmers of the former country being less dependent upon corn for their livelihood than those of the latter, and scarcely at all upon wheat. This remark also applies to Ireland. For many years, too, the grazing and dairying districts of England suffered comparatively little; but all classes of farmers in all parts of the kingdom shared to some extent in the disaster sooner or later.

Its Results.   A full account of the changes produced by the depression in agriculture would carry us far beyond the period under notice. The most remarkable are the decrease in the area of land under corn—wheat especially, and the increase in the acreage of pasture. Up to 1859 the area of wheat in the United Kingdom had not fallen below 4,000,000 acres, and in 1874 it was still as much as 3,821,655 acres. After that season, however, there was an almost constant decline, the extent of land under wheat having fallen to 2,549,335 acres by 1885, to fall 1,000,000 acres more in the next decade.[1] Between 1866 and 1885 all corn crops together fell off in area by 1,444,641 acres. In the same time the area of permanent pasture in the kingdom had been extended by nearly 5,000,000 acres, as closely as can be ascertained. The Irish statistics of the earlier year did not distinguish between permanent and temporary pasture; but in the two together, including clover, there was an increase of about 6,000,000 acres in the United Kingdom, half being derived from an addition to the total cultivated area. In the same period, again, cattle increased from 8,569,693 to 10,868,760; but it is doubtful whether sheep or pigs had increased or diminished. The year 1866 was the first in which the Agricultural Returns were collected, and they were far from perfect.

The Rural Exodus.   The decrease of arable land and the poverty of the farmers greatly reduced the number of persons employed on the land, and the migration of people from the rural districts to the towns became excessive. Some time before depression commenced, the employment of women and children in agriculture had been steadily falling off. The women gave up

[1 In 1900 the wheat acreage was 1,901,038. That of all corn crops together had declined since 1885 by 1,307,023 acres. Cattle numbered 11,455,009.]

the work when their husbands earned enough to do without
their help as wage-earners, and school regulations interfered
with the employment of young children.   Between 1871 and
1881 the number of males of all ages employed on the land
in England and Wales in various capacities fell from 1,200,920
to 1,137,810, showing a decrease of 63,110, or 5·3 per cent.;
but about half the decrease consisted of boys under fifteen
years of age.   A much greater decrease of labourers over

THE BAD SEASON, 1879.

(Reproduced by special permission of the Proprietors of " Punch.")

fifteen took place after 1881; in the next decade the decrease
was 82,499, or 7·7 per cent.[1]   In Scotland also there was a
decrease, but not as great in proportion.   There was no fall in
the rates of wages up to 1885.

So long as farming paid fairly, the improvement in agriculture, which had been active for many years up to 1865,
continued its progress, and it was not till after 1879 that any
noticeable check took place.   But as the resources of landlords

[1] In 1901 there was a considerable further decrease. The total number of
persons employed in agriculture in England and Wales in 1891 was 1,099,592;
in 1901, 988,340. The number of women employed, however, increased considerably in the decade.]

and tenants became reduced, economy in expenditure upon the land was inevitable. Such expensive work as land-draining was almost entirely given up, and a large area of land formerly yielding good crops of corn reverted to its early condition of rough pasture, not a little having been left to "lay itself down" with indigenous grasses and weeds.

Dairying.   There never was a time in the history of British agriculture in which so much progress was made in the dairy industry as during the period under notice and subsequently. Shortly after it began, Mr. H. M. Jenkins, Mr. J. C. Morton, Dr. Voelcker, Mr. (afterwards Professor) Sheldon, and a few others, made successful efforts to create an interest in the improvement of dairying, especially by describing the advances made in certain foreign countries; and at about the same time, or later, Professor Long, Lord Vernon, and Dr. Bond, in England, and Canon Bagot and Professor Carroll, in Ireland (to name only a few out of many), became active advocates of a movement in favour of the application of science in dairy practice. One result was the formation, in 1866, of the British Dairy Farmers' Association, which has done a great deal, by holding shows and conferences, and by establishing a Dairy Institute at Aylesbury, to improve the industry which it represents. The Bath and West of England Society some time afterwards started a travelling dairy school, and the example was followed by other bodies. The great multiplication of dairy schools, however, was reserved for a later period. Professor Sheldon, assisted by authorities in several countries, brought out his great work, "Dairy Farming," shortly after the first Dairy Show of 1877 was held, and that book did much to enlighten the backward dairy farmers of the United Kingdom. At that time the use of a thermometer in an English farm dairy was a great rarity. Butter was churned into a lump and made up by hand, as a rule, and was seldom twice alike in quality from the same dairy. A great improvement has since taken place, helped in no small degree by the enterprise of makers of dairy utensils, implements, and other appliances, some of which will be mentioned in connection with agricultural implements. The first cheese factory in England was established in 1871. A few others were afterwards started, but the system did not find much favour. Butter factories, or creameries as they are usually termed, were of later introduction, and they too have multiplied but slowly, except in Ireland, where they became somewhat numerous after the end of the period with which this section is concerned.[1]

Of the course of improvement in agricultural implements and machinery during the period under review only a general notice can be attempted. With respect to steam cultivation, it Imple-
ments and
Machines.

THE LONGFORD CHEESE FACTORY, DERBYSHIRE.
(*Professor Sheldon:* "*Dairy Farming,*" 1881.)

will suffice to state that early in the period Fowler's double-engine ploughing and cultivating system came into use, and subsequently held its ground, with improvements, against all rivals. Towards the end of the period, or a little later, Darby's steam digger was introduced, and other similar implements followed it. By 1869, when the Manchester field trials were held, no fewer than 84 reaping-machines were selected by the judges for testing, and as many as 52 competed, including those of

[1 Their development was afterwards encouraged by an unofficial body called the "Recess Committee" (1895), presided over by Mr. (now Sir) Horace Plunkett, M.P., whence was developed the Irish Board of Agriculture and Technical Education.]

delivery in sheaf bundles (not tied), swath delivery, one-horse manual delivery, and two-horse manual delivery machines. The winners of prizes in the several classes were Hornsby, Samuelson, Bamlett, Burgess and Key, and Cuthbert, and others were commended. The mowing-machines tried numbered 23, Hornsby, W. A. Wood, Burgess and Key, and Samuelson (for a combined mower and reaper) being the winners. About 1870, the self-binding reaper was brought out in the United States by McCormick, Wood, and others, wire first and string or straw afterwards being used for binding the sheaves. This wonderful labour-saving machine was shortly afterwards introduced to this country, but was not greatly used until string took the place of wire for binding, because of the danger to stock of possibly swallowing wire in the chaff made from the straw. Horse-rakes, hay-making machines,

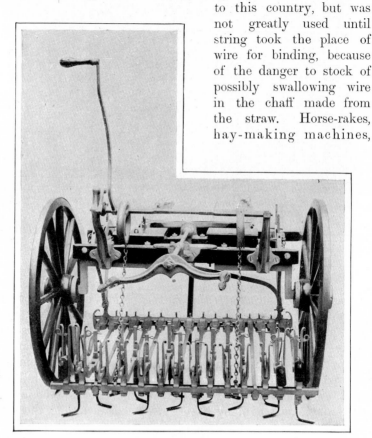

MODEL OF A LEVER HORSE-HOE IN 1851.
(Victoria and Albert Museum, by permission of Messrs. R. Garrett & Sons.)

CLOD CRUSHER, 1845.
(Victoria and Albert Museum, by permission of Messrs. R. Garrett & Sons.)

drills, thrashing-machines, straw-elevators, traction and stationary engines, ploughs, harrows, and all other kinds of
implements and machines were also greatly improved. In
1877, the centrifugal cream-separator, a machine which has
revolutionised dairying, was invented by Lefeldt; but it was
only the embryo of the separator as improved, and indeed
transformed, by Laval and other makers. At about the same
time the butter-worker was introduced in this country. Many
other new and improved dairy implements and utensils were
brought into use later on, including wonderfully improved
churns, butter-driers, milk-testers, refrigerators, heaters, and
cheese-making apparatus.

A number of elementary books on science in relation to **Science**
agriculture, which it is not necessary to specify, came out **and**
during the period, and Lawes and Gilbert continued to **Education.**
publish records of their valuable and diversified experiments
at Rothamsted (p. 483). Field experiments were commenced
by the Royal Agricultural Society on a trial farm at
Woburn, granted by the Duke of Bedford in 1877, and
feeding experiments followed. As to educational establishments, a grant was given by the Government in 1868 to the
Chair of Agriculture at the University of Edinburgh. In

1869, the Senior Examinations of the Royal Agricultural Society were started, leading to the teaching of agriculture in some of the middle-class schools. In 1874, the Aspatria Agricultural School was founded in order "to carry out with greater efficiency the improved ideas of practical and scientific farming." In the following year, the Science and Art Department added the Principles of Agriculture to the subjects for which grants were made to elementary schools, and afterwards provided courses of lectures on the subject, mainly for teachers in those schools. The Downton College of Agriculture, a private venture, was established in 1880 by Professor Wrightson, assisted by Professor Fream. A much greater multiplication of agricultural schools and classes was reserved for a later period.

Legislation. Space is not available for tracing the history of agricultural legislation. It may be mentioned, however, that a permissive Agricultural Holdings Act, providing for compensation for tenants' improvements, was passed in 1875, and proved abortive; and that a second Act, under the same name, was passed in 1883, which did more good indirectly than directly (pp. 528, 537). As long ago as 1848 Mr. Pusey endeavoured to get some such measure through the House of Commons, but in vain. In Ireland some important measures, securing to tenants their improvements, and enabling them to purchase their holdings on easy terms, were passed (pp. 523, 884), though the latter arrangement was not made extensively operative until 1891 and, still further, in 1903.

Agricultural depression was only in its childhood in 1885, and although our period ended with rents and prices falling, and gloomy prospects for the owners and occupiers of the soil, fate had in store for them many years of trials more severe than any which, up to that time, they had been called upon to endure.

J. E. SYMES. The Economic Conditions. THE prosperity which marked the closing years of the period dealt with in the last chapter was interrupted by the failure of Overend, Gurney and Co., and of other firms, in the spring of 1866. The panic of that year bore a general resemblance to those of 1847 and 1857, already described (pp. 489, 497).

In each case the crisis was due to over-speculation, and the sinking of vast sums of money in enterprises that would never pay, or only begin to pay after the lapse of years. The firms that had been too reckless in advancing money for such schemes were, in 1866, the first to suffer. The Joint Stock Discount Company failed in February; Barnard's Bank in March. Then began a rapid contraction of credit, and a drain of gold from the Bank of England. The directors tried to check this by raising the rate of discount to seven per cent. (May 3rd), to eight per cent. (May 8th), and then to nine per cent. (May 9th). Meanwhile the Mid-Wales Railway Company had failed, and among their creditors was the great firm, Overend, Gurney and Co. The Court of Common Pleas decided on May 9th that a railway company had no right to incur debts in the way in which not only the Mid-Wales, but many other railway companies, had incurred them towards this same firm. On the following day Overend, Gurney and Co. stopped payment, with liabilities exceeding £10,000,000. This was the greatest failure that had ever taken place in the City. The panic that followed was of unparalleled intensity, but the Government once more suspended the Bank Act. The directors raised their rate to ten per cent., and began lending vigorously to individuals and firms that could offer good security. £12,225,000 was thus advanced in eight days, and, although there were many failures and heavy losses, the panic very soon subsided. Once more the air was cleared by the storm. Weak and rotten firms had been swept away; but strong ones held their ground, and credit soon revived. So far the events of 1866 followed a somewhat similar course to those of 1847 and 1857. There are, however, two exceptional features to be noticed. Hitherto the crises had taken place at intervals of rather more than ten years. In this case the interval was less than nine years. The speedier recurrence was probably largely due to the increased facilities for joint-stock trading (pp. 498, 556), and the consequent encouragement to over-speculation and undue giving of credit. A more interesting fact is that the panic of 1866 is the last really extensive panic that England has had. Since then there have, of course, been periods of failure and commercial disaster, but there has been nothing corresponding

to the great decennial panics of 1826 to 1866, which at one
time seemed to be almost inevitable incidents of the complicated
modern mechanism of trade and finance, largely based upon
credit. This happy cessation of panics is largely to be
attributed to increased knowledge and prudence, though it
is also probable that the fall of prices from about 1873
has greatly tended to check the excessive speculation which
invariably precedes one of these great panics.[1]

Friendly Societies. From 1867 the material prosperity of England increased
by leaps and bounds, and in particular the condition of the
working classes steadily improved. Not only were they
earning better wages, but they were steadily building up their
own organisations, by means of which the hardships of their
lot were mitigated. This will be a convenient place to refer
to the growth of the friendly societies, both in this period
and in earlier times. Friendly societies may be defined as
the Mutual Assurance Societies of the Poor, and in many
respects they overlap trade unions, so far as the latter are
also benefit societies. Some important distinctions must,
however, be noted. A friendly society is hardly ever limited
to the members of a single trade. It has nothing to do
with strikes. It cannot, as a rule, give " out-of-work "
benefit, since it has no means of determining whether a
member is out of work through his own fault. It generally
makes some provision for social entertainment, and frequently
for religious services. Some of the existing friendly societies
date back to the very beginning of the eighteenth century,
and an Act of 1793 seems to imply that many such societies
were then in existence. The Act sought to encourage them,
especially by exempting members from removal under the
old Poor Law. This seems to have greatly stimulated the
movement. Within a few years, in Middlesex alone, more
than a thousand societies were enrolled. The " goodfellow-
ship " element was prominent in most of these. The scale of
payment usually under-estimated the risks ; and though in
many cases members abstained from claiming benefits to

[1 A great panic, however, was nearly brought about in 1890 by the failure of
Messrs. Baring Brothers & Co., consequent on a political and economic crisis in
Argentina, and was only averted by the steps taken by the London banks, on the
initiative of the Governor of the Bank of England, Mr. Lidderdale, to guarantee
payment of the liabilities of the firm, before the failure became known.]

which they were entitled, most of the societies had to be
wound up. The Act of 1819 tried to remedy this by requiring
rules and tables to be submitted to justices, who were to
consult two actuaries or other competent advisers before
authorising a society. The Act, however, was so badly
administered that there was very little improvement till 1829,
when Mr. J. Tidd Pratt was appointed as an official to whom
all societies must submit their rules. His authority was slight,
but he did much by moral influence to get sound principles
adopted. A series of further Acts in 1834, 1846, 1850, and
1855 modified their legal status. The last of these was the
most lenient, and under it 21,875 societies were formed. A
Royal Commission, which sat from 1870 to 1874, published very
full information on the subject. It was found that the largest
societies consisted of a number of almost independent branches,
affiliated to a central body. Thus, the Manchester Unity had
in 1878 526,802 members, and funds amounting to £4,325,000.
The Ancient Order of Foresters had 521,416 members, and
£2,497,000. The other kinds of friendly societies are divided
by the Commissioners into twelve distinct classes. Some
are confined to particular counties, some to particular towns,
some to women, and some to particular trades. Some divide
their balance every year, and start afresh ; some combine the
functions of a savings bank with other friendly society
objects. The most successful with the poorest and most
ignorant classes were the collecting societies, so called because
the subscriptions were called for by agents. In many of these
a very undue share of the contributions found its way into
the pockets of the officials. Yet the system made way among
those who were too lazy or unintelligent to join the other
kinds of societies. The Commissioners found two hundred and
fifty-nine of these "collecting societies" with over two million
members, and funds amounting to nearly £700,000. The Act
of 1875 was founded on the report of the Commission, and
extended the means of ascertaining and remedying fraud or
mismanagement. Every society was obliged to send to the
Registrar an annual balance-sheet, and also a quinquennial
return of its assets, liabilities, sickness, and mortality. A
reasonable proportion of the members were to have power
to insist on a general meeting, or an official inspection, and

the Registrar might insist on the dissolution of a society. There were also various provisions to check abuses in " collecting societies," and in relation to infant insurance. These last need further extension, but with all their defects the societies have conferred immense benefits on the working classes, who have built them up by their own energy.

**Co-opera-
tion.** The principles of the co-operative stores (p. 495) continued to be very successfully applied. Stores increased greatly, both in numbers and size. They ceased to be mere local ventures. They began to hold annual congresses. Moreover, the co-operators successfully extended their functions from retail to wholesale transactions. The following figures show the rapid progress of the Co-operative Wholesale :—

Year.			Business.			Profits.
1865	...	...	£120,755	...	...	£1,859
1870	...	...	£653,608	...	...	£6,818
1875	...	...	£2,103,226	...	...	£23,816
1880	...	...	£3,339,681	...	...	£42,000
1885	...	...	£4,793,151	...	...	£77,630
[1902	...	...	£18,397,559	...	...	£336,369]

Meanwhile the number of co-operative societies had grown to 1,441, containing 850,659 members, and doing business to the amount of £31,305,910; but the success of the movement continued to be mainly confined to the distributive department. The societies that undertook productive work, such as manufacturing, continued to be comparatively few and small, and only moderately successful, except some few, which were indeed called co-operative, but where the principle of dividing profits among employees as such hardly existed, or did not exist at all.

**Trade
Unions.** From about 1863 the number of strikes and lock-outs, and the formation of employers' associations to fight the trade unions, had called much attention to the trade disputes. Apprehension was increased by an outrage at Sheffield (June, 1866).[1] It was vainly pointed out that the connection of any trade union with the outrage was not proved, and that

[1 The Sheffield outrages, planned and paid for by one Broadhead, the secretary of the Saw-Grinders' Union, were revealed by him and other participants to the Special Commission of 1867, under an indemnity. They had no connection with the general body of Trade Unionists.]

in any case the whole movement could not be regarded as responsible.

Even the Courts of Law seem to have been influenced by the general feeling. At any rate they now decided that trade unions were so far " in restraint of trade " as to be practically illegal associations, which the law would not protect from fraud on the part of their own officials. This was a serious matter. Positivists like Frederic Harrison, Henry Crompton, and E. S. Beesly, and Christian Socialists like Thomas Hughes exerted themselves to remove the prejudices of their own class. A Royal Commission was appointed, but the case of the unions proved so strong that its report was on the whole rather in their favour. The Commission advised that legal protection should be extended to those societies that did not insist upon certain restrictions (such as limitation of apprentices, prohibition of piece-payment, etc.). The minority maintained that nothing done by a *workman* ought to be illegal, unless it would also be illegal for other persons to act in a similar way, and that nothing done by a *society* should be illegal. unless it would also be illegal if done by an individual. The Reform Act of 1867 gave the franchise to a large number of trade unionists, and their opponents did not attempt any restrictive legislation. In 1869 Messrs. A. J. Mundella and Thomas Hughes introduced a Bill representing the trade union views. This was withdrawn on an undertaking from the Government to deal with the subject speedily, and meanwhile to pass a provisional measure for the protection of trade union funds.

This was actually done, but the Act of 1871 was accompanied by a Criminal Law Amendment Act, which affixed severe penalties to intimidation and coercion, without in any way defining these words. The unionists and their friends knew that much in their policy was coercive, and might even be said to be intimidatory, even though they considered it reasonable, and thought that it should be legal. The Liberal Government refused, however, to go further, and many trade unionists revenged themselves by abstention from the polls, or by running Labour candidates at the General Election of 1874. This policy was successful. The new Conservative Parliament repealed the Criminal Law Amendment Act of 1871, and expressly declared peaceful picketing to be permissible (1875 and 1876). (Cf. p. 830.)

Labour Legislation of 1871.

Federation.   Meanwhile the growth of the Miners' and of the Cotton Operatives' federations had been so remarkable as to practically make the North of England the headquarters of trade unionism. The chief part in the building up of the Miners' National Union was taken by Alexander Macdonald, a Scottish pit-boy, who attended Glasgow University in the intervals of his work. The Union was effectively established by the year 1863. Macdonald and his colleague, Thomas Burt, were elected to Parliament as the first two " Labour " members in 1874. The great Cotton Operatives' Organisation devoted itself chiefly to the shortening of the hours of labour and to the drawing up of elaborate " lists "— detailed remuneration tables of every process, and piece-work in their complicated industry. These two great federations and the Society of Amalgamated Engineers were pursuing, on the whole, a peaceful policy, developing the " benefit " side of trade unionism and organising the workers, but using their influence against strikes, except in extreme cases. This line tended to alienate

Strike of 1871.   some of the more active spirits, and in 1871 the public were surprised by a great strike, in which unionists and non-unionists combined. This was the five months' strike of men engaged in the engineering trades at Newcastle for a " Nine Hours Day." It was conducted so judiciously that even the *Times* supported the men. Funds poured in from all parts of the country, and ultimately the employers accepted fifty-four hours a week as the recognised time limit.

Prosperity, 1872-74   This victory, combined with the changed state of public opinion, and the good trade of the years 1872, 1873, and 1874, led to a great increase in both the number and the strength of unions. The agricultural labourers, instigated by Joseph Arch and others, formed extensive unions. The old societies prospered and multiplied. In days of rapidly rising prices the unionists were disposed to accept the employers' principle that " wages should follow prices." Hopes were widely entertained that by means of boards of conciliation, sliding scales, division of profits, and such devices, the long war between capital and labour would be brought to an end; and even when, in 1874,

Depression, 1875-1880.   there was a general contraction of demand, especially in the great coal and iron industries, the men at first peaceably submitted to serious reductions in their wages. But things went from bad to worse. The employers demanded more and more

Photo: Bassano, Old Bond St., W.

THE RT. HON. A. J. MUNDELLA, M.P.

Photo: Braconnier. Clerkenwell Close, E.C.

J. M. LUDLOW.

Photo: Braconnier, Clerkenwell Close, E.C.

THOMAS HUGHES, M.P.

Photo: Bassano, Old Bond St., W.

HENRY FAWCETT, M.P.

SOME SYMPATHISERS WITH LABOUR.

reductions of wages and longer hours of work. The high hopes of 1874 were shattered. Strike followed upon strike; but the men were in almost every case defeated. In the three years 1878, 1879, and 1880 the Amalgamated Engineers paid out £287,596 in "out-of-work" relief. The Agricultural Unions, and hundreds of small societies, ceased to exist; and in 1881 the number of members of unions represented at the annual Congress had sunk to one-third of what it had been in 1874.

The New Unionism.
    It was natural that the depressed trade of 1875–80 should lead to wide difference of opinion among workmen as to the wisdom and adequacy of the policy hitherto pursued by the unions. The movement known as the "New Unionism" was the outcome of some of these divergences; and although it mainly belongs to the years subsequent to 1885, its beginnings were plainly discernible by the close of our period. Broadly speaking, the chief distinctions between the old and the new unionism are, firstly, that the "old" was mainly individualistic. It said to the State, "Hands off. Leave us freedom to combine and to make use of the peaceful pressure of public or class opinion. Only protect our property and our rights to freedom of contract, and we ask nothing more from you." The New Unionists, on the other hand, were frankly Socialistic. They wanted to obtain an eight-hour day by legislation, and municipal organisation of workshops. They looked forward to the nationalisation of land, and even of the instruments of production. Again, the old unions aimed mainly at a policy of peace. Only a small proportion, probably less than an eighth part, of their funds went to support strikes, and since their legal position has been secured they have steadily denounced violence. The new unionists, on the contrary, looked upon trade unions as essentially fighting machines. They formed societies in which no provision was made for superannuation, sickness, or funerals, and they showed some tendency to apologise for violence and for intimidation. The fact that they tried to raise the condition of a poorer and more oppressed class will partly explain the difference. The old trade unionism has been called "the aristocracy of labour." The new movement tried to organise and elevate the unskilled labourers, the sweated, and all the other victims of modern industrialism.

Photo: London Trades Council.

GEORGE ODGER.

Photo: Lock & Whitfield, Regent St., W.

ALEXANDER MACDONALD, M.P.

Photo: Pitt & Son, Bethnal Green Road.

GEORGE HOWELL, M.P.

Photo: The London Stereoscopic Co.

THOMAS BURT, M.P.

SOME LABOUR LEADERS.

**Labour
Disputes.**

Little space can be spared here to describe the attempts that have been made to mitigate the evils of the conflicts between employers and employed by schemes of arbitration and conciliation. The first moderately successful Board of Conciliation was started in the Nottingham hosiery trade as early as the year 1860. Others were soon afterwards founded in the lace, iron, coal, and other industries. They undoubtedly prevented many conflicts, and brought about a better mutual understanding between the two parties, whose interests are in some respects identical and in some respects opposed. Arbitration, again, has often been resorted to with advantage, and the historian of the future may be able to record that some combination of the two methods has reduced industrial warfare to a *minimum.* The highest authority on the subject wrote, in 1875 :

" Industrial conciliation is an economical success. This is a mere truism, so far as the putting a stop to strikes or lock-outs is concerned. Industry, instead of being subject to constant interruptions, is continuous. The waste and the misery consequent on stoppage, even for a short time, are avoided."

But the hopes of 1875 were damped by the experience of the following years, or at least were relegated to the future. The same must be said of the various schemes of sliding scales and profit-sharing, which are, indeed, only forms of conciliation.

**Labour
Laws,
1874-1878.**

We turn now to speak of various statutes passed between the years 1874 and 1880, which directly affected the interests of the labouring classes, but which we have not yet had occasion to speak of. These laws may conveniently be divided into two classes : (1) those which directly affected the conditions of labour, such as the Factory Act of 1874, the Merchant Shipping Act of 1876, and the Employers' Liability Act of 1880 ; and (2) those which affected the life of the working classes, and, therefore, *indirectly* their labour, such as the Dwellings Act of 1875, the Alkali Act of 1874, and the Pollution of Rivers Act of 1876. We will deal with these briefly in the above order.

**Factory
Act, 1874.**

An Act of 1874 still further reduced the hours of labour for women and children in factories, and thereby indirectly brought the labour of many adult males down to the same *maximum,* viz. fifty-six hours a week. In support of this Bill it was contended with much force that the growing complexity of machinery and other changes were adding to the strain on factory workers. On the other side there were the usual prophecies about foreign competition. The Bill happened to be passed just towards the end of a period of exceptional good trade; and the contraction of 1875 and the following years might have been plausibly used as a proof that the prophecies of 1874 were being fulfilled. It is a striking proof of the triumph of the more Socialistic view, that

Photo: Russell, Baker St., W.
SAMUEL PLIMSOLL, M.P.

even in the worst time there was no perceptible reaction against the Factory Laws. It was rightly felt that they strengthened rather than weakened us in the world's rivalry.

The Merchant Shipping Act of 1876 was less fortunate. It attempted to deal with very real evils. The overloading of ships and the sending them to sea in bad repair had roused great indignation, and Mr. Plimsoll's efforts induced the Government to interfere. By the Act of 1876 every owner was required to mark the load-line on his vessel, and the Board of Trade was to have extended powers and duties of supervision. It seems doubtful, however, whether the Bill did any good. Load-lines were marked so as to allow unreasonable loads, and this tempted

Merchant Shipping Act, 1876.

captains, in foreign ports, to load up to the line. The other provisions of the Bill tended to shift responsibility from owners on to the Board of Trade ; and it seems that the evils both of overloading and of unseaworthiness were aggravated by this well-meant attempt to check them.

Employers' Liability Act, 1880. The Employers' Liability Act of 1880 made employers liable in cases of accident when they had not been guilty of any personal negligence. It sufficed to prove negligence in any one to whom the employer had delegated his authority.

Other Laws. A few further instances of the tendency of legislation to extend the sphere of State action may be here introduced. The Artisans' Dwellings Act of 1875 aimed at empowering ratepayers to provide better dwellings for the working classes. This Act was so hedged in with precautions that little came of it. The whole risk and expense was to fall on the rates. Owners were to be compensated at market price, and this was to be largely based on the income hitherto derived from dwellings so bad as to call for demolition. In other words, the cost would be prohibitive. The Alkali Act of 1874 and the Pollution of Rivers Act of 1876 may be included in the same group. The former aimed at restricting the injuries to health and vegetation caused by alkali works. It took the form of testing smoke and laying down a *maximum* proportion of muriatic acid that should be tolerated. The pollution of rivers was more difficult to deal with, because there was less agreement among experts as to the tests that should be applied.

Socialism. While Parliament was thus tentatively extending the sphere of State action, an agitation in favour of a more thorough Socialism was beginning. Since the decline of Chartism and the development of commerce and industry under the Free Trade policy, English Radicalism had been mainly individualistic. The prominent trade union demand had been for liberty to combine without State interference. The popular agitation for an extension of the suffrage, *e.g.* in 1886, had been singularly free from indications that the poor meant to use political power (when they got it) to improve directly their material condition, except by insisting on economy and a peaceful foreign policy, and a freedom from vexatious interferences. Disestablishment was advocated, not so much because it might provide funds to be used for national objects, as because it would do away with a form of inequality and of State interference. In these days much of the moral and intellectual fervour of artisan leaders was absorbed in the "Bible smashing" of the Secularist lecturers; and of these lecturers, Bradlaugh in particular was strongly opposed to Socialism. The results of Free Trade seemed a convincing argument of the evils of State interference, and the commercial prosperity made men hope that poverty was going to be got rid of (so far as was humanly possible) by liberty. Presently the tide turned. The prosperity of 1867 to 1874 had been largely stimulated by the amount of gold poured into Europe from California and Australia. Now the mines were becoming less productive, and suddenly a great demand for gold set in, chiefly through the policy of the German and American Governments. Germany substituted a gold for a silver standard (1873). The United States contracted their paper currency. Other Governments began to fear that they would be denuded of gold, and modified their currency or mint systems. Naturally gold became appreciated, and the fall of prices set in. This in turn led to a fall in profits and discouraged employers from extending their business. Wages fell, and, what was even more serious, the amount of employment (even at reduced wages) contracted. All this tended naturally to call forth bitter cries from the poor, and warm sympathy from the benevolent, and many of both sorts were attracted to Socialistic schemes.

The appearance of Henry George's "Progress and Poverty" **Henry George.** marks the transition of Radicalism to Socialism. George (a Californian) was, in theory, a strong individualist, a champion of the rights of capital no less than of labour. The great success of his book was undoubtedly partly due to its appearing at a time when there was an unusually strong predisposition to accept the bold paradox that what is usually called progress brings with it an increase of extreme poverty. His proposed remedy was one which fitted in well with the teaching of some of the dominant political economies.

But of those who at first accepted the doctrine many soon **Land Nationalisation.** advanced to a Socialistic position. The attack on land-owning passed into an attack on monopolies, and thence to an attack on the virtual monopolies which the possession of capital creates. Socialistic organisations and Socialistic newspapers began to multiply. The Secularist societies practically turned Socialistic in spite of the efforts of Bradlaugh. Meanwhile the two political parties began to seek the Socialist vote. Free Education was established in 1887 ; and proposals for a legislative limitation of labour to eight hours a day, for old age pensions subsidised or wholly provided by the State, for a reform of the Poor Law in the direction of greater leniency and greater generosity, began to be advocated by people who would repudiate the charge of being Socialistic. Another side of the same tend-

Municipal Socialism. ency was seen in the extension of municipal functions. Large towns began to take over the gas and water supply, and to work the same for the advantage of their populations. Free libraries, parks, museums, baths, and other institutions supported out of the rates began to multiply. In some cases the trams were taken over by the municipality. In Nottingham, a University College was started out of the gas profits ; and almost everywhere the ratepayers showed a readiness to vote rates for educational purposes, far beyond what the authors of the Act of 1870 had contemplated or desired. It would be beyond the scope of this book to discuss the policy which has thus been gaining ground ; but no reasonable account of the history of the period dealt with in this chapter can ignore the fact that it brought in a strong movement in a Socialistic direction on the part of Parliament and of the local authorities, as well as in the thought and literature, and in the popular demands. It is satisfactory to note that the popular agitation has been singularly free from violence in comparison with the earlier agitations of the century for the People's Charter or for Parliamentary Reform.

Popula- tion. During the period 1865–85 the population continued to increase, but the *rate* began to fall off from about the year 1878. The census figures are (for England and Wales):—

Year.			Population.			Increase per cent.
1871	...	...	22,712,266	...	...	—
1881	...	...	25,974,439	...	...	14·3
1891	...	...	29,002,525	...	...	11·6
[1901	...	...	32,526,075	...	...	12·1]

The birth rate per thousand rose pretty steadily till 1877, when it began to fall. By 1885 it stood at 33·3, which is lower than it had been since 1853. The death rate also fell, but

not quite so fast. The Emigration rate (English) reached a
minimum in 1887, when the emigrants were 63,711 ; and a
maximum in 1883, when they were 183,236.

The fluctuations in the national wealth are less easy to   Wealth.
trace, but they probably corresponded pretty closely with those
of the population. In other words, England grew in wealth
from 1865 to 1885, but the *rate* of increase probably diminished

UNIVERSITY COLLEGE, NOTTINGHAM.

after 1875. Our foreign trade fluctuated considerably, but a
general upward tendency may be clearly seen by grouping quinquennial periods.[1] By 1885 a decline was seen. The fall in
almost all prices since 1875 must, of course, be kept in mind. The

[1 The figures to 1902 are as follow (the later ones being taken from the
" Fiscal Blue Book," c. 1761, 1903 ; the earlier from a return of 1896) :—

Annual Average (in million pounds).

Groups of Years.			Imports.			Exports.			Re-exports.
1865–9	...	..	285	...	...	181	...	...	48
1870–4	...	...	346	...	...	230	...	...	55
1875–9	...	...	375	...	...	201	...	...	56
1880–4	...	...	408	...	...	234	...	...	64
1885–9	...	...	379	...	...	226	...	...	61
1890–4	...	...	419	...	...	234	...	...	62
1895–9	...	...	453	...	...	238	...	...	60
1902	...	...	528	...	...	277	..	...	66]

opening of the Suez Canal, and various improvements in steam engines, and inventions for economising fuel, led to an astounding development of shipping business (pp. 464, 748). This helped to cheapen raw material and food. The better organisation of labour, the growing economies from production on a large scale, and the immense accumulation of capital (with the consequent fall in the rate of interest) acted in the same direction. On the other hand, the bad harvests of 1876, 1877, 1878, and 1879, and the Protective Tariffs of foreign and colonial governments, checked the growing prosperity; and the fall of prices and of the rate of profit caused considerable depression. The classes who suffered most from this were (1) the owners of agricultural land; (2) the smaller employers, including most of the farmers; (3) those who were displaced by new processes, and especially the more elderly members of the working classes, who could not adapt themselves to the changes that were going on, or who did not possess the efficiency which modern conditions of labour required. The success of trade unions in maintaining a *minimum* wage (in each trade for each locality) operated hardly on those whose labour was not worth this *minimum*, and the conflicts between employers and employed caused grave distress.

Progress.   Nevertheless, the wealth of England, and of the working classes in particular, greatly increased between 1865 and 1885. The gross annual value of the property and profits assessed to the income tax rose from 395 millions in 1865 to 571 millions in 1875, and to 631 millions in 1885,[1] and the statistics of consumption, especially of the consumption per head of meat, tea, sugar, tobacco, and other comforts of the working classes, prove that these, on the whole, advanced greatly in material prosperity. The progress of Friendly Societies, Trade Unions,[2] Co-operative Stores, Savings Bank Deposits, Building Societies, etc., gives additional evidence that the power and will to save have increased side by side with the increased consumption of comforts and luxuries.

AT the beginning of the nineteenth century, when the evils of the Poor Law system were under discussion, the general condition

[1 In 1900 it was 788 millions.]   [2 Since this was written the position of Trade Unions has been weakened by the decisions affecting picketing in *Lyons* v. *Wilkins* (1896), *Quinn* v. *Leatham* (1901), and the Taff Vale case (1902).]

of the poor received an unprecedented amount of attention. **MARY BATESON. Education in England, 1807-1885.**
During the eighteenth century the primary education of the
poor had been left to the zeal of voluntary workers, prompted
by religious, charitable, and other motives. But it was beyond
dispute that a large proportion of the population was entirely
without the means of education, and that England was behind
many foreign countries in recognising the educational duty of
the State. The first effort to establish the principle as accepted
abroad had been made by Whitbread in 1807, in a Bill which **Primary Education.**
proposed to create parochial schools through the agency of
local vestries empowered to draw on the rates. The Bill was
thrown out in the Lords, who failed to see what a severe
check such a scheme might have given to the Dissenters, who
were exerting themselves strenuously to secure as large an
influence as possible through elementary schools. While the
pupil-teacher or monitorial system which Bell had introduced **Bell and Lancaster.**
was being adopted in the schools where Church of England
doctrine was taught, the Quaker Lancaster was using a very
similar plan for teaching large classes in the Borough Road.
In 1808 some leading Dissenters took over Lancaster's school
and founded the Royal Lancastrian Institution, which became
in 1814 the British and Foreign School Society. In their
schools, which were intended for children of all religious
persuasions, the Bible was read, but no catechism was taught.
To counteract the results expected from this institution, the
Church of England was compelled to organise a rival society,
and in 1811 the National Society for Promoting the Education
of the Poor in the Principles of the Established Church began
its work, and in 1817 was incorporated by royal charter.

In 1816 Brougham's Commission sat to inquire into the **First Commission.**
state of the education of the lower orders in London, but the
evidence taken concerned chiefly the abuse of charitable
endowments. In 1818 its inquiry was made to extend to
the whole country, and it continued to sit for many years.
There were shown to be 19,326 infant and day schools of
all kinds, attended by 605,704 pupils of all classes; whereas
it was estimated that the number of children requiring
elementary teaching was over two millions. To remedy the
defective supply Brougham brought forward a Bill in 1820, in
which he proposed a local rate, placing local control in the

hands of the magistrates of Quarter Sessions. Still further to conciliate the Churchmen, he suggested that all teachers must be members of the Church of England; to conciliate Dissenters he suggested that parents should be free to withdraw their children at the hours when the catechism or liturgy was taught. The Bill was rejected, as being equally displeasing to both parties.

The educational needs of the country were first recognised

Photo: Walker & Cockerell.
JOSEPH LANCASTER, BY JOHN HAZLITT.
(National Portrait Gallery.)

First Grant. by the State when, in 1833, a Government grant was made to the National and the British Schools. Nearly all the primary schools then belonged to one of the two societies, but the connection was purely formal. There was no real union, no common superintendence, no direction, no code of regulations, no uniform standard of teaching. The numbers under daily instruction were now stated to be 1,276,947 children. But in contrasting these figures with the statistics of a later time, it must be remembered that all classes of schools, for children of all ages, for rich and poor alike, were included in the estimate, and the census, which was never complete, was only roughly calculated. The number of children receiving some sort of elementary education in the first half of the century cannot be ascertained.

Although the increase in numbers appeared to augur well, it was generally acknowledged that of the scholars thus accounted for, many were included who merely left home to be taken charge of by some decrepit person, incapable of either physical or mental activity. The distribution of schools was wholly irregular; so that while in some parts of the country

MADRAS COLLEGE, ST. ANDREWS.

there was even an excess of provision from charitable endowment, in many of the large manufacturing towns of recent growth there were no endowed elementary schools at all, sometimes not even a dame-school. Religious differences, however, made it impossible that any adequate remedy should be accepted ; all that was done was to continue for six years the grant which was administered by the Treasury. Doctrinal hostilities had been instrumental in bringing the educational problem within the sphere of practical politics, but they served no less effectually to prevent a solution of the problem. Select Committees sat almost annually without arriving at any conclusions. But in 1839 the control of the grant was, by an Order in Council, taken away from the Treasury and vested in a Committee of the Privy Council, and two further proposals

Proposals of 1839.

305

were made which excited violent opposition. The Committee of Council determined to make inspection a condition of their grants, and further projected the creation of a normal school for teachers, with schools for practice in teaching attached to the same. In the training-school the members of each religious communion were to be taught their own religious dogma. This proposal to put the denominations on a footing of equality in a normal school, which it was believed would be the pattern for all normal schools, enabled the Church party to carry a motion through the House of Lords which was lost by two votes in the Commons—a motion to rescind the Order in Council. This action was rebuked in a Royal reply, but the scheme for a State training-school had to be abandoned, and the religious societies were left to form their own. The Dissenters had already established one in the Borough Road. The first Church training-school was planned by Dr. Kay, secretary to the Committee of Council, who, aided by Mr. Tufnell and Robert Eden, Vicar of Battersea, had started a school for teachers in Battersea, where it was at first intended to train workhouse boys only. In 1842 this school got a grant from the Committee, and was handed over to the National Society to become a normal school for the training of adult teachers.

The monitorial system came to be generally regarded as a failure, and an improved pupil-teacher system was established in 1846, on the model then used in Dutch schools. The best of the former monitors and other promising children aged over thirteen years were kept on at small salaries, and bound over by indenture to serve an apprenticeship of five years. Teachers were to be encouraged by gratuities to instruct the apprentices, and scholarships were offered to them at the training-schools. The salaries of teachers also were raised and made in a measure dependent on the annual report, and further a pension for old age was provided. A new departure was made in the requirement that all schools which were to receive grants should be well furnished and provided with books and apparatus.

A unanimous resolution of the Commons that more education, moral and religious, was a necessity for the working classes—a resolution which showed that all were

A DAME'S SCHOOL, BY THOMAS WEBSTER, R.A.

(National Gallery of British Art.)

53

united as to the end in view, differing only as to the means
—resulted in an increased Parliamentary grant, and the
Committee of Council worked steadily on without legislative
interference.

In 1858 the Duke of Newcastle's Commission began to **Commis-**
inquire into the merits and defects of the existing system, and **sion of**
it fell to Mr. Lowe (afterwards Lord Sherbrooke) as Vice- **1858.**

A VILLAGE SCHOOL IN 1840, BY HABLÔT K. BROWNE.
(*" Master Humphrey's Clock," by Charles Dickens.*)

President of the Committee of Council, the officer who in
1856 had been made responsible to the Commons, to take
steps to amend the state of affairs described by the Commission.

In 1861 he first proposed that the grant should be a **The**
capitation grant, a principle which had been in part accepted **Revised**
for rural districts in 1853, and extended to towns in 1856. **Code.**
The grant was to depend almost entirely on the number of
scholars who should pass an examination in reading, writing,
and arithmetic. The scheme was ultimately modified, and in
1862 it was agreed that one-third of the grant should be
awarded on attendance, two-thirds on examination. This is the

basis of the system subsequently known as " payment by results." [1]
At this time, too, the "standards" or classes still in use were
established, and the old classification by age was given up.
The steady diminution in the Government grant that followed
in 1861–5 showed that many of the schools which had hitherto
received it were unworthy to do so.   The proposer of the
Bill obtained the result he sought; for if elementary teaching
was still inefficient, it was at least cheaper.   One drawback,
however, was quickly discovered.   The code was found to
encourage teachers to give an undue amount of time to the
three standard subjects, and statistics were worked out to
show that a child under the Revised Code spent 2,920
hours in learning to read.   To amend this, an arrangement was made in 1867 by which the higher subjects were
allowed a certain measure of encouragement in the form of
grant.

In 1869 it was estimated that the accommodation in
inspected schools could supply places for 2,000,000 children,
or nearly double the number provided for in 1859.   The
average attendance had also doubled; still the accommodation was only half of what was required, the attendance only
a quarter of what it should have been.

The Act
of 1870.   In 1870 Mr. Forster's Elementary Education Act was passed
to remedy the deficiency in the supply of efficient elementary
schools.   The country was mapped out into school districts,
coinciding generally with the boundaries of boroughs or parishes;
and on the complaint of the inspectors of returns that the
school accommodation in any district was insufficient, a School
Board was to be formed, elected by ratepayers in a parish,
or burgesses in a borough.   There were two saving clauses :
first that the complaint could be challenged by ten ratepayers
or the school-managers, when fresh inquiry would be made;
and, secondly, six months' grace was given, during which the
want might be voluntarily supplied.   It was made possible to
remit school fees on account of poverty, and where the poverty
of the inhabitants of a particular district required them, free
schools were to be established.

The religious difficulty was met by requiring that in all
public elementary schools, whether Board or Voluntary schools,

[1 Its last remnant, individual examination, was abolished in 1893.]

attendance at religious worship or instruction should not be made a condition of admission: if the parent chose to withdraw his child he was free to do so, and, further, any religious observance or instruction must be at the beginning or end of school hours. In Board schools the Act requires that no religious formulary distinctive of any denomination shall be taught, and that parents shall be free to withdraw their children from religious observance at the beginning or end of school hours. All public elementary schools are to be open to inspection at all times, but the teaching in religious knowledge is not to be examined. The aid to Voluntary schools was limited by the rule that the grant in any year should not exceed the income of the school derived from voluntary contributions, fees, or other sources during that year. This rule was changed in 1876, when it was ordered that no reduction of grant should be made on this ground unless the grant exceeded 17s. 6d. a head. The Act of 1870 used only tentative measures to secure the attendance of children. School Boards were empowered, but not compelled, to pass bye-laws fixing the standard of exemption, and it was left to the magistrates to deal with the offenders as they thought fit. In 1876 the principle of compulsion was extended; the duty of the parent to have his children educated in the "three R's" was formally propounded, and a minimum requirement was fixed which the bye-law, if accepted, must enforce. Where there was no School Board, school-attendance committees might enforce bye-laws. In 1880 the acceptance of bye-laws was made compulsory on all school districts.

Public education has been assisted in Great Britain by steadily increasing Government grants. Thus:—

1833–39	...	...	...	... £20,000
1839–41	...	...	...	... 30,000
1842–44	...	...	...	... 40,000
1851 ...	...	...	...	... 150,000
1879–80	...	...	...	... 2,854,000
1884–85	...	...	...	... 4,410,000
1893–94	...	...	...	... 8,409,000
[1902–03	...	...	...	... 10,851,000]

The growth of the system described above in outline can be most easily set forth by a table:—

Year.	Number of Primary Schools in *Great Britain*.	Annual Grant to the same (000 omitted).	Number of Inspected Schools *England and Wales*.	Number of Voluntary Schools *England and Wales*.	Number of Children on their Register (000 omitted).	Number of Board Schools.	Number of Children on their Register (000 omitted).	Number of Teachers Certificated.	Accommodation per cent. of Population.	Attendance per cent. of Population.	Subscription (£000 omitted).	Rate (£000 omitted).	Grant (£000 omitted).	Average Attendance (000 omitted).	Cost per child.
															£ s. d.
1854	3,825	—													
1855	4,800	—	3,853					2,484							—
1860	7,270	—													
1861	—	813	5,438				—	7,072	8·75	5·5					
1865				—			—				311	—	378	848	1 5 5
1870	10,949	840	8,281					12,467			419	—	563	1,152	
1871	—	—		9,772	—	82									
1872	—	—	9,854								493	5	790	1,336	1 7 5
1875	—	—									676	236	1,158	1,837	—
1877	18,118	—													
1879	—	2,732													
1880	20,670	2,854	18 289								739	726	2,130	2,751	—
1882	—	3,101	—	14,421	—	3,868					725	808	2,393	3,015	1 16 8½
1885	21,976	3,664	18,895	14,600	2,859	4,295	1,553	40,703	18·18	12·26	756	1,140	2,867	3 371	2 0 6¾
[1900	23,204	4,911	20,100	14,359	3,054	5,758	2,361	64,038	20·28	14·53	811	2,959	10,048	4,666	2 11 7

Boys and girls leaving elementary schools half taught, before the period closes, could in many places continue their education by means of evening classes. The University Extension Lectures, too, since 1873, in all populous districts had begun to bring educational opportunities within the reach of the working classes. The popular desire for greater intellectual advantages has been shown in the large towns throughout the period. The Mechanics' Institutes in Manchester, Liverpool, Sheffield, Coventry; the Birkbeck Institute (1823), the Polytechnics, are among the older institutions founded to satisfy these needs, and since 1854 working men's colleges, and since 1860 working men's clubs, have shown that the movement is real and lasting. Cheap popular literature found a market early in the period. The Society for the Promotion of Useful Knowledge began its work in 1825, and soon after there poured forth Family Libraries, Libraries of Entertaining Knowledge, penny magazines, and cheap encyclopædias, which needed no charitable society to support them, and the cheap issues of English and foreign classics followed in the way thus prepared. Free Libraries, since the Acts of 1845 and 1850, have supplied many large towns with the means of every form of literary enjoyment.

As early as 1835 the educational methods pursued at the

THE EDUCATION PROBLEM.

Master Forster. "PLEASE, M'M, I'VE DONE IT, M'M!"

Schoolmistress (Britannia). "AND *HOW* HAVE YOU DONE IT, WILLIAM?"

Master Forster. "PLEASE, M'M, I'VE REDUCED ALL THE FRACTIONS TO THE LOWEST COMMON DENOMINATION."

Schoolmistress. "GOOD BOY! *GO UP!*"   [*The Good Boy enters the Cabinet.*

THE ELEMENTARY EDUCATION ACT, 1870.

(*Reproduced by special permission of the Proprietors of "Punch."*)

Boys' Secondary Schools. great public schools for boys were widely censured by popular opinion. At Eton the number of school hours was said to be only eleven a week, and there were complaints of the tyranny exercised by the elder scholars, of the constant assembling of too many boys in one hall, of the unequal treatment of the rich and noble, of the excessive exercise of

Photo: Rodger, St. Andrews.

DR. ANDREW BELL.

(From an old engraving.)

memory, the few subjects taught, and the antiquated methods used. The education was almost exclusively classical, and it was contended that even Greek and Latin were ill taught, with bad grammars and by means of mere fragments of the great writers. The greater part of the boys' time was spent in the composition of Greek and Latin verse. At Charterhouse Bell's "Madras system" was in use, and the elder boys were set to teach classes in the Lower School, after the fashion of the monitors in the National Schools. The education at Westminster, according to Sydney Smith, cost his son from £150 to £200 a year. He writes that the first year there is severe, " an intense system of tyranny, of which the English are very fond, and think it fits a boy for the world—but the world, bad as it is, has nothing half so bad."

Brougham's inquiry into the abuse of charitable endow-

SCHOOL ROOM, WESTMINSTER SCHOOL, 1883.
(*By permission, from a drawing by H. M. Marshall.*)

ments was long in bearing fruit, but in 1840 an Act for improving the condition of grammar schools was passed which declared that whereas there were many foundations for teaching boys wholly or principally in grammar, and whereas the term "grammar" had been construed by the Courts to have reference only to Greek and Latin, the Courts of Equity were to be empowered to remodel such schools. According to the Charity Commissioners' report of 1842, there were 705 grammar schools and 2,200 other non-classical schools. But no steps were taken as yet towards ascertaining what kind of teaching was given in these schools. In 1861 a Royal Commission was appointed to inquire into the conditions of nine of the chief endowed schools—namely, Eton, Winchester, Westminster, Charterhouse, Harrow, Rugby, Shrewsbury, St. Paul's, and the Merchant Taylors' School. The result of this, the Clarendon Commission, was the Public Schools Act, 1868, which reformed the administration of the first seven, arranging particularly for the admission on favourable terms of a larger number of day scholars. The Commission of 1864 discussed next those schools not hitherto included. It was ascertained that there were nearly 800 endowed schools, 80 proprietary, and over 10,000 private schools. The report of the Commission filled twenty volumes. The principal result of this, Lord Taunton's Commission, was the Endowed Schools Act, 1869, from which sprang the Endowed Schools Commission, with power to deal with charitable trusts " in such manner as may render any educational endowments most conducive to the advancement of the education of boys and girls, and either of them." In 1874 the Commission was merged into the Board of Charity Commissioners.

The Endowed Schools Commission.

At the close of the period there were already many signs of the growth of public interest in questions of educational theory and practice, which in the past the English have, as a rule, neglected, leaving them to be dealt with on the Continent or in the United States. The change is probably partly due to the great increase of sympathy with children and childhood that is characteristic of the present day.

Girls' Schools.

In the first half of the century girls of the richer classes were sent almost exclusively to boarding-schools, or were taught by private governesses whose educational merits could not be tested by any examinations. The school-books were Mrs. Mangnall's " Questions," Pinnock's " Catechisms," Mrs. Marcet's " Conversations," Keith's " Use of the Globes," Mrs. Trimmer's " English History," and other elegant abridgements. The one intellectual faculty that was trained in girls was verbal memory, and for them knowledge existed only in epitome. While boys read the classics, girls learnt lists of the names of gods and goddesses ; they were expected to be familiar with all the great names of ancient and modern history, but with the names alone. A few were suffered to reach the classics through Valpy's translations and Hamilton's keys. Even those domestic interests which have at times been credited with educational powers were now neglected, and it was considered discreditable that a lady should subject herself to what little of mental discipline may be derived from cooking or making caps. She was at as much pains to conceal household occupations as she was to avoid all signs of blue-stockingism.

The subject of girls' education was first seriously handled by the Royal Commission of 1864. It was shown that the number of girls' schools was very large, while the number of pupils in each averaged only twenty-five. There was no system of classes or of examinations, no definite course of studies: each pupil learned such accomplishments and at such times as her parents thought fit. The best education for the female mind was believed to be steady application to vocal and instrumental music and to the subject of ladylike manners and deportment. For what were technically known as "accomplishments" expensive schools had expensive masters, whilst the teaching that was educational was in the hands of one or two teachers, who had neither separate classes nor separate rooms.

Royal Commission of 1864.

Instead of gymnastics or games, instruments of torture were used for modelling the figure. A contemporary writer says that " could the modern schoolroom (1831) be preserved, it would pass for a refined Inquisition. There would be found stocks for the fingers [the cheiroplast] and pulleys for the neck with weights attached." Fanny Kemble, to whom Nature had been by no means unkindly, was found wanting in deportment; and she writes that she wore a " back-board made of steel, covered with red morocco, which consisted of a flat piece placed on my back, and strapped down to my waist with a belt, and secured at the top by two epaulettes strapped over my shoulders. From the middle of this there rose a steel rod or spine with a steel collar, which encircled my throat, fastened behind." The machine proved a failure, and she was put under the tuition of a drill-sergeant, who did for her all that was required.

There were no means of testing the competence of the women who entered the teaching profession, and as the position of teachers in boarding schools and of governesses in private families was, as a rule, unenviable, this profession was too often the refuge of the destitute. A change, however, was at hand.

Teachers.

About the middle of the century a few of the more intellectual among the governesses studied at the Literary Institutes and the London Institution, and in 1848 some professors of King's College, London, gave lectures to the Governesses' Benevolent Society, which, under F. D. Maurice's care, developed into Queen's College. In 1849 Bedford College was founded, chiefly through the influence of Mrs. Reid and some intellectual

THE GYMNASIUM, NORTH LONDON COLLEGIATE SCHOOL FOR GIRLS.
(*By permission of the Head Mistress.*)

Unitarians. In 1854 Cheltenham College, the first proprietary girls' school, was opened, and not long afterwards Miss Buss's private school (which eventually became the North London Collegiate School for Girls) was well established. After the Commission of 1864 had dealt with the question of girls' education, and proposed the restoration of some endowments to girls' schools which had been alienated from them, the Women's National Educational Union was founded, largely through the agency of Mrs. William Grey, and in 1872 this Union became the Girls' Public Day Schools Company. The tendency in the secondary education of girls, since these changes took place, has been, on the whole, to approximate their education to that of boys.

The admission of women to University teaching and examination followed close upon the change in secondary education, and in their origin and subsequent history the two movements are closely connected. In 1867 women were admitted to examinations in the University of London. Two years later the first scheme for a collegiate institution with academic teaching took shape, and in 1872 it was incorporated as Girton College, Cambridge. In the following year members of this college were first informally admitted to Tripos examinations. In 1871, after the University of Cambridge had opened the Higher Local Examinations, to stimulate the education of women aged over eighteen, Miss Clough opened a house for students in Cambridge, which in 1875 became Newnham Hall, afterwards Newnham College. In 1881 the same University formally admitted women, who have resided the statutory terms and satisfied prescribed conditions, to the Tripos examinations, and in 1884 somewhat similar privileges were given at Oxford. The opportunities thus afforded have been seized, with results that serve year by year to establish what once was strongly contested, that mental cultivation is desirable for women as for men.

Higher Education of Women.

The exclusion of Dissenters from matriculation at Oxford and from degrees at Cambridge led to the proposed creation of a London University, in 1826, which two years later took shape as London University College. Crabb Robinson writes that he has bought a hundred-pound share in this Gower Street Company, as it was called by the scoffers, for it was a private enterprise; but he thought the share worthless and took it only as "a debt to the cause of civil and religious liberty." The Church party, in alarm lest Londoners should be taught exclusively by schismatics, opened King's College in 1831. In 1834 University College applied to the Crown for power to grant degrees, those in theology alone excepted. The Universities of Oxford and Cambridge and the College of Surgeons agitated in opposition, and for a time successfully. But in 1837 the University of London was incorporated as an examining and degree-giving body, while University and King's Colleges still continue as separate teaching bodies.

London University.

Provincial Colleges and Universities.

The first movement towards the creation of a provincial University was made by the Dean and Chapter of Durham, who obtained a charter, and opened their buildings in 1833. Victoria University received its charter in 1880, but its component colleges—the Owens College, Manchester, and the Yorkshire College, Leeds—had already been in existence for some time. Liverpool University College got its charter of incorporation in 1881. Birmingham, Bristol, Newcastle, Nottingham, Sheffield, had all established local colleges before the period closed.

Oxford and Cambridge.

The changes which have taken place at Oxford and Cambridge during the present century have tended, by the abolition of divers monopolies, to admit a greater number of persons to those benefits which the Universities bestow upon education; by the elaboration of a system of examinations, to provide tests of qualification; and by changes in internal administration, to increase the influence of the Universities upon education and learning. At the beginning of the century the excellence of a student's merits were tested at Cambridge only in one way, by the Mathematical Tripos; not till 1824 was the first Classical Tripos held, and to that examination until 1850 none were admitted who had not gained honours in the Mathematical Tripos. At Oxford there had been no examination for degrees till the beginning of the century, when classical and mathematical honours lists began. Until 1850 no other radical change was effected at either University. There had been an attempt in 1834 to secure for Dissenters admission to the degrees of Cambridge, but the Bill was thrown out in the Lords. In 1838 Whewell became professor of Moral Philosophy at Cambridge, and it was largely through his influence that a wider range of studies began to be regarded as proper to the University. As a consequence of this movement, two new triposes were held for the first time in 1851, in Natural Science and in Moral Philosophy, with Law and History. At Oxford, in 1850, there was a reorganisation of examinations, resulting in a system not different in essentials from that now established.

Royal Commissions.

These changes came from the Universities themselves, unassisted by pressure from without. Although at Cambridge Dean Peacock's "Observations on the Statutes of the University" had excited some enthusiasm, the need of a change in the constitution of the Universities was felt rather by the educated

classes as a whole than by the resident members of the Universities. It was generally thought that the number of persons
admitted to share in the benefits of the Universities was unduly
small ; and even at Cambridge, where there had been some increase in the number of students, the increase was not
proportionate to the growth of the population. In 1850 a
memorial was signed by some Oxford and Cambridge graduates
and some members of the Royal Society, which set forth " that

Photo : Mason & Basébé, Cambridge.

NEWNHAM COLLEGE, CAMBRIDGE.

the present system of the English Universities had not
advanced, and was not calculated to advance the interests of
religious and useful learning to an extent commensurate
with the great resources and high position of those bodies," and
pointed to the need of changes in their constitution. This was
sent to the First Lord of the Treasury, and a Royal Commission
was appointed to inquire into the state, discipline, studies and
revenues of the University and Colleges of Oxford and Cambridge in 1852. At Oxford the inquiry was met with violent
hostility ; it was pronounced illegal and unconstitutional, the
Commissioners' letters were not answered, and Fellows were

told that they would violate their oaths taken on election
if they provided materials for the inquiry. The Commissioners had to turn to the British Museum for copies
of college statutes. Their verdict was that University teaching was nearly extinct, and that professorial lectures had
suffered something more than what the friends of the existing
system called "a temporary interruption." The Hebdomadal
Board, with which rested the sole power of initiation in legis-

BALLIOL COLLEGE, OXFORD—SOUTH FRONT.

lative affairs, was described as "an organised torpor." It consisted of the heads of colleges and the proctors. Congregation,
consisting of resident Masters of Arts, had merely formal
functions and no power of debate; Convocation might debate
only in Latin, which very few members could speak. By the
Act of 1854 and subsequent ordinances the representation on
the Hebdomadal Board of Professors and resident Masters of
Arts was secured, Congregation was allowed to discuss questions
of academic policy, the test oath was removed from matriculation and the B.A., but was kept for the M.A. degree; the opening
of private halls was allowed, local preferences and other restrictions on competition for endowments were removed, but the
restriction of Fellowships to clergymen was to be annulled only
when three-fourths of the Fellows were found to be already in

orders. Oxford had hitherto been drawing about 300 students a year, of whom the larger number were destined for holy orders. Before long the matriculation doubled.

Phot⟩: Gillman & Co., Oxford.

CHAPEL OF EXETER COLLEGE, OXFORD.

At Cambridge the chief suggestions of the Commissioners, embodied as the New Statutes, 1858, led to very similar changes. In ten years' time a fresh movement for reform was started. The "Essays on a Liberal Education" (1867) explained the views of the reforming party. Mark Pattison's "Suggestions on Academic Organisation" (1868) raised similar questions in

306

Oxford.   In 1871 the Fellows of Trinity College, Cambridge, drafted of their own initiative a new code of statutes.   In the next year a second Royal Commission was appointed to inquire into the revenues and property of both Universities.   By the Universities of Oxford and Cambridge Act, 1877, two Executive Commissions were appointed to revise college statutes.   In 1882 the work was finished; the principles involved in celibate, clerical, and life fellowships were given up; the college system of teaching, by which each college provided, as far as possible, its own teachers, to the neglect of University and inter-collegiate teaching, was discouraged: the financial relations of colleges to the University were revised, so that the colleges were made to contribute to University funds.   By these means, and by the admission of women students to college lectures and University examinations, the character of academic life was greatly changed within a short period.   The creation of sectarian colleges (Keble, founded in 1870, being one of the largest) has opened new opportunities for the development of ecclesiastical influence.

ARTHUR GRIFFITHS. Prison Discipline, 1846-1885. THE cessation of transportation, even in a modified form, imposed a serious obligation upon prison administrators (p. 316).   In the early 'fifties they were faced with the necessity for finding an outlet for the convicts, hitherto so comfortably disposed of, now constantly accumulating on our hands at home.   Hence the form of punishment known as penal servitude.   Great public works were started and carried through.   These are to be seen now, mostly completed, at Portland, in the breakwater and the vast fortifications on the **Convict Labour.** Verne; at Portsmouth and Chatham, in the development of the dockyards and the large basins constructed there, capable of holding half our fleet; at Borstal, in the chain of forts protecting the Medway; at Dartmoor, where great areas of good land have been reclaimed from the barren wastes.   The system first invented is practically that still in force.   It is possibly irksome to all those who go through it, but the main idea of crime to be expiated cannot be forgotten; yet pains are taken that the moral and material well-being of the convict is not neglected.

QUADRANGLE, KEBLE COLLEGE, OXFORD.

NEW BUILDINGS, TRINITY COLLEGE, OXFORD.

(*Photos: Gillman & Co., Oxford.*)

The whole sentence is divided into three stages: of these the first is a period of probation, nine months, passed in separate confinement, at a time when the prisoner is supposed to be susceptible to better influences, and will be benefited by reflection and good counsels. The second stage takes him to the public works, where he is permitted to labour in association, but always under observation and control. All this time his industry is encouraged, his best energies secured by a judicious method of deferred reward, not in mere money— although he can earn a small fixed sum, to be paid on release —but in the boon a convict prizes most of all, release from durance. The marks gained for daily labour, if at the highest rate, secure remission of sentence, one-fourth of the whole term. But the premature release thus obtained is only conditional, and the convict issues forth with the clear understanding that he will be re-incarcerated if he falls into bad ways. This is the third and last stage—that of the license-holder, or ticket-of-leave man, whose character and conduct while at large are strictly watched, and freedom is only permitted pending good behaviour.

A system is best judged by its results, and that now in force can assuredly answer this test. Not only have the great works above mentioned been completed, and at considerable saving to the country, but there has in recent years been a marked diminution in crime. Not only have offenders *in esse* been wisely handled, but those *in posse* have been presumably deterred from taking to evil ways. There can be no question of this decrease. The population of the convict prisons has diminished steadily year after year, and whilst the number in 1875 was 9,815, in 1885 it had fallen to 8,836, and in 1895 to 3,309. It has been urged that this decrease is in a measure due to the greater leniency shown by all courts of jurisdiction, which often choose now to inflict a lesser penalty than penal servitude. If this were so the minor sentences should show a corresponding increase, and the smaller local prisons should be much more full. But here the same marked diminution is apparent. Where, in 1878, the lesser offenders in prison numbered 26,000, they are now barely 13,000, and this notwithstanding an increase in the general population of 4,000,000 during that period, which would in itself excuse a corresponding increase in the criminal class. The same explanation is offered that the sentences are much shorter, and the prisons are in consequence more quickly cleared. But this is not sufficient to account for the whole decrease. Many other causes contribute, each different, but all issuing from the same general origin—a more humane and intelligent appreciation by the State of its duty towards those who lapse into or are predisposed towards crime.

Crime has been well defined as a failure to abide by or live up to a standard deemed essential by society. Criminals are such by accident or inclination, and under a perfect system of government they should be saved from the one and cured of the other. We do much nowadays in the first direction by our care of the youthful, by dealing with crime in embryo, and before it takes concrete form. Reformatories and industrial schools now cut off the supply of young recruits to the great army of criminals; wide-reaching machinery for child rescue is now in full operation, and is very effective while the general spread of education has undoubtedly contributed to the same end. But uniformity in prison discipline has been a potent factor, and has told upon the contingent floating continually in and out of prison. The convicted offender is certain that wherever he may find himself he will be under precisely the same rules, will eat the same scanty fare, do much the same labour. There is no distinction now between localities; the punishment is alike in all. No administrative reform in recent years has been more beneficial than the concentration of prison management under the central authority **Reform of 1877.** of the State. This was effected by the Prisons Act of 1877, when full powers were vested in a Board of Prison Commissioners. Great economy was the immediate result, for prisons were at once cut down in number from 114 to 56, with a corresponding saving on staff. Another obvious advantage in State control is the publicity afforded. Where the servants of the public are responsible there can be no secret abuses; everything must be carried on in the light of day, by officials who can be held strictly to account. The prisons of England can challenge the most searching investigation, and all who have compared them with the best in foreign countries must admit that ours are inferior to none.

Shortened Sentences.

Of English prison discipline and penal legislation the whole tendency is towards leniency, in dealing both with law-breakers and the ever-present but narrowing problems of crime. This is plainly shown in the determination of all courts to inflict light, even minimum, sentences; it is still more apparent in the many wise and humane modern enactments intended to keep all offenders possible from going to gaol. The Summary Jurisdiction Act was one of the chief of these; another was the First Offenders Act. Under the first named, where an alternative is offered of fine or imprisonment, time may be given to pay the money; before its passage non-production of cash meant immediate incarceration. The other Act, based as it is upon humanity and common-sense, saves all whose first lapse does not place them beyond hope of reform, from the indelible brand of the gaol-bird. The fewer people committed to prison the better for them and for the country. Equally true, on the other hand, is the proposition that all who, by repeatedly offending, offer themselves again and again for punishment should be retained within four walls until they can afford reasonable hope that they mean to go straight on release. These are the so-called habitual or professional criminals, and they constitute the greatest of unsolved difficulties in penal science. In some countries, as in the United States of America, a special penalty exists, known as the "indefinite" or "indeterminate" sentence, under which a persistent offender may be kept *sine die* in gaol. This punishment has been enforced to a limited extent beyond the Atlantic, and has, it is said, achieved considerable success. But it has been carried out there with an elaboration of costly means that rather condemns it as a practical method of dealing with a large number of offenders

MARY BATESON. Dress, 1840-1885.

THE period 1840–50 was one of the worst in the history of tight-lacing; all dresses pretending to fashion laced up the back, where the lady's maid could bring any amount of muscular force to bear upon the unfortunate victim. The crinoline, introduced in Paris in 1854, was welcomed as a way

Photo: Grove, Brompton Road, S.W.

CONVICTS AT WORK IN THE DARTMOOR QUARRIES.

Crinoline. out of the difficulty, for, as the advertisements announced, it made the dress appear sufficiently full and in proper contrast to the waist, "thereby sparing the necessity and agony, as well as injury, of tight-lacing." The term crinoline was applied to the stiff material of horse-hair used to distend skirts, and then to the ribbons of steel which took its place. To make a crinoline four narrow steels covered with tape were run into a calico slip or petticoat; the steel nearest the waist should be distant $1\frac{3}{4}$ nails from it, and should be $1\frac{3}{4}$ yards in

DRESS AND COIFFURE, 1845.
(" *World of Fashion*," 1845.)

length. The other three steels should be $2\frac{1}{2}$ yards long, and at 6 nails distance from each other. The ends of only the top steel should meet in the front. Before this invention was made, and while skirts were merely stiffened or held out by a dozen or more petticoats, true gentility was best shown by the way in which the arms were drawn down to keep the voluminous mantle, Paisley or cashmere shawl, in its proper folds, while the hands, clasped in front, held a lace pocket-handkerchief or reticule. The shawl was fastened with a large cameo brooch. During the same period (1840–50), silk and satin aprons trimmed with lace or guimp were worn indoors, as in the Queen Anne period.

In 1860 the skirt over the crinoline was trimmed with three deep flounces, scalloped and vandyked to break the size of the circle. A long loose jacket bodice was worn

Dress in 1860.
("World of Fashion.")

Dress in 1875.
("World of Fashion.")

DRESS IN 1860 AND IN 1875.

with sleeves made *en pagode*, wide at the cuff and set in low on the shoulder, where a muslin under-sleeve was attached which fitted tightly to the wrist. In 1864 there was a short rage for scarlet "Garibaldi bodies" held in by tight waist-belts. Boots to the ankle, white stockings, little round hats with a single pen-feather at the side, complete the costume.

DRESS AND THE LADY, 1856.
(Reproduced by special permission of the Proprietors of "Punch.")

The changes in the shape and size of bonnets were rapid; within the space of a few years there were velvet and beaver bonnets with lace curtains at the back, filled with lace quilling

Headgear. and artificial flowers under the brim which surrounded the face, the coal-scuttle bonnet, the bonnet of drawn white silk, the bonnet fitting close in front, and bonnets with long veils hanging from a string. While very large bonnets were worn, tiny fringed parasols were in fashion. The hair showed very little out of doors, and from 1840–50 the best effect was made by those who had well-shaped heads, with only a small quantity of straight hair. About 1836 the wicker-work plaits then in fashion, made of eight or nine strands plaited in an elaborate pattern, put nature to severe trial, but in 1840 ringlets over the ears and side-partings drove out the stiffer fashion. In 1846 came the smooth bandeaux plastered down with

LADY IN SHAWL, 1853.
("World of Fashion.")

bandoline, and whereas in 1836 every girl had one artificial flower over the left ear in the evening, so in 1845 she wore

a wreath. At the beginning of the crinoline period the hair
was covered with a net spangled with jet beads, and at this

A *THÉ DANSANTE*, 1845.
(*Reproduced by special permission of the Proprietors of " Punch."*)

time wide flapping straw hats came in. In 1865 the Alexandra curl and the chignon were fashionable, necessitating
much false hair, for the bonnet was worn tip-tilted at the
back to display as much hair as possible.

In 1865–70 Dolly Varden dresses of gaily-flowered muslin
were fashionable for summer wear; the bodice was pointed, and

Dress
after 1885.

EARLY VICTORIAN BONNETS.
(*" World of Fashion,"* 1845.)

the flowered polonaise was tucked up over a coloured skirt. The
crinoline had gone, leaving only the bustle. In 1875 the alpaca
skirts were trimmed with a quantity of small frills of kiltings

and tied tightly back across the knees, the polonaise being looped with bows and buckles. The dress was worn partially open at the neck, and the bell-sleeve exposed the lower part of the arm. This was the period when much jewellery was worn in the daytime, and when it was the fashion for all young married women to wear caps indoors. In the period of "Princess" robes, 1875–80, the skirt and bodice were cut in one piece, and made

A DOLLY VARDEN FAREWELL KISS, BY G. DU MAURIER.
(Reproduced by special permission of the Proprietors of "Punch.")

very plain. The skirt clung closely to the figure, and was made with a train. To the same period belongs the "fringe." From 1880 date the "æsthetic" and other "dress reform" movements, and from this time there are signs that fashion begins to rule over a smaller number of subjects, and fails to exercise such unchecked tyranny as in the periods which precede. The democratic movement seems in the matter of dress to have worked rather towards variety than towards uniformity.

Men's Dress.   In the time of the black satin stocks of 1840 men shaved their faces, and only cavalry wore moustachios. In the early 'forties whiskers began to be encouraged; but the beard and the moustache (for civilians) only came in after military rules on the subject had been relaxed by the Crimean War. Soon afterwards the abundant locks which had been worn throughout the reign began to be cropped close in military fashion. In 1840 no white was worn round the neck other than a fold of white waistcoat, which showed above the coat collar and below the stock, but by 1855 white collars and bows had come in. French tall silk hats were made lighter and cheaper than the English beavers, and

AN IMPARTIAL STATEMENT IN BLACK AND WHITE, BY G. DU MAURIER, 1881.
(Reproduced by special permission of the Proprietors of " Punch.")

natural beaver was no longer used when new methods of waterproofing had been discovered. Ankle-jacks or jack-boots reaching to the ankle were characteristic of the same period. Already in 1825 Charles Macintosh had applied some important discoveries to the waterproofing of clothes (p. 514), and Hancock was able to induce the Guards to use his drab cambric waterproof capes on the way to field exercise. This colour began to take with the public generally, and all travellers by 1830 had macintoshes for coach travelling.

WRITING in 1825, Sir Walter Scott says, " Drinking is not now the vice of the times," and again, to his son, he says, " The habit of drinking wine, so much practised when I was a young

MARY BATESON. Social Life.

man, occasioned many of my cruel stomach complaints. You
had better drink a bottle of wine on any particular occasion
than sit and soak and sipple at an English pint every day."
"Sots are excluded from the best company."   Habitual or
violent drunkenness was already a social offence, but occasional
total lapses and regular haziness after dinner were still weak-
nesses in men which all must tolerate.

Drink.   Gin-drinking among the lower classes had again reached
alarming proportions in 1830.   The numbers entering fourteen
of the largest gin-shops in London were counted, and in one
week the number of men was 142,453, of women 108,593, of
children 18,391.   Throughout the war, malt, hops and beer had
been heavily taxed, and the consumption had not increased in
proportion to the consumption of spirits, or even of tea and
coffee.   It was hoped that if the sale of beer were encouraged
the sale of spirits might still further diminish, and in this belief
the taxes on beer, hops, and malt were reduced, and cheap beer
Beerhouse   licences were sold at two guineas each.   In the first year 31,000
Act, 1830.   of the new licences were taken out for "Tom and Jerry shops."
Already in 1834 it was seen that some revision of the system
was needed, and new licences, more costly for the sale of
beer to be consumed on than off the premises, were issued.
Nevertheless the number of "swankey shops," or "ons," continued to increase, and the "offs" to diminish.   In ten years
the quantity of malt paying duty increased by ten million
bushels.   A slight diminution in the consumption of spirits
followed, but was not long maintained.

Public-   The statistics of the number of publicans' spirit licences in
houses.   England and Wales show a continuous diminution in proportion
to population.   In 1889 the total of intoxicating liquor licences
was 181,297.   The licences in 1830–9 amounted to 6·30 to every
1,000 of population; in 1860–9, to 5·57.   After Selwin-Ibbetson's
Act there was a drop from 124,173 in 1869 to 116,759 in 1871,
or in beer-house licences from 48,967 to 42,607.   In 1885 the
proportion was at about 4·54 per 1,000.

The statistics of consumption show an increase over the
years 1831–85 as compared with 1761–1821 in the consumption
of British spirits per head, with a diminution in malt; but
this increase is more apparent than real, for the statistics are
estimated on duty-paid spirits, and in the earlier period the

THE DRUNKARD'S CHILDREN. BY GEORGE CRUIKSHANK.

quantity of spirits which escaped duty cannot be ascertained. Smuggling and illicit distillation, whenever duties were high, deprived the Government of a large part of the dues that should have been paid for home consumption. During the war and till 1823, duty was charged at 11s. 8½d. for English spirits, for Scotch and Irish 5s. 6d. a gallon; then the duty fell, on English to 7s. 6d., on Scotch to 3s. 4d., on Irish to 2s. 4d. Between 1823 and 1839 the consumption of duty-paid English and Irish more than doubled, and Scotch trebled; yet this increase doubtless does not point to an actual doubling of consumption. The increase was maintained after the tax on spirits was made uniform at 10s. a gallon in 1860. It would appear, then, that in the present century increase of duty within certain limits has not prevented increased consumption, and no longer leads, as once it did, to smuggling and illicit distillation.

Committee of 1834. In 1834 a Select Committee of the House of Commons sat to consider means to prevent drunkenness, and came to the conclusion that the vice had declined in the upper classes but increased in the lower. The committee were prepared to enforce drastic measures, such as Sunday closing, the opening of retail-shops to the view of passers-by, the reduction of duties on tea, coffee, and sugar, the abolition of the issues of spirits to the Army and Navy, with a view to the ultimate prohibition of all foreign importation and of home distillation. These proposals were out of harmony with the public opinion of the time, and only the mildest of the suggestions have since been put in force. The evidence collected by the Lords' Select Committee on intemperance, 1877–8, led them to report that recent legislation had not diminished drunkenness, that it had not increased in rural districts, but had increased in towns, especially during the five or six years of prosperity which followed 1868. They held that there was a vast increase of female intemperance, and summed up that there was no evidence to prove that the country was in a *worse* condition than it was thirty years ago. This verdict was certainly not unduly optimistic.

Drunkenness. The statistics of drunkenness, which, of course, bear no necessary relation to the consumption of spirits per head of population, are not easily ascertained, for the tables of apprehensions and convictions at police courts are often affected by

changes of magisterial practice. On the whole, the tendency
has been to make drunkenness more distinctly a petty criminal
offence; drunkards are no longer, as before 1833, "taken care
of" by the police, and dismissed, when sober, without being
entered on the charge-sheet. But it seems that 1865, looking
back on 1835, saw an improvement; this included the period
when the taxes on all British spirits were made uniform, and
the tax on tea was reduced by one-half; 1885, looking back on
1860, saw neither improvement nor the reverse. But as there
was greater police vigilance and an increased readiness to convict,
it is possible to escape the conclusion that there was as much
drunkenness as ever.

The Cobden Treaty of 1860 to encourage the lighter French **Wines.**
vintages had a marked effect on the consumption of light
wines in the United Kingdom. In 1801–3 only 274,000 gallons
of French wines were drunk, with over 7,000,000 gallons of other
wines. In 1880, of over 17,000,000 gallons imported, the French
contribution was nearly 7,000,000. From 1858–60 the average
annual consumption of all foreign wines was about 6,600,000
gallons; from 1882–4 over 14,000,000 gallons. According to
Porter's statistics, the consumption of British spirits per head
was, 1721–91, an average of ·62 gallon; 1791–1871, ·46 gallon, or
a diminution of 25 per cent., but foreign and colonial spirits
showed an increase. Malt showed a decrease from 3·76 bushels
to 2·11 bushels, a fall of 43 per cent.; whereas the amount of
wine imported per head of population increased by about 200
per cent., 1860–85.

The earliest temperance societies were American, and date **Tem-**
from the end of the eighteenth century. In England temperance **perance.**
societies of the modern type date from 1829, when Professor
John Edgar at Belfast, G. W. Carr at New Ross, and John
Dunlop at Glasgow, acting independently, started societies with
members pledged to abstain from intoxicating liquor. A year
later H. Forbes started one at Bradford; in 1832 Joseph
Livesey, of Preston, and six others pledged themselves to total
abstinence, and one of their friends created a word when he
declared in a speech that "nothing but te-te-total would do."
In 1834 the Commission on drunkenness proposed that temperance societies should be encouraged and established throughout
the country. This recommendation, however, was little likely

307

to find acceptance in high quarters; for William IV., though he hated drunkards, hated water-drinkers no less. When King Leopold was dining with him, the king exclaimed, "What's that you are drinking, sir?" "Water, sir." "G—— d—— it, why don't you drink wine? I never allow anybody to drink water at my table." He himself drank a bottle of sherry daily at dinner.

It was not long before the advocates of temperance and of teetotalism found their differences irreconcilable. But the movement was unchecked. Father Theobald Mathew, President of the Total Abstinence Society in Cork, began in 1838 to become famous for his marvellous influence over drunkards, and crowds took the pledge at his hands (p. 337). A fruitful source of evil, in the belief of the Commissioners of 1834, had been the meeting of benefit and friendly societies in public-houses, where a part of the funds was always spent in drink. In 1835 was founded the first benefit society on temperance principles, called the Independent Order of Rechabites. Total abstinence was shown to be an important factor in insurance statistics of health and longevity, and many other insurance societies were founded for pledged members. Co-operation with societies in all parts of the world has become a leading feature of temperance work. A special branch of periodical literature is devoted to the question, and the bibliography of temperance is rich in songs, recitations, and tracts. In 1878 the Blue Ribbon Army made its first appearance, in Hoxton. Whilst temperance as a doctrine was spreading, its practice was helped on by the opening of coffee-taverns, temperance hotels, and other places intended to offer as many of the comforts of the public-house as are possible in the absence of its temptations.

Liquor Laws. The example of the Maine Liquor Law of 1851 led the temperance reformers to look to legislation for drastic measures against the liquor trade. In 1853 a Select Committee inquired into the public-houses, but no legislation followed their report. The first step gained was the Wine and Beerhouse Act of 1869, which made it impossible for any excise licences to be granted without the sanction of the justices. In 1872 the hours of sale were reduced from twenty-one to an average of seventeen, and the penalty on infringement was increased.

Any licensed person who allowed riotous or drunken conduct
on his premises or who sold liquor to a drunken person was
to be fined, and the conviction might be recorded on his
licence. In 1874 the Licensing Act required Sunday closing
during certain hours. In 1882 the justices were allowed
a more extended discretion in the refusal of licences for

THE TRUE LOVERS' KNOT: THE COBDEN TREATY.

(Reproduced by special permission of the Proprietors of " Punch.")

consumption of beer on and off the premises than had been
given in 1869, which had allowed refusal only in flagrant
cases. Two important Acts are the Sunday Closing (Wales)
Act, which enforces general closing except for the refresh-
ment-rooms of railway-stations; and the Act of 1883, which
forbade the payment of wages in public-houses, and embodied,
after long delay, one of the proposals of the Commissioners
of 1834.

Tea.

Before the war, tea had been charged an *ad valorem* duty, but in 1806 the necessities of the Government led to the raising of the tax to a uniform rate of 96 per cent. on all teas. Still in 1819 the tax was not reduced; all teas worth less than 2s. a pound paid at this rate; those worth more paid at the rate of 100 per cent. An attempt was made to restore the differential duties in 1834, but in 1836 a uniform duty of 2s. 1d. the pound on all sorts was again tried, and the consumption fell from 49,000,000 lb. to 31,000,000 lb., so that not till 1849 did the amount again stand at 49,000,000 lb. The *ad valorem* duty had enabled the poor to buy the cheapest bohea at only 1s. a pound. The new duty kept the inferior teas out of the market, and made tea cheaper for the rich and dearer for the poor. At the time when the tax on tea was 2s. 1d. a pound, the gallon of Irish whisky was paying but little more. But when the tax on whisky rose to 10s., and the duty on tea fell to 1s. 5d., the consumption of tea doubled. In 1865 the tax was 6d., and the total consumption in 1885 was 175,000,000 lb., or 4·87 lb. per head of the population, instead of 1·25 lb. as in 1837. The amount of coffee consumed has diminished in proportion to the increase of population. The consumption of sugar has increased nearly five-fold, from 15 lb. a head in 1837 to 70 lb. in 1887. In 1843 tobacco yielded to the revenue £3,711,000, in 1885 £9,250,000. This increase is perhaps partly due to the change of fashion about 1865, when the men who formerly would have been snuff-takers became smokers.

Wealth.

Elizabeth's reign is the only parallel in our history that can be suggested to illustrate the increase of wealth in the first fifty years of the Victorian era. It is estimated that the amount of income which would have been liable to income-tax assessment in 1837 was not more than £270,000,000; in 1887 it was £630,000,000, or, per head of population, £17 instead of £10. In 1837 the total income of the country divided among the population would have given £150, in 1887 £256 per head. Savings had increased from £14,000,000 to £90,000,000; houses of over £10 rental from £12,500,000 to £60,000,000.

Comfort: Matches.

But the period is unlike the reign of Elizabeth in that the growth of comfort has been due less perhaps to increase of wealth than to the powers of human invention. Not only do a larger number of people enjoy luxuries formerly confined to the few, but the nineteenth century is rich in discoveries which help to increase the comfort of all classes. The inventor of the first practical friction matches deserves a high place in the list of the benefactors of humanity. The old method of obtaining light by letting sparks, struck from flint and steel, fall on tinder, whence the sulphur-tipped spunk or match was ignited, was the only method in general use at the beginning of the century. In Paris a small quantity of phosphorus matches had been made since 1805. In 1827 John Walker, a druggist, of Stockton-on-Tees, invented matches tipped with sulphur, sulphide of antimony, and chlorate of potash. These he called Congreves, after Sir William Congreve, inventor of the Congreve rocket. They were sold at the rate of 1s. per box, containing eighty-four matches, with a piece of glass paper folded, through which each match had to be drawn to strike it. The Congreves were followed in 1830 by the noisy Pro-

TINDER BOXES, FLINTS AND STEELS. (*Victoria and Albert Museum.*)

metheans, which were made of paper, rolled and tipped with chlorate of potash and sugar, with a thin glass globule attached containing sulphuric acid, which was liberated when the glass broke as it was rubbed on a rough surface. In 1833 phosphorus matches began to be imported from Austria and South Germany in quantities of commercial importance.

Mineral Oil.

The uses of mineral oil were unknown commercially till 1859. Petroleum springs till then were suffered to run to waste ; all that was drawn was sold as a liniment called " American oil." In 1847 E. W. Binney had found that the oil from a Derbyshire spring could be used for lamps, and when the Alfreton spring was exhausted Mr. James Young, of Glasgow, decided to distil from the Boghead coal near Bathgate, and carried on the works till 1866. By that time the American springs were sending immense quantities into the market at cheap rates.

By the use of mineral instead of fixed oils it was possible to greatly simplify the mechanism of lamps. By the use of paraffin and stearine, candles of the cheaper sort were improved. Gas was introduced more freely into private houses as it became less expensive, as the service pipes and burners were improved, and the fear of explosions passed off. In 1821 it was still thought a great luxury.

Minor Comforts.

The cleansing properties of paraffin have also made great changes. Soap has been improved and cheapened. Blacking was a source of constant trouble to the Georgian dandy, who failed to produce with champagne so good an effect as Day and Martin secured with their cheap mixture, sold in stone jars to escape the glass-tax. Numbers of such small changes can easily be called to mind. Of much importance as affecting the public health and the appearance of towns was the withdrawal in 1831 of the tax on slate-roofing, and in 1851 of the window-tax.

Food.

The duties of housekeeping have been lightened in innumerable ways. Bought jams, preserved foods, tinned, bottled, fresh and dried foreign productions of all kinds, make it no longer necessary for the housekeeper to be generally a year in advance of time, with a store-room that would supply the needs of a besieged garrison, which yet must be continually replenished as the preserving seasons come round.

The nineteenth century had made it usual among the upper and middle classes to eat meat at three meals in the day. Meat-breakfasts are modern institutions. In 1845 Sir W. P. Lennox, recounting the pleasures of a stay at Horton, says there was at breakfast always a bill of fare sent up from the kitchen. Instead of having the sideboard covered with dishes of cutlets, grills, kidneys, eggs and bacon, etc., which get cold and clammy unless quickly attacked, a *carte* was put in the hands of every guest as

THE FIRST FARMHOUSE JAM FACTORY, 1873.
(By permission, from a photograph supplied by Messrs. Chivers.)

he entered the room, from which he made his choice. Tea, coffee, etc., were handed, and not poured out by the hostess; to see the hostess pour out he found as odious as for the guest to be asked to carve. How shocked would William Harrison have been had he been present at this breakfast! (Vol. III., p. 540.) Among the poor, too, it is certain that much more meat is eaten than at the beginning of the period. The importation of foreign meat at low prices has done much to bring this about. Many more are the minor changes affecting domestic comfort. Lennox speaks with enthusiasm of the supply of baths at Horton. Hot water, fires in bedrooms, armchairs, were comforts rarely enjoyed by the middle classes till the last half of the period. The poor of London were provided with the first public bath and wash-house in Glasshouse Yard in 1845. The catalogue of such details may be almost indefinitely prolonged.

Provincial Life. The vast growth of the urban population has changed the character of English provincial life within the period. By the middle of the century more than one-third of the population of England and Wales dwelt in towns of over 20,000 inhabitants, and the great centres of population have changed with a rapidity unknown to previous centuries. In 1825 Dublin was second only to London; in 1851 Manchester, Liverpool, and Glasgow stood **Growth of Great Towns.** before it. Manchester, which in 1825 had 140,000, in 1851 had 401,321; Liverpool rose from 120,000 to 375,955. Glasgow stood fourth in 1825 instead of second as now. Edinburgh and Birmingham followed, and only these six towns had over 100,000 inhabitants. Bristol with 80,000, Leeds, Sheffield, Plymouth with from 50,000 to 60,000, brought up the rear. In 1851 Leeds had risen to 172,270; Bristol and Sheffield followed with over 135,000. In 1816 no Middlesbrough existed; Swansea was a village. With this vast growth has come an increase in the importance of local interests, in local opportunities of every kind. A large number of wealthy people can enjoy a varied life without staying long in London. A country holiday, long or short, is now considered a necessity by all classes except the very poor. Although the importance of London to the whole country is fully as great as ever it was, London influences now go out to the country; it is less necessary to be constantly in London in order to be in touch with the world. The harder it was in old times to reach London, the more determined were the efforts of fashionable people to get there; now that it is easy to go people come and go incessantly. All classes know each other somewhat **Mingling of Classes.** better now; the arrogance of the aristocracy is less insolent, the bitterness of the democracy less uninformed and ignorant. It is no longer only in "contests with the clods" that rich men and poor have their one opportunity of meeting on equal terms. In every large town now there are many who take to heart the existence of an "East End," who are concerned with the problem of the social duties of the rich to the poor, and who realise something of the difficulties of philanthropy; where formerly it was possible to number the more energetic philanthropists, now their name is legion.

Precedence and etiquette in the first half of the century had **Home Life and Society.** been supremely important matters in provincial society, and those who loved the artificialities of civilisation found in them compensation for the dreariness of life. The importance assumed at one time by small domestic incidents which would nowadays be ignored makes it appear that our lives are flat and colourless in comparison with those of our ancestors. Those, again, who

TOYNBEE HALL, WHITECHAPEL.
(By permission, from a photograph supplied by the Secretary.)

enjoyed nature and the charms of a simple life had opportunities which rarely come to us. It was not then, as now, only the favoured few who can keep pigs, kill them, and make black puddings, sausages, and hams at home. It was suffered then in the heart of the largest towns. It was easier with a little energy and invention to create a sensation and to dazzle the neighbourhood; a little intellectual effort went a long way. Outside the family circle women, it is true, had not much to look for, but within there was freedom, even variety. It is possible that more pains were taken then to make home happy by those whose gifts lay that way, since in the home life lay the only chance of happiness. The naturally gay were, it would seem, more gay; the little excitements of life were more exciting. But those were not happy times for the gloomy-minded, for provincial people who had any sorrows to forget; there was no chance to escape from woes in the hurry of an active existence. As life becomes busier for all classes the desire for pleasure grows stronger, and with larger educational and intellectual opportunities for both sexes the possibilities of pleasure have become more varied, while the development of taste has given fuller consciousness to the sense of enjoyment. The demands made on life are greater, and to him that asks much, much shall be given. Goodness becomes more attractive, for it is not identified now, as once it was, with religious strictness, with the forbidding of pleasure, of theatres, of dancing, of cards; it is no longer conceived as a mere negation of evil, it has more of positive quality. Blake has as a motto of Hell: "Damn braces, bless relaxes." Who knows but it may yet prove to be a motto of Heaven?

JAMES COLVILLE. Scotland. SCOTTISH legislation has tended more and more to assimilation with that for England, but certain great movements, reflected in the English statute-book, have had their counterparts in the North as adapted to the special circumstances of Scotland—notably, Elementary Education, Endowed Schools, Public Health, Road Reform, and Local Government. Crofter Acts, again—a conspicuous feature—may be regarded as a reflex of the Allotments Act and the Irish Land Bill.

Education Not till 1872 was there secured a settlement of the long-pending question of education. The Act transferred control from the clergy to School Boards, relieved landlords from the burden of maintenance of schools and of teachers' salaries, and laid this on the general community. The religious difficulty was solved by neither prescribing nor proscribing, all being left to the arbitrament of the local ballot. The Presbyterian churches practically withdrew from the field, so that the Voluntary schools difficulty has no existence in Scotland. All parties find in the cumulative vote a tempting instrument for keeping alive sectarian ambition and jealousies. The old system had broken down most seriously in the larger towns, and here the secondary education, long supplied by grammar schools, soon found itself in competition with that developed by the Act. To remedy this the Endowed Schools Act (1882) secured for secondary education enormous funds, the fruit of ages of pious bequest, thus handing over to the well-to-do what had in most cases been designed for the poor and needy.

The Act of 1858 enormously stimulated the higher learning

GLASGOW UNIVERSITY.

on lines laid down by Dr. Chalmers in his evidence before the Commission of 1828, but did little to remove the weakest point in the Scotch University system, the preponderance of professorial lecturing over teaching. The later Act of 1890 has effected radical changes in the constitution of the Universities. The most notable academic event of the time was the removal of Glasgow College from its old and limited site in the heart of the city to the commanding eminence of Gilmour Hill (1869), at a total cost of little short of half a million. In the same year Edinburgh Medical School was successfully stormed at last by five women students.

Universities.

Public
Health.

Under the Act of 1867, amended 1879, rural and urban sanitary districts were created, and for the first time the duty of guarding our social and industrial environment was made a legal claim on the whole community.   The period has seen the fruits of such measures as the Improvement Acts for Edinburgh (1865) and Glasgow (1866).   The marvellous advance in the standard of well-being and taste is shown by the fact that all the large towns have been almost entirely rebuilt within living memory, and this on a scale that marks a revolution in public feeling. Open spaces in towns, long overlooked, are now appreciated. Edinburgh led the way in this direction by laying out the Meadows as a public park in 1853.   The tramway appeared first in Glasgow in August, 1872, immediately after the lead of Liverpool and London.   A change, equally vital to the country districts, was the much older measure of Road Reform, originating in 1845 and consummated by the Act of 1881, which substituted a general assessment for the machinery of tolls and local trusts, heavily burdened with debt.   After June, 1883, tolls ceased to exist.   The supply of water and gas in large towns was gradually assumed by municipalities.   Here the example of Glasgow and Edinburgh spread to the rural districts, where the Local Government Act (1885) has given corporate life to scattered communities.   It restored the office of Scottish Secretary, combined shortly after the Union with that of the Lord Advocate.

Industry.

Scotland has played a leading part in the greatest engineering advance of recent times, the manufacture of steel and its applications on the largest scale.   The Steel Company of Scotland, first at Newton in 1871 and next at Blochairn in 1880, has made the Clyde the centre for the manufacture of Siemens steel (p. 746).   The Forth Bridge (p. 740) was a colossal triumph for the new material.   The steel for the structure was made in Glasgow, and put in place by Sir William Arrol, an engineer of that city.   The bridge was begun in 1882, and opened in 1889. Previously a substantial railway-bridge over the Tay at Dundee had taken the place of the slight iron structure blown down in the terrific winter gale of 1879.   Lord Kelvin's vast and varied services to physical and electrical science have been mentioned elsewhere (pp. 711, 729).

The Admiralty led the way in applying steel to shipbuilding

when Denny of Dumbarton turned out the *Redoubtable* (1874). The success of the manufacture led to a crowd of Clyde indus- tries, notably to the building of warships. No sooner had Clyde engineers triumphed in building powerful ships of iron and sub- sequently of steel than they turned to such agents in effecting the best results in economy and efficiency as the surface con- denser, the compound engine (pp. 464, 730), and the triple- Marine Engineer- ing.

Photo: *Wilson, Aberdeen.*

THE TAY BRIDGE AFTER THE DISASTER OF 1879.

expansion principle. Kirke of Dumbarton successfully applied triple-expansion to the engines of the *Propontis* in 1874. There, too, William Denny, with the help of the famous Leven Experi- mental Tank (1883), established data for calculations which are indispensable to the modern shipbuilder. The Clyde Harbour The Clyde Trust has kept pace with this rapid progress in the building of long, deep, powerful steamships. The first steam-dredger began work in 1824, and for long thereafter the material removed was used to build up the banks of the river, but in 1862 steam hopper barges were introduced for removing the dredgings to the deeper waters. Now the river from Port Glasgow to Glasgow is practically a deep-sea canal, adapted for the largest of ships. Till 1869 the river-bank supplied the quayage of the port of Glasgow, but in that year an Act was obtained for a magnificent new dock, opened in 1873, and this has been followed by others.

The Church.
The great blow of the Disruption roused the Church to fresh efforts.   By the Robertson Extension Scheme, 351 new charges were founded and endowed (1854–86).   This was a striking contrast to the policy of the pre-Disruption days, when the Moderates deprecated the creation of small, struggling churches.   Within the Church itself a notable liberalising process has been in progress, and this both in creed and ritual.   An extremely unpopular church rate, the annuity tax, a long-standing grievance in Edinburgh, was satisfactorily disposed of in 1871.   The Assembly, after a vigorous attack extending over several years (1857-69), was at last got to condemn patronage, and this led to the Act abolishing this fruitful source of trouble (1874).

Agriculture.
Economic changes have sorely crippled the oldest of industries, agriculture, bringing in their train what is almost a social revolution.   Clyde triumphs in shipbuilding have contributed to this result in keeping the foreign supply of food-stuffs lucrative and expeditious.   The Bell-Colman refrigerating process, a Clyde invention, was first successfully applied, about the close of the period, to sea-going vessels, when a cargo of frozen meat was brought from Australia in good condition.   Extensive depopulation and consequent unequal distribution of labour have brought about changes in rural economy, which have in turn stimulated invention.   Few contrivances have had more notable effects than the reaper, invented by the Rev. Patrick Bell of Carmyllie (1799–1869), and in successful and extensive operation after the middle of the century (p. 477).   But the economic distress of the Lowland farmer is mild in comparison with that of his Highland compatriot.   His story is told in the **The Crofter Question.** Report of the Crofter Commission, 1884.   In the agrarian movement of which it was the outcome the Highlander made no claim to dual ownership, limiting himself to a demand for enlarged holdings, especially for grazing, and security of tenure. The period 1748–1825 (end of the clearances) witnessed far-reaching changes in the formation of big sheep-farms, entailing the appropriation of township lands, long farmed in common, and the removal of the peasant cultivators or crofters to the arable sea-coast strip, generally poor in soil and limited in area. The large farmers who took their place were often absent tenants

of absent landlords, leaving but few natural and intelligent leaders of the community, and these scattered over wide areas. Latterly this reversion to pastoral conditions has not been a success for the sheep-farmers any more than the needy and unprogressive crofter, who, regardless of consequences, allowed the squatting of cotters to go on unchecked—a process aggravated by the perilous subdivision of his petty croft among his dependent relatives. For awhile kelp-burning diffused much

CROFTER'S HOME IN ISLAY, 1787.
("*Britannica Curiosa.*")

money, but the industry collapsed after 1851. Fishing, too, of which much had been expected, was impossible to this farming population in the absence of harbours, access to markets, and capital. Government has done very little to help. Commercial enterprise, however, stimulated by this age of sport and touring, has done and is doing far more than legislation or imperial doles. Orkney and Shetland started for itself a direct service to Leith in 1833. About the same time Burns began the West Highland trade, subsequently taken up by the firm of Hutcheson (now Macbrayne). After Queen Victoria passed over the Royal Route in 1847, an immense impetus was given to Highland touring.   Railways followed, beginning with the Highland (1865), extended ultimately to Wick.   The Callander and Oban Railway tapped much of the west coast.   But to reach the more central districts, and ultimately the remoter north-west, a railway from Glasgow to Fort William was projected.   Thrown out in Parliament (1883), it was not opened till more than ten years later, and was subsequently extended towards loch Ness and Skye.

Photo: Wilson, Aberdeen.

CROFTER'S HOME IN SKYE, 1885.

P. W.
JOYCE.
Ireland.
The
Fenian
Society.

THE Fenian Society, which took definite shape in 1862, had for its object to effect the independence of Ireland by force of arms; and the members were sworn in and the proceedings were carried on in secret council.   The leaders, like those of the Young Ireland party, were men of education and high moral character; and their organ, the *Irish People*, which decried constitutional agitation and openly advocated armed resistance, was conducted with great ability.   In 1865 a number of the leading Fenians were arrested, including the chief organiser, James Stephens; but a few days later Stephens escaped from prison by the help of his warders, who themselves had been sworn in as Fenians.   The others were sentenced to various terms of penal servitude. The movement spread, however, not only in Ireland but also in England and America; and the ranks were swelled by the accession of large numbers of Irishmen who had fought through the recent American War. In 1867 there was a rising on a small scale. which was suppressed without any difficulty. A plan to seize Chester Castle with its store of arms was disclosed to the authorities in time enough to prevent its execution. Shortly afterwards, on the occasion of the rescue of two Fenian prisoners from a prison van in Manchester, the police officer in charge was unintentionally shot dead; for which three of the rescue party, Allen, Larkin, and O'Brien, were tried and hanged. Near the end of the same year (1867) an attempt was made to blow up Clerkenwell Prison, with the idea of rescuing a Fenian prisoner who was confined in it, which caused the death of several men and other scarcely less dreadful consequences to many people in the neighbourhood (p. 520).

These events, happening in quick succession, seriously turned the minds of Englishmen to the necessity of adopting some measures of restoring Ireland to a condition of tranquillity. It was felt that reform was needed in three directions, or, as Mr. Gladstone expressed it, that the Irish Upas tree had three branches—the Established Church, the system of land **The Irish** tenure, and the system of national education—meaning chiefly **Church,** University Education. At the end of 1868 there was a general **1867.** election, and Mr. Gladstone became Premier with a great Liberal majority (p. 520). Attention was first directed to the state of the Protestant Church in Ireland. It had been originally established and richly endowed with the direct object of converting the Roman Catholic people to the Protestant faith; but so far was it from accomplishing this, that the Catholics had relatively increased, and at this time the Established Church Protestants formed only about a tenth of the whole population. After most determined opposition and vehement denunciations, the Protestant Church of Ireland was disestablished by the Gladstone Government in 1869, due regard being had to vested interests.

The next question was the land. In 1870 Mr. Gladstone **The Land** had a Bill passed intended to secure for the tenants com **Act, 1870.** pensation for improvements and for disturbance in case of eviction, and also to encourage peasant proprietorship (p. 523).

308

But the landlords in various ways impeded the working of the measure, so that the intention of the Legislature was carried out only to a trifling extent. Compensation for disturbance afforded little or no security; evictions went on as busily as ever—two or three thousand a year—and the population still continued to run down.

The University Problem. Next came an attempt to settle the question of University Education (p. 526). There were at this time in Ireland the Dublin University—or Trinity College, as it is usually called—a purely Protestant institution, though admitting Catholics to degrees; and the Queen's University, with its three colleges, in Belfast, Cork, and Galway, founded in 1845, but having no provision for religious teaching. The Catholics demanded a University of their own, endowed and chartered, and in all respects on an equality with Trinity College. Twenty years previously the Catholic bishops had established a Catholic University in Dublin, which was supported by subscriptions and was well attended; but it had no charter and no power to confer degrees. In 1873 a Bill was introduced by Mr. Gladstone to abolish both the existing Universities and to create a central one, to which Trinity College, the three Queen's University Colleges, and the Catholic University should be affiliated; but the Bill was thrown out. Thus, so far, only one branch of the Upas tree had been dealt with successfully.

Home Rule. Under the leadership of Isaac Butt, a Protestant barrister, the Home Rule agitation was revived; and in the General Election of 1874 more than fifty Irish Home Rulers were returned to Parliament. Butt's motions in Parliament in favour of Home Rule were, as usual, easily voted down, on which the Home Rulers turned their attention to the land; but their efforts in Parliament for land reform were fruitless.

Secondary Education. The Irish Intermediate Education Act, which was passed in 1878, provides for intermediate (or secondary) education, by yearly public examination of students, by awarding prizes and exhibitions to successful students, and by paying results fees under certain conditions to managers of schools. The expenses are defrayed from a portion of the funds of the Disestablished Church. This, like the National System of Primary Education, has been very successful.

The condition of the small farming classes continued so **The Land** alarming that the land question now overshadowed all others; **League.** and about 1879 the Land League was formed by Michael Davitt, a league destined to exercise a most important influence on Irish affairs.   In the following year Charles Stewart Parnell, the greatest figure in Irish political history of the latter half of the century, became the leader of the Irish party.   In the same

AFTER THE EXPLOSION IN CLERKENWELL, 1867.
(Reproduced by permission of the Proprietors of the "Illustrated London News.")

year (1880) there was a General Election (p. 533), and the Liberals came into power with an overwhelming majority. The land agitation grew more violent than ever, for evictions rather increased than diminished, and the practice of boy-cotting began to be resorted to.   The methods of the people were similar to those carried on during the tithe war (p. 148), and for a time boycotting became a leading feature in the land agitation.   An unsuccessful attempt to convict and punish the leaders of the Land League was followed by Mr. Forster's Coercion Act, giving power to arrest all persons "reasonably suspected" of certain specified offences.   While this Bill was passing through Parliament, the system of Parliamentary Obstruction, which had been brought to great perfection by Parnell and Biggar, came into full play, and the proceedings were greatly protracted.   But the Bill became law in March, 1881.

The first real attempt to go to the heart of the land question was made by the Land Act of 1881, passed by the Gladstone Government (p. 534).   While passing through the

VENUS ATTIRED BY THE GRACES, 1869.
(Reproduced by special permission of the Proprietors of " Punch.")

Commons, what is called the " Healy Clause," exempting the tenants' improvements from rent, was inserted at the instance of Mr. T. M. Healy.   Before becoming law the Bill was twice sent back to the Commons by the House of Lords, so altered as to render it almost useless; but the Commons were determined, and the Lords passed it in the end, much against their will.   A Land Court was formed for fixing fair rents and for settling disputes between landlord and tenant. The rent once fixed by this court remained stationary for fifteen years, during which there could be no eviction except for serious breach of contract, such as non-payment of rent. The Irish members, whose ideas had expanded as the land contest in

HIBERNIA WATCHING FOR THE GOOD SHIP LAND ACT, 1881.
(Reproduced by special permission of the Proprietors of "Punch.")

Ireland grew more bitter and protection for the tenant more necessary, accepted the measure as an instalment of what was due; and expressed their determination to have the landlords bought out, and the land put in possession of the tenants. The Act was, however, extensively made use of; and the Land Court and its branches fixed fair rents in a vast number of cases, with an average reduction of about twenty per cent.

The Coercion Act, 1881.

Meantime, under Mr. Forster's Act, great numbers of persons had been imprisoned on "reasonable suspicion"—no offence specified. At length, in October, 1881, matters came to a climax when Mr. Parnell and many of the other chief leaders were arrested and lodged in Kilmainham Gaol. This was followed by the No-rent Manifesto from the imprisoned leaders, which, however, was universally condemned by the clergy, and was not obeyed to any extent. But it led to the suppression of the Land League by Government proclamation. After the imprisonment of the leaders the state of the country became worse than ever, and murders and other outrages increased. At length the conviction forced itself on the Government that the arrest of Parnell and the others was a mistake, and did harm instead of good; and a conciliatory policy was resolved on. Mr. Forster's Act was dropped, and the suspects were all released; whereupon Mr. Forster resigned the Chief Secretaryship, and Lord Frederick Cavendish was appointed in his place. But the hopes of peace and tranquillity were dashed by a terrible crime. There had grown up in Dublin a secret society calling themselves "Invincibles," whose chief agency in carrying out their plans was assassination; and on the 6th of May, 1882, Lord Frederick Cavendish and Mr. Thomas Burke the Under-Secretary, were murdered in the Phœnix Park, Dublin (p. 537)—a crime which created no less horror and grief in Ireland than elsewhere. This terminated for a time the policy of conciliation, and a stringent Coercion Bill was passed. After some further attempts at assassination the murderers were brought to justice; five of the Invincibles were hanged, and others were sent to penal servitude. These events

Photo: Lawrence Dublin.

CHARLES STEWART PARNELL.

The Phœnix Park Murders.

were followed by a series of dynamite outrages in London in 1884 and 1885, which had been concocted in America; but these, too, ceased on the lapse of the Coercion Act. The remaining events of 1885 (p. 540), need no special detail here.

Of late years the ancient Language and Literature of Ireland have attracted much attention. The movement began

SCENE OF THE PHŒNIX PARK MURDERS.

about half a century ago; and it will be interesting to sketch the progress of Celtic learning during that time, so far as it concerns Ireland, and to indicate its present position and future prospects. The study is a difficult one, for the Gaelic texts preserved in manuscripts comprise specimens of the language dating from the seventh century downwards; and as Irish underwent, from century to century, those gradual changes that every living language is subject to, the Gaelic of the early centuries differs at least as much from the modern language, in vocabulary, orthography, and inflection, as the language of Chaucer does from that of Tennyson. In the case of Irish, moreover, there is this additional element of

P. W. JOYCE.
Celtic Scholarship.

difficulty: that the continuity of the written language was broken by the wholesale destruction of manuscripts during the Danish and Anglo-Norman invasions; so that we have now numerous early pieces containing words, phrases, and allusions which no one has hitherto been able to explain. These obscure old texts are chiefly contained in manuscripts preserved in Dublin.

The Keys to the MSS. In Continental libraries there are numerous copies of the Latin classics, full of interlined and marginal glosses or explanations, in Irish, of the words and phrases of the Latin text, written by Irish teachers, mainly for the use of those of their Irish pupils who were learning Latin. They were written during those ages when Irish scholars and missionaries frequented the Continent and were employed as professors in many of the French, German, and Italian schools and colleges. By the help of these glosses, which date from the seventh to the ninth century, the meanings of innumerable Irish words and phrases, long lost, have been recovered, by reversing the original intention—the Irish being now explained by the Latin, instead of Latin by Irish. By means of these glosses also, and of those of the other Celtic dialects, the great German scholar, Johann Kaspar Zeuss, constructed his " Grammatica Celtica," a complete grammar of the four ancient dialects of Celtic—viz. Gaelic, Welsh, Cornish, and Breton—which first directed the attention of Continental scholars to the importance of the subject. This great work, which was published in 1853, laid the foundation of Celtic philology. Since his time a great many of the Continental glosses have been published, chiefly by German, French, and Italian scholars.

Irish Celtic Scholars. About fifty years ago the Celtic and Archæological Societies were established in Dublin, under whose auspices Dr. John O'Donovan translated and annotated, with great learning and research, a number of Gaelic texts, forming several volumes. The most important of all his works, however, was his edition of the Annals of the Four Masters, which has been mentioned already (Vol. IV., p. 276). In these several works O'Donovan rediscovered, as it were, and restored the ancient historical topography of Ireland, which, when he began his labours, had been all but lost. His fellow-labourer, Professor Eugene O'Curry, delivered a series of lectures in the

Catholic University, Dublin, on the Manuscript Materials of Irish History, which were published in one volume in 1861, and at once turned attention to the vast amount of ancient Celtic lore contained in the collection of manuscripts preserved in the libraries of Trinity College and of the Royal Irish Academy in Dublin. Another series of his lectures, of equal importance, on the Manners and Customs of the Ancient Irish People, was published after his death, edited by Dr. W. K. Sullivan, of Cork. O'Donovan and O'Curry translated the Brehon Laws, a task of enormous difficulty, on account of the technical nature of the subject and the archaic and elliptical forms of expression. Four volumes of these ancient laws have been lately published, and two more, under the editorship of Dr. Robert Atkinson, are on the eve of publication. What Zeuss did on the Continent these two great scholars, O'Donovan and O'Curry, did in Ireland; they led the way in the proper scientific method of investigating and illustrating the contents of our ancient Gaelic

Photo: Lawrence, Dublin.
EUGENE O'CURRY.

manuscripts, and laid the foundation of Gaelic scholarship at home. Contemporary with O'Donovan and O'Curry were three other scholars—the Rev. Dr. William Reeves, author of several important works on Irish literature, among them his edition of Adamnan's Life of St. Columba, a monument of exhaustive accurate learning; the Rev. Dr. Todd, who edited the Irish Book of Hymns, the "Wars of the Irish with the Danes," with translation, and left several other important works; and Dr. George Petrie, who set at rest the question of the origin of the Irish Round Towers, in his great work on the "Ecclesiastical Architecture of Ireland," and who, though not himself a Gaelic scholar, was in fact the guiding spirit in the

movement for the study of the language and antiquities of
Ireland.

The MSS. Published.   The circumstance which gave, perhaps, the greatest stimulus
of all to Celtic investigation was the publication in *facsimile*
by the Royal Irish Academy, since 1870, of the most important
of the Dublin Gaelic manuscripts—viz. "The Book of the Dun
Cow," "The Book of Leinster," "The Speckled Book of MacEgan,"
"The Book of Ballymote," and "The Yellow Book of Lecan"—
which contain nearly all the important texts. Copies of these
books are now in all the principal libraries of Europe, so that
scholars everywhere have opportunities of studying them without
coming to Dublin; and the opportunities have been turned to
excellent account. Several periodicals are now published on
the Continent and in Great Britain devoted either wholly or
partly to Celtic learning, such as the *Revue Celtique, Melusine,*
the *Archæological Journal,* etc.

Celtic Scholars at the close of the Century.   Among living workers, Dr. Whitley Stokes must be singled
out as by far the most distinguished. He has translated and
edited a great number of Gaelic glossaries, ancient romantic
tales and lives of saints, the Tripartite Life of St. Patrick, the
"Feilirè," or poetical catalogue of saints, written by Aengus the
Culdee, with many other texts; and the results of his labours
will be found partly in separate volumes, and partly in the
pages of the *Revue Celtique* and other periodicals. Dr. Standish
Hayes O'Grady gave to the world in 1892 a most important
work, "Silva Gadelica," consisting of text and translation of
thirty-one ancient tales, with annotations. The Rev. Edmund
Hogan, S.J., among other works, published the "Battle of
Rossnaree," with original text and translation; and the Rev.
Dr. B. McCarthy translated the latter part of the "Annals of
Ulster," in continuation of the translation of the earlier part by
the late W. M. Hennessy, who also translated the "Annals of
Loch Ce" and the "Chronicon Scotorum." All the scholars
hitherto named, except Zeuss, are, or were, Irishmen. But many
others are working with equal enthusiasm and success in the
same field. In Germany Ernst Windisch and H. Zimmer, and
in France H. D'Arbois de Jubainville, have brought a vast
amount of learning to bear in illustrating ancient Irish lore of
every kind; they have published texts and glossaries, essays
on Irish mythology, laws, literature, philology, descriptive

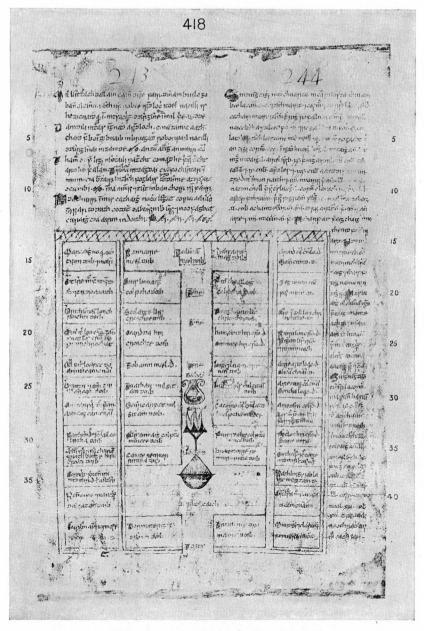

PAGE FROM "THE YELLOW BOOK OF LECAN."

(Reproduced from the Facsimile by permission of the Royal Irish Academy.)

catalogues of manuscripts, etc. In Dublin Dr. Robert Atkinson has printed several texts with glossaries, some with and some without translation; and he has in preparation a glossary of the Brehon Laws, and a still more important work, a complete lexicon of the Gaelic language, both ancient and modern. Professor Kuno Meyer, of Liverpool, has published a number of Irish tales with translations, some in separate volumes and some in the *Revue Celtique* and other periodicals. Notwithstanding what has been done, however, the principal text of all still remains untranslated and unpublished. This is a long story called the " Táin bo Chuailnge," or the " Cattle Spoil of Quelna," the Irish epic, contained in " The Book of the Dun Cow," and " The Book of Leinster," which, from its great difficulty, has hitherto deterred Celtic scholars from dealing with it. It is, however, understood that Ernst Windisch has prepared a German version, and it is to be hoped that the text with the German translation will be soon given to the world.

From the foregoing sketch some idea may be formed of the amount of learning and labour expended in illustrating the ancient lore of Ireland. Moreover, the subject is attracting more and more attention, and the number of persons engaged in the investigation increases year by year; and it may be asserted that it excites almost as keen an interest among scholars as we see manifested by the public of learning in the study of Egyptian and Assyrian literature and antiquities.

J. SCOTT KELTIE. British Exploration, 1815-1885.

THE continuous and almost world-wide war which was waged from 1793 to 1815 was not favourable to the work of exploration; but when the Napoleonic incubus was removed in the latter year, an impetus was given in this, as in other directions, to British activity, which grew with the century. But even in these oppressive years explorers were not entirely idle.

The Arctic Regions.

Soon after 1815 Polar exploration was renewed with increased zeal. Captain Scoresby, it may be mentioned, in 1806 reached, on the north of Spitzbergen, a latitude of 81° 12′ 42″. In 1818 two Government expeditions were despatched—one under Captain Buchan, with Lieutenant John Franklin as second in command, to Spitzbergen, and the other under Captain John Ross, with Lieutenant Edward Parry as second, to Davis

Straits. The former was unfortunate, but the latter may be said to have rediscovered Baffin's Bay. In the following year Parry succeeded in pushing through Lancaster Sound and Barrow Strait, passing the Parry Islands on his right to Melville Island, about half-way to Behring Strait. In a second expedition (1821–3) Parry discovered Fury and Hecla Strait, separating Melville Peninsula from Cockburn Land;

PASSAGE THROUGH THE ICE, JUNE, 1818.
(*Sir J. Ross, "Voyage of Discovery in H.M.S. 'Isabella' and H.M.S. 'Alexander,'" 1819.*)

and in a third attempt (1824) entered Barrow Strait, and explored the channel leading to the south, which he named Prince Regent's Inlet. At the same time that Parry tried to push his way from the east, Captain Beechey entered the Arctic Sea by Behring Strait (1826), and succeeded in reaching Point Barrow, 156° 31′ W. With these two expeditions a third co-operated by land under Captain John Franklin. Before this, however, Franklin had succeeded in laying down a considerable stretch of the coast of Arctic America. In 1819–22, accompanied by Dr. Richardson and two midshipmen, Back and Hood, Franklin made his way by the Saskatchewan and the Barren Grounds to the Coppermine river, which he followed, descended, and explored the coast to the east for 500 miles, as far as Cape Turnagain. On his next expedition—that of 1826—Franklin, again accompanied by Dr. Richardson, descended the Mackenzie river, and laid down the coast of the continent through 37 degrees of longitude—as far east as the Coppermine river, and as far west as the 150th meridian, within 160 miles of Beechey's farthest. Meantime, on the east coast of Greenland, Captain Scoresby succeeded (1822) in penetrating the ice-barrier and carrying out a survey from 75° N. to 69° N.; and in 1823 Captain Sabine conducted a series of pendulum observations on the same coast, in 75° 30′ N., surveying the coast from 72° to 76° N. One of the most interesting attempts to penetrate northwards was that made by Captain Parry in 1827, when he proceeded to Spitzbergen in the *Hecla*, and, setting out upon the ice in sledge-boats, reached 82° 45′ N., which for nearly half a century was the record northern latitude.

The next important Arctic expedition was equipped by Felix Booth, and placed under the command of Captain John Ross and his nephew James Ross. This expedition left England in 1829 in the *Victory*, and proceeded down Prince Regent's Inlet to its continuation, which was named the Gulf of Boothia, the projecting peninsula on its left receiving the same name, Boothia. Expeditions were made across the peninsula, on the west side of which, on June 1st, 1831, the Magnetic Pole was discovered. King William's Land, on the west of Boothia, was discovered and named, and to some extent explored. The Rosses—who passed four winters on the shores of Boothia and North Somerset, and had at last to abandon their vessels—were rescued (1833) by a whaler in Barrow Strait. In 1833 Captain Back was sent out by land to search for the Rosses. In 1834 he descended the Great Fish river, but want of supplies prevented him from proceeding beyond its mouth. Nor was he more successful in 1836 in his attempt to complete our knowledge of the northern shores of America. This work was ultimately achieved by employees of the Hudson's Bay Company. Simpson and Dease in 1837 connected the work of Franklin with that of Beechey at Point Barrow, and in 1839 they traced the coast from Cape Turnagain eastward past the mouth of the Great Fish river to Castor and Pollux river.

In 1853–4, Dr. John Rae completed the work of Dease and Simpson on the east, exploring the west coast of Boothia and proving King William's Land to be an island. Before this, however, in 1846–7, Rae had explored the great gulf (Committee Bay) on the south of Boothia Gulf. Thus, after about thirty years' work, the outline of the northern coast of America was completed.

Partly owing to the strong representations of Sir John Barrow, in 1845, the Government of the day resolved to make another attempt to discover a practicable north-west passage, and in June of that year despatched the *Erebus* and *Terror*, under the command of Sir John Franklin, who was well supported by Captain Crozier, Captain FitzJames, and other naval officers, and by a well-selected body of men. Proceeding up Baffin's Bay, Franklin passed through Lancaster Sound and Barrow Strait, sailed up Wellington Channel to 77° N., circumnavigated Cornwallis Island, and returned to winter at Beechey Island, off the south-west coast of North Devon. In 1846 the ships proceeded down Peel Sound and Franklin Strait between North Somerset and Boothia on the one side and Prince of Wales Land on the other, towards the passage lying between King William's Land and Victoria Land, and were apparently caught in the ice near Cape Felix to the north-west of King William's Land, where they passed the winter of 1846–7. In June of the latter year Franklin died, and in the year following, no news of the party having reached England, a search expedition was sent out. Between that year and 1854 some fifteen expeditions were sent out from England and America with the hope of rescuing or, at least, of finding traces of the missing explorers. Their searches left no room for doubt as to the fate of Franklin and his men. The ships were abandoned on April 22nd, 1848. The officers and crew, consisting of 105 souls under Captain Crozier, landed on King William's Island in 98° 41′ W., and started for the mainland in the hope of being able to make their way up the Great Fish river to the Hudson's Bay Company's stations. From the testimony of the Eskimo and of the subsequently discovered relics of the expedition, it was evident that one by one the poor men fell by the way, dying of cold and starvation, most of them before reaching the mainland at all. In-

Sir John Franklin.

directly, the expedition led to great additions to our knowledge of the Arctic region lying to the north of America. By far the most important of the search expeditions was the double one despatched in 1850, four ships under the command of Captain Austin being sent out by Barrow Strait, while from the other side Captains Collinson and M'Clure with two ships proceeded by Behring Strait. By the former branch of the expedition Cornwallis Island was explored, M'Clintock—who had accompanied Captain Austin—proceeding to Melville Island, and his comrades Osborne and Ommanney discovering Prince of Wales Island. On the other side Captain Collinson succeeded in

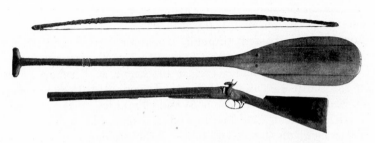

BOW, PADDLE, AND SHOT GUN FROM SIR JOHN FRANKLIN'S EXPEDITION.
(Greenwich Hospital.   By permission of the Lords Commissioners of the Admiralty.)

navigating his ship from Behring Strait along the northern coast of America, to within a short distance from where Franklin's ships were beset. But before this, Collinson's party had examined Prince of Wales Strait between Banks Land and Prince Albert Land, the latter of which was traced in a southerly direction. The shores of Victoria Land were also explored before Collinson's ship, the *Enterprise*, returned to Behring Strait in 1853. Meantime M'Clure almost circumnavigated Banks Land, visited Melville Island, and after three years he and his companions were obliged to abandon their ship; proceeding across the ice, they reached, in June, 1853, the *Resolute*, under Captain Kellett, which had been despatched through Lancaster Sound in 1852. As they returned with her crew by the same route, M'Clure may be said to have first traversed the North-West Passage. Kellett's vessel was one of four sent out in 1852 under Sir Edward Belcher by

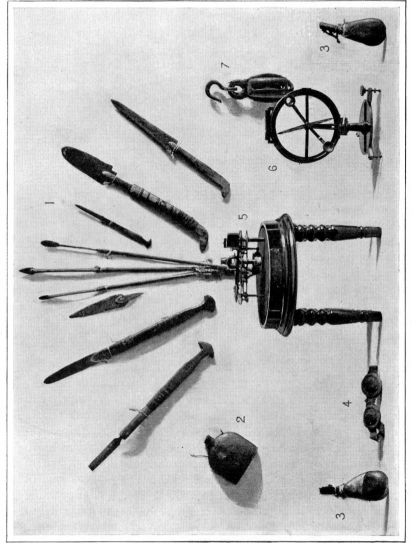

RELICS OF SIR JOHN FRANKLIN. (GREENWICH HOSPITAL.)

(By permission of the Lords Commissioners of the Admiralty.)

way of Lancaster Sound. Some thousands of miles were traversed in sledges in the course of this expedition, and our knowledge of Cornwallis, Bathurst, Melville, and Prince Patrick Islands, as well as of the channels and islands to the south, was thereby completed.[1] The final expedition (1857–9), sent out at Lady Franklin's expense, under M'Clintock, not only cleared up the fate of Franklin and his men, but completed our knowledge of the shores of Boothia, King William's Land, and Prince of Wales Island. When to all this we add the work of the American search parties, it will be seen that the terrible tragedy of the Franklin expedition was productive of the richest geographical results.

Nares' Expedition, 1875. It was not until thirty years after the departure of the *Erebus* and *Terror* that the British Government equipped another expedition for purely exploring purposes in the Arctic regions. This expedition was placed under the command of Captain Nares (p. 927), and, in the *Alert* and the *Discovery*, left England in May, 1875. It made its way through Baffin's Bay, Smith Sound, Kennedy Channel and Robeson Channel, to Lady Franklin Bay in Grinnell Land, where the *Discovery* was left, the *Alert* pushing on about forty-five miles further, to 82° 27′ N. The most striking incident in connection with this expedition was the sledge journey of Commander (afterwards Admiral) Albert Markham, who in the spring of 1876 succeeded, in the face of enormous difficulties owing to the state of the ice, in pushing his way northwards to 83° 20′ 26″, the highest latitude which had ever been attained, a latitude surpassed by only a mile or two during the Greely expedition of 1882–4. Besides this, Lieutenant Aldrich explored some 200 miles of coast on the north of Grant Land, and Lieutenant Beaumont a long stretch of the north-west coast of Greenland. On the opposite side of the Arctic area, Leigh Smith, in 1880–2, succeeded in adding considerably to our knowledge of Franz Josef Land, discovered by the Austrian expedition under Payer and Weyprecht. England took her share in 1882–3 in the international schemes

[1 Sir Edward Belcher abandoned all but one of his ships, against the opinion of his subordinates. The *Resolute* eventually drifted into the Atlantic, was picked up by an American whaler, bought by subscription in America, and presented to Queen Victoria.]

for circumpolar observations, by establishing a station on
Great Slave Lake.

British enterprise was neither so extensive nor so continuous   The
in the Antarctic as in the Arctic. Between Cook's memorable   Antarctic
voyage (1773 : Vol. V., p. 302), when he reduced the " Great   Regions.

THE COUNTRIES ROUND THE NORTH POLE AS KNOWN IN 1875.
(By permission from the contemporary chart published by Edward Stanford.)

Antarctic Continent " within reasonable limits, and 1815, barely
anything had been done for the exploration of this part of the
world. A few outlying islands, not strictly within the Antarctic
area, had been discovered by British vessels in the early years
of this century. Enderby Land and Graham's Land were reached
by Captain Biscoe in 1831, but most knowledge was gained by
the expedition sent out by the British Government in 1839–43

in the *Erebus* and *Terror* under Captain (afterwards Sir) James Ross. In the first year Kerguelen Island was surveyed; in the second year Ross pushed southwards with his two sailing vessels, and in the longitude of New Zealand land (Victoria Land) was sighted in about 70° S., with lofty mountain ranges. The land was followed to about 77° 30′ S., where an active volcano, Mount Erebus, 12,400 feet, was sighted, and an extinct volcano, Mount

ANTARCTIC ICE, 1874.

(By permission from a photograph supplied by the "Challenger" Office, Edinburgh.)

Terror, 10,900 feet. Further progress southwards was impossible, owing to an impenetrable ice barrier rising to a height of 150 feet, which was traced to several degrees east, the highest latitude reached being 78° 11′ S., in February, 1842. In 1874 the *Challenger* just crossed the Antarctic circle to the south of Kerguelen Island; since then, so far as British enterprise is concerned, nothing was done for the exploration of the Antarctic till the twentieth century.

One of the greatest enterprises for the exploration of Asia by England has undoubtedly been the survey of India. Begun in 1800 at the suggestion of Major Lambton, it has been steadily carried on under a succession of able officers. The principal triangulation of the whole peninsula was, indeed, practically completed in 1883, so that the great features of the geography of our Indian Empire are known with almost mathematical accuracy. Alongside of the trigonometrical work, topographical and cadastral surveys have been carried out, with the result that a vast amount of varied geographical information has been collected, a summary of which has been embodied in the great Government " Gazetteer of India," compiled under the direction of Sir W. W. Hunter. The coasts of India and neighbouring countries have at the same time been surveyed by officers of the Indian Navy. The official work has been supplemented by a multitude of books by officials and others, but the work of the Indian survey has extended far beyond the frontiers of the country itself. Under the superintendence of men like Sir Andrew Waugh, Colonel Montgomerie, and General J. T. Walker, the great mountain mass of the Himalayas has been sur-

CHRISTMAS HARBOUR, KERGUELEN ISLAND.

(By permission from a photograph supplied by the "Challenger" Office, Edinburgh.)

veyed with approximate completeness, and many of its loftiest
peaks measured, from Mount Everest (29,000 feet) downwards. In 1855 the survey of Kashmir and of the mass of
mountains up to the Tibetan frontier was begun by Colonel
Montgomerie, who also organised the plan of employing
native explorers to make their way into Turkestan and Tibet
and other parts of Central Asia, which has led to considerable
gains to geographical knowledge between the meridians of
66° and 102° E. longitude. One of the most important contributions to a knowledge of Kashmir during the period was made
by F. Drew, who for many years resided in the country in an
official capacity. W. Moorcroft, with G. Trebeck, in 1819–25,
visited Ladak, and Kashmir, Peshawar, Kabul and Bokhara.
Alexander Burnes's residence in Kabul (1836–8) added much
to our knowledge of Persia, as did the reports obtained by him
in Sind, Afghanistan, and neighbouring countries. Lieutenant
Wood, of the Indian Navy, in 1838, pushed beyond the Hindu
Kush, reached the "Bam-i-Dunesh" (Roof of the World), and
discovered Lake Sirikol, supposed by some to be the source of
the Oxus. Dr. (afterwards Sir) Joseph Hooker, in 1847–50,
traversed the valley of the Ganges, and through Sikkim reached
the higher Himalayas, adding not only to our knowledge of their
geography, but collecting material which has resulted in his
great "Flora Indica." Dr. Thomas Thomson was the first to
cross the Karakoram Pass (1848). In 1860 Colonel Godwin
Austen made a careful survey of the Mustagh region. In
1848 R. B. Shaw entered Eastern Turkestan, at the same time
as Mr. G. W. Hayward reached Yarkand City. Shaw collected
material for a general map of the country. The mission under
Sir Douglas Forsyth in 1873 went to Yarkand and Kashgar.
Colonel Henry Trotter accompanied the mission and made
excursions as far as the Artysh district, and over the Pamirs
into Wakhan, visiting Lake Sirikol, and throwing a flood of
light over the geography of the Pamirs and Eastern Turkestan.
In 1885 A. D. Carey made a journey round Chinese Turkestan
and along the northern border of Tibet; and in the following
year Colonel Mark Bell and Captain Younghusband went from
Peking across Central Asia to Kashmir, the latter crossing the
formidable Mustagh Pass.

In the early years of the century, Captain Basil Hall, while in command on the China station, took advantage of his opportunities to visit places about which Englishmen were then peculiarly ignorant—*e.g.* Korea and the Luchu Islands. Admiral Collinson in the 'fifties investigated and surveyed the coasts of China and Tartary as far as the Sea of Okhotsk, as did Sherard Osborn the coasts of Japan and the Gulf of Pechili. Robert Fortune, a botanical specialist and excellent observer, travelled extensively in China in the 'forties and 'fifties. In 1862 Captain Blakiston surveyed the Yang-tse-Kiang for 900 miles, being the furthest point up to that date reached by Englishmen. Mr. Ney Elias in 1868 surveyed the new course of the Yellow river, and in 1872 the same excellent traveller made a remarkable journey through Western Mongolia and South-Eastern Siberia, by Uliassutai and Kobdo. In the same year Major E. R. Sladen made an important journey from Bhamo on the Irawaddy, to Momien in South-West China, partly by the same route on which a few years later A. R. Margary was assassinated, after he had successfully led an expedition from Shanghai to Bhamo. In 1877 Captain W. J. Gill made his way overland from Hankau on the Yang-tse-Kiang to Batang on the borders of Tibet, and thence by Talifu to Bhamo, making a careful survey of his route. Still more extensive studies of the geography of China were made by E. Colborne Baber, who undertook several important journeys between 1876 and 1880, particularly in the provinces of Yunnan and Sze-chuen. Another important journey across Southern China, from Canton to Bhamo, was accomplished by A. R. Colquhoun in 1881. Among the few missionaries who have been geographers, Mr. J. McCarthy in 1877 ascended the Yang-tse-Kiang to the centre of Sze-chuen province, and then proceeded south and west to Bhamo.

One of the most important British contributions to a know- ledge of Japan before the country was thrown open to foreigners was the narrative of Sir Rutherford Alcock, who was British Minister in Tokyo for three years. Mrs. Bishop's journey through the interior of the main island in 1879 deserves mention, as she visited parts of the country not previously seen by Europeans. In 1871 Captain Blakiston made a journey round the northern island, Yezo.

In 1882 and following years, Mr. Carles, British Consul, made

China.

several journeys through the interior of Korea. In North China, Manchuria and Mongolia, two missionaries, A. Williamson and James Gilmore, travelled extensively in the 'sixties, 'seventies, and 'eighties. Though rather beyond the limit of this period, the journeys of Mr. H. E. M. James and Captain Younghusband in Manchuria should be mentioned, when they succeeded in ascending the " Great White Mountain."

Siberia.

During the first half of the century Siberia was as unknown, to Englishmen at least, as Central Africa. Captain Dundas Cochrane in 1820 traversed the country from west to east, making excursions into the north-east of the country into Kamchatka. In the 'forties and 'fifties Charles Herbert Cottrell, S. S. Hill, and T. W. Atkinson travelled over a great area of Siberia ; the last-named penetrated into Chinese Turkestan, especially the mountainous region between Lakes Balkash and Baikal, noting the advances of Russia into Central Asia. H. Seebohm's visit to the valley of the Yenissei in the spring and summer of 1877 was of special value from the point of view of physical geography and natural history.

Western Asia.

The countries of Western Asia, during the nineteenth century, have been traversed by many British travellers. Colonel Leake journeyed in Asia Minor in 1800-2 ; his map, compiled from his own and other observations, was the best of its time. In 1808 C. J. Rich settled as British Resident in Bagdad, and till his death, in 1823, travelled extensively in that region and in Kurdistan. He visited Babylon, Nineveh, and Persepolis. In 1808-16 Morier's two journeys through Persia, Armenia, and Asia Minor were fruitful in geographical and antiquarian information, while the maps by Rennell and others were of special value. Mountstuart Elphinstone, in his important mission to Kabul in 1808-9, was accompanied by a number of specialists, all of whom made observations during their stay in the country, which still renders Elphinstone's work an authority on Afghanistan. The travels of James Baillie Fraser in Persia, in 1821 and 1833, made considerable additions to the existing knowledge of the country. One name associated with Persia, Afghanistan, and Baluchistan and neighbouring regions, for half a century, is that of Sir Henry Rawlinson. He first went to Persia on an official mission in 1833, and during five years visited various portions of the Persian Empire,

accumulating stores of geographical and archæological information. In 1843 he was appointed British Consul at Bagdad,
which gave him exceptional opportunities of carrying out those
researches in connection with the decipherment of Cuneiform
inscriptions with which his name is so intimately associated
(p. 672).

Charles Masson's extensive journeys through Afghanistan **The**
and Baluchistan in the 'thirties and 'forties deserve mention on **North-**
Western
account of the fulness and value of the information which he **Frontier**
collected. Sir A. Burnes, already referred to, travelled from **of India.**
India by Kabul into Bokhara in 1831–3. Stoddart and Conolly's
journey through Persia and Bokhara, in 1842–3, can only be
mentioned in connection with the sad fate of the travellers;
Wolff's mission to inquire into the fate of the Englishman
added something to our knowledge of Central Asia. In 1840
Captain J. Abbott's journey from Herat, through the desert to
Khiva, yielded fresh and valuable results. Lieutenant Selby's
ascent of the Karun and Dizful rivers to Shiraz in 1842 remained
for forty years our only source of information on this important
district. Of great importance were the labours of the Persian
Boundary Commission, under Sir Frederic Goldsmid, in 1870–2.
At various times between 1861 and 1872 Sir F. Goldsmid had
travelled not only throughout Persia, but in neighbouring countries, in connection with the Indo-European telegraphs. One
important result was St. John's six-sheet map of Persia. Between
1857 and 1872 H. W. Bellew made considerable contributions
to a knowledge of Baluchistan, Afghanistan, and Persia. The
name of Houtum Schindler, an Englishman in the Persian
service, should also be mentioned for the many contributions
he has made to a knowledge of the topography of Persia.
Sir Charles Macgregor began his journeys in Persia in 1875.
He travelled right across Persia, passing through Shiraz, Yezd,
and Birjand, to the Afghan border. In 1877 he and Captain
Lockwood explored the uninviting waste between the sea-coast
and the Helmund in Afghanistan. In 1875 E. A. Floyer travelled
through the almost unknown region of Bushakand, in Western
Baluchistan, and by Kerman, Yezd, Isfahan, and Bagdad, reached
Europe. In 1878 the surveys of various officers accompanying
our army in the Afghan War made important additions and
corrections on the map of Afghanistan. This led ultimately to

the Afghan Boundary Commission, under Sir West Ridgway and Sir Peter Lumsden. A host of other names (including some of newspaper correspondents) are connected with this region and with Central Asia, especially about the period of most energetic Russian advance (1870 *seq.*). The name of Lieutenant Wood is connected with an attempt, in 1840, to solve the question of the source of the Oxus; while in the 'seventies Major H. Wood explored the Lake Aral region and the Lower Oxus.

Asia Minor. Lieutenant Wellsted, in 1829–35, besides exploring the Sinai Peninsula, and surveying the Arabian as well as the Nubian coast of the Red Sea, made an extensive journey through Omân. The Euphrates Expedition (1835–7), under the command of Colonel Chesney, was fruitful in results in many directions. Its objects were the establishment of steam communication with India, and its route lay through almost unexplored countries. Materials for a correct map of a very large portion of Northern Syria were collected; while the Euphrates and Tigris, and a large extent of their basins, were carefully explored. At a subsequent period two ascents were made of the Karun river and two descents of the Bahameshir. A new country was thus opened to navigation, commerce, and civilisation, and the practicability of the route for steam navigation established. Besides the reports of Chesney himself, W. J. Ainsworth, the surgeon and geologist of the expedition, published his special researches on the antiquities of Assyria, Babylonia, and Chaldæa, and the antiquities and geology of Asia Minor, Pontus, and Armenia were described by W. J. Hamilton. This may be said to have led to the expedition under Ainsworth and Rassam in 1839–40. From Skutari the party traversed Asia Minor in a south-east direction to the Persian frontier, their route covering thousands of miles. In the exploration of this interesting region since 1840 England has taken an important part, especially so with respect to ancient sites of Babylon and Nineveh, and other great cities of antiquity, the topography of which, the architecture, the inscriptions, and the monuments have been worked out in great detail by such men as Rawlinson, Layard, Loftus, George Smith. Further north, James Bryce[1] has described Ararat and Armenia, and in the

[1 President of the Board of Trade in 1892–1895, and perhaps best known as author of "The Holy Roman Empire" and "The American Commonwealth"; sometime Regius Professor of Civil Law at Oxford.]

Caucasus good work has been done by Freshfield, Grove, Telfer, and Dent in revealing the extent and character of the glaciation of that mighty range. Of the work of Beke in Palestine a bare mention must suffice, as also of the journey of Tozer and Crowder in Armenia (1877). In 1837–44 Sir Charles Fellows made several journeys in Asia Minor, mainly for antiquarian researches, during which he did much to clear up the ancient geography, especially of the western peninsula of Asia Minor (p. 668).

VIEW OF THE SOURCE OF THE RIVER TIGRIS.
(Gen. F. R. Chesney, " Expedition for the Survey of the Euphrates and Tigris," 1850.)

Of the labours of Sir Charles Wilson and his colleagues in Asia Minor (1879), the geographical results were, briefly, a complete military survey of the Taurus range, from the mountains of Lycia to the Persian frontier, of the Anti-Taurus, and of the Giaour Dagh to Mount Amanus, from the Taurus to the Beilan Pass. Surveys were also made of the Cilician Plain, of the country round Mount Argæus, of portions of Paphlagonia and Pontus, and every important road in the country was examined and sketched. In 1883 *et seq.* Prof. W. M. Ramsay carried out a careful exploration of Asia Minor, his chief aim being to identify ancient sites and roads.

Since 1840, besides special surveys of the coast referred to Arabia. below, there are several important journeys by Englishmen in

Arabia to record.   First of all there must be mentioned Richard Burton's daring visit to Mecca and Medinah in 1853, by which he was able to give to the world so much valuable and new information concerning these cities and the pilgrims that flocked to them.   In 1862–3 Gifford Palgrave made his famous journey through Arabia, from Damascus by Gaza, through Nejd, by Djuf, Haïl-Riad, the capital of the Wahabites, to the Persian Gulf, by the Bahrein Islands to Maskat, up the Tigris to Bagdad.   Mr. Doughty's many years' sojourn and journeys in North-Eastern Arabia and in Nejd (1876 *et seq.*), as far east as Hodeida and south to Mecca, were fruitful in valuable additions, not only to geography, but to ethnology, archæology, geology, and natural history.

Palestine and Syria.   The Palestine Exploration Fund, founded in 1865, has effected a complete topographical survey of the whole of Western Palestine, and with this the names of Wilson, Warren, Conder, Kitchener, Tyrwhitt Drake, and others, are intimately associated. Not the least important of the Society's productions is the beautiful and accurate map in six sheets.

Of individual researches in this region, we need only refer to Layard's journeys through Syria in 1839 *et seq.*, the results of which have only been recently published; Churchill's long residence in Mount Lebanon, 1842–52; Allen's survey of the Dead Sea, 1849 *et seq.*, with the view of a new route to India; Porter's important researches during his five years' stay, 1849 *et seq.*, in Damascus.   Burton and Tyrwhitt Drake's explorations in Syria in 1872 are a valuable supplement to the work of the Palestine explorations.   Finally, the surveys conducted by the Indian Navy have completed our knowledge of the Asian coast from Suez to Singapore.

Africa.   At the beginning of the century Africa was a blank from 10° N. lat. to the confines of Cape Colony.   Meantime the African Association was founded in 1788.   Under Captain Tuckey an expedition was sent to explore the Congo in 1816, but it did not get beyond the first rapids.   Nothing fresh was added to Tuckey's discoveries till Stanley's descent of the river sixty years later.

From the Mediterranean Lyon and Ritchie reached Murzuk, while Denham and Clapperton made their memorable journey from Tripoli to Lake Chad and Sokoto.   In a second expedition Clapperton, having thus completed a march across Africa, started from the Bight of Benin, reached Sokoto again from that side, and died there in April, 1827. His companion, Richard Lander, completed his work, and determined the course of the Quorra and Niger ; Major Laing reached Timbuktu in 1826. In 1820–7 Captain F. W. Owen made a survey of nearly the whole of the west and east coasts of Africa, while in 1821 much of the north coast was surveyed by the Beecheys.

To the 'thirties belong the expeditions of Lieutenant Washington and John Davidson in Morocco, Sir James Alexander's expedition into Damaraland, and James Hamilton's journey from Suakin to Khartum. In 1840 Dr. Beke made his first journey into Abyssinia, exploring the kingdom of Shoa and the province of Gojam, and visiting the source of the Abai. Our knowledge of Abyssinia was greatly increased by the journeys of Mansfield Parkyns (1843–6), and still more by Chichele Plowden, who journeyed up the Nile to Abyssinia. The invasion of Abyssinia in

SIR RICHARD F. BURTON, K.C.M.G., IN PILGRIM'S DRESS.
(*From his "Pilgrimage to Almadinah and Mecca,"* 1853.)

1867–8 by an English army, accompanied as it was by several scientific specialists—Blanford, Markham, and others—resulted in large contributions to our knowledge of the country in its varied aspects. John Petherick was in Africa in 1846, when he travelled from Keneh to Kosseir. In 1853 and afterwards he traversed the Bahr el Ghazal into the country of the Jur. In 1861–3 he, with two naturalists, Murie and Browell, traversed a great stretch of country west of the White Nile into the Jur and Niam-Niam countries. In 1845 James Richardson undertook a journey from Tripoli to the Sahara, and proceeding to Ghadames,

was the first European to enter Ghat, and after traversing
Fezzan returned to Tripoli in 1850. The same traveller took
command of an expedition into the Central Sudan, his companions being Barth and Oberweg. Richardson, after accomplishing much good work, died in March, 1851, at Ungurut, six
days' journey from Kuka. The expedition, which was essentially
an English one, was continued, with abundant results to science
and geography, under Dr. Barth. The Central Sudan States,
Lake Chad, the Shari, Binue, Niger, and the region watered by
them, were explored during four years, and Timbuktu itself was
visited. In 1850 Francis Galton travelled through the country
of the Damara and the Ovampo, in a journey covering upwards
of 2,000 miles. His companion, Mr. Andersson, extended his
wanderings to Lake Ngami, and afterwards to the Okovango and
Cunene rivers.

Living-
stone.

David Livingstone went out to South Africa as a missionary
in 1840, and he settled at Kolobeng in the far interior in 1847.
His first important journey was to Lake Ngami in company with
Oswell and Murray; in his second he reached the Zambezi river.
After a course of study at Cape Town, he set out on his most
important and famous expedition, reaching Linyanti, the capital
of the Makololo, in May, 1853, and the Portuguese settlement of
São Paulo de Loanda in May, 1854. From Loanda Livingstone
marched across the continent along the line of the Zambezi,
accompanied by his faithful Makololo followers, during which
he discovered the Victoria Falls of the Zambezi. Livingstone
reached Kiliman in May, 1856, and returned to England
to receive that enthusiastic welcome which he had so well
earned. He was appointed Consul for the Interior of Africa,
and he was placed at the head of the Government Zambezi
expedition. In March, 1858, Livingstone again started for
the Zambezi, accompanied by Dr. (afterwards Sir John) Kirk
and others. During this expedition the great explorer traced
the course of the River Shire; and in September, 1860, he
discovered the beautiful Lake Nyasa and the smaller Lake
Shirwa. Livingstone returned to England in 1864.

The Livingstone Zambezi expedition (1858–64) was the
forerunner of much work by English travellers and missionaries in this direction, of which the limits of our space
preclude further mention. Next to Livingstone and Baines

at this period, perhaps the most fruitful traveller in South Africa was the trader and hunter, James Chapman. From Natal he visited Bechuanaland, Lake Ngami, discovered in

DAVID LIVINGSTONE.

(From the painting in the possession of the London Missionary Society.)

1852 the great Saltpans into which the Ngami discharges its waters ; in 1855 he went from Lake Ngami to Walfisch Bay, and thence with Baines back to Lake Ngami and down the Zambezi to the Victoria Falls and on to the Indian Ocean. Baines visited in 1859 the Tati goldfields and the Matabele country, gathering much information as to its resources.

Our knowledge of the Limpopo and the region through which it passes is largely due to the explorations of St. Vincent Erskine in 1868 and 1871-2. In 1870 J. F. Elton went from Tati to the Limpopo, and traversed the region between that and the Indian Ocean. After other journeys south of the Zambezi, Elton, between 1873 and 1877, visited the Lufiji, and died while with Cotterill, pushing his way by the shore and Lake Nyasa, north and east, to Zanzibar. F. C. Selous went to South Africa since 1873. He has traversed a large area of South Africa between the Cape and beyond the Central Zambezi, and between Bechuanaland and Matabeleland, and has contributed much to the cartography of the region as well as to a knowledge of its natural history and resources.

Photo: aull & Fox, Piccadilly, W.
LIEUT.-COLONEL JAMES GRANT.

While Livingstone was making his important discoveries in Southern Africa, the expedition of Burton and Speke (1857) from Zanzibar succeeded in reaching the shores of the great

The Source of the Nile. Lake Tanganyika at Ujiji, at a distance of seven hundred miles from the coast. On their return Speke made a journey northwards from Unyanyembe, and discovered the southern shore of a vast inland fresh-water lake, which he named the Victoria Nyanza. The expedition of Speke and Grant reached Unyanyembe in 1861, and during that and the following year they marched northward to the Victoria Nyanza, skirted the western shore of that great lake, and reached the kingdom of Uganda, discovering the outlet of the Nile at Ripon Falls. They followed the river to Gondokoro on the White Nile, which they reached in February, 1863, where they were met by Samuel Baker. Thus Speke and Grant, by their discovery of the main source of the Nile, solved a question that had exercised the imaginations of geographers since the dawn of history.

Before Sir Samuel Baker met Speke and Grant at Gondokoro he had already made discoveries in the basin of the Atbara. He continued his explorations to the south, and discovered the Muta Nzige of Speke, a second great lake, to which he assigned the name of Albert Nyanza. In 1871 Baker, in the service of the Khedive of Egypt, while engaged in expelling the slave - traders and kidnappers, explored the kingdom of Unyoro. In 1874–9 Gordon Pasha (p. 538), Baker's successor, did much directly and indirectly to clear up still further the hydrography of the Upper Nile and obtain a know-ledge of the country to the right and left of the river and Lake Albert.

Photo: Lyd. Sawyer, Maida Vale,
CAPTAIN JOHN HANNING SPEKE.

The English expedition for the relief of Emin Pasha (1887–9), under H. M. Stanley, shed much light on the hydrography of the Nile and the Congo; traced the course of the Aruwimi to its source; added much to our knowledge of the forest region of Central Africa and of its inhabitants, of the country on the west of the Albert Nyanza, of the lake itself, of the Semliki, which connects it with the southern lake (Albert Edward), and of Mount Ruwenzori. **West Africa.**

On the west coast of Africa, the British expeditions up the Niger met with some success. In 1832 Laird and Oldfield, accompanied by R. Lander, further explored the Niger (p. 910), Oldfield ascending the Benue for 105 miles. Captain H. D. Trotter in 1841–2 added much to our knowledge of the Niger mouth and neighbouring regions. The *Pleiad*, to the command of which Dr. William F. Baikie, R.N., succeeded in 1854, went

310

250 miles higher up the Niger than had previously been reached. A few years later he formed a settlement called Lokoja, at the confluence of the Quorra and Benue, and explored the surrounding country.   In 1868–70 Winwood Reade, from Sierra Leone, in two journeys reached the source of the Niger and explored its upper course.   He had previously (1861–3) spent fourteen months in the Gorilla country on the west coast.   In 1879 Ashcroft, in the *Henry Venn*, carefully surveyed the Benue for forty miles beyond Yola.   In 1885, on behalf of the Niger Company, Joseph Thomson ascended the Niger to the neighbourhood of Sokoto, and the company's agents have done much to explore the Benue and other affluents.   Among other names connected with exploration in West Africa since 1845 are those of John Duncan, Commander F. E. Forbes, Richard Burton, J. A. Skertchly, Hewett, and Gouldsbury.

From the mouth of the Rovuma Livingstone, in April, 1866, entered on his last great African expedition.   Between that and his death on Lake Bangweolo in 1873 he explored the region between Lakes Nyasa and Tanganyika, visited Lakes Mweru and Bangweolo, went on to Ujiji, thence westwards to Nyangwe on the Lualaba (the Upper Congo), back to Ujiji, where, in October, 1872, he was succoured by H. M. Stanley, with whom he explored the north end of Tanganyika.   From Ujiji he proceeded south to Bangweolo, where he died.   Most of the ground traversed by Livingstone was new.   As an explorer, Livingstone trod some 29,000 miles of African soil, and laid open nearly one million square miles of previously unknown country. Commander Lovett Cameron, R.N., reached Ujiji from Zanzibar in February, 1874, explored the southern half of Lake Tanganyika, and solved the great problem of its outlet.   He then advanced across Manyuema to the Lualaba or Congo, crossed that river, and reached the capital of Urna.   Thence he pushed forward across the continent, and arrived at Benguela, on the west coast, in October, 1876.

Sir H. M. Stanley, 1840–1904.

H. M. Stanley's first journey in 1872, an enterprise of the *New York Herald*, was undertaken to relieve Livingstone.   At the cost of the *Daily Telegraph* and *New York Herald*, Stanley undertook a second journey into the interior of Africa.   In March, 1875, he reached the southern shore of the Victoria Nyanza, which he circumnavigated.   He visited Uganda, crossed

towards the Albert Nyanza, and discovered the southern lake
Muta Nzige (Albert Edward).   Proceeding to Ujiji, he explored
the southern half of Lake Tanganyika ; he then marched across
Manyuema to Nyangwe, and embarked on the Lualaba, which
river he eventually proved to be the Congo.   The distance from
Nyangwe to the mouth of the Congo is calculated at 18,000 miles,
and Stanley was navigating the river from November, 1876, to

LAKE NYASA, FROM THE ISLAND OF LIKOMA.

(From a photograph by the Universities' Mission to Central Africa.)

August, 1877, amidst dangers in every form.   This discovery has
led to consequences of great commercial and political importance
among other things to the founding of the Congo Free State, in
which Stanley took an active part.   The Rev. George Grenfell's
explorations of the Mobangi, the Lomami, and other tributaries
of the Congo, give him a high rank among explorers.

Alexander Keith Johnston was sent out by the Royal **Keith**
Geographical Society in 1879 from the east coast, to proceed by **Johnston.**
the north end of Lake Nyasa and between Lakes Nyasa and Tanganyika.   He was accompanied by Joseph Thomson, a young
Scotch geologist, and they landed at Dar-es-Salaam on May 19th,

Joseph Thomson.

1879. Keith Johnston died on the 23rd of June; Thomson, at the age of twenty-two, resolved to go forward and do his best. He proceeded to the north end of Lake Nyasa and thence to Tanganyika, and proved the Lukuga to be an outlet of that lake. On his return he discovered Lake Rikwa, east of the south end

CENTRAL AFRICA IN 1815.
(*Portion of Map published by C. Smith.*)

of Tanganyika, and marched thence to Zanzibar.   In 1883-4 Thomson was again sent out by the Society. Starting from Mombasa, he went by Mount Kilimanjaro, was the first to explore the Masai country, visited Mount Kenia, Lake Baringo, and the Kavirondo countries, and added greatly to our knowledge of African geography and geology.   Thomson's subsequent work in Africa lies beyond the limit of the period.

It was two German missionaries in the employment of the
Church Missionary Society, Krapf and Rebmann, who in 1848
were the first Europeans to get a glimpse of Kilimanjaro. In
1865 and following years Wakefield and New not only visited
Kilimanjaro, but partly by personal travel and partly by inquiries

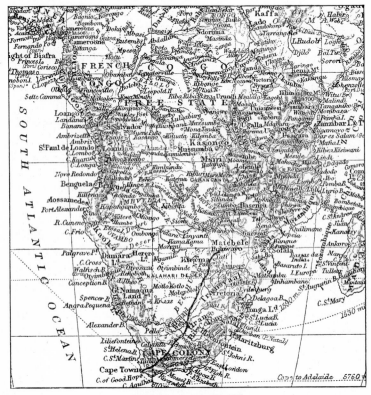

CENTRAL AFRICA IN 1890.

(Portion of Map by F. S. Weller, F.R.G.S.)

among native traders, obtained much information as to the
region to the north and west of Kilimanjaro and Mount Kenia,
including the Masai country. In 1871 Wakefield ascended Kilimanjaro to its snow-limit. In 1884-5 Sir H. H. Johnston visited
Kilimanjaro and ascended to within 2,000 feet of the summit.

In Somali and Galla lands we find Smee exploring the Jub
in 1811. In 1848 Captain Cruttenden, of the Indian Navy,

Somali-
land.

succeeded in penetrating some distance into the mysterious Somaliland, while one of Burton's most memorable and hazardous feats was his visit to the city of Harrar. Subsequently, at the end of 1884, the Somali country was penetrated southward from Berbera, by F. L. James (who died in 1890) and his companions, to the Shebeli, a distance of 350 miles.

Morocco. Since Jackson's work, the most important addition to a scientific knowledge of Morocco has been made (1871) by Sir J. D. Hooker and John Ball, who made an extensive journey into that country, visiting the city, penetrating into the Great Atlas, reaching a height of over 10,000 feet, investigating its botany, and, with the aid of Maw, its geology, as well as its geography and inhabitants.

During the nineteenth century Englishmen did much for the geography and ethnology of Madagascar, with which are connected the names of Captain W. F. W. Owen, the Rev. W. Ellis, J. L. Macleod, Captain S. P. Oliver, the Rev. J. Sibree, the Rev. Mr. Baron, and other English missionaries.

North America. Both in North and South America during the seventy years under consideration there have been many English travellers, some of whom have done good exploring work. The explorations in the northern region of Canada have been dealt with in the Arctic section. In 1840 Logan began the survey of Canada, which under Selwyn, assisted by an able staff, has surveyed a large portion of the Dominion. Of explorers outside the survey only a few demand notice. In 1857–60 Captain Palliser's great expedition was sent out for the exploration of the region between the great lakes and the Saskatchewan and the Rocky Mountains, to the Cascade Range and Vancouver, partly with a view to survey a railway route to the Pacific. As the expedition was accompanied by a staff of specialists—Sullivan, Hector, S. J. Dawson, Blakiston, Hind, and others—not only were the geographical acquisitions of great extent and value, but important studies were made on the geology and natural resources of the region. In 1862 Milton explored the Red River, and with Cheadle sought to find a route to British Columbia, exploring what was then, to a considerable extent, an unknown region.

South America. Pentland, who resided for many years in South America (including Bolivia) as British Consul, and who was an accomplished geologist and botanist, carried on a series of explorations

(1825–37) which gained the praise of Humboldt and Cuvier. He traversed a great part of Peru, Chili, and Bolivia. He measured the most important summits of the Andes, Chimborazo, Illimani, and Sorata; Titicaca Lake was carefully surveyed by him. In 1826–36 King and Fitzroy, and subsequently Fitzroy alone, in the *Adventure* and *Beagle,* at various times carried on the survey of the coasts of South America, from the La Plata to Cape Horn, and up the whole of the Pacific coast to Guayaquil. During the later years of this long-continued survey-voyage Darwin was on board as naturalist, and his observations, including his journeys into the continent, added greatly to the value of the scientific results of the expedition. Smith and Lowe in 1834–6 journeyed down the Ucayali, Maranhão, and Amazon, and indicated the great water-routes for conveying the products of the Cordilleras to the Atlantic, the Pachitea, Ucayali, and Amazon. In 1848 Bates and Wallace proceeded to South America for the special purpose of investigating the natural history of the Amazonian region; Bates devoted eleven years to the purpose. The name of Spruce should also be mentioned in this connection. In 1852–4 Clements Markham travelled in Peru, and explored the forests of the Eastern Andean range. Again in 1860–1 he visited Peru for the purpose of obtaining cinchona plants to transfer to India, a mission which he accomplished with complete success. The extensive and fruitful explorations of Chandless in 1862–9 in the Amazonian region can only be mentioned. In 1873–5 Barrington Brown, accompanied by the botanist Traill, and Lidstone traversed the Amazon and several of its tributaries, the Tapajos, Madeira, Rio Negro, Purns, Jurua, Javary, Solimoens, and others.

Further south a noteworthy journey was made by Commander Musters, R.N., in 1872, through Patagonia, over 960 miles of latitude, in 780 of which he traversed a country previously quite unknown to Europeans. R. H. Schomburgk's extensive and invaluable botanical explorations (1835–44) in British Guiana were carried out by means of funds supplied in England. He traversed the rivers of the country to their sources, and explored in the basins of the Amazon and Orinoco. Other names connected with the exploration of British Guiana in recent years are those of Barrington Brown and E. F. Im Thurn.

In 1879–80 the journeys of E. Whymper in Ecuador were

notable, not only for the fact that he succeeded in ascending some of the great summits of the Andes, but for the observations which he made on the physical geography and natural history of the region traversed, and especially for his fresh contributions to our knowledge of the glaciation of this great mountain chain. Before this, A. Simson crossed the Ecuadorian Andes from Guayaquil.

In Brazil, besides those already referred to, there have been several English travellers and explorers who have helped to increase our knowledge of that vast region. The work of Gardner (1836–41), Burton (1864 *et seq.*), Bigg-Wither (1872–5) and Wells (1868–84) can but be barely mentioned here.

Coming further south, we must notice the varied observations of Sir Woodbine Parish in the La Plata region. At a later period the *Beagle* survey was supplemented in many important directions by that of the *Nassau*, in 1866–9, and by the very careful observations conducted in the region of Magellan Straits in 1876, by the *Challenger* staff, who landed both in Tierra del Fuego and the mainland, to carry out their scientific investigations. Still later (1878) another of her Majesty's surveying ships, the *Alert* (first under Sir G. Nares and afterwards Captain J. Maclear), visited the Tierra del Fuego region, and examined still more minutely the land on both sides. In other parts of South America, both the *Beagle* and the *Alert* expeditions did good service; the former, *e.g.*, in the Galapagos Islands, and the latter on the coast of Chile.

Australian Exploration. In 1815 "Botany Bay" was still a convict settlement; no colonies in the proper sense existed, and the continent was as unknown as the heart of Africa. The survey of the coasts had been begun by Cook, Bass, and Flinders, continued by King in 1817–24, and by the *Beagle* (on which was Charles Darwin) in 1837–43, and since then in still further detail by her Majesty's survey ships. The exploration of the interior was begun immediately after the founding of the settlement. It is impossible to refer in detail to all the expeditions with which the names of Oxley, Hume, Sturt, Mitchell, Kennedy, Gregory, Eyre, and others are connected. By 1850 the continent had been penetrated for several hundreds of miles at various points, and before 1885 it had been crossed in several directions. Reference can only be made to some of the greater expeditions. One of the earliest journeys of any extent was that of Edward John Eyre, who in 1841, in order to ascertain whether there were fertile lands in the interior, made his way from Adelaide to King George's Sound, a distance of 1,040 miles. Owing to the scarcity of water, the party suffered the greatest hardships. A few years afterwards Captain Sturt explored the courses of the rivers Darling and Murray. In 1844–5 Sturt, starting from the *Darling*, travelled north-west and north to the Grey Ranges, through great sand-

MOUNT SARMIENTO.
(*C. Darwin and Admiral R. Fitzroy's "Voyage of the ' Beagle,' " 1839.*)

ridges, mud-planes, and the spinifex which covers so much of the interior, to a point within 150 miles of the centre of the continent. Augustus Gregory commanded an expedition which in 1856 went by sea from Sydney, through Torres Straits, and landed on the banks of the Victoria river. Ascending this stream to its source, Gregory crossed the water-parting at a height of 1,660 feet above the sea, and descended a stream flowing south, which ended in a salt lake. Returning down the Victoria, he next advanced to the Gulf of Carpentaria, and explored the region on its eastern side, ending his labours at Brisbane. He had marched over 6,500 miles in a country previously unknown. Attempts to cross the continent from Adelaide continued to be made. M'Douall Stuart, in 1860, got within 245 miles of the northern shore.   At length Richard O'Hara Burke, with his companions Wills and Gray, accomplished this arduous achievement, crossing the continent from south to north.   But they nearly all perished ; one man, named John King, alone surviving.   In 1862, however, M'Douall Stuart, in a second attempt, successfully made the journey from Adelaide to Van Diemen Gulf on the north coast, along the route which has since been adopted for the electric telegraph (1872).

Queens-land.

In 1843–6 Leichardt explored Queensland from the south to the Gulf of Carpentaria, crossing the Fitzroy river to the head of the gulf, whence he made his way westwards along the north coast as far as Port Essington.   In 1845–58 the Queensland interior was still further explored, the Barcoo discovered, and other intermittent streams flowing towards Torrens, and other lakes by Mitchell, Kennedy, Gregory, and others.

West Australia.

In 1829 the colony of West Australia was founded, and the exploration of the continent began from that point.   In 1857–60 great activity was shown in the exploration of the region around Torrens Lake, east and west, by such explorers as Swindon, Warburton, M'Douall Stuart, and others, during which other lakes and mountains were discovered, the physical features filled in with fresh accuracy, and the economical value of the country ascertained.   The search expeditions that were sent out after Burke and Wills in 1861 and 1862 greatly extended our know-ledge of the country.   M'Kinley crossed the frontier twice.   In South Australia he proceeded to the mouth of the Barcoo, the remarkable formation of which he was the first to make known. By a route a little to the east of that of Burke and Wills he reached the Gulf of Carpentaria, and on the return journey crossed through Queensland.   The information obtained by all these expeditions on the physical geography and natural resources of the country was of substantial value.   In 1860–74 much was done to obtain a better knowledge both of the back country of Queensland and of Western Australia, though the results of the latter were not encouraging to industry.   The most energetic of these explorers were the brothers Forrest, especially John. We can only mention the expedition by John Forrest and Kennedy, in 1874, across the centre of the continent from west to east, and south to Adelaide.   Other important names connected with the exploration of the interior are those of Giles and

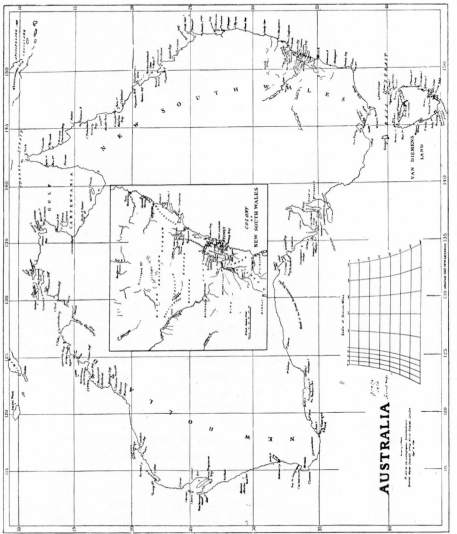

MAP OF AUSTRALIA IN 1830 BY L. HEBERT.

Carmichael (1872), the Gosses (1873), Giles and Tietkens (1873–6). In 1873 Warburton made his famous journey from Alice Springs, on the telegraph line north-west and west to the west coast, between 20° S. and the tropic of Capricorn, revealing more strikingly than had been done before the terrible nature of the interior. In 1875–6 Giles crossed from Lake Torrens by Lake Moore to Perth, and recrossed from Perth by the Ashburton to the telegraph line. Between 1875 and 1885 expeditions were continually in the field, opening up the continent, and seeking for lands that might be turned to account for agricultural or mining purposes. In 1896, however, it might be said that about one-half of the continent was unexplored.

New Zealand. The exploration of New Zealand has been mainly carried out by the well-organised Colonial survey, under Sir James Hector and the late Sir Julius Von Hoast. The coasts of New Zealand and the surrounding regions were fully surveyed by Captains Stokes and Byron-Drury, in the *Pandora* and *Acheron*, between 1848 and 1858. The adjacent island of New Guinea is only separated from Australia by Torres Strait, and its south-eastern portion has been partially explored and surveyed, first by British surveying ships, and in later times by missionaries and **Malaysia.** others. In the Malay Archipelago, also, English surveying vessels and English travellers have done much good work, the name of A. R. Wallace (p. 434) being intimately connected with this region.

The Pacific. The work of exploration and survey by English navigators was continued after Cook's death (Vol. V., p. 307) with unabated vigour; and as each vessel had, as a rule, a naturalist on board, much good work was done for science. During the voyage of 1872–6 the *Challenger* visited many of the Pacific islands, with results to scientific geography of the first value.

Europe. During the period under review Europe was overrun by British travellers, some few of them entitled to be regarded as explorers, especially in the field of physical geography. With the exploration of the great Alpine region and the investigation of its glaciers, the English Alpine Club has been intimately associated; and if we gave the names of all who have done something for Alpine topography and physical geography the list would be a long one. The Alpine Club map of Switzerland is an achievement worthy of record. The names both of J. D. Forbes and of Tyndall are intimately associated with the Alps,

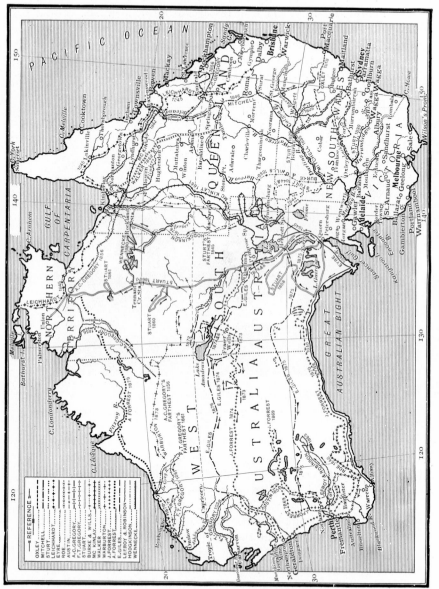

MAP OF AUSTRALIA, SHOWING ROUTES OF EXPLORERS UP TO 1889.

not only for the light they threw on their topography, but also, and mainly, for their classical researches into glaciation. For a knowledge of the scientific aspect of the great Alpine groups John Ball did much. Forbes's researches on the glaciers of Norway, though not so extensive as in the case of Switzerland, were not of less scientific value. Murchison's investigations of

BREADFRUIT TREE, KI ISLAND, THE MOLUCCAS.

(By permission, from a photograph supplied by the "Challenger" Office, Edinburgh.)

the Ural Chain, and Murchison, Lyell, and Sedgwick's journeys in the volcanic region of Auvergne (p. 80), while mainly for geological purposes, yielded valuable results in physical geography; so have Lyell's investigations of the volcanic region of Sicily and of the coasts of Denmark. Some topographical work has been carried out in Greece and the Balkan Peninsula, both by private travellers and through the Hellenic Society.

The Ordnance Survey of the British Islands, initiated about the beginning of the century, was nearly completed by 1885. The Royal Geographical Society was founded in 1830, and during the period did much to promote exploration all over the world and to raise the standard of geography at home.

Deep-sea research (oceanography) may be said to have been The Ocean Depths. initiated during the period under review, and to have culminated in the voyage of the *Challenger*, equipped by the Government, which under Captain (afterwards Admiral Sir George) Nares and the late Captain F. T. Thomson, from 1873 to 1876, ex-

A LAVA STREAM, KILAUEA, HAWAII.
*(By permission from a photograph supplied by the
"Challenger' Office, Edinburgh.)*

tended research over the Atlantic and Pacific oceans, and added largely to our knowledge of the physical geography of the sea.

WHEN Englishmen from the mother country visit the colonies Greater Britain. and learn to appreciate the wealth and the prosperity of Greater Britain, they find it hard to realise that nearly all this vast and apparently stable empire has virtually been created within the last hundred years. When, to avenge the loss of Canada, France aided the American colonists to throw off the yoke of

George III., England as a colonial power sank low among the five European nations who strove for dominion beyond the seas. The Dutch had great possessions in Asia, at the Cape of Good Hope, and in South America; the Spaniards and the Portuguese held Mexico, Central America, and, with the exception of the country now known as Guiana, all South America also; the French owned Mauritius and many of the West Indies. The nucleus of colonies left to England, and on which she built up her second empire, consisted only of Gibraltar, Canada (at that time virtually bounded on the west by the Great Lakes), Jamaica, Barbadoes, and a few of the smaller West Indian islands, St. Helena, and some trading stations on the west coast of Africa.[1]

Growth of the Empire. From these small beginnings has grown a world-wide empire; and now the larger half of North America, the whole of Australia, Tasmania, and New Zealand, vast territories in the south, the east, and the west of Africa, British Guiana, the Malay peninsula, innumerable islands, and priceless fortresses which command the highways of commerce, own allegiance to the British Crown. The various methods by which this extraordinary expansion has been effected cannot be described in detail in this chapter, for the history of many of the colonies cannot be dissevered from that of our foreign policy. England emerged empty-handed from very few of the long series of wars which ended at Waterloo. Before the fall of Napoleon most, if not all, of the over-sea possessions of France and her allies had surrendered to our flag. At the Peace many were restored to their original owners, but Ceylon, Mauritius, Cape Colony, Trinidad, and Guiana were then permanently added to the British dominions. On the other hand, most of the great countries which are now known as the self-governing colonies were founded and developed by the restless energy of the Anglo-Saxon race. Thus in Ontario, the first province of British North America settled after the United States obtained their independence, the pioneers were Englishmen and Scots from the revolted colonies. These men, known in Canadian history as the "United Empire Loyalists," refused to throw in their lot with the young Republic, and, following the old flag into

[1 India does not come within the scope of this section.]

Canada, became backwoodsmen in Ontario. With indomitable energy, and strengthened by a considerable immigration from Scotland, they slowly and painfully converted their forest wilderness into the "garden of Canada"; and their descendants have been the pioneers of the army of emigrants from Britain, who have now begun to people the prairies of Manitoba and the North-West, and, tunnelling through the Rocky Mountains, have joined hands with their fellow-Britons on the shores of the Pacific Ocean. Australia, Tasmania, and New Zealand have been entirely settled by emigrants from the mother country; and though many of the original settlers in Tasmania, New South Wales, and Western Australia were of undesirable material, hundreds of thousands of active, energetic English emigrants have now not only completely obliterated the convict taint, but have built up a second England in the Southern ocean. In South Africa, too, there has been a considerable influx of population from Great Britain. Besides these great colonies, which claim a nationality of their own though not independence, there are a number which possess representative government, the Crown retaining a veto on legislation; a number of Crown Colonies, governed by British officials (the British and native population, however, enjoying varying degrees of representation); and of Protectorates, which retain their native governments under British supervision. The two last classes, like the Indian Empire, have developed in Britons a capacity for governing uncivilised races hitherto unparalleled in history.[1]

Growth of Imperial Sentiment. It is difficult for this generation to believe that the pride and interest with which the mother country now regards the self-governing groups of colonies is quite of recent growth; harder still to realise that in the middle of the nineteenth century British statesmen contemplated, and even sometimes hoped for, separation. Happily, although the Australians and Canadians were deeply wounded by this attitude of the Colonial Office, always unsympathetic and often insolent, they refused to "take the hint and cut the painter"; and thus by their pride of race, their common-sense, and their sturdy

[1 The revived colonial activity of foreign states in recent years has caused a renewal of the "expansion of England" which lies beyond our scope in this chapter.]

patriotism, they preserved the British Empire from dismemberment. The English public were at that time so ignorant in all concerning the colonies that they were indifferent as to the continuance of the connection. They were unable to distinguish between the nationality of the inhabitants of British North America and the United States, and, to the intense disgust of the Canadians, used to speak of them as Yankees; while even the Colonial Office was known to address despatches to "Melbourne, South Australia, New South Wales," which in Europe would be equivalent to sending a letter to "Lisbon, Spain, France." But this is now a thing of the past; and British indifference to the fortunes of the colonies has given place, from about 1875 onwards, to keen pride in the Empire. An Imperial Federation League was founded in that year, under the auspices of statesmen of both political parties; the conferences of colonial statesmen in London at the Jubilees of the coronation of Queen Victoria in 1887 and 1897 have drawn the great self-governing colonies closer to the mother country, and opened up at least the possibility of a customs union; the aid given by Canadian *voyageurs* and New South Wales cavalry in 1885 to the mother country in the Soudan prepared the way for the more extensive and more needful support accorded to her by both Canada and Australia during the South African War in 1899–1902, and for the assumption by them of part of the burden of Imperial defence.[1] The Canadian colonies were federated in 1867, the Australian in 1900, the South African will follow in good time.[2] The practical experiments of the Australian colonies and of New Zealand in state ownership of railways, in the simplification of the transfer of land, in the extension of the suffrage to women, in old age pension schemes, in payment of members, in laicising the State by disestablishment and

[1] In some degree, moreover, the Imperial connection was strengthened towards the end of our period by the change in the system of appointing Colonial Governors which began with the despatch of the Marquis of Lorne to Canada in 1878. Formerly they constituted almost a special profession, not unlike the provincial Governors of the Roman Empire. Now, at least in the great self-governing Colonies, they are men of high social and political position in England. Naturally they tend to carry more weight in the Colonies. and their experience on their return commands more attention from the British public than those of their more specialised but less eminent predecessors.]

[2 See page 974]

THE ROYAL NAVAL DEPÔT, SYDNEY HARBOUR.

(By permission, from a photograph supplied by the New South Wales Government.)

unsectarian or secular education, in compulsory arbitration in
labour disputes, are instructive attempts at solving some of the
social problems which await treatment in the United Kingdom.
The national devotion to sport has been frequently gratified by
the visits of Australian cricket elevens to England, and of English
elevens to Australia.   The Colonial Procession at the Queen's
Jubilee of 1897 brought vividly before the British public the
extraordinary variety of the races and countries ruled by men of
British birth.   Improved steam communication, Imperial penny
postage, and an all-British cable route to Australia, have helped
to draw closer the bonds of the Empire.   Whatever may be the
form ultimately taken by the constitutional relations of Great
and Greater Britain, it may be said with certainty that the
indifference of a generation ago is ended for ever.

Photo : London Stereoscopic Co.

PORTION OF THE COLONIAL PROCESSION AT QUEEN VICTORIA'S JUBILEE, 1897.

AUTHORITIES.—1865-85.

GENERAL HISTORY.

Justin McCarthy, *History of Our Own Times;* Fyffe, *Modern Europe;* A. Debidour, *Histoire Diplomatique de l'Europe;* H. M. Stanley, *Coomassie and Magdala;* Winwood Reade, *Ashantee War;* Lord Roberts, *Forty-one Years in India;* C. G. Gordon, *Journals;* Wingate, *Mahdism and the Egyptian Soudan;* T. F. Carter, *History of the Boer War;* Sir Wemyss Reid, *Life of W. E. Forster;* A. Lang, *Life of Lord Iddesleigh;* Davidson and Benham, *Life of Archbishop Tait;* Ashwell and Wilberforce, *Life of Samuel Wilberforce;* Macdonnell, *Life of Archbishop Magee;* Hodder, *Life of Lord Shaftesbury;* Sir W. Hunter, *Life of Lord Mayo;* Lord Lytton, *Despatches;* Leslie Stephen, *Memoir of Henry Fawcett;* Lord Sherbrooke, *Autobiography;* G. Barnett Smith, *Life of W. E. Gladstone* and *Life and Speeches of John Bright;* Busch, *Our Chancellor;* Taxile Delorde, *Histoire du Second Empire* (6 vols., Paris, 1869-75) ; John Morley, *Life of W. E. Gladstone,* 1903 ; Lord Wolseley, *Story of a Soldier's Life* (his own), 1904.

SPECIAL SUBJECTS.

Law.—See the Acts in the text referred to and the Acts amending them ; *see also* Stephen's *Commentaries on the Laws of England* passim ; Maitland, *Justice and Police* in the "English Citizen" Series ; Fitzjames Stephen, *History of English Criminal Law, Law of Criminal Procedure,* and *Law of Evidence;* Pollock, *Land Laws* in the "English Citizen" Series ; Williams, *Principles of the Law of Real Property;* Digby, *History of the Law of Real Property;* Pollock, *Law of Contract;* Anson, *Law of Contract;* Buckley, *The Companies Acts,* etc.

The Army, 1815-1885.—Marshall, *Military Miscellany; The Army Book;* Wrottesley, *Life of Sir John Burgoyne;* Gleig, *Life of Wellington;* Hamilton, *History of the Grenadier Guards; Camp and Barrack Room,* by a late Staff-Sergeant in the 13th Regt. (London, 1845) ; *Report of the Select Committee on the Army before Sebastopol,* 1854-55 ; Kinglake, *Crimea;* Wood, *The Crimea in 1854 and 1894;* Colin Campbell, *Letters from Camp during the Siege of Sebastopol* (with preface by Lord Wolseley) ; Stevens, *A Campaign with the Connaught Rangers; Historical Record of 30th Regiment;* Holden, *The Green Jacket,* in *United Service Magazine,* IV., N.S.; Hamley, *The Crimea;* W. H. Russell, *The Great War in the East;* Articles on *The English Soldier* by Colonel Knollys, in *Blackwood's Magazine,* 1895 ; Hamley, *The Operations of War;* Hume, *Précis of Modern Tactics,* revised by Pratt ; Lord Wolseley, *Story of a Soldier's Life,* 1904.

The Navy, 1815-1885.—*The Nautical Magazine,* 1832-85 ; *The Navy List,* 1815-85 (for Admiralty orders, etc.) ; *The Queen's Regulations and Admiralty Instructions;* Papers read at the Royal Naval Exhibition, 1891 ; *The Naval Chronicle,* xxxiii-xl ; Hans Busk, *The Navies of the World,* 1859 ; *Report of the United States Commissioner at the Paris Exhibition,* 1867 ; Lieutenant-Colonel Owen, R.A., *Modern Artillery* (1873) ; *Textbook of Gunnery* (1887) ; Laird Clowes, *History of the Royal Navy.*

The Church, 1815-1885.—It is difficult to select from the large mass of contemporary literature, but attention may be called to the following works :—Perry, *Student's History of the Church of England,* part iii.; Wakeman, *Introduction to the History of the Church of England;* Dean Church, *The Oxford Movement;* Liddon, *Life of Pusey;* Newman, *Apologia; Autobiography of Isaac Williams;* Coleridge, *Life of Keble;* Lock, *Life of Keble;* Gladstone, *Gleanings;* Mark Pattison, *Memoirs;* Smith, *Life of Bishop Heber;* Stanley, *Life of Arnold;* Prothero, *Life of Dean Stanley;* W. Ward, *William George Ward and the Oxford Movement;* Purcell, *Life of Manning;* Hare, *The Gurneys of Earlham; Life of Charles Lowder; Life of James Skinner; Life of A. H. Mackonochie;* Stephens's *Life of Dean Hook;* Churton's *Life of J. Watson; Life of Bishop Wilberforce.* For a severe Nonconformist criticism (the purely historical value of which is marred by a number of inaccuracies), *see* Dr. Rigg's *Oxford High Anglicanism.*

Music.—Sir G. Grove, *Life of Beethoven ;* Dr. Hueffer, *Music in England under the Reign of Queen Victoria ; Programmes of the Philharmonic Society ;* C. Kenney, *Life of Balfe ; Memoirs of Moscheles ; Recollections of J. H. Mapleson.*

Art.—*See* chap. xxiii.   *Philosophy.*—*See* chap. xxiii.   *Literature.*—*See* chap. xxii.

English Scholarship since 1742.—Some account of the leading representatives of classical scholarship in England is given by Urlichs in Iw an Müller's *Handbuch,* i. 104–7, and by Bursian in his *Geschichte der classische Philologie,* pp. 1218–1227.   On Porson, the principal authorities are his *Correspondence,* edited by H. R. Luard for the Cambridge Antiquarian Society (1867), and the *Lives* by Luard in *Cambridge Essays* (1857), J. S. Watson (1861), and Professor Jebb in *Dictionary of National Biography* (1896); on Parr, the *Memoirs* by Johnstone (1828); on Wakefield, his own *Memoirs* (1792–1804), and his *Correspondence with Fox* (1813); on Dobree, Burges, and Gaisford, Bake's *Scholica Hypomnemata,* pref. to vol. ii. (1839); on C. J. Blomfield, the *Life* by his son (1864); on E. V. Blomfield, an article in the *Museum Criticum,* ii. 520; on Samuel Butler, Mayor's *History of St. John's College, Cambridge,* pp. 898–964, and the *Life* by his grandson.   There are articles in the *Journal of Philology* on Conington (ii. 334), Shilleto (vii. 163), W. G. Clark (viii. 173), Munro (xiv. 107), and W. H. Thompson (xv. 306); in the *Eagle* on Churchill Babington (xv. 362), Paley (366), T. S. Evans (477), Kennedy (448, 475), and Merivale (xviii. 183); and in Bursian's *Biographisches Jahrbuch* on W. G. Clark in 1879, George Long in 1880, Pattison and Badham in 1885, Blakesley, Munro, and Veitch in 1886, Paley, Kennedy, Babington, and Chandler in 1890, and Sellar in 1891. There are also articles on Kennedy in the *Classical Review,* iii. 226, 278.   Pattison's *Memoirs* appeared in 1885 ; Jowett's *Life,* by Abbott and Campbell, in 1897.   The best account of Sellar is by Mr. Andrew Lang, in Sellar's *Horace* (1892); of Nettleship in vol. ii. of his *Lectures and Essays* (1895).   Grote's *Life* was published in 1873, and Thirlwall's *Letters* in 1881.   Sir Charles Newton is the theme of an Address by Professor Jebb, published in *Journal of Hellenic Studies,* vol. xv.   To the archæologists named on p. 668 may now be added Sir E. H. Bunbury (1812-95), the well-known numismatist and writer on ancient geography.   Among Orientalists Cureton was the subject of an article in the *Times,* 30th June, reprinted as Appendix to Dean Stanley's Sermon of 19th June, 1864 ; there is a *Life* of Professor Lee (1896), an article on Professor J. Palmer in the *Journal of Philology,* vol. vii. 264, and a *Life* of Professor E. H. Palmer, by Besant (1883).   There is also a notice of Alexander Hamilton (1765-1824) in Benfey's *Geschichte der Sprachwissenschaft,* p. 358 ; a *Life* of William Carey, by Marsham (1859), and also by G. Smith (ed. 2, 1888) ; and, lastly, a *Life* of Bryan Hodgson, by Sir W. W. Hunter (1896).   For notices of other scholars, see *Dictionary of National Biography ;* and for those of recent date, the successive editions of *Men of the Time.*

Astronomy, 1815–1885.—Grant, *History of Physical Astronomy ;* A. M. Clerke, *Popular History of Astronomy during the Nineteenth Century,* and *The System of the Stars ;* Proctor, *Saturn and its System ;* Proctor and Ranyard, *The Old and New Astronomy ;* Ranyard, *Observations made during Total Solar Eclipses,* forming vol. xli. of the Royal Astronomical Society's *Memoirs ;* Young, *The Sun ;* Gore, *The Visible Universe ;* Sir R. Ball, *The Story of the Heavens ;* Huggins, *Presidential Address at the Cardiff Meeting of the British Association,* 1891 ; Scheiner and Frost, *A Treatise on Astronomical Spectroscopy ;* Young, *General Astronomy.*

Geology and Medicine.—*See* chap. xxi.

Physics, 1815–1885.—O. Lodge, *Pioneers of Science* (1893) ; Garnett, *Heroes of Science* (S.P.C.K., 1885) ; A. Guillemin, *Electricity and Magnetism,* translated and revised by S. P. Thompson, F.R.S. (1891) ; T. Preston, *Theory of Light* (1890) ; Arago, *Biographies of Distinguished Scientific Men* (London, 1857) ; *Memoirs of Sir Isaac Newton* (2 vols., London, 1855) ; Tyndall, *Heat a Mode of Motion,* and *Light and Sound ;* Garnett, *Heat ;* A. R. Wallace, *The Wonderful Century* (1898) ; Glazebrook, *Clerk Maxwell and Modern Physics ;* Clerk Maxwell, *Collected Papers* (Camb.

Univ. Press); P. G. Tait, *Life of Sir W. R. Hamilton* **and** *Recent Advances in Physical Science;* Notices in the *Dictionary of National Biography, Encyclopædia Britannica,* Articles on Magnetism, Heat, Light, etc. ; Cajori, *History of Physics,* 1899.

Chemistry, 1715-1885.—For fuller accounts of Price, Priestley, Boyle, Cavendish, etc., *see* the *Dictionary of National Biography.* Accounts of the various processes used by alchemists, and stories of transmutation, may be found in the *Bibliotheca Chemica Curiosa* of Mangetus, Stahl's *Fundamenta Chemiæ,* and Junker's *Conspectus Chemiæ.* There is no complete modern history of the science, but Kopp's *Geschichte* is one of the best, and Hoefer's *Histoire de la Chimie* is good. *See* also E. Meyer, *History of Chemistry,* trans. M'Gowan (incomplete as regards English and French work): *Reports* on the Exhibitions of 1851 and 1862, chemical sections; *Philosophical Magazine; Journal of the Chemical Society.*

Medicine.—See chap. xxi. For the history of medical journalism, *see* Sprigge, *Life and Times of Thomas Wakley,* 1897.

Engineering to 1885.—*Spon's Dictionary of Engineering* (1874); Rankine, *Civil Engineering* (ed. 1884) ; H. Law and D. Clark, *Civil Engineering* (1881) ; Galloway, *The Steam Engine and its Inventors;* Thurston, *The Steam Engine* (International Science Series); E. Clark, *The Britannia and Conway Tubular Bridges* (1880) ; J. Claxton Fidler, *Practical Treatise on Bridge Construction* (1887); Smiles, *Lives of the Engineers; Minutes* of the Proceedings of the Institution of Civil Engineers.

Mining and Metallurgy.—Percy, *The Metallurgy of Iron* (1864) ; Turner, *The Metallurgy of Iron* (1895) ; R. Nelson Boyd, *Coal Pits and Pitmen* (1892) ; Galloway, *History of Coal Mining* (1882) ; Hull, *The Coalfields of Great Britain* (1881) ; Meade, *Coal and Iron Industries of the United Kingdom* (1882) ; Jevons, *The Coal Question* (1866) ; *Coal, its History and its Uses* (by the Professors of the Yorkshire College, Leeds) ; W. E. Hunt, *British Mining; Journal of the Iron and Steel Institute,* especially the Presidential Address of Mr. David Dale (1895) ; *Reports* of the various Royal Commissions to which reference has been made in the text.

Pottery and Porcelain.—Art Journal's Illustrated Catalogues of the Exhibitions of 1851, 1862, 1871 ; *Reports* by juries of the Exhibition of 1851 and 1862 ; *Rapport des Délégués des Ouvriers Parisiens* (on the 1862 Exhibition ; *Porcelain* by MM. Bédigie, Légier, E. Solere, and Troisvallets père) ; *Official Reports* of the London Exhibition of 1871, by Drury-Fortnum, Magniac, Soden-Smith, and Arnoux : Léon Arnoux on *Ceramic Manufacture* (Society of Arts, 1853) ; G. Wallis, *Ceramic Manufacture* (Staffordshire, Coalport, Worcester), 1862 ; Binns, *Worcester China* (1897) ; Burton, *English Porcelain.*

Applications of Electricity, to 1885.—Lodge, *Pioneers of Science;* Garnett, *Heroes of Science* (S.P.C.K., 1885); S. P. Thompson, *Dynamo-Electric Machinery,* 4th ed. (1892), and *The Electro-Magnet* (1891) ; S. P. Thompson, *Philipp Reis, Inventor of the Telephone;* Prescott, *Bell's Speaking Telephone;* Fahie, *The Electric Telegraph* (1889); A. Guillemin, *Electricity and Magnetism,* trans. and revised by S. P. Thompson (1891); J. A. Flemming, *The Alternate Current Transformer,* 4th ed., 2 vols. (Electrician Series); Preece and Stubbs, *Manual of Telephony* (1893); Preece and Maier, *The Telephone* (1889); *Journal of the Institution of Electrical Engineers;* G. Kapp, *Dynamos, Alternators and Transformers,* and *Electrical Transmission of Energy.* [For electric lighting and traction, which have been mainly developed since 1885, the student must be referred to the Supplement to the *Encyclopædia Britannica* and works there cited. A recent popular work on electricity is G. Iles's *Flame, Electricity, and the Camera,* 1900, covering colour photography and the Röntgen rays. Blount, *Practical Electro-Chemistry,* London, 1901, and McMillan, *Treatise on Electro-Metallurgy,* 2nd ed., London, 1899, cover developments of more recent date than the text.]

Textiles, 1815-1885.—*Reports of Artisans on the Paris Exhibition,* 1889; Evan Leigh, *Cotton Spinning* (1882); J. Watts, *Cotton Manufacture* (1887); Bonwick, *Romance of the Wool Trade;* Barlow, *History and Principles of Weaving;* Archer, *Wool and its Applications;* W. T. Charley, *Flax and Linen Manufacture; Reports* of the Flax Improvement Society; Fox, *Mechanism of Weaving* (only incidentally historical) ; and in general, *British Manufacturing Industries.*

Education.—Kay, J., *Social Condition and Education of the People ;* Fyffe and Arnold in T. H. Ward, *The Reign of Queen Victoria ;* Brodrick, *Oxford*, and Bass Mullinger, *Cambridge*, in Creighton's *Epochs of Church History ;* Craik, *The State in its Relation to Education* (" English Citizen " Series); Hamilton, *Journal of Statistical Society*, 1883 and 1890.

Dress.—E. Hill, *History of English Dress ; Punch*, from 1840.

The Modern Convict System.—Sir E. Du Cane, *The Punishment and Prevention of Crime ; Reports* of Directors of Convict Prisons, 1854–96 ; Crawford, *Secondary Punishment ;* Griffiths, *Chronicles of Newgate*, and *Secrets of the Prison House.*

Economic History.—See chap. xxi. *Agriculture.*—See chap. xxiii. *Social Life.*—See chap. xxii. *Scotland.*—See chap. xxiii.

Ireland, 1800–85.—Plowden, *History of Ireland* (1800–10) ; Cloncurry *Personal Recollections ;* Lecky, *Leaders of Public Opinion in Ireland ;* Grattan and O'Connell, *Lives and Speeches of O'Connell, Sheil, and Grattan ;* Hamilton, *Life of O'Connell ;* State Trial of O'Connell, 1843 ; Shaw-Lefevre, *Peel and O'Connell ;* McLennan, *Life of Thomas Drummond ;* Duffy, *Young Ireland ;* A. M. Sullivan, *New Ireland ;* W. O'Connor Morris, *Ireland*, 1794–1868 *;* Barry O'Brien, *Fifty Years of Concession to Ireland*, and *Irish Wrongs and English Remedies ;* T. P. O'Connor, *The Parnell Movement ;* J. H. McCarthy, *Ireland since the Union ; Report of the Financial Relations Commission ;* Lough, *England's Wealth and Ireland's Poverty ;* Blennerhassett, *Reign of Queen Victoria ; Ireland.* For *Celtic Language and Literature*, the principal authorities have been named in the text (p. 888 *seq.*).

Exploration, 1815–1885.—Sir C. Markham and J. S. Keltie, *Review of British Geographical Work during the last Hundred Years* (Royal Geographical Society, 1892). There is a bibliography to this, giving the titles of all the works of the leading British travellers and geographers during the century ; but, though printed, it is not published. It is impossible to give the titles here of the works of all the travellers referred to in the text. The following works, however, may be mentioned : Sir John Barrow, *Chronological History of Voyages into the Arctic Regions* (1818) and *Voyages of Discovery and Research within the Arctic Regions from the year* 1818 (1848); Sir C. Markham, *The Threshold of the Unknown Region* (4th ed., 1875); General A. W. Greely, *Handbook of Arctic Discovery* (1896) ; H. D. Traill, *Life of Sir John Franklin ;* Dr. John Murray, *The Renewal of Antarctic Exploration*, in the *Geographical Journal*, vol. iii. (1894) ; *Journal* and *Proceedings of the Royal Geographical Society*, 1830–92, and *Geographical Journal*, 1892–97 ; *Alpine Journal*, 1844–97 ; Dr. Robert Brown, *The Story of Africa and its Explorers* (4 vols., 1892–95). For the history of Australian Exploration, *see* the works of the Rev. J. E. Tenison-Woods (1865), Ernest Favenc (1888), and A. F. Calvert (1895–96). There is no good history of exploration in Asia or America. This is to some extent supplied by the Annual Reports of the Indian and Canadian Surveys. *See also* the articles on those continents in the *Encyclopædia Britannica* and St. Martin's *Dictionnaire de Géographie Universelle.* For a history of Oceanography, *see* the final volume of the *Challenger* publications, by Dr. John Murray, F.R.S.

Greater Britain.—Sir C. Dilke, *Greater Britain* (1868), and *Problems of Greater Britain ;* Sir G. Cornewall Lewis, *Essay on the Government of Dependencies ;* Lucas, *Historical Geography of the British Colonies* (new introduction, 1903, by H. Egerton, published separately) ; Dodd, *History of the British Colonies ;* Willison, *Sir Wilfrid Laurier and the Liberal Party*, 1903 *; Histories* of Canada by Kingsford, South Africa by Theal, of Australia and of New Zealand by Rusden, of the West Indies and the Spanish Main by Rodway ; Jenks, *The Australasian Colonies ;* Goldwin Smith's *Canada and the Canadian Question ;* W. P. Reeves, *The Long White Cloud* and *State Experiments in Australia and New Zealand*, 1903 *;* H. de B. Walker, *Australasian Democracy ;* Lord, *The Lost Possessions of England.*

CHAPTER XXV

EXPANSION AND CONSOLIDATION OF THE EMPIRE.   1885-1909

THOUGH a quarter of a century is but a moment in the life
of an Empire, the events of the period with which the
present chapter is concerned reveal incessant change in the
political and social organism.   In foreign affairs, in inter-
Imperial relations, in domestic policy there has been an
increasing activity, while the conflict for better conditions
of life for the masses of the people has taken, under the
influence of Socialist thought, a new form which has
alarmed the propertied classes.   The years have been fruitful
in developments of Imperial policy and action; in wars and
changes abroad and new alliances with foreign Powers; in
domestic political strife which has swept Home Rule for
Ireland—for the time being, at any rate—into the background
and resulted in the emergence of a Labour-Socialist group
that threatens to end the two-party system and reduce internal
politics to a war of classes to determine the conditions under
which wealth shall be produced and distributed.   It will be
convenient if the principal facts of the period in question be
marshalled in the three broad divisions thus suggested to
the mind.

Foremost among the developments of Imperial policy and
action stands the work achieved by English sword and brain
in Africa.   In that continent our race has made history with
a prodigality not to be foreseen when the first edition of
this work was published.   In this chapter the record has
to be carried forward to the reconquest of the Soudan and
the consolidation of our position in Egypt, the overthrow
of the Boer republics and the emergence of a United South
Africa, the expansion of British power from the Cape to

H. R.
WHATES.
A Period
of Change.

the Zambesi, from the Indian Ocean to the sources of the Nile, from the Atlantic to the deserts of the Western Soudan.

Egypt and the Soudan.

By a death-bed declaration, the Mahdi transmitted his mastery of the Soudan to the Khalifa Abdullah. The latter entered into an inheritance menaced in the north by Egypt, by England from Suakim, by Abyssinia from the east; and, as we know from Slatin Pasha's dramatic record of years of captivity, his kingdom was torn by dissensions and formidable revolts. Such ruthless resolution did Abdullah display that by the early 'nineties his sway was absolute. Rival military leaders and prophets who escaped death in the field met their fate at the hands of the executioner or rotted in chains in the prisons of Omdurman. Reorganising the Mahdi's army and reducing the personal retinues of the semi-independent emirs, Abdullah destroyed the possibility of an armed confederacy against himself. The nucleus of his military power was provided by his own tribesmen, the Taisha branch of the Baggara Arabs, seven thousand of whom were brought to the capital. Their courage and military skill were equal to their ferocity. They were given a monopoly in Omdurman of the cannon and rifles and ammunition, while other tribesmen of the valley were allowed only swords and spears, except when serving in the frontier wars. Thus these ferocious herdsmen, though few in numbers, were able to hold down many millions of Soudanese. But the successes the Khalifa gained through them were won at the cost of innumerable lives and by a savage oppression for which modern times afford no parallel. In the remoter regions, not easily overawed from Omdurman, the Khalifa had the astuteness to maintain his authority by playing off one emir against another, one tribe against its rival. But he was ill-advised enough to invade Abyssinia with an immense army, and though, in 1889, the head of King John was displayed in Omdurman as the trophy of victory, the success had been dearly bought, and only a remnant of the Khalifa's army returned.

Meanwhile war was made on the Egyptian frontier and Wad-el-Njume was sent, with five thousand men, north from

Dongola. It was an act of madness, having regard to the
English occupation. Sir Francis Grenfell met the invaders
at Toski on August 3rd, 1889, and inflicted a crushing defeat.
The emir perished, and few of his force returned whence
they came.

The worthless victory over the Abyssinians and the disaster
at Toski mark the beginning of the end of the Khalifa's power.
Famine added its horrors to those of war. It seems to
have been general throughout the Soudan. Slatin Pasha has
drawn a terrible picture of its effects. Cannibalism was not
infrequent; social life was utterly disorganised; the mortality
was appalling; the streets and fields were littered with the
dead, and the Nile bore corpses innumerable. The tyranny
of the Mahdi and his successor, and internecine war among
the tribes, had decimated the region; the famine did more—
it depopulated vast tracts. The magnitude of its effects was
not appreciated for a decade, when the victors of Omdurman
found, to their astonishment, that the population was but a
fraction of what they had believed it to be.

The victory of September 2nd, 1898, was the fruit of
years of silent preparation. If England, as a nation, averted
her face from the Soudan after the death of Gordon, and
closed her ears against its tragedies, her servants in Egypt,
though held back by the home Government, cherished
the idea of an eventual reconquest of the lost provinces.
The army of Egypt was reformed simultaneously with the **Prepara-**
reorganisation of the administration. The fellaheen were **tions for**
drilled into fighting men. At Toski they proved that, in the **Advance**
company of white troops, they could withstand the dreaded **the**
Dervish rush. Sir Herbert (afterwards Viscount) Kitchener **Khalifa.**
succeeded to the Sirdarship in April, 1892, and thenceforth
organised for an advance. Meanwhile the attention of the
Khalifa was commanded by Italy, which, in retaliation for a
Dervish raid into Eritrea, seized Kassala. He thus found
himself threatened by Europeans on the east. This move
was, however, the prelude to a succession of disasters for
Italy, culminating in the defeat at Adowa by the Abyssinians
in 1896; and Kassala, on Italy's retirement to the Red Sea
littoral, was transferred by her to the Egyptian Government.
More important than these events, as affecting the fortunes

of the Dervish power, was the creation, by Major (afterwards
Lieut.-General Sir Reginald) Wingate, of the Intelligence
Department of the Egyptian Army, which, during these years
of preparation, had spies in Omdurman through whom masses
of information—political, topographical, military and personal—
were accumulated. In 1891 Father Ohrwalder escaped from
Omdurman and enriched these stores, giving also to the
world a story of his ten years of captivity, which had its
effect in turning public opinion in England in favour of
the recovery of the Soudan. Four years later Slatin Pasha,
the Governor of Darfur, who had been a prisoner since the
Mahdi overthrew the Egyptian power, and had succeeded in
gaining the ear of the Khalifa, contrived to escape. Not
only was he able to place unrivalled knowledge at the service
of the department, the staff of which he joined, but in his
"Fire and Sword in the Soudan" he gave an account of the
region since Gordon's death which decided the public mind
in favour of a policy of reconquest.

Meanwhile, in 1895, a Unionist majority was returned,
and Lord Salisbury found himself in a position to retrieve
the past in the Soudan. Mindful of the treacherous nature
of desert operations, that cautious statesman held back his
party. Events, however, moved apace. The defeat of the
Italians at Adowa reacted at Omdurman, as well as in the
capitals and upon the policies of the European Powers, and
it was decided, by relieving the Italians from possible peril
at Kassala and by a southward move from Wady Halfa, to
demonstrate both to the Khalifa and to the world that the
disasters sustained by our ally did but stiffen the British
resolve to maintain our supremacy in Egypt and regain the
lost prestige of the European in the south. A demonstration
on the frontier was developed into a resolve to seize and keep
the province of Dongola. A fortnight after the battle at Adowa
a column of Egyptian troops marched out of Wady Halfa
and, without resistance, seized the village of Akasha. The
war that was to end two and a half years later at Omdurman
had begun.

The limits of space prohibit any narrative of the war.
An Anglo-Egyptian army under Sir Herbert Kitchener crossed
the desert, following a railway laid from Wady Halfa south-

ward. After fighting several battles along the course of the river the army reconquered the province of Dongola and, on the morning of September 2nd, 1898, came within sight of Omdurman. After a fierce battle, the issue of which was once in doubt, but in which Dervish valour was powerless against modern artillery, the Khalifa's host was scattered and the city taken.

The Battle of Omdurman.

Photo: Dittrich, Cairo.

THE RIGHT HON. THE EARL OF CROMER, O.M.

The pride of England at the success of the Anglo-Egyptian army, and the rejoicings at the liberation of the peoples of the Soudan from the yoke of the Khalifa, were swiftly succeeded by anger against France and apprehension of war with that Power. Steaming with a flotilla up the White Nile, establishing posts and scattering bodies of armed Dervishes on the way, Sir Herbert Kitchener arrived at Fashoda. He found the country under the French flag, and M. Marchand, seven other white officers and eighty Senegalese

The Fashoda Incident.

in occupation of a fort, from which they would surely have
been evicted and massacred by the Dervishes but for the
Sirdar's journey. Wisely refraining from forcing the situation against M. Marchand, who would not haul down his flag
without instructions from his own Government, the Sirdar
reported to his superiors. There were dramatic negotiations
at Paris. Confronted with the fact of French intrusion
into the Nile Valley, the French Government would not
admit that their "emissary of civilisation" had no right to
be there. Sir Edward Monson, our ambassador, told M.
Delcassé bluntly that the Government were determined not
to compromise on the issue: they had no wish to pick
a quarrel, but M. Marchand must be withdrawn. This
was six days after the battle of Omdurman. When the
situation became known by the publication in this country
of the Foreign Office papers, there was intense and anxious
interest on both sides of the Channel. On October 6th Lord
Salisbury and Baron de Courcel fought the matter out in a
notable conversation at the Foreign Office, but without result.
Six days later there was another futile conversation in which,
however, the Baron's rhetorical attempts to "explore the
question" were met by an immovable determination to cede
no rights to France.

A united country rallied to Lord Salisbury's support.
Lord Rosebery made a public speech applauding the Govern-
ment for its firmness in upholding the Grey declaration
of 1895, and warning France or any other Power against
any attempt to "encroach and infringe on the rights of
England." With one accord Mr. Asquith, Sir William
Harcourt, and other leaders of Liberalism echoed his words.
Faltering at the imminence of war, M. Delcassé disregarded
the ravings of the French press and consented to withdraw
M. Marchand, who would have starved but for the food the
Sirdar had supplied. The British Government concerted
means with M. Delcassé by which the fall could be softened
and M. Marchand withdrawn with as little loss to French
dignity as possible; and at the Guildhall banquet on November 9th (1898) Lord Salisbury was able to announce, to the
relief of the nation, that the crisis was over. But he vetoed
a suggestion that a British protectorate should be established

over Egypt and the provinces. A convention was signed (January 19th) with the Egyptian Government vesting the command of the Soudan in a Governor-General (Sir Reginald Wingate) with absolute power, and excluding the Mixed Tribunals, and therefore foreign influence, from the region south of the 22nd parallel. Under this arrangement, with the British and Egyptian flags flying together, a system of administration was built up which has brought peace and order to the desert tribes. M. Marchand returned to Europe *viâ* Abyssinia, with which country, by the way, a treaty had been made barring Abyssinian interference with the advance to Khartoum. France did her best to forget a humiliating incident, handled with great moral courage by a ministry which had dared to retreat from an untenable position. Some consolation was provided for her by a partition of the Soudan, which closed the era of French aggression alike in the hinterland of our West African possessions and in the Nile Valley, and ended the "policy of pin-pricks" that for some years had imperilled the peace between the two nations. Under a convention signed in June, 1898, the Soudanese region beyond Nigeria and the British West Coast colonies had been recognised as the French sphere, France evacuating certain points which she had seized and held on the assumption that "priority of occupation" superseded British treaties with native chiefs; and to this was added, in March, 1899, a clause drawing a line from north to south, which cut France off for ever from the Nile Valley, leaving the Bahr-el-Ghazal and the former Egyptian provinces west of the Nile to Great Britain as her sphere, and the Thibesti region

Peace in the Soudan.

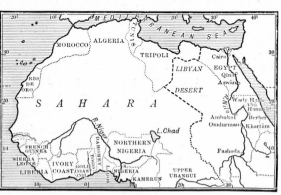

MAP SHOWING THE ENGLISH AND FRENCH
SPHERES IN THE SOUDAN.

south-east of Tripoli and north and east of Lake Chad to France.

Prosperity in Egypt.

After the triumphs of war and diplomacy there came a period of organisation and consolidation in the Nile Valley and in West Africa. The emergence of Egypt to solvency and prosperity under Sir Evelyn Baring (afterwards Earl of Cromer), greatest of modern proconsuls; the completion and economic effects of the irrigation works on the Nile carried out by Sir William Garstin; the transformation of the Khalifa's capital into a centre of civilisation; the gradual building up of a semi-military rule extending to the remotest parts of the provinces east, west and south; the creative and recuperative energy which has been diffused along the Nile Valley from the Delta to the Lakes, form a story unique in modern annals. It was told, year by year, in a series of reports from the Commissioner in Cairo which are remarkable not less for their literary excellence than for their statesmanship; and on his retirement in 1907 the Earl of Cromer, as he then became, gave it anew, in brilliant and authoritative form, in his book on "Modern Egypt."

Turkey and the Sinai Peninsula.

One incident only can here be touched upon, and one additional observation made. The incident was furnished by Turkey, which, in 1906, occupied certain posts on the Gulf of Akabah and set up a claim to sovereignty over the peninsula of Sinai, thus imperilling our command of the Suez Canal and the route to India. After a sharp crisis, when war seemed imminent, the Porte withdrew the posts and agreed to a settlement confirming Egyptian rights over the peninsula, which has since been more effectively occupied and administered from Cairo. The observation is that since

Nationalist Movement in Egypt.

the reconquest of the Soudan the Nationalist movement in Egypt has grown in strength and is a cause of anxiety to Sir Eldon Gorst, Lord Cromer's successor. Partly as a result of Turkish intrigue preceding the seizure of the posts on the Gulf of Akabah, partly because of the general unrest among Eastern peoples, an Islamic movement was threatened in Egypt during 1906 and 1907, and there were some ugly incidents, notably at Denshawi, where English officers were maltreated and one killed—Captain Bull, of the 6th Dragoons —in an affray arising out of a pigeon-shooting trespass. Four villagers were publicly executed, and several were flogged and afterwards sent to prison. The affair caused much excitement in Egypt and some acrimonious discussion in England. But the agitation died away in both countries. Nationalism in Egypt, which aims at the termination of the English occupation and self-government under a parliament in Cairo, is, however, an active force; and a new era of political agitation and constitutional development in Egypt seems to have opened.

A brief survey of affairs in West and East Africa will give **Ashanti.** completeness to the story of English activities in the tropical belt of that continent. The Wolseley expedition of 1874 left Ashanti an independent kingdom. We went to Coomassie, and we conquered, burnt, fined—and returned. As the lesson faded from the native mind the old horrors were resumed. Coomassie again became a human slaughter-house; trade with the coast was interrupted and sometimes wholly blocked; barbaric anarchy prevailed over the hinterland. The conditions were a reproach to British vigour in protecting the inland tribes of the Gold Coast region from Ashanti aggressions. France, moreover, was rapidly extending her rule over the hinterland from Senegal, and threatened to sweep away the Ashanti kingdom in her march. The situation ripened in the early 'nineties, and in 1894 Mr. Chamberlain, then Colonial Secretary in Lord Salisbury's third Administration, decided to forestall France and require King Prempeh to accept a British protectorate with a Resident at his capital. The demand was treated with contempt, and in December, 1895, an expedition, under Sir Francis Scott, marched on Coomassie. The town was occupied on January 17th, 1896, without a shot being fired; the king was brought to the coast, and the kingdom annexed to the Crown. Coomassie was found to be a veritable charnel-house, but no foe was encountered more formidable than disease. Among its victims was Prince Henry of Battenberg, who succumbed on January 20th, 1896. By the establishment of posts among the northern tribes subject to Ashanti, the African troops left to garrison Coomassie came into conflict with Samory, a Mahommedan slave raider, against whom French Senegalese troops also were operating. A force under

312—N.E.

Lieutenant Henderson was surrounded at Wa, and the young officer courageously went alone into Samory's camp to treat for peace. He was kept a prisoner for a month, and was then released, and found his way back to civilisation. The civilian official, Mr. Ferguson, who had accompanied him to Wa, was less fortunate. In the fighting there he had been wounded. The beleaguered troops succeeded in getting away into the bush, but Mr. Ferguson's carriers disburthened themselves of him by cutting off his head. Colonel Northcote —who was to lose his life in the Boer War—took a strong force northward and, after sharp fighting in the spring of 1898, pacified the region. Samory eventually was disposed of by the French, whose activities brought them into touch with our outlying posts.

Native Rising in Sierra Leone. Meanwhile there was a serious native rising in the hinterland of Sierra Leone, and several white missionaries were massacred. The ostensible cause of the insurrection was the imposition of a hut tax when a protectorate over the hinterland was declared in 1896 ; and the home Government sent out the late Sir David Patrick Chalmers, a retired Colonial Chief Justice, to investigate and report. He advised a cessation of operations and condemned the tax; but Mr. Chamberlain disregarded his counsels, and under the stern but judicious control of the Governor, Sir Frederick Cardew, the insurrection was suppressed and the hut tax retained.

The Royal Niger Company. In the vaster region lying aback of the Niger delta and the Coast Protectorate, with its magnificent waterway, its Hausa empire of Sokoto and tributary emirates, its populous centres connected by caravan routes crossing the continent to Tripoli in the north and the Red Sea in the east, the Royal Niger Company had pursued an active policy of treaty-making since the grant of a charter in 1886. But the capacity of the Company's officers to make local treaties outstripped the power of the Company effectively to occupy the ceded territories. or to exercise the rights conferred. For ten years Mr. Goldie Taubman (afterwards Sir George Taubman-Goldie), with a far-seeing judgment, had been organising, under stupendous difficulties, a system of military and civil administration, and had built up a considerable trade. In 1887 the Imperial Government proclaimed a protectorate over the basin of the Niger and

its affluents wherever the Company were or might be established. Thereafter began a struggle between the Fulah rulers
of the Hausa states and the Company for the mastery of the

Photo: Russell & Sons, Baker Street, W.
CECIL J. RHODES.

policies of the region. Meanwhile, however, the French,
sweeping past the hinterland of Ashanti and Dahomey, had
penetrated Nigeria and established posts in regions covered by

British treaties, which they claimed to have invalidated by virtue of priority of occupation. Partly to arrest this process, partly forced by local necessities, the Company hazarded its fortunes in 1897 by an expedition against the Emir of Nupe. It was brilliantly successful, despite the valour of the Fulah cavalry, and Bida was captured after two days' fighting. Ilorin next fell to the Company's arms and thus the way was cleared for the assertion of British treaty rights from both banks of the upper waters of the Niger.

Imperial Control in Nigeria. Imperial control now became a necessity alike for international and administrative reasons. The French and British spheres in the West African Soudan having been defined by the Convention of June, 1898, the Government relieved the Company of its administrative powers and established a direct Imperial system. Sir Frederick Lugard, who had done brilliant service in Uganda and afterwards as chief military officer of the Niger Company, was appointed High Commissioner, and he set himself to consolidate and extend our occupation of Nigeria. He proved a bold, sagacious and successful administrator—a little too bold for the Imperial Government, in whose imagination the Fulah power held, as events were to prove, a disproportionate space, and whose minds were haunted by fears of a great Mahommedan rising. The policy of Sir Frederick Lugard was to break down the outlying emirates of Sokoto and establish in every centre an emir subservient to himself. That it was a hazardous policy was indisputable; but in the hands of a man of energy and daring, with a military capacity strengthened by much experience of African warfare, it was successful. The first dramatic blow was struck in the autumn of 1901, from a point five hundred miles up the Benuë river, when an expedition attacked Yola and captured it after severe fighting. Setting aside recalcitrant emirs here and there, wherever the argument of a Maxim gun could be brought to bear, and replacing them with puppets of his own, Sir Frederick prepared for further exploits.

Overthrow of the Hausa Power. Kano—the great walled city known to every Soudan merchant as the emporium of the west—was his next objective. The Emir, who paid tribute to the Sultan of Sokoto, was defiant. Zaria was then our advanced post. Mr. Chamberlain was in South Africa at the time, and Lord Onslow was in charge of the Colonial Office. Without taking the home authorities so fully into his confidence as Lord Onslow and others could have wished, Sir Frederick forced the situation and extorted assent to his plan to attack forthwith. On February 3rd, 1903, he dashed at Kano, and after a sharp fight the place was in his hands. Sokoto followed suit, and the Fulah ascendency came to a dramatic end. Since then, though there has been much sporadic fighting, British rule has been firmly established from the Delta to the boundary in the French desert. But the pagan region in Southern Nigeria has presented great difficulties. Benin, however, was opened up to civilisation in 1907, and since then it has been possible to traverse the recesses of the Delta territories. This achievement was precipitated by an adventurous indiscretion on the part of Acting-Consul Phillips, who in January, 1896, took a party of European officers and two civilians to treat with the king. They were massacred in the bush; but two—Captain Boisragon and Mr. Locke—notwithstanding their wounds, escaped to tell the tale. An expedition was organised and the city captured. It was little else than a place of human sacrifice. This part of the record may be brought to a close with the statement that Sir Percy Girouard succeeded Sir Frederick Lugard as High Commissioner of Nigeria in 1907, that the railway now extends from Lagos to Kano, and that a policy has been framed, and is indeed in partial operation, for threading the entire region with a branch system.

In East Africa England has entered into the inheritance unconsciously prepared for her during many centuries by the explorers and traders of Arab race who put to use the geographical knowledge handed down from the days of Ptolemy. The quarter of a century covered by this chapter has witnessed the subjection of the ascendant Arab class who carried Mahommedanism into Central Africa; the liberation of the negroid peoples from the merchant enslaver; the substitution of a European and Christian administration— two such administrations, for Germany is co-partner by partition of the region—for independent native kingdoms; the building of a trunk railway from the sea to the heart of the continent; the acquisition of the great lakes which are the source of the Nile; and the establishment of such conditions as may enable the aboriginal peoples to ascend the scale of humanity. Civilisation found them in much the same condition, subject to much the same horrors and oppressions from without and within their territories, as those disclosed by the Arabs and Persians who, centuries before the advent of Mahomet, sailed down the coast and ventured inland for spoils of gold and ivory, frankincense and spices. Diplomatic and other changes must now be sketched in outline as evidence of the opening of a new chapter in the life of Africa and the relations thereto of the English race now and hereafter.

Anglo-German Treaty. The Anglo-German scramble for East and Central Africa was terminated by a treaty of July 1st, 1890, which reserved to Great Britain an enormous block of territory from the Indian Ocean to the Nile springs. A decade of war and confusion in the early stages of Imperial administration following the administrative collapse of the British East African Chartered Company, was closed by the construction, at a cost of £5,500,000, of a railway from Mombasa to the lakes. The Pax Britannica is now established securely everywhere on that side of Africa except in the Somaliland Protectorate on the north-east, where an Arab mullah has given much trouble.

South Africa. During the period under review the lives of two great personalities, Cecil Rhodes and Paul Kruger, were interwoven with the history of England, their hostile activities culminating in a war which lasted for three years, cost over nineteen thousand British lives, consumed a hundred and fifty millions of British money, extinguished the two Dutch republics, and led to the political unification of South Africa. Cecil Rhodes, the younger son of a Hertfordshire clergyman, went to South Africa as a youth, returning yearly to Oxford, where he took his degree at Oriel College in 1873. His tenure of life was then of the slightest, for phthisis claimed him: but in the dry and invigorating air of the veldt he threw off the disease. Establishing himself at Kimberley, he built up in a few years a great fortune in diamond mining, and carried through an amalgamation of interests under the name of the

De Beers Mines which gave him a predominant position in finance and politics in the sub-continent. But money-making was with him only a means to an end, and the ideal and the dream of his life was an illimitable extension of British rule northward from the Cape Colony frontier. "It is no use," he observed to General Gordon in 1882, "to have big ideas unless you have got pounds, shillings and pence to carry them out." He had both the ideas and the money. Foreseeing, after Majuba and the Transvaal Convention of 1884, that the one question of the future was whether South Africa would remain under the British flag or become a gigantic Dutch republic, he used brains and purse to frustrate the ideal of the Boer President at Pretoria.

His first move was to influence the acquisition of Bechuana- *Acquisi-* land, which was cleared of Boer freebooters by Sir Charles *tion of* Warren. This carried the British flag to the 22nd parallel *Territory.* of south latitude. His next was to extend British rule to the Zambesi. Portugal had a shadowy claim from the coast; the Boers were feeling their way into the region from the north. Forestalling Kruger by a treaty with Lobengula, the king of Matabililand, Mr. Rhodes sent agents into the country; they found Boer emissaries there also who had likewise made treaties with Lobengula at Buluwayo. Loben- gula was playing off one aggressor against another, his army being the real barrier against the Dutch and the British alike. The situation ripened in 1888, when Mr. C. D. Rudd, a Kimberley partner of Mr. Rhodes, Mr. Maguire, an Oxford associate, and Mr. F. R. Thompson struck a bargain with Lobengula, buying of him the concession of mineral rights for an income of £100 a month with 1,200 Martini- Henry rifles and a million rounds of ammunition. The latter items of the deal have a significance which comment would mar. A charter was then obtained from the British Govern- *Birth of* ment, and in 1889 the British South Africa Company came *Chartered* into existence. Enlisting the services of Mr. Selous, the *Company.* famous African hunter, Mr. Rhodes sent out from Kimberley, in March, 1890, an armed expedition of two hundred pioneers and two troops of mounted police, whose object was the occupation of Mashonaland. Dr. Leander Starr Jameson, another of Mr. Rhodes's early Kimberley associates, had been in Buluwayo and, by the exercise of medical skill and diplomacy, was understood to have obtained Lobengula's consent to the passage of this expedition, which the doctor joined. Though in peril of attack from the Matabili impis, the force got safely past the Matabili country and, on September 12th, 1890, planted the flag at Mount Hampden, now the town of Salisbury. Treaties were made eastward which brought England into diplomatic conflict with Portugal, and the extension of the authority of the Chartered Company to the coast was checked only by the orders of the Crown. These difficulties were settled in November, 1890, by a *modus vivendi* which reserved the greater part of Swaziland to Portugal and gave Great Britain a preferential right of purchase over all the Portuguese territories south of the Zambesi. But the extension northward went on unchecked, Sir H. H. Johnston getting ahead of Major Serpa Pinto and his Portuguese force in 1891, and making treaties establishing British rights as far as Lake Tanganyika. Thus Nyasaland came into existence.

The effect of these doings was finally to shut off the Transvaal from expansion northward. Meanwhile the Company carried the railway from Kimberley to Mafeking and the telegraph to Fort Salisbury, and daring pioneers, in search of gold, spread themselves over Mashonaland, where Dr. Jameson was Administrator.

Matabili-land.

Lobengula remained to be overthrown and his territories subjected to the like exploitation. It had been his custom to raid the Mashonas at will, and the continuance of this practice was inconvenient to the Chartered Company. Remonstrances were made ; Lobengula was defiant ; the Company organised a force against him, and in 1893 war broke out. In an engagement on the Shangani River Major Wilson, with a body of forty horsemen, pursued a retreating impi in a daring attempt to capture the king ; but the pursuit was pushed too far and the pursuers were trapped and surrounded. They fought till their last cartridge was spent, and fell in hand-to-hand conflict with the spearmen. It was an heroic incident in a campaign that ended in the capture of Buluwayo and the temporary conquest of the country—temporary because, in 1895, the entire area of Matabililand and Mashona-

land was aflame with revolt. The Company's forces having
been withdrawn to the south for the purposes of the raid into
the Transvaal, the natives rose and massacred the settlers on
every side. Dr. Jameson, who at this time was in Pretoria
jail, was succeeded as Administrator by Earl Grey. Sir
Richard Martin was sent out as Deputy High Commissioner,

Photo: G. F. Ferneyhough, F.R.P.S., Pietermaritzburg.

S. J. PAUL KRUGER.

and Sir Frederick Carrington was given command of the
forces. After much fighting the war was brought to an end
in 1897, Mr. Rhodes risking his life in the Matoppo Hills' in
an effort, happily successful, to persuade the recalcitrant chiefs
to accept terms of peace. Then the country entered upon a
period of slow recuperation. The railway was carried to Buluwayo, and then northward across the Zambesi to Victoria Falls.

Earlier and more momentous events now claim attention. The Convention of 1881 granted the Boers of the Transvaal "complete self-government subject to the suzerainty of her Majesty," and specified certain rights as retained by the Crown. Boer discontent with these limitations led to a demand for a treaty of amity and commerce as between two independent Powers. This was not conceded, but a new Convention was signed (February 27th, 1884) which, while not specifically abrogating the preamble of the 1881 instrument defining the suzerainty, substituted for the articles certain others which weakened Imperial rights. The Volksraad treated this new arrangement as an abandonment of the suzerainty. For some years the position was that the Imperial Government allowed the suzerainty to fall into the background; the Transvaal acted as though it enjoyed an independence as complete as that of its neighbour and ally the Orange Free State. The difference of view and of attitude would not have
become of practical importance but for the gold discoveries on the Witwatersrand in 1885 and 1886. These brought into the Transvaal a swarm of prospectors, miners and traders, and millions of British and other foreign capital. By 1887 there was a population of ten or twelve thousand non-Boers on the Rand, and Johannesburg had come into being. The marvellous richness of the Rand reacted on the Boer Treasury. In 1886 the revenue was just under £200,000; in 1892 it was £1,255,830; and year by year it rose by leaps and bounds until in 1899 it was £4,087,852.

The riches accruing to the republic by the rise of the new industry confirmed Mr. Kruger in his political ambitions. The oligarchy of which he was head taxed the new-comers up to the hilt, refused them any share in the government unless they became burghers of the republic, and proved itself both corrupt and incapable. But of that more anon. We have seen how the Boers were headed off from expansion in the north. They turned their attention to the east, swarmed into Swaziland, and built the Netherlands Railway to Delagoa Bay in order to be independent of supplies from the Cape Colony and Natal lines. In pursuance of a policy to obtain for this line a monopoly of the Transvaal traffic, Mr. Kruger imposed disabilities on the southern traffic, and finally, in 1895, "closed the drifts." This was a flagrant breach of the commercial stipulations of the London Convention. Mr. Chamberlain, who had just taken his seat at the Colonial Office, at once demanded the reopening of the drifts. Mr. Kruger, not prepared to fight on such an issue, complied, and the peril passed for a time. Meanwhile the Uitlander population of the Transvaal had grown to sixty thousand people, who paid nine-tenths of the taxation and had become dangerously restive under the misgovernment of the Boer oligarchy. Mr. Kruger disliked them, seeing in them, though an apparently inexhaustible source of wealth, a menace to his rule and to the political ambitions of his race in South Africa; and the feeling was cordially returned, though not unmixed with admiration for his rugged and masterful character. The Uitlanders would have welcomed war over the railway question, for war would then surely have ended in the overthrow of the Pretoria government.

Thwarted in that by Mr. Kruger's change of front, they applied themselves to political agitation, while the oligarchy, secretly but lavishly, spent its abounding revenues on arms and ammunition and other preparations for an appeal to force. The agitation in Johannesburg was organised by the Transvaal National Union, and the wires were pulled by Mr. Rhodes, then Prime Minister of the Cape Colony, member of the Privy Council, head of the De Beers Mines, the ruling spirit of the British South Africa Company, managing director of the Goldfields Company at Johannesburg, and, next to Mr. Kruger, the most influential man in the sub-continent. With him, in closest confidence, were his co-directors of the Chartered Company: Mr. Alfred Beit, a German subject and head of the firm of Wernher, Beit and Company; Dr. Jameson; Mr. Rutherfoord Harris, the secretary of the Company; Mr. Lionel Phillips, a Johannesburg partner of Mr. Beit; and Mr. Leonard, a Johannesburg solicitor, who was chairman of the National Union. Repeated representations by the Union having failed to secure any redress of Uitlander grievances, Mr. Rhodes and Mr. Beit met at the Cape in May, 1895, and, in apprehension of a rebellion in Johannesburg, concerted means by which they could "assist" that cause. War was

meant, but the leading Uitlanders looked askance at the
intention. Mr. Phillips, for example, would have preferred
to spend a few millions "to improve the Raad." Counsels of
bribery, however, were overborne, and it was agreed that a
rising should occur late in the year and that simultaneously
Dr. Jameson, with the military police of the British South
Africa Company, should invade the Transvaal from the
Bechuanaland border.

For the better furtherance of this plan, which was kept
a profound secret, it was desirable to cajole the Imperial
Government into adding a frontier strip of the Bechuanaland Protectorate to the territory of the Chartered Company.
Mr. Chamberlain gave up the strip for railway purposes.
Mr. Harris carried out this negotiation in London, and he
was authorised to "sound" Mr. Chamberlain as to what that
gentleman's course would be if there were a rising in Johannesburg. There was some conversation on the unrest in that
city, and Mr. Harris appears to have thought that he communicated more to Mr. Chamberlain than that statesman's
astute brain actually comprehended. It seems that he was
about to say something which he wished to be regarded
as confidential, but was stopped by Mr. Chamberlain, who
declared that he could hear nothing in confidence but
only that of which he could make official use. Mr. Harris
left, however, under the impression that among the reasons
he had given for wanting the strip was that it was required
as a suitable "jumping-off place" for an invasion of the
Transvaal; and he claimed to have spoken in the same
sense to Mr. Fairfield, of the Colonial Office, who, equally
with Mr. Chamberlain and Lord Selborne, denied that any
such information had been conveyed to his intelligence. Be
these things as they may, Mr. Harris telegraphed to Mr.
Rhodes that the Colonial Office knew of the double purpose
for which the territory was needed.

The grant being made, arms and ammunition were bought
freely with the Chartered Company's money, ostensibly for
Rhodesia, and smuggled into the Transvaal through the
agency of the De Beers Company; and Colonel Frank Rhodes,
a brother of Cecil, organised the Johannesburgers for a
rebellion. Stations were fixed and stores collected on the

route the invaders would have to follow. Meanwhile the High Commissioner, Sir Hercules Robinson, afterwards Lord Rosmead, was kept wholly in the dark by Mr. Rhodes, the Prime Minister ; but the real reason for the presence of the troops was confided to Mr. Newton, the Chief Magistrate of Bechuanaland, who also concealed his knowledge from the High Commissioner. While the plan was ripening Dr. Jameson paid a flying visit to Johannesburg, and there, with Mr. Charles Leonard, Mr. Lionel Phillips, Colonel F. Rhodes, Mr. John Hays Hammond and Mr. George Farrar, concocted a letter drafted by Mr. Leonard, intended to be used to delude the British public. It was undated, addressed to Dr. Jameson, and the date—December 20, 1895—filled in afterwards by the doctor. With this letter in his pocket he returned to the frontier early in December, having arranged to start for Johannesburg with his force on the same night as a rising was to occur in that city, two dates being fixed provisionally— December 28th and January 4th. This invented and deceitful letter spoke of conflict between the Government and the Uitlander population and recapitulated the latter's grievances, represented thousands of unarmed men, women and children as being at the mercy of well-armed Boers, and called upon Dr. Jameson to come to their aid should disturbance arise.

No sooner had Dr. Jameson left than the Johannesburgers **The Jameson Raid.** began to repent. Their rifles and ammunition had not all arrived ; to seize Johannesburg fort was an uglier job than it seemed ; they were not sure that Dr. Jameson's force would be so large as it ought to be ; some of the " Reformers " were not enamoured of the plot ; others were not sure whether the Transvaal flag or the British should be flown after a successful rebellion ; some wanted one flag, some the other. These and other excuses cloaked an uneasiness that grew as the month advanced. Mr. Leonard was sent post-haste to Mr. Rhodes to insist that the British flag should not be flown. That, it was alleged, was the compact with Dr. Jameson. The upshot was that it was agreed to postpone the rising until January 6th. Dr. Jameson was commanded both from Cape Town and from Johannesburg to stay his hand. But his troopers were in the saddle on the 28th, waiting for the word to start, and on Sunday the 29th, when these countermanding instructions were received, Dr. Jameson broke the leash. "I shall leave to-night Transvaal," he telegraphed to Mr. Rhodes. "My reasons are, final arrangement with writers of letter was that without further reference to them . . . I was to take my troops immediately to prevent loss of lives as letters state." "On no account whatever must you move," telegraphed Mr. Rhodes; "I most strongly object to such a course." But that message was not delivered. Dr. Jameson had cut the wires. With 480 men, eight Maxims and four field pieces—as reckless a company of freebooters as ever mounted horse—he was racing eastward across the veldt.

Late at night Mr. Rhodes confided his news to Sir Graham Bower, the Imperial Secretary to the High Commissioner, who thought fit to sleep upon it, and told Sir Hercules Robinson the next morning. Sir Hercules ordered Mr. Newton to send his fleetest horsemen after Dr. Jameson and command his return; and he urged Mr. Rhodes publicly and forthwith to disavow complicity with the doctor, which Mr. Rhodes naturally would not do. The messengers overtook Dr. Jameson at mid-day on Tuesday, the 31st. Their command was disregarded. On the same day Mr. Harris telegraphed the concocted letter from the Rand to Miss Shaw, a lady who, in Mr. Rhodes's language, "did the colonies for the *Times*," and "did" them with remarkable knowledge and high literary ability. The *Times* published the letter in full on January 1st, and the country was dazed with surprise. Meanwhile Mr. Chamberlain did all he could by telegraph to compel the retreat of the force; but Dr. Jameson was racing onward full of confidence and hope. He sighted Krugersdorp on the afternoon of Wednesday, January 1st, and there found

Failure of the Raid. his advance contested. A preliminary fight was opened and maintained until darkness set in. The troopers fell back and camped for the night. In the morning they found themselves enveloped by Boers and in an untenable position. They fought for a time and then ran up the white flag. A score of troopers lay dead, many more were wounded, the rest were marched off to Pretoria and there laid by the heels, while the Maxims and field guns were added to the artillery of the defending force, which had utterly outgeneralled the invaders. Johannesburg had not risen. The city had sent no force to meet

Dr. Jameson. The Boers had lured the wearied troopers into a strategic trap and inflicted upon a British force a humiliation which was read of in England with mingled rage and shame.

From this moment Mr. Chamberlain superseded Mr. Rhodes as Mr. Kruger's antagonist. But the President held,

THE RIGHT HON. VISCOUNT MILNER.
(From the painting by P. Tennyson Cole.)

for the moment, all the winning cards. A great wrong had been done to the republic, and technically he would have been justified in hanging every one of the raiders and also the co-conspirators in Johannesburg, many of whom likewise were lodged in jail. He was at the head of the richest and best-armed State in South Africa; his burghers held the Uitlander population as in a vice which could be tightened at will. The only thing he had to fear was such an explosion of wrath in England as would make immediate war a necessity; and even this was counterbalanced by the consideration that he had the violent sympathy of Europe and might reckon on the active help of Germany. "I express to you," telegraphed the German Emperor, in a moment of political aberration that definitely changed for the worse the relations of the English and German Governments and peoples, "my sincere congratulations that, without appealing to the help of friendly Powers, you and your people have succeeded in repelling with your own forces the armed band which had broken into your territory and in maintaining the independence of your country against foreign aggression." This implied denial of the suzerainty and admission that the republic was an independent sovereign State caused intense anger in England, not less to those who were shamed and shocked by the wickedness and folly of the raid than to those who were mortified only by its failure. Whatever our difficulties might be with the Transvaal, there was no intention of allowing Germany to profit by them and get a foothold there. The Cabinet answered the telegram, to the immense satisfaction of the people, by forming a naval squadron, by otherwise marshalling the fleet in home waters, and by diverting home-coming troops from India to the Cape. President Kruger replied in a sense which eased the critical situation in so far as he showed that he had no mind to exchange the whips of England for the scorpions of Germany. He sent his "very deep and heartfelt" thanks to the Emperor, and observed significantly—using, be it noted, the language of a sovereign State—that, with the help of God, he and his people "hope to do everything further that is possible for the holding of our dearly-bought independence and the stability of our beloved republic." Henceforth the German Government observed a strict neutrality, though asserting itself aggressively during the subsequent war, when it became necessary to interfere with German vessels carrying contraband. In these cases Lord Salisbury sharply reproved the blustering German diplomatists, but cautiously refrained from pressing his contentions to the breaking point.

Meanwhile Mr. Chamberlain, through the High Commissioner, had expressed "sincere regret at the unwarrantable

The German Emperor's Telegram.

raid by Jameson," and had thanked the Boer Government "for the moderation shown under trying circumstances," this moderation being a demand for the unconditional surrender of Johannesburg within forty-eight hours, a denial that it was intended to shoot Dr. Jameson and his companions, and an offer to hand them over to the Imperial Government for punishment. These matters being arranged and the Jameson raiders handed over, Mr. Chamberlain pressed for reforms for the Uitlander population. But he found Sir Hercules Robinson in bad health, disgusted at the duplicity with which he had been treated by Mr. Rhodes—who at once resigned his office of Prime Minister—and disinclined to act with the confident vigour Mr. Chamberlain thought necessary. In these circumstances Mr. Chamberlain's negotiations for local autonomy for the Rand, subject to the veto of the President and the Executive Council of the republic, came to nothing. After a year, in which no advance was made, Sir Hercules retired and was awarded a peerage, which he lived to enjoy only for a few months, and Sir Alfred (afterwards Viscount) Milner, with a brilliant reputation earned in Egypt and at the Board of Inland Revenue, was appointed High Commissioner.

With Sir Alfred Milner's arrival at the Cape in May, 1897, **Trial of the Raiders.** a new chapter opened. Meanwhile, dramatic events had occurred in England. Dr. Jameson and five officers of the British army—Sir John Willoughby, Bart., the military commander of the raiding party; Henry F. White; Raleigh Grey; Robert White, and Charles John Coventry—were put on their trial under the Foreign Enlistment Act. The various counts of the indictment may be epitomised in the charge that within the limits of her Majesty's dominions and without the licence of the Crown they prepared and fitted out a military expedition against the dominions of a friendly State. The trial took place in the High Court before the Lord Chief Justice—the late Lord Russell of Killowen—Baron Pollock and the late Sir Henry Hawkins. The troopers were not proceeded against. A verdict of guilty was followed by sentence of fifteen months' hard labour upon Jameson and lesser terms for the other prisoners. The Lord Chief Justice delivered a brief, but dignified and powerful, address which had much influence in correcting public opinion, for the raiders had been regarded

313—N.E.

less as reckless disturbers of the world's peace than as heroes in misfortune. The lightness of the sentences caused much irritation in the Transvaal, and no one either there or in England could understand why Mr. Rhodes—"the man who set the dog on to me," as Mr. Kruger observed—was not also put on his trial. An explanation, however, may be found in the suggestion that, had this been done, Mr. Rhodes might have returned to South Africa and, with or without Mr. Kruger, formed an Afrikander Confederation independent of the British Crown. The belief in the Transvaal was that the Government dared not punish Mr. Rhodes because Mr. Chamberlain was privy to his offence.

A Committee of Inquiry. Colour was given to this suspicion by the proceedings of a Select Committee appointed in 1896 to inquire into the origin and circumstances of the affair. Its investigations were conducted with a certain delicacy which Mr. Labouchere, one of its members and a persistent critic of the British South Africa Company, failed to modify, though he compensated himself by writing a searching and caustic Minority Report. Certain telegrams came to light and certain others did not, though these were published subsequently in Europe from a doubtful Dutch source; but there was nothing in the evidence adduced, or which Mr. Chamberlain had seen at the time, "which caused him [Mr. Chamberlain] in any way to modify or qualify the statement he made that he had no foreknowledge of the raid nor of the preparations for the raid, and had given no approval to it." Lord Selborne, and Mr. Fairfield, who had died since, had been equally unsuspicious. "Your Committee"—again we quote from the Majority Report—"fully accept the statements of the Secretary of State for the Colonies and the Under Secretary, and entirely exonerate the officials of the Colonial Office of having been in any sense cognisant of the plans which led up to the incursion of Dr. Jameson's force into the South African Republic." One fact was clearly brought out: that the conspirators had put it abroad that their project was known at, and approved by, the **Mr. Rhodes Censured.** Colonial Office. Mr. Rhodes had been examined with unwonted gentleness, notwithstanding his refusal to produce certain telegrams relating to this phase of the matter; and he was allowed to return to South Africa, where he applied himself as best he could to the pacification of Rhodesia. The Report mildly censured him. After outlining the facts and Mr. Rhodes's relation to them it said : "Such a policy,"—*i.e.* that of rebellion and invasion—"once embarked upon, inevitably involved Mr. Rhodes in grave breaches of duty to those to whom he owed allegiance. He deceived the High Commissioner representing the Imperial Government, he concealed his views from his colleagues in the Colonial Ministry and from the Board of the British South Africa Company, and led his subordinates to believe that his plans were approved by his superiors." The wrath of the Committee was reserved for Sir Graham Bower and Mr. Newton. A debate on the Report took place in the Commons, but there was an arrangement between the two front benches to foil the attack on the Committee. The issues raised were : Whether the Committee had screened Mr. Rhodes, and if so, why, and whether Mr. Chamberlain had been privy to the raid. Mr. Chamberlain vigorously repelled the insinuations against himself and made the singular assertion that, while the fault of Mr. Rhodes was about as great a fault as any statesman could commit, there existed nothing which affected his personal character as a man of honour.

While these events were happening in England the sentences of death on four of the Johannesburg "reformers" had been commuted by the payment of fines of £25,000 each. Others bought their liberty, and the Pretoria Government pocketed £212,000 in fines. But two stalwarts, Mr. A. Wools Sampson and Mr. W. D. Davies, refused to purchase their freedom and stayed where they were until, on the Queen's Jubilee Day, in 1897, Mr. Kruger turned them out of prison. Mr. Kruger had also presented his account for damages arising from the raid and had definitely repudiated the suzerainty, which Mr. Chamberlain as definitely asserted. The little bill, at which even Lord Rosmead was astonished and all the world was amused, amounted to £1,677,938 3s. 3d. —£677,938 3s. 3d. for material damages, and £1,000,000 for "moral and intellectual damages." Mr. Chamberlain repudiated the claim for £1,000,000, and asked for further particulars as to the rest.

This was the situation when Sir Alfred Milner arrived in

Uit-
landers'
Petition to
Queen
Victoria.
South Africa. For a year he travelled, observed, thought, probed the minds of Dutch and British alike, but contented himself with keeping the issues between London and Pretoria open and negotiable. Mr. Kruger also did much thinking; and he acted vigorously, though warily, purchasing in Germany the best artillery money could buy, accumulating vast stores of Mauser rifles and ammunition, and otherwise preparing secretly for war. He ruled the humiliated Johannesburgers as with a rod of iron. With the Orange Free State he made an alliance for common action against Great Britain, and it was believed that one of the conditions of this pact was that Mr. Steyn, the President at Bloemfontein, and a much younger man, should succeed him in the headship not merely of the united republics, but of the great Afrikander Confederation that was to arise after a war. Between himself and Mr. Chamberlain's insistent arguments for reform on the Rand he interposed Dr. Leyds, an astute young Hollander, and afterwards Mr. F. W. Reitz, each of whom had a brain as keenly argumentative as that of Mr. Chamberlain and a pen of much force. Evasive and obstructive answers were made to specific complaints of breaches of the Convention. In vain did Mr. Chamberlain endeavour to extort from the President an admission of the reality of the suzerainty; equally in vain did the Boer diplomatists endeavour to obtain from the Imperial Government recognition of the independent sovereign rights which Mr. Kruger claimed for the republic. It is unnecessary to say more regarding this long epistolary wrangle about words and phrases. The reality was that the Uitlander grievances, out of which the raid had partly arisen, still remained wholly unredressed.

Kruger
Prepares
for War.
An incident in Johannesburg in which an Englishman named Elgar was shot dead by a Boer policeman whom he had resisted helped to give a new turn to the controversy, and in March, 1899, the Uitlanders sent a petition to the Queen, bearing nearly twenty-two thousand signatures, recounting their wrongs and asking for recognition of their rights as British subjects. This petition Sir Alfred Milner supported in an eloquent despatch in which he declared that the case for Imperial intervention was overwhelming.

"The spectacle of thousands of British subjects kept permanently in the position of helots," constantly chafing under undoubted grievances and calling vainly to her Majesty's Government for redress, "steadily undermined the influence and reputation of Great Britain in South Africa. A section of the Press preached openly and constantly the doctrine of

Photo: B. Grant, St. Helena.

COMMANDANT CRONJE.

a republic embracing all South Africa, and supported it by menacing references to the armaments of the Transvaal, the alliance with the Orange Free State, and the active sympathy of a section of her Majesty's subjects." This doctrine, "supported as it is by a ceaseless stream of lies about the intentions of her Majesty's Government," was producing a great effect on a large number of our Dutch fellow-colonists. He could see nothing that would put a stop to this mischievous propaganda "but some striking proof of the intention of her Majesty's Government not to be ousted from its position in South Africa. And the best proof of its power and its justice would be to obtain for the Uitlanders in the Transvaal a fair share in the government of the country which owes everything to their exertions." On this despatch Mr. Chamberlain acted by suggesting a conference between Mr. Kruger and the High Commissioner. It was held at Bloemfontein on May 31st, and lasted for six days. The issue was whether or not Mr. Kruger would concede a franchise to the Uitlanders. Sir Alfred Milner made suggestions which Mr. Kruger professed to regard as "tantamount to handing over his country to the foreigner." But he was willing to give a franchise on a two years' naturalisation period and five years' continuous residence, provided that the suzerainty and other disputatious questions were referred to some arbitral body with foreign jurists. The conference failed. Mr. Chamberlain raised the tone of his despatches. The British War Office, under the Marquis of Lansdowne, let things take their course notwithstanding the worsening condition of diplomacy and despite information on the military strength of the Boers which the late Sir John Ardagh had accumulated in the Intelligence Department.

Thus things dragged on until September, when the rains were due, and soon the veldt would be grass covered and the horses of the peasant soldiery would not need to carry provender. The diplomatists kept up their disputes, Mr. Chamberlain giving a qualified acceptance of a five years' franchise but refusing to drop the suzerainty or arbitrate upon it through any body on which the Orange Free State was represented. Thereupon Mr. Kruger withdrew the five years' franchise and reasserted the claim that the republic was "a Sovereign International State." On September 8th, 1899, the Cabinet met and despatched an answer reiterating that the Government were prepared to accept a five years' franchise with ten seats for the Rand and equal rights in the election of a president of the republic. If the reply of the republic is "negative or inconclusive," wrote Mr. Chamberlain, "her Majesty's Government must reserve to themselves the right to reconsider the situation *de novo* and to formulate their own proposals for a settlement."

Those proposals were never formulated. September passed in squabbles between the Boer Government and Mr. Conyngham Greene, and between Mr. Steyn and the High Commissioner, Mr. Steyn vociferously protesting against certain reinforcements of our troops in Natal. On October 9th Mr. Reitz handed to Mr. Greene a strongly-worded ultimatum, reviewing the Boer case against Great Britain, complaining of the increase of British troops in South Africa, demanding that those troops be instantly withdrawn and that other troops then on the high seas be diverted from any South African port. "This Government," the clumsy translation of the document concluded, "must press for an immediate and affirmative answer, . . . and earnestly requests her Majesty's Government to return such an answer before or upon Wednesday, the 11th of October, 1899, not later than 5 p.m., and it desires further to add that in the event of unexpectedly no satisfactory answer being received by it within that interval it will with great regret be compelled to regard the action of her Majesty's Government as a formal declaration of war, and without holding itself responsible for the consequences thereof, and that in the event of any further movements of troops taking place within the above mentioned time in the nearer direction of our borders this Government will be compelled to regard that also as a formal declaration of war." The Cabinet met, and on the 11th telegraphed that the Government had received this peremptory communication with great regret and that "the conditions demanded by the Government of the South African Republic are such as her Majesty's Government deem it impossible to discuss." The High Commissioner was instructed to invite President Steyn to declare himself. The Orange Free State threw in its lot unreservedly with the Transvaal Republic.

Diplomacy had said its last word. Pouring through Laing's Nek, the Transvaalers entered Natal from the north while the Free Staters streamed through the western passes. On the 15th was fought the battle of Talana Hill, and the English public learned, with wonder and apprehension, of an indecisive engagement which had cost us 50 lives—among them that

[margin note: Boer Ultimatum.]

[margin note: Beginning of the War.]

of the general in command, Penn Symons—180 wounded, and a body of cavalry *en route* to Pretoria as prisoners. Then on the 21st came the fight at Elandslaagte, where we lost 41 killed and 220 wounded. Dundee was hastily abandoned and the wounded left behind. On the 24th there was another fight, at Rietfontein, and the total loss was 109. The apex of Natal was in the hands of the enemy. England marvelled, and waited for better news. The press of Europe, which with few exceptions was bitterly hostile to this country throughout the verbal warfare, resounded with praise of the Boers, and prophesied the loss of South Africa and the downfall of the British Empire.

Criticism of Mr. Chamberlain. The untoward issue of the negotiations had aroused mixed feelings in these islands. Among those to whom Mr. Chamberlain's pugnacious qualities made little appeal there was a feeling that his policy was provocative in spirit and purpose. A strong pro-Boer party existed among his opponents in Parliament and in the country, and this group identified his methods with those of the men whose unscrupulous intrigues and political crimes now found their outcome in Boer and British dead on the hillsides of northern Natal. There were many Conservatives also who had been unable to overcome their distrust of Mr. Chamberlain, and would have been better pleased had Lord Salisbury taken the negotiations into his own hands or otherwise imposed his own prudent will upon his colleagues before Mr. Chamberlain imperilled the negotiations by complicating the question of a franchise—to which, in principle, Mr. Kruger had agreed—with other issues, thus conveying the impression to the Transvaal that the only choice was between war and a complete surrender on all points. But once the situation had passed out of our keeping by the publication of the Boer ultimatum, all parties in the country united in support of the Government. Parliament met on October 17th, and the Speech from the Throne asked that the Reserves should be called out and provision made for further military expenditure. During the debate in both Houses Mr. Chamberlain's conduct of the negotiations was sharply criticised and, except by Mr. Chamberlain himself, rather feebly defended. The "new diplomacy" of the Colonial Secretary was not at all to the

liking of those bred in the traditions of the older methods of
secretiveness and reserve. One hundred and thirty-five members of the Commons voted for an amendment to the Address,
moved by Mr. Philip Stanhope, expressing "strong disapproval
of the conduct of the negotiations." The effect of the debate,
however, was to increase the determination of the country that,
war having been begun by the Boers, it should be continued
until British paramountcy was established once for all south
of the Zambesi.

Neither Lord Lansdowne and his advisers, nor the country,
had any adequate conception of the magnitude of the task.
Sir Michael Hicks-Beach (afterwards Viscount St. Aldwyn),
the Chancellor of the Exchequer, submitted supplementary
estimates for £10,000,000 ; it would be necessary, he thought,
to raise £8,000,000 only, and he believed he would then
have a margin of £1,000,000. It was rumoured that the
Army Corps sent out under Sir Redvers Buller confidently
expected to eat its Christmas dinner in Pretoria. Under
the influence of these illusions the nation assured itself
that the battles in Natal were of little military significance,
and that the enforced retirement of our troops to Ladysmith
was merely a strategic move preliminary to striking a blow
which would clear British territory of the enemy. Such a
blow was attempted by General Sir George White, in command at Ladysmith with a composite force of some 12,000
men, at Lombard's Kop and Nicholson's Nek on October 30th.
It failed disastrously. Sir George White had to fall back
upon Ladysmith, leaving a column hung up on Nicholson's
Nek, where, the ammunition having run out, it had to surrender. Nine hundred of the flower of the British infantry,
under Boer escort, were marched to Pretoria.

No story of the war can be told here. The Boer siege of
Ladysmith, the repeated attempts of General Sir Redvers
Buller's army to relieve the town, General Lord Methuen's
effort to relieve Kimberley, the British disasters at Magers-
fontein, at Colenso, and at Stormberg aroused the nation to
an appreciation of the magnitude of its task. England was
denuded of regular troops, and Lord Roberts was given
command of the army. With an overwhelming force he
swept northward through the Orange Free State, and after

*Annexa-
tion of
the Two
Republics.*

the defeat and capture of a Boer army under Cronje at Paardeburg, occupied Bloemfontein on March 15th, 1900, and Pretoria on June 5th. On September 1st he issued a proclamation incorporating the two republics into the British Empire.

Guerilla Warfare.

Unhappily the war was not over with the seizure of Pretoria, the act of annexation and the flight of President Kruger to Europe; nor could the British generals bring it to an end until June, 1902, though they had a quarter of a million of men in the field, command of the sea and the railway lines, the world to draw upon for horses, and the capacious purse of the British taxpayer at their service. The Boer generals—Botha, De Wet, Delarey, and others—maintained a vigorous guerilla resistance everywhere except on the ground that could be swept by our rifles and artillery. Time and again their commandos outwitted and out-raced the numerous columns sent up and down the country in pursuit; and they frequently inflicted more punishment than they received. Lord Roberts seems to have regarded this persistence with a pained surprise, and to have thought that, with the Boer capitals in our hands and no main Boer army left to strike at, the burghers ought to have surrendered forthwith. In proclamations during 1900 he appealed to reason and to fear without result, and, a general election in England becoming imminent, an elaborate pretence was made in Government and military circles that the war was "practically over." Lord Roberts having left South Africa, Lord Kitchener took over the command. Time and numbers were on his side. Throughout 1901 he steadily wore down the Boer resistance, which, however, owing to the exploits of De Wet, more than once flamed up so dangerously that the end of the war could not be foreseen. The Boer farms being used as places of refuge, many dwellings were destroyed, and wide tracts of country devastated, a procedure denounced by the leader of the Opposition, Sir Henry Campbell-Bannerman, as war by "methods of barbarism." The civilian population was gathered together in "concentration camps" and there maintained at the cost of the British Treasury. Relieved of responsibility for maintaining their wives and children, the men-folk were able to keep the field so long as their ammunition held out. The sanitary conditions of these camps were unsatisfactory, and the infant mortality in particular was alarming. A report by Miss Hobhouse led to a painful controversy in England and to efforts to organise the camps on more hygienic principles. Except at the coast towns, where contractors and others who thrive on war continued to amass wealth, industry and commerce were paralysed, and the condition of the region was one of ruin and misery.

In these circumstances, Lord Kitchener, supported indirectly by mediations through Holland, endeavoured to accomplish by negotiation that which might have taken his columns many months to bring about by force. A conference was arranged at Vereeniging, and on June 1st, 1902, at Pretoria, a treaty was signed under which the Boers laid down their arms and recognised King Edward VII. as their lawful sovereign. The British Government agreed to restore all prisoners—there were many thousands at St. Helena and in the Bahamas—to their homes under generous conditions, and undertook to supersede military by civil government and to introduce representative institutions leading to self-government as soon as circumstances should permit. They also agreed not to levy any special war tax on the Transvaal and Orange River Colonies and to make a free grant of £3,000,000 for the restoration of the burgher families to their homes. British rebels who surrendered were to be returned to their localities subject only to the discipline of local laws disqualifying them for ever for the franchise—a disqualification since removed.

So great was the relief at the termination of the war that there was little inclination to scrutinise closely the clauses of the treaty. With the conclusion of peace South Africa entered upon a period of painfully slow recovery. Though the country had been nearly ruined, high hopes were entertained that prosperity would come with a rush. These were disappointed. Labour was slow in returning to the mines; the Boer families, replaced amid the *débris* of their ruined farmhouses, exhibited an apathy in marked contrast with the energy and courage their men-folk had shown in the field; costly plans for attracting British settlers to the new colonies failed; almost

The Vereeniging Conference.

End of the War.

Effects of the War.

every war-worn soldier who left South Africa was an influence against, rather than in favour of, British immigration. The native population, which had waxed rich in the service of the armies during the three years' war, remained in their kraals and would not go underground in sufficient numbers at the price which the mining magnates combined to offer them.

Photo: Reginald Haines, Southampton Row, W C.
SIR HENRY CAMPBELL-BANNERMAN.

In view of this alleged shortage of labour the mining interest sought to introduce Chinese, and was able to convince Lord Milner of the expediency of that step.

Financial Situation in the Transvaal   In 1903 the Transvaal was verging upon bankruptcy and was unable to meet its obligations. Mr. Chamberlain, with high courage, had visited the new colonies after the war and, by personal intercourse and a series of public speeches, had encouraged a reconciliation between the two races. He

SIGNING OF THE TREATY OF PEACE AT PRETORIA.

also arranged a "deal" with the Transvaal under which the mining magnates guaranteed £10,000,000 of a loan for the colony. The Transvaal was under a liability of £30,000,000 towards the cost of the war. Lord Milner found himself unable to pay any instalment of this sum, or any interest on the loan if it were floated. The financial situation at the close of 1903 was such that, notwithstanding sweeping economies in administration, aid from the Imperial Exchequer would become necessary if nothing were done to provide the mines with an abundant supply of cheap labour.

Introduction of Chinese Labour. In these circumstances the Imperial Government agreed, as "a regrettable necessity," to an ordinance passed in the Legislative Council—the Transvaal and the Orange River colonies being then ruled as Crown Colonies—regulating the admission of Chinese indentured labour. With an influx of cheap Orientals the mining industry revived and the financial crisis was thus staved off. In 1905 Lord Milner was succeeded in the High Commissionership for South Africa by Lord Selborne. The Boers pressed for a fulfilment of the stipulation of the peace treaty regarding self-government, and in that year the Unionist Government offered a representative system as a stepping stone to full self-government. The return of the Liberals to power in 1906 was followed by a withdrawal

Self-Government. of this legislation, and Sir Henry Campbell-Bannerman forthwith gave responsible government with a Legislative Assembly elected by manhood suffrage on a six months' residential qualification. A similar concession was made to the Orange River Colony. By this bold and far-reaching step, which will give the late Sir Henry Campbell-Bannerman a place of high honour in the annals of the British Empire, the Boer population, which returned Boer majorities in the Chambers, and, therefore, Boer Ministers, became reconciled to the new *régime;* the British element, which had apprehended disaster for itself, also in time accepted the situation. Dutch and British throughout South Africa thereafter worked harmoni-

South African Constitution Act 1909. ously together for a federated South Africa, and in 1909 a Bill for the union of the four colonies—Cape Colony, Natal, the Transvaal, and the Orange River Colony—received the royal assent.

In this work of racial reconciliation and political reorganisation on the basis of a unified South Africa, Lord Selborne laboured with ability and steadfast zeal. He put the case for union or federation in a State paper of convincing power. That the Act of 1909 should have been passed in the colonies is chiefly due to the impetus he gave to South African opinion. In a searching argument, stated with no slight literary skill, he showed that the South African colonies had no choice between organic unity and the perpetuation, and likely settlement by the sword, of inter-state problems and differences, political, economic and racial.

Turning from Imperial to Foreign Affairs, the second division of this survey is opened. The Administration formed by Lord Salisbury on the defeat of the Liberals in the General Election of 1886 found itself confronted by a menacing situation in South-Eastern Europe, where Prince Ferdinand of Bulgaria was kidnapped by revolutionists, who were believed to be acting on Russian instigation. The disturbance threatened a reopening of the Eastern Question and led to apprehensions of war, but the Prince was allowed to return to his kingdom. He abdicated in 1887, and was succeeded by Prince Ferdinand of Saxe-Coburg, a grandson of Louis Philippe. For eight years Russian enmity towards Bulgaria was foiled by the ability of M. Stamboulov, the Prime Minister, who was murdered by political foes in 1895. A new minister, M. Stoilov, of pro-Russian tendencies, reconciled Prince Ferdinand with the Czar, and the compact was sealed by the baptism of the heir to the throne, the infant Prince Boris, in the Greek Church, with the Czar as godfather. **Foreign Affairs.**

Since the Treaty of Berlin there had been no improvement in the government of Turkey, and Asia Minor was in a state of spasmodic civil war. These troubles culminated in a series of massacres in 1893 and 1894, when 25,000 Armenians were slain by Kurds and Turkish troops. The Armenians were treated by the Porte as being in revolt, and horrible excesses were proved against the soldiery. Public opinion in Europe was so shocked by what there was reason to regard as an attempt to exterminate the Armenian population of the Vilayet of Biltis, that the Powers signatory to the Treaty of Berlin were forced to act, and the Concert of six was brought **The Armenian Atrocities.**

into being by Lord Kimberley, then Foreign Minister in Lord Rosebery's Administration. He would have acted with vigour. The Rosebery Government was on the point of issuing a forty-eight hours' ultimatum to Turkey, requiring her to accept a scheme of reform or war, when the Ministry was defeated on a minor issue—the stores of cordite. The matter then passed into Lord Salisbury's hands. The issue was whether Christian Valis should be appointed to reorganise an administration on lines which would give the Christian population reasonable security against slaughter. The Sultan would not have such Valis. Prince Lobanoff, the Russian Foreign Minister, was opposed to the use of force, and his defection brought the Concert to a standstill. There were people in England who would have had this country act alone against Turkey at the risk of an Armageddon ; others deprecated such a course and found justification for caution in the undoubted evidence of a widespread Armenian conspiracy. Lord Salisbury struck out a middle course, and a new programme of reform was drafted to which the Powers agreed. The Sultan protested his solicitude for his Armenian subjects, but would have none of it, putting in motion administrative measures of his own. At the Guildhall Banquet, on November 9th, 1895, Lord Salisbury expressed publicly his distrust of these measures, and upon a letter of remonstrance afterwards addressed to him by the Sultan made no comment except to say that whatever was done must be by consent of the Powers.

Isolated action by England being thus staved off, affairs drifted. Among the Armenians there was an outburst of revolutionary activity, which was suppressed with ruthless barbarity by the Porte. Asia Minor was drenched with blood. In vain did the ambassadors protest. The Sultan went his way, and the Moslem populace, with the connivance and even with the active aid of the soldiery, slaughtered at will. "Has even one foreigner's nose bled either in the capital or the provinces?" was the Sultan's answer to Sir Philip Currie's protests. He knew full well that the cabinets of St. Petersburg, Vienna and Berlin would not act against him except for the protection of Europeans. In August, 1896, a party of Armenian anarchists seized the

Ottoman Bank at Galata, and while the troops dealt with
them the Moslem mob was let loose and slaughtered between
five and six thousand Armenians in the streets of Constantinople. The anarchists had failed to terrorise the Sultan into
submission; they had brought an awful vengeance upon their
compatriots; and they had stereotyped the attitude of non-

Pho'o: Russell & Sons, Baker Street, W.

THE THIRD MARQUIS OF SALISBURY.

interference which the central Powers imposed on their
colleagues in the Concert.

Finding the main problem insoluble except at the risk of
a general war, Lord Salisbury applied himself to a minor
and local aspect of misrule in the Turkish dominions. Crete
was in insurrection. There, also, Moslem and Christian
were engaged in a war of extermination. Lord Salisbury
set himself to obtain the liberation of Crete. The situation

The Græco-Turkish War.

314—N.E.

was complicated by a raid of Greeks led by Colonel Vassos, the landing of a Greek force under Prince George and a proclamation of union with Greece. But in this the Powers would not acquiesce, and each sent detachments from their warships, and the island passed under joint military occupation. The Greeks, however, were spoiling for a fight with Turkey, and, egged on by injudicious friends in England, disregarded the advice and remonstrances of the Powers, and appealed to arms. A Turkish army under Edhem Pasha poured through the passes and drove the Greek forces across the plain of Thessaly. A stand was made at Velastinos, but Edhem pushed the Greeks pell-mell to Domokos. On May 19th, 1897, a battle was opened south of Lamia, but it had not proceeded far when the Crown Prince, who was in command, saved his army from destruction by hoisting the white flag. The Powers intervened to protect Greece from extinction, and she was let off by the payment of an indemnity of £4,000,000 and the loss of territory on the northern frontier. One of the mysteries of the war was the inactivity of the Greek fleet, which had Salonika at its mercy; one of its lessons was that Turkey was still a formidable military Power. The Concert withstood the strain of these events because Lord Salisbury took the view that for any one Power to go further than other Powers willed would result in "a bloody and desolating war"; the Opposition, however, were angered by his caution, and complained that he had allowed England to be dragged at the heels of the three Emperors. During, and for some time after, the Turkish campaign in Greece, matters in

End of Turkish Rule in Crete. Crete and the Near East were stationary. The Concert marked time; but the Cretan revolutionists did not, nor the Mussulmans, who, in September, 1896, attacked a British force at Canea. Admiral Noel bombarded the town; more troops were sent to the island, and the upshot was that Lord Salisbury induced the three other Powers to demand the withdrawal of the Turkish garrison. The Porte yielded to the ultimatum, the garrison was deported, and on December 21st Prince George took over the Governorship of the island. Turkish rule there was at an end. As for Asia Minor, the fratricidal warfare subsided by exhaustion. The Sultan continued master in his own house.

As the years passed Macedonia supplanted the Armenian vilayets as the field where diplomacy had to deal with the problems of Turkish mis-government. Here again the principle followed by our Foreign Office was that of action by common consent of the Powers, and marking time when general assent was unobtainable. Better that Moslem, Bulgar, Serb, Greek and Armenian should perish by mutual extermination than that the continued existence of the Ottoman Empire should operate to set the armies of the Powers on the march against each other. It was not an heroic policy. Many in England to whom certain of the provisions of the Treaty of Berlin were a charter for the Christian subjects of the Sultan which we were bound to enforce, with or without the aid of our co-signatories, deemed it a cowardly and shameful policy ; but it served to avert war on a grand scale. One of its minor results was to furnish Macedonia, after a long course of yearly raids by Bulgar and Greek bands and of murderous reprisals under Moslem direction, with a gendarmerie officered by Europeans. This force, however, could effect no appreciable improvement save on the spots where detachments were posted. It expressed the inertia of the Powers and the pretensions by which diplomacy cloaked refusal to discharge the common obligation to enforce the reforming clauses of the Treaty of Berlin.

When the Liberals returned to power in 1906, Sir Edward Grey, the Foreign Minister, endeavoured to act with greater vigour. He found the Balkan States in a ferment, Bulgaria hot for war, a powerful Turkish army within easy reach of her frontiers, and Macedonia swarming with raiding bands. He was urging a large increase of the gendarmerie, its organisation into columns which would sweep the region and rid it of marauding Bulgars and Greeks, the withdrawal of the Turkish army of occupation and the allocation of its cost to the administrative needs of Macedonia, when the situation underwent a sudden change. The Young Turks wrung from the Sultan in July, 1908, a firman restoring the Constitution of 1876. Europe was incredulous. It had been taught to regard the Reform Party in Turkey as a thing of naught. So badly was the English public served by the Press that it had no knowledge that such a development could be

The Revolution in Turkey.

attempted, still less accomplished. Never was a bloodless revolution prepared with so much secrecy or carried out with more address. Even more marvellous than the peaceful extinction of the Sultan's despotic powers, and his reduction to the status of a sovereign ruling through ministers liable to be impeached by Parliament, was the apparent reconciliation between the Moslem and Christian races. In the twinkling of an eye the condition of Macedonia had ceased to be a European question and had become one for exclusive settlement by a regenerated Turkey under a parliamentary system. That was the surface fact of the situation, and England, at least, accepted it with thankfulness and relief.

The revolution, however, was followed by a dramatic event which filled the world with apprehensions of war. No sooner had the Turkish ministry got to work than Bulgaria repudiated the Turkish suzerainty, and Austria-Hungary formally annexed the provinces of Bosnia and Herzegovina, which she had administered for thirty years. Thus opened an era of profound distrust—that "hush in Europe" which Lord Rosebery described with almost dread significance to delegates of the colonial Press who visited England in the summer of 1909.

Deposition of the Sultan. One startling fact has to be added to this narrative. The submission of Abdul Hamid was to *force majeure*. A conspiracy to overturn the Constitution in the spring of 1909 restored the old state of things for a few days in Constantinople. But the reformers marched an army to the capital, and the revolt collapsed. On April 27th Abdul Hamid was deposed and his brother, Mahommed Reshad Effendi, placed on the throne. Abdul was taken to Salonika to end his days in obscurity. The necessary brevity of this record must limit comment to the statement of fact that English policy, admirably expressed by Sir Edward Grey, was warmly sympathetic towards the new *régime* in Turkey, and that the wisdom and restraint shown throughout by the Constitutionalists, especially under the provocation of Bulgaria and Austria, won high approval.

The Venezuela Dispute. Scarcely had the nation realised its helplessness to check the massacres in Armenia when a staggering blow to its

SIR JULIAN (AFTERWARDS LORD) PAUNCEFOTE AND MR. OLNEY SIGNING THE ANGLO-
AMERICAN TREATY OF ARBITRATION.

self-esteem came from an unexpected quarter owing to a frontier dispute whose existence was unknown in England outside the Government offices. Diplomatists alone saw any significance in Mr. Cleveland's references, in his Message to Congress early in December, 1895, to the debatable territory lying between Venezuela and the colony of British Guiana; but when he issued his Special Message of December 18th, with its accompanying despatch by Mr. Richard Olney, the State Secretary, war with the United States became imminent. President Cleveland, in brusque language, demanded that Great Britain should submit the controversy to arbitration. It turned upon obscure questions of geography, jurisdiction, Dutch occupancy, and British rights acquired from Holland by conquest and treaty. These Mr. Olney had discussed in a sense adverse to Great Britain, and the President, whose assumption was that this country was denying to a small State the justice that would have been conceded forthwith to a great Power, advanced a new version of the Monroe Doctrine. This would have given the United States an overlordship of the American continent from the Arctic Circle to the Straits of Magellan—a right of supremacy and dictation to which Great Britain, France and Holland would be subject equally with the South American republics. In a despatch of much power and dignity Lord Salisbury denied the right of the United States to interfere and

**Immi-
nence of
War.**

refuted Mr. Olney's history. The blustering demand for arbitration thus produced a deadlock from which no way of escape could be seen by either nation. The majority of the people in the United States, misled by an anti-British press which foresaw the acquisition of Canada as one of the fruits of war, suffered a frenzy of passion against this country. In England public opinion remained cold and calm. The fury of the United States jingoes, however, was checked by the financial consequences of the apparent imminence of war. There was a panic in Wall Street. A sudden realisation of the inability of the United States fleet to protect the coasts combined with criticism of Mr. Cleveland's diplomacy to bring about a reaction. Distinguished men in both countries set to work to find a way of retreat such as the United States could use and Great Britain permit without humiliation. In this country there was an intense desire to keep the peace, not alone because of the immense commercial interests at stake and the insensate folly and wickedness of war from causes in themselves trivial, but also because it was felt that though, through our immense naval superiority, we could inflict untold injury upon the United States, the people of that country might prove unconquerable in the land war in which we should be compelled to engage for the protection of Canada.

These being the chief factors in the case, negotiations went on during the spring and summer of 1896, anti-English passion across the Atlantic swiftly dying down meanwhile. At the Guildhall banquet in the autumn Lord Salisbury was able to announce that a solution had been found by which there would be arbitration, but that the area under actual British settlement would be excluded from the arbitrators' consideration. A treaty was signed constituting a tribunal of five jurists: two British—Lord Russell of Killowen and Sir Henn Collins—M. Martens, of St. Petersburg, and two members of the United States judiciary. It met at Paris and delivered its award in October, 1899. We lost some territory which we had claimed, and Venezuela lost much more. Each gained a definitive frontier, and a dispute that had lasted for fifty years was closed without the war which President Cleveland had almost precipitated. *Dispute settled by Arbitration.*

Since then our relations with the United States have improved steadily. They changed definitely for the better when Lord Salisbury declined to have anything to do with an intrigue for bringing joint European pressure to bear at Washington when the condition of Cuba and the destruction of the United States warship, the *Maine*, led to war between the States and Spain. The expulsion of Spain from the Philippines brought the United States within the ambit of Far Eastern policies, and she found it to her interest to act with us in maintaining "the open door" in China. Other issues between the two countries Lord Salisbury managed so as to gratify American desires, but not until after severe diplomatic difficulties and the breakdown of a Commission of which the late Lord Herschell was president—a breakdown attended by his death at Washington owing to an accidental fall. *Growth of Better Relations with the U.S.A.*

It is worthy of remark that on this Commission Canada

The Anglo-American Commission. was directly represented, all the questions—the Alaska boundary, sealing in the Behring Sea, fishing in the north Atlantic and in the Great Lakes, and reciprocal trade— affecting her. Her relations with the United States had not been cordial, owing partly to the United States' love of a hard bargain, and partly to a revival of Imperial senti- ment in the Dominion by which an intrigue for commercial union with the States was frustrated, the real aim of the intrigue, on the evidence produced by Colonel G. T. Denison, the leader of the Imperialists in Canada, being the political incorporation of the Dominion. The crowning difficulty of the Commission was the Alaska boundary dispute, the United States, as heirs of Russia, claiming the Lynn Inlet and other arms of the sea to a line inland, thus cutting off Canada from access by the ocean to the Klondike region, which then offered a prospect of illimitable wealth to the miner because of rich finds of gold along the course of the Yukon. A better feeling was produced in England and throughout America by the high honours paid in the United States to the memory of Lord Herschell, whose body was sent home in a United States man-of-war; and, undaunted by failure, Lord Salisbury resumed the negotiations. His guiding principle was that there must be no rupture with the United States, and for the sake of peace he was prepared to make considerable sacrifices. In this broad aim he was finely assisted by Sir Julian Pauncefote—the late Lord Pauncefote—our Minister at Washington, who owed his opportunities in life not less to Lord Salisbury's discernment in earlier years than to his own high abilities. Together they negotiated a *modus vivendi* as to Alaska, with which Canada had, perforce, to be content. In the early stages of the South African War the United States was presented with the exclusive British rights for naval purposes over Tutuila, in the Samoan group, thus giving the United States control over the finest harbour in the Pacific. At the same time British rights over Upolo and Savii were ceded to Germany. These incidents help to explain why both Governments disregarded the clamours of sections of their people for intervention in the Boer interest.

The Panama Canal. In further pursuance of a conciliatory policy a Convention was signed in 1900 abrogating the Clayton-Bulwer Treaty of

1850 in such a way as to give the United States exclusive rights to construct an isthmian canal, subject to complete neutralisation. The canal, the greatest engineering work of modern times, is now in course of construction, and all

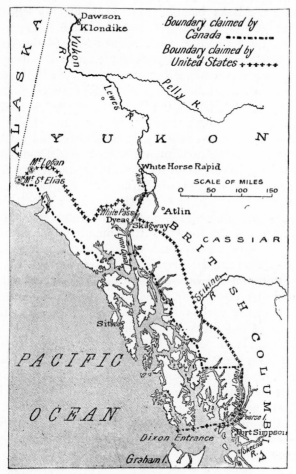

MAP SHOWING THE ALASKA BOUNDARY CLAIMS.

difficulties seem likely to be surmounted within the next decade. One feature bearing upon this Empire, apart from the maritime advantages we shall enjoy when ships can steam through the isthmus, is that the work has reacted upon the distressed West Indian colonies. From the negro population the many thousands of shovelmen are drawn, to the profit of the men and of the families to whom the wages are remitted.

**Settle-
ment of
the Alaska
Boundary
Dispute.**
Heedless of criticism that he was giving important rights and getting nothing in exchange, Lord Salisbury pegged away at the Alaska boundary question, and at length succeeded in getting it referred to arbitration. Lord Alverstone, the Lord Chief Justice, as president of the tribunal, courageously gave a casting vote for an award substantially in favour of the United States. It caused bitterness in Canada, where the public had assimilated an overstatement of the British case ; but as the defence of four thousand miles of frontier by the British army, plus a numerically feeble colonial militia, was a military impossibility, the settlement of the question was an immense gain to the Dominion. It established Anglo-American relations upon a sure and friendly foundation which has since been undisturbed, though, unfortunately, there have been difficulties over the North Atlantic fisheries, Newfoundland exhibiting an impracticable spirit which compelled the Imperial Government to coerce her into the acceptance of a *modus vivendi* pending a final settlement of the issues at the Hague Arbitration Court.

**Progress
made by
Canada.**
Something should be said here of the extraordinary progress made by Canada in population, in wealth, and in the settlement of her vast prairie lands. Year by year, since the completion of the great trunk railway from ocean to ocean, many thousands of people—latterly at the rate of some fifty thousand every season—have left these shores and spread over the interior. The population is now nearing seven millions, and patriotic Canadians, for whom the winter climate has no terrors and whose knowledge of the latent resources of the Dominion is indisputable, foresee the rise of a nation as populous and as prosperous as that which lives south of the forty-ninth parallel.

**Affairs
in Asia.**
Across the Pacific Ocean, among the countless millions of Asia, events have occurred which have given a new direction to the history of the world and have twice brought this country to the edge of the precipice of war—once when Russia ordered British warships away from Port Arthur, and again

when Admiral Rodjestvensky, in a moment of aberration while in command of the Baltic Squadron on its way to the Far East against Japan, fired upon British fishermen in the North Sea. The first incident occurred during the third Administration of Lord Salisbury, 1895–1902. During the 'eighties our relations with the Asiatic Powers had been undisturbed by anything worse than an occasional massacre of missionaries in China. In the early 'nineties Japan and China were in hot dispute about Korea, then an independent kingdom over which China claimed suzerainty. The two Powers fought for control of the Korean peninsula. The army of China was an ill-organised rabble, badly armed; that of Japan was modelled on the German system and armed with the latest weapons. The Chinese were hopelessly outmatched, both on land and on sea. Korea fell an easy prey to Japan, which advanced north and, after tremendous slaughter, captured Port Arthur and occupied the Liao-Tung peninsula. China then made peace, paid a heavy indemnity, and ceded the peninsula. Russia, Germany and France came to the aid of China, and the result of a diplomatic intrigue, in which Lord Rosebery, then Prime Minister, would take no part, was that Japan was ordered out of Port Arthur and the Manchurian mainland. In default of English aid Japan accepted the inevitable, retired, tightened her grip upon Korea, and prepared for another war.

Then ensued a series of events which kept England in constant apprehension of participation in a general scramble for supremacy in the Far East. By a treaty with China Russia not only acquired railway rights through Manchuria, thus bringing the railway from Moscow to the warm waters of the Pacific, but also obtained a lease of Port Arthur itself. During these negotiations China had granted harbourage at Port Arthur to Russian men-of-war, the plea being that these vessels could not anchor at Vladivostok until the arrival there of an exceptionally powerful icebreaker. Russia, however, denied that she had any design upon Port Arthur, and obliged China to declare that she had no intention of giving any preference to Russia there or elsewhere in Manchuria. Lord Salisbury was dissatisfied with these statements, and, in the ordinary course of their duties, two vessels of the China

Russia's Movements in the Far East.

Squadron looked in at the naval fortress. Russia remonstrated so energetically that it seemed she meant to have Port Arthur even if she had to fight Great Britain; and she complained so significantly of the presence of British warships in the harbour that Lord Salisbury, though protesting that the one remaining vessel had every right to be there, said she "would be leaving in a few days; her visit was by orders of the admiral, issued at his own discretion, and not under the directions of her Majesty's Government." She left, and it was learned with chagrin at home that our fleet had moved at Russian dictation. The fundamental fact was that Lord Salisbury was quite willing that Russia should get a warm-water port, but objected to her possession of a naval base and fortress which would put north China within her grasp and disturb the balance of power in the Gulf of Pechili. Rather than force this objection to the stage of war, he abandoned it and obtained compensation—for what it might be worth, which proved to be little—in an arrangement with China leasing to Great Britain the island of Wei-hai-wei, which Japan retained pending payment of the arrears of the China War indemnity. This was at the suggestion of Japan, with whom our relations had been consolidated in 1894 by the surrender of our rights of consular jurisdiction, and with whom henceforth Great Britain acted in Far Eastern diplomacy.

The "Open Door" in China.   The diplomatic ferment continued throughout 1898, China being apparently at the point of dismemberment and division into spheres of influence, Germany having established herself at Kiao-Chau, in compensation for the murder of some missionaries, and threatening to eat up the province of Shantung, Russia menacing the north, and Great Britain preparing to take over the control of the Yangtse valley provinces. The convulsion that would have followed upon the collapse of the Chinese Empire and a scramble for its territories by the Powers was, however, averted. Russia, satisfied for the time being with Port Arthur, made an agreement with Great Britain on railway and other interests, and the keen irritation her diplomacy had excited in England subsided. Then followed a long wrangle on the subject of the "open door" in China. Japan, the United States and Great Britain were united against Russia in asserting treaty rights affecting commerce, the aim of Russia being to coerce China into giving her preferential concessions.

Scarcely had these differences been composed, at least in principle, when China asserted herself against Europe by an unexpected outburst of anti-foreign fury. In January, 1900, Mr. Brooks, an English missionary, was murdered barbarously in Shantung at the instigation of an anti-foreign secret society which became known colloquially as "the Boxers"—or the Righteous Harmony Fists. The Boxer movement spread over north China, and the Powers sent guards to their legations in Pekin. The evidence proves that the Boxer movement was encouraged by the Empress Dowager, who had set the Emperor aside and made herself Regent. When the guards arrived the Boxers swarmed about the legations and besieged the quarter. In answer to an appeal for help from Sir Claude MacDonald, our Minister at Pekin, Admiral Seymour, with a force of 1,700, started from Tientsin for the relief of the legations on June 10th. He found the road blocked by Boxer hordes and had to fight his way back to Tientsin, the native quarter of which, by this time, was in the hands of the Boxers. The peril of the legations aroused deep anxiety in England, and Lord Salisbury, while acting for himself by ordering troops from India, concerted measures with the Powers for united military action. These were stimulated by the news on July 1st that the German Minister, Baron Ketteler, had been murdered in Pekin, and on the 2nd by a message from Sir Robert Hart, the Director of Chinese Customs, who had also taken refuge in the legations: "Situation desperate. Hasten your coming. Sunday, 4 p.m." It had been sent off eight days before it reached Tientsin. What had happened since? *The Boxer Movement.*

Fearing the worst, and yet hoping against hope, the nation watched for news of the gathering of a force at Tientsin strong enough to cut a way to the capital. Two newspapers published circumstantial accounts of the overpowering of the legation guards and the massacre of all the Europeans, thus giving a terrible shock to the public; but the news was promptly contradicted. On August 4th a composite army of 13,000—German, British, Indian, Russian, French, and *Relief of the Legations.*

Japanese—started from Tientsin. One engagement was fought on the road, and on August 14th Pekin was attacked and the legations relieved. The Dowager Empress and the Court by this time had fled into the interior, and the allied forces, heavily reinforced and placed under the command of Count von Waldersee, re-established order in north China. The story of the siege and of the frightful massacres of missionaries which preceded it—over a hundred Europeans (men, women and children) being butchered—is one of the most dramatic and painful in the annals of Western intercourse with the East. Nor was the conduct of the international armies without reproach. After infinite difficulty terms were arranged by which the allied forces were withdrawn, and the Dowager Empress returned to her capital, where she died in 1908, apparently on the same day as the Emperor and in circumstances of grave suspicion.

The Russo-Japanese War. In 1903 Russian intrigues and military preparations for ousting Japan from Korea had reached such a pass that Japan resolved upon war. Again it seemed that the Far Eastern question would be reopened, and that other Powers would be drawn into the strife. It must suffice here to say that the world looked on with astonishment as the Japanese passed from victory to victory at sea and on land. At last both sides were glad to accept the peace overtures of President Roosevelt. That these should have been made from such a quarter brings out in sharp relief the emergence of the United States into Asiatic policies, a consequence in part of the war with Spain and the acquisition of the Philippines, and in part of the determination of her people to maintain a place in the markets of Asia. The Japanese and Russian plenipotentiaries signed a treaty of peace at Portsmouth, United States, on September 5th, 1905.

The Anglo-Japanese Alliance. With a sureness of instinct and a far-seeing wisdom which sorely perplexed those of Lord Salisbury's friends who had failed to appreciate the power of Japan, England had, in 1902, made a treaty of alliance with Japan which was obviously intended to counteract the aggressive aims of Russia in the Far East. It was received with astonishment in Russia, where it was regarded, when war broke out, as evidence that Great Britain was behind Japan and had, in fact, egged that

Power on to try conclusions with Russia. The Jingoes in Russia clamoured for war with Great Britain, and during the early stages of the hostilities with Japan peace between Russia and Britain was kept with difficulty. On the night of October 21st, 1904, the Baltic Squadron under Admiral Rodjestvensky was steaming through the North Sea

Photo: London Stereoscopic Co.

THE RIGHT HON. A. J. BALFOUR, M.P.

to meet its fate in the China seas when it passed through the Hull fishing fleet on the Dogger Bank. By some inexplicable blunder or crime fire was opened on the fishing fleet and the steam trawler *Crane* sunk, two men being killed and several wounded. It was an act of war to which, it seemed, there could be only one answer. Mr. Balfour, then in temporary charge of the Foreign Office, instantly demanded an explanation, and the Home, Channel, and

Dogger Bank Episode.

Mediterranean fleets were combined for action. The Czar as promptly expressed his sincere regret and disavowed Admiral Rodjestvensky's conduct, which, he averred, must have arisen from some regrettable misunderstanding. By an acceptance of this expression war was averted and a convention hastily agreed upon referring the matter to commissioners of both nations for adjustment. They met at Paris, and substantial damages were paid by Russia to the families of the men who were killed and to those who were injured. Mr. Balfour's skilful handling of the matter was cordially approved by the nation as a whole; but he did not escape criticism from the victims of Russophobia, who saw in the admiral's behaviour not the freak of a man temporarily bereft of his senses, but a wilful provocation to war at the instance of the anti-British element in St. Petersburg.

Renewal of the Alliance with Japan.   During the armistice which preceded the peace at Portsmouth, Lord Lansdowne, who in 1900 had succeeded Lord Salisbury as Foreign Minister, negotiated a renewal, for ten years from August 12, 1905, of the alliance with Japan. It provided for the integrity and independence of China, for equal opportunities for all nations in the commerce of that Empire, and for the maintenance of the territorial rights of the contracting parties in Eastern Asia and in India. It was agreed that whenever, in the opinion of either Great Britain or Japan, any of the rights and interests in question are in jeopardy, the two Governments will communicate with one another fully and frankly, and in the event of either being the subject of unprovoked attack upon its territorial rights—Japan in Korea or Great Britain on the Indian frontier —"the other contracting party will at once come to the assistance of its ally and will conduct the war in common and make peace in mutual agreement." It was further agreed that neither party would enter into separate arrangements with another Power to the prejudice of the interests defined in the preamble, and that if any other Power or Powers joined with Russia in the then pending war, "Great Britain will come to the assistance of Japan and will conduct the war in common and make peace in mutual agreement with Japan."

In 1908 Sir Edward Grey, the Foreign Minister in Sir

Henry Campbell-Bannerman's Administration, achieved a **Treaty with Russia, 1908.** diplomatic success which closed the long era of Anglo-Russian hostility. A treaty was made with Russia which freed India from all apprehensions of invasion from the north and ended our rivalries in Persia, allowing Russia the region along her frontier as her exclusive sphere of interest, and giving Great Britain an unquestionable supremacy in the Gulf region. This treaty re-established the relations of the two Powers on a sure and friendly basis; and the concession of a parliamentary system in Russia, after a fierce struggle, scarcely distinguishable at times and in some districts from civil war, helped further to reconcile the British and Muscovite peoples. The value of the treaty as an instrument of peace between Russia and Great Britain was attested in 1909 in Persia, where violent internal discord resulted in the overthrow of the Shah and the placing on the throne of a boy of eleven. The good feeling existing between the two Powers was undisturbed by this upheaval in a country in whose destinies both had for many years taken a distinctly jealous interest.

A few words should here be added regarding affairs in India. **The Indian Frontier.** Three events stand out in the interminable record of frontier troubles: the occupation of Chitral in 1894, an extensive campaign in the Afridi country in 1897–1898, and an advance into Thibet in 1904—to the very walls of the sacred city of Lhassa. Great Britain, however, withdrew from Thibet upon the Indian Government's commercial claims being conceded, and is now, under the Anglo-Russian treaty already mentioned, debarred, equally with Russia, from occupying the region or otherwise seeking to change its status, China being the suzerain Power. Broadly stated, there has been a great improvement during the past quarter of a century in our relations with the border states and independent tribes along the north-west frontier, and the frontier campaigns of the 'nineties and the new treaties with Russia and with Afghanistan have minimised dangers to India from that quarter. A greater **Unrest in India.** peril, however, has arisen in India itself owing to the diffusion of Western ideas and the growth of a demand for self-government. The agitation assumed a criminal form in 1908, and events showed that anarchism had found a

315—N.E.

congenial soil in the Dependency. The Indian Government, under Lord Minto, grappled with the evil courageously and firmly, freely exercising their powers of arbitrary deportation of agitators and suspicious characters. But it was felt that the political unrest was too deep-seated and widespread to be cured by repressive measures alone, and Lord Morley, who had become Secretary for India under the Liberal Government of 1905, concerted plans of reform on the principle of the representation of Indian opinion in the councils of the Government both in London and in India. An Act was passed through both Houses in 1909, and under the influence of this reform the danger of an upheaval in India seemed to be minimised. But sanguine views were sharply checked by the murder of a distinguished Indian official, Sir William Curzon Wyllie, at a social gathering at the Imperial Institute in London in June of that year. The murderer, a native student named Dinghra, who avowed the political purpose of his crime, was tried and executed.

Home Affairs.   In the General Election of 1885, 335 Liberals were returned against 249 Conservatives. The 86 Nationalists held the balance. Disappointed in an effort to secure Lord Salisbury's co-operation, Mr. Gladstone had allowed his conversion to the principle of Home Rule to be announced in the press. With the aid of the Irish vote he defeated the Salisbury Ministry in the debate on the Address, which had expressed resolute opposition to any disturbance of the Act of Union and had foreshadowed a Coercion Bill as well as an extension of the Ashbourne Land Act. Mr. Gladstone took office in February, 1886, and set himself to form a Cabinet on the basis of a memorandum for the creation of a legislature in Dublin to deal with Irish, as distinct from Imperial, affairs. Lord Hartington, Lord Derby, Mr. Bright, Lord Northbrook **The Home Rule Split.** and Mr. Goschen—all of whom have since passed away—declined office on account of this condition. Mr. Chamberlain joined the Cabinet on the understanding that the issue was not prejudged. Lord Rosebery became Foreign Minister and Mr. John Morley Chief Secretary for Ireland. A fierce agitation arose in the country for and against Home Rule. It overshadowed every other question, although a riot of unemployed in Trafalgar Square, on February 8th, in which Mr. John Burns figured in company with other leaders of the Socialist movement, caused much uneasiness, and showed that other forces were arising in England. Lord Randolph Churchill appealed to the loyalty of Ulster in passionate speeches. He expressed their attitude and his own in a famous epigram: "Ulster will fight; Ulster will be right"; and in a speech at Manchester he coined the words "Separatists" and "Unionists," as descriptive of the opposing parties. In March Mr. Chamberlain left the Cabinet on the ground that the Bill Mr. Gladstone had prepared was "tantamount to a proposal for separation"; and Mr. (Sir George) Trevelyan, who had been Chief Secretary, accompanied him. In his speech introducing the Bill, Mr. Gladstone described it as a measure for the establishment of a legislative body sitting in Dublin to make laws for Ireland and control Irish administration. The new body was to impose taxes other than customs and excise. It would have no concern with matters affecting the Crown, the army and navy, foreign and colonial relations, trade and navigation, coinage and the like. The new Parliament was to consist of two Houses, one of twenty-eight Irish peers supplemented by seventy-five elected members, and the other of two hundred and four members elected on the existing franchise. Irish members would cease to sit at Westminster. The Bill was received in the House and in the country with a storm of criticism. One of its first-fruits was the birth of the Liberal Unionist Party, for Liberal defections were many. The Bill was accompanied by a measure of land purchase to which the Conservatives were bitterly hostile. Lord Salisbury, in a speech calling for twenty years of resolute government for Ireland, declared that he would rather spend treasure in emigrating a million Irishmen than in buying out the landlords; and he excited bitter feelings by a gratuitous suggestion that the Irish, like the Hottentots and Hindoos, were incapable of self-government. The second reading of the Bill was fixed for May 10th. Mr. Gladstone outlined some changes he was willing to make. These failed to satisfy the dissentients, and on the 14th a meeting at Devonshire House, called by Lord Hartington, sealed the fate of the measure.

First Home Rule Bill, 1886.

With Lord Hartington, Mr. Bright, Mr. Chamberlain, Mr. Goschen and nearly a hundred other members of his party against him, Mr. Gladstone fought for the principle of the Bill in vain. On the night of June 8th he brought the second reading debate to a close in a speech of surpassing eloquence. Amid a scene of interest and excitement unparalleled in the recent annals of Parliament, the House went to a division, and the Government found themselves in a minority of thirty. Ninety-three Liberals voted with the majority, and eight absented themselves. Mr. Gladstone, on June 10th, announced a dissolution. The election was fought with a vigour and passion which stirred the country to the depths, and Mr. Gladstone threw himself into the fray with an energy that seemed inexhaustible. The elections resulted in a conclusive victory for the Conservatives and Liberal Unionists. Of the former there were 316, of the latter 78 —a combination of 394 against 191 Gladstonians and 83 Parnellites. On July 30th Mr. Gladstone surrendered the seals of office.

Lord Salisbury's second Administration, 1886

The Queen sent for Lord Salisbury, a Minister much more to her liking than Mr. Gladstone, whose policy, domestic and foreign, she had long distrusted. Lord Salisbury had offered to give way to Lord Hartington, but that leader preferred to leave the way open for a reconciliation with the Liberal Party. He explained to a meeting of dissentient Liberals at Devonshire House on August 5th that he had thought it best that a Ministry should be formed out of the Conservative majority of the combined Unionist parties. Liberal Unionists had not ceased to be Liberals, and their function, while co-operating to maintain the Union, was to prevent the Conservatives from becoming a party of reaction. A Conservative Ministry was therefore formed, and Lord Randolph Churchill, whose speeches had made him a power with the democracy, became Chancellor of the Exchequer. In this Government Mr. Arthur Balfour had a minor place, which was soon to be exchanged for the Chief Secretaryship to the Lord Lieutenant, a position in which he was to display unsuspected courage and energy. The surprise of the Cabinet was the selection of Churchill as Chancellor of the Exchequer, for he had had no experience of finance, and his brilliant but adventurous qualities were not those that appeal to the counting-house mind. An autumn session showed that the Irish question was still predominant. The policy of the Ministry was to let Ireland share in what Lord Randolph called "equality, similarity and simultaneity" of treatment in local government reform throughout the United Kingdom. Pending Home Rule, Mr. Parnell wanted a Tenants' Relief Bill which, in effect, would have reduced rents 50 per cent. Simultaneously a "Plan of Campaign" was launched, though not with Mr. Parnell's approval, under which tenants, in combination, were to offer rents which they thought fair, and if these were not accepted they were to refuse to pay anything. This course was followed by innumerable evictions, much agrarian crime, and, over large areas, a state of war between landowners and occupiers—a war which the landlords, in the majority of cases, waged through local agents without peril to themselves. *Irish Land-lords and Tenants.*

In December (1886) attention was distracted from Ireland by the announcement that Lord Randolph Churchill had re-signed the Chancellorship. He had failed to impose upon his colleagues his views as to the necessity for economies in the army and the navy, and he had aroused hostility among reactionary Conservatives, within and without the Cabinet, by the advocacy of measures framed to attract the "Tory democracy." Moreover he saw no need for a strong foreign policy in the Near East, then overshadowed by war-clouds, the result of Russian interference with Bulgaria. Lord Randolph's calculation seems to have been that his resigna-tion would not be accepted; but he was wrong. Lord Salisbury would not allow himself to be overruled in foreign affairs and in domestic legislation by his youthful colleague, and, with the assistance of Lord Hartington, he re-formed the Ministry, Mr. Goschen, a Liberal Unionist, becoming Chancellor, and Mr. W. H. Smith, Leader of the House. In the re-arrangement of offices Lord Iddesleigh was retired from the Foreign Office, and on taking leave of the staff there, on January 11th, 1887, he crossed to 10, Downing Street, to call on the Prime Minister, in whose presence he died from an attack of syncope. *Resigna-tion of Lord R. Churchill.*

These Ministerial changes were accompanied by negotiations

The "Round-Table Conference." by which Mr. Chamberlain, now one of the staunchest opponents of Home Rule, who had carried Radical Birmingham and the greater part of the Midlands against Mr. Gladstone's policy, sought for a way back to the Liberal fold. A "round-table conference" was held at Sir William Harcourt's house in London in January and February, and a provisional arrangement arrived at for submission to Mr. Gladstone. But the conference was, either purposely or clumsily, wrecked by a communication from Mr. Chamberlain to a Nonconformist journal, and its only result was the final severance of the Liberal Unionists from the Gladstonian Liberals. Sir George Trevelyan, however, rejoined his chief as a Home Ruler.

Parnell and the "Times." The next session (1887) was spent on Irish affairs, Mr. Balfour, who had become Chief Secretary, introducing a Coercion Bill and waging in Ireland and in the House implacable warfare against law-breakers and instigators of disorder. During this session the *Times* published a series of articles entitled "Parnellism and Crime," and on the morning of the second reading of the Crimes Bill one of the set contained what purported to be a facsimile letter signed by Charles Stewart Parnell, in which the writer was made to appear to regret his public condemnation of the murder of Lord Frederick Cavendish and Mr. Burke. Those who were in the House will not readily forget the scene that night. Mr. Parnell denounced the letter as a forgery, but he was widely distrusted, and the second reading was agreed to by a larger majority than was expected. Throughout this session and the next the strife about Ireland continued, and the condition of the country, which was that of ill-suppressed civil war, enabled Mr. Gladstone and his following to push forward their claim that Home Rule was the only remedy. The imprisonment of Mr. William O'Brien, M.P., was made the occasion of disorders in Trafalgar Square on Sunday, November 13th, 1888, when Mr. R. B. Cunninghame Graham, M.P., and Mr. John Burns, the Socialist Labour leader who was afterwards to become a Cabinet Minister in a Liberal Government, were arrested and imprisoned for six weeks for taking part in an unlawful assembly.

On July 2nd, 1888, in an action for libel brought by Mr.

Frank Hugh O'Donnell against the *Times*, certain incriminating letters were produced by the *Times* which were alleged to have been written by Mr. Parnell. From his place in the House the Irish leader repudiated all knowledge of them and demanded a Select Committee. This the Government refused, but appointed a Special Commission of three judges—Sir James Hannen, Mr. Justice A. L. Smith, and Mr. Justice Day—to inquire into all the charges against Mr. Parnell and his colleagues in the "Parnellism and Crime" series. This Commission sat in the Law Courts day by day from September 17th, Sir Richard Webster (afterwards Lord Alverstone and Lord Chief Justice) being principal counsel for the *Times*, and Sir Charles Russell—the late Lord Russell of Killowen, Lord Chief Justice—leading counsel for the Irish Party, with Mr. H. H. Asquith, afterwards Prime Minister, as junior. On February 18th, 1889, a certain Richard Pigott, an elderly, white-bearded man known to have been familiar with the subterranean paths of politics in Ireland, was called as a witness to the authenticity of the Parnell letters. He had supplied them to the *Times* writer. He told a story which fell to pieces under cross-examination. The Court adjourned on Friday, February 22nd, while the cross-examination was proceeding, but not before the bubble of the chief incriminating letter had burst. On the following day Pigott called on Mr. Labouchere, M.P., and signed a confession. On the Monday he fled, and his name was called in vain. A warrant was issued for his arrest, and he was traced to an hotel in Madrid, where he shot himself dead on the arrival of the police officer. From that moment it was plain what the findings of the Commission would be. The public did not wait for the judges' report—which was not issued until February, 1890—to acquit Mr. Parnell of having written the *Times* letters, or of being otherwise a party to the crimes of the "Invincibles" and the "Clan-na-Gael." As to the other charges against the Nationalists, most of them, in the judgment of the Special Commission, were proved. Mr. William O'Brien, Mr. Davitt, Mr. Dillon and others, excepting Mr. Parnell, were held to have started the Land League to bring about the independence of Ireland; to have conspired,

The Parnell Commission.

by a system of intimidation, against the payment of rents;
to have encouraged seditious publications, knowing that crime
and outrage would follow; to have invited and obtained the
co-operation of the physical force party in the United States
and of the Clan-na-Gael. There was a great debate in the
Commons on March 3rd. Mr. W. H. Smith moved that
the House thank the judges and adopt the report. To this
Mr. Gladstone moved an amendment condemning the charges
in very strong language and expressing regret for the wrong
done to the Irish members. Lord Randolph Churchill made
a speech of exceptional violence, condemning the appointment
of the Special Commission; in a paroxysm of anger he used
an expression which shocked and revolted the House. It was
his last notable appearance on a great occasion. His health
gave way, but a trip to South Africa seemed to restore his
powers. One night, however, during the early days of the
Rosebery Government, he rose to take part in an important
debate, but in a short time became confused. His words were
inarticulate, and he had to sit down. After this painful scene
his public appearances were few. The end came on
January 24th, 1895. He was but forty-six, and no man of
his day in England had, at so early an age, made so deep
an impression upon his contemporaries.

**Downfall
of Parnell.**
It is not possible within the limited space of this chapter
to follow the details of the incessant struggle between the
Government and the Land League in Ireland. It must
suffice to say that Mr. Balfour crushed opposition and enforced order of a sort, meanwhile making a sure reputation
as a debater in the House. Under the stimulus of the
Pigott disclosures the Gladstonian Liberals renewed their
attacks upon the Ministry, which was losing ground appre-
ciably in the country. In November, 1890, however, the Home
Rulers were thrown into confusion by revelations in the Divorce
Court concerning Mr. Parnell, who had for some time
been carrying on an intrigue with the wife of a former
member of his party. The husband obtained his decree,
and Parnell was covered with dishonour. The Nationalists,
as a Roman Catholic party, could not tolerate a leader
who had entered into a liaison with another man's wife,
even though he should marry her as soon as the decree

MR. GLADSTONE INTRODUCING THE SECOND HOME RULE BILL.

(From the painting by R. Ponsonby Staples.)

was made absolute; nor could the Gladstonian Liberals, who were supported by the Nonconformist vote, consent to act with a man who had been found guilty of misconduct. From within the Irish Party and within the Gladstonian ranks there arose an outcry for his removal. Parnell defied both the Irish malcontents and "the English wolves who howl for my destruction"; but the Gladstonians and the Roman Catholic Bishops in Ireland were too strong for him. Parliament met for an autumn session, and the Irish Party gathered in Committee Room 15 to fight out the question of his continuance in the leadership. The battle waged for a fortnight, and there were stormy scenes and a fierce war of tongues. On December 6th it ended in the deposition of Mr. Parnell and the election in his stead of Mr. Justin M'Carthy, journalist, novelist and historian, who filled the position with much tact and a quiet dignity until ill-health compelled him to retire. For a while the Nationalist Party was split into two sections, but some time after Parnell's death Mr. John Redmond became the leader of a re-united party.

In 1891, on October 6th, Parnell died. Like Lord Randolph Churchill, he was only forty-six. His life was an enigma, which, on its personal side, has been explained in an indiscreetly painful volume. His reserve, the cold scorn with which he treated even his followers, prevented him from being popular among his associates; but his unconquerable courage, his intense determination, and his political intuition made him a commanding and magnetic figure. Landlord and Protestant though he was, he dominated Catholic Ireland. Men called him the "uncrowned king," and the name expressed the realities of the case. On the same day died Mr. W. H. Smith, the Leader of the House. Mr. Smith's devotion to duty and inaptitude for parliamentary rhetoric made him the embodiment of the common sense of the English man of business. His unpretentious capacity for getting the House to do its nightly work, coupled with his unfailing good humour and modesty, had endeared him to the nation. Mr. Balfour gave up the Irish Office to become Leader, but not before he had convinced the Nationalists of his ability, and, in some measure, won the regard even of those whom he had imprisoned. In Lord Randolph Churchill's opinion this promotion was a death-blow to "Tory democracy"; the phrase became a memory, the expression of a phantasmal body of political opinion. In December (1891) the Duke of Devonshire died and the Marquis of Hartington went to the House of Lords, Mr. Chamberlain being elected leader of the Liberal Unionists when the session opened in 1892.

Throughout the session of 1892 both parties prepared for a General Election. Mr. Gladstone kept Home Rule to the front, but took up also the Newcastle Programme, which covered franchise reform, special legislation for labour, disestablishment, and local option—the last two items throwing the Anglican clergy and the liquor interest into the arms of the Conservative Party. The Conservative claim to support rested upon opposition to Home Rule, certain restrictions in taxation which Mr. Goschen had carried out, the passing of a new Factory Act, and free education—the last a most notable reform which had long figured in Liberal programmes, and had been stoutly opposed by the Conservatives on the ground that to relieve parents of the payment of school fees would tend to weaken their sense of responsibility for the upbringing of their children. Each party had thus been compelled to hearken to the popular demand for social legislation; and the Conservatives had made it clear that they were prepared to go a long distance in the direction of "State Socialism," and regarded themselves as endowed with peculiar skill in the art of constructive reforms suitable for a clamorous but ignorant democracy. The General Election, fought in July, carried Mr. John Burns and Mr. Keir Hardie into Parliament, a more significant circumstance, perhaps, than the net result of the battle between the two orthodox parties, to whom the Socialism of these gentlemen was abhorrent. The Conservatives were in a majority of seventy-two in English constituencies, but Scotland and Wales were loyal to Mr. Gladstone and Home Rule, and, with the aid of the Irish Nationalists, he found himself with a majority of forty in the Commons. In his new Cabinet Mr. Asquith was Home Secretary, Sir William Harcourt Chancellor of the Exchequer, Mr. John Morley Chief

The General Election of 1892.

Secretary to the Lord Lieutenant. Lord Rosebery again became Foreign Secretary.

Second Home Rule Bill, 1893. Parliament met in the new year, and on February 13th, 1893, Mr. Gladstone introduced his second Home Rule Bill. It differed essentially from the first by providing for a representation of Ireland by eighty members in the Imperial Parliament, expressly asserting the Imperial supremacy—a subject upon which Lord Rosebery and Mr. Asquith had made firm declarations—and, as before, it excluded foreign affairs, the army, navy, customs and trade from the scope of the autonomous Irish Parliament. Mr. Balfour called the Bill an abortion; Mr. Chamberlain assailed it as a surrender of the Imperial power in Ireland; the Irish Party accepted it in default of anything better, and many Liberals regarded it with scant enthusiasm. Mr. Gladstone fought for it with a magnificent energy, a fertility of mental resource and a wealth of eloquence which were the admiration of friends and foes alike. After heated debates and much obstruction, finally crushed by the "guillotine" process, invented by the Unionists when passing the Crimes Act in 1887, the Bill, slightly remodelled, reached the House of Lords by a majority of thirty-four on the third reading. This was on September 1st. On the 12th the second reading in the Upper House was moved by Lord Spencer. Lord Rosebery asked for a settlement of the controversy by agreement between the two parties. The Unionist peers rejected these overtures and threw out the Bill by 419 votes to 41.

The country accepted this decision, and an attempt to rouse it to hostility against the Peers failed. Public attention was distracted by the danger of a war with France over the Siamese question, which had been handled with high determination and courage by Lord Rosebery, and by the dramatic extension of the Empire by the conquest of Matabililand. Other Government measures were rather roughly handled by the Peers, and in the session of 1894, on March 1st, Mr. Gladstone made an historic pronouncement on the constitutional aspect of the conflict between the two Houses. The differences had resulted in "a state of things of which we are compelled to say that, in our judgment, it cannot continue."

On March 3rd Mr. Gladstone resigned office, ostensibly because of his great age and failing eyesight, but in reality because he objected to the increased Navy Estimates which his colleagues thought necessary. The resignation was not unacceptable to the Queen, and his sixty years of service to the Crown and the nation elicited from her but a brief note commending his decision to seek relief from the burden of his duties. "The Queen would gladly have conferred a peerage on Mr. Gladstone, but she knows he would not accept it," ran this singularly dry communication. Lord Rosebery succeeded Mr. Gladstone as Prime Minister, and put the Home Rule question out of the sphere of practical politics by speaking, in the debate on the Address, of England as the predominant member of the partnership of the three kingdoms, who would have to be convinced of the justice of Home Rule before Home Rule could be granted. Mr. Gladstone made a brief reappearance in public affairs in 1896, in the cause of the massacred Armenians, for whom he wished England to go to war, unaided if no ally could be had. The nation heard again, with wondering admiration and delight, "the old man eloquent," but it responded faintly to his appeals to incur so tremendous a risk. He died on May 19th, 1898. Thousands passed before his bier in Westminster Hall, and throughout the kingdom the day of his interment in the Abbey, May 28th, was a day of mourning.

Resignation of Mr. Gladstone, March, 1894.

Death of Gladstone.

Queen Victoria survived the statesman who had played so great a part in her reign by nearly three years, dying on January 22nd, 1901. As old age came upon her she abandoned the seclusion in which she had lived since the death of the Prince Consort. The brilliant celebrations of the Jubilee of her reign in 1887 had revealed to her the affection of her people here and in the colonies; and the even more enthusiastic demonstrations on the occasion of her Diamond Jubilee in 1897 led her to place herself in still closer touch with her subjects. Her death was mourned with a sorrow universal and sincere. Her body was taken on a gun-carriage from Buckingham Palace to Windsor, to be laid by the side of her husband in the mausoleum at Frogmore, and the scenes in the crowded streets and parks on the route to Paddington were unforgettable by all who witnessed them.

Death of the Queen.

Corona-
tion of
Edward
VII.

The coronation of Edward VII. was fixed to take place on June 26th, 1902, but his Majesty was stricken with illness, and it was necessary to perform a severe operation. Its success relieved the nation of an intense anxiety, and on August 9th the coronation ceremonies were conducted in Westminster Abbey with traditional pomp and splendour, the royal procession to and from the building being witnessed by a multitude which gave unrestrained expression to its loyalty.

With the re-establishment of his health, his Majesty applied himself to the improvement of our relations with foreign Powers. The Sovereign of England can act in such matters only by the advice of his Ministers. Within the limits of this constitutional principle his Majesty was able to exercise his personal influence in foreign Courts to the advantage of his country. The *entente* with France and the treaty with Russia disposing of the difficulties with that Power in the Middle East are diplomatic achievements in which King Edward shared. The activities with which he was credited in these respects, however, produced an unfortunate impression in Germany that an object of British policy was to isolate that Power. A State visit of the King and Queen to Berlin in the spring of 1909 was officially thought to have done much to counteract that view; and although distrust between the two peoples is not yet removed, and rival naval policies have excited excessive attention in both countries, a marked tendency to drift apart seems, at present, to have been partially arrested. Without entering further on this debatable and delicate topic, it can confidently be said that by his labours in the cause of peace, his Majesty has strengthened the monarchical principle, which now has a vitality in England which it assuredly did not possess in the early decades of the nineteenth century.

Lord Salis-
bury's
Third Ad-
ministra-
tion, 1895.

We must now retrace our steps to follow the fortunes of Lord Salisbury's third Administration, formed in 1895. Lord Lansdowne took office as Secretary for War, Mr. Chamberlain as Secretary for the Colonies, Sir Michael Hicks-Beach (afterwards Lord St. Aldwyn) as Chancellor of the Exchequer, and Mr. Balfour as First Lord of the Treasury and Leader of the Commons. Lord Salisbury was his own Foreign

Photo: Russell & Sons, Baker Street, W.

QUEEN VICTORIA'S COFFIN ARRIVING AT ST. GEORGE'S CHAPEL, WINDSOR.

Minister. The General Election resulted in a Unionist majority of 152 over Liberals and Nationalists combined. The next five years were crowded with historic events which distracted the attention of the nation from domestic policy. These have already been reviewed, and it remains only to note the principal legislative achievements. These included a new Land Act, which further weakened the position of the landlord class in Ireland; an Employers' Liability Act, which has since been extended to cover almost every class of worker, including seamen and domestic servants; an Act creating County Councils for Ireland similar to those set up in England and Wales during Lord Salisbury's second Administration; an Act substituting Borough Councils for the Vestries of London; a number of minor social measures; and an Act constituting the Commonwealth of Australia.

General Election of 1900.   In the autumn of 1900 the Government dissolved and appealed for a new lease of life on their South African policy. The war, then supposed to be "practically over," was the dominant issue of the election, and it was believed that the guerilla fighting would soon be stamped down and the way opened for the supersession of military by civil administration. The electorate committed the completion of this task to those who had been unable to prevent the war, and the Unionists obtained a majority of 134. South African and Far Eastern affairs, and the rise of a new problem in North Africa, where the apparently "dying State" of Morocco was the objective of rival French and German ambitions, absorbed public interest to the exclusion of domestic concerns. The life of the Ministry was marked by growing political discontent among the people as the evil economic effects of the war in South Africa made themselves felt. With two exceptions the legislative achievements were unimportant. An Education Act was passed which placed the voluntary schools on the rates, and an Act providing a scheme of compensation, at the cost of the liquor trade, for extinguished public-house licences. Sanction was also, as we have seen, given to the introduction of Chinese into South Africa. All three Bills were hotly opposed by the Liberals, and the Chinese influx to the Transvaal caused a revulsion of feeling among the democracy, who had been led to believe that the war would

open a larger market for white labour in the mines. Army
and administrative scandals arising out of the war helped to
weaken public confidence, nor did Mr. Brodrick's attempt at
War Office and army reorganisation convince the public that
the nation would have an army more effective for its purpose
than the quarter of a million of regulars and volunteers who
had spent nearly three years in subduing a nation of sixty
thousand men who knew how to shoot.

Lord Salisbury retired after the coronation, and Mr. Balfour **Death of**
became Prime Minister (July, 1902). On August 22nd, 1903, **Lord Salis-**
Lord Salisbury died. His death was an irreparable loss to **bury.**
Conservatism, for it deprived the party of the one man whose
authority in its councils was unchallengeable. To the nation
it meant the passing of a great Foreign Minister, who, with
singular caution and sagacity, had kept the peace abroad
through a series of exceptional difficulties, and had laid the
foundations of British policy in the new conditions that had
arisen in the Far East.

In 1903 Mr. Chamberlain caused a convulsion in the **Mr. Cham-**
party and in the country by announcing his conversion to **berlain**
the fiscal views of those who would set up a general tariff **and Tariff**
with preferential rates for the British colonies. His mind **Reform.**
had long been working in this direction, and at the Conference of the colonial premiers at the second Jubilee, in
1897, he had spoken in favour of a reorganisation of inter-
Imperial relations such as would produce a closer working
partnership between the parent state and the oversea communities; and he had met the colonial desire for preferential
commercial arrangements by what amounted to an offer
to denounce the commercial treaties with Germany and Bel-
gium which entitled those powers to the same tariff terms
in British colonies as those granted to Great Britain. The
chief outcome of the Conference was the termination of
the treaties in July, 1898. But the Conference passed a
resolution declaring that, under existing conditions, it is not
practicable to establish Free Trade between the colonies and
the mother country, approving the granting by the colonies
of substantial preferences to the produce and manufactures of
the United Kingdom, and declaring that the Imperial Government "should be invited to consider the expediency of giving

a preferential treatment to the products and manufactures of
the colonies." There the matter remained, though not dormant
in Mr. Chamberlain's mind, until his return from the South
African tour.

On May 15th, 1903, in a speech at Birmingham, he
announced that he was in favour of establishing preferential
tariffs between the mother country and the colonies. It was
not a sudden conversion, he explained, but the outcome of reflection on the "solitude of the illimitable veldt." The present
was a creative period; we were at the beginning of a new
era. How were we to keep and increase and promote trade
with the colonies, even at the risk of lessening trade with
foreign nations? The chief colonies had given preferences;
Canada had made him a definite offer. They said: "We
have done for you as much as we can do, voluntarily and
freely and without return. If you are willing to reciprocate
in any way, we are prepared to reconsider our tariff with a
view of seeing whether we cannot give you further reductions,
especially in regard to those goods in which you will come
into competition with foreigners; and we will do this if you
will meet us by giving us a drawback on the small tax of
1s. per quarter which you have put on corn"—a part of the
war taxes, which Sir Michael Hicks-Beach, the Chancellor
of the Exchequer, withdrew later because it had enhanced
the price of bread. In a later speech Mr. Chamberlain
deprecated duties on raw-material imports, but admitted that
if preference is to be given to the colonies "you must put a
tax on food."

Mr. Chamberlain's speeches on this topic were lacking
in that coherency of argument and accuracy of detail which
distinguished his previous utterances on great questions; but
they made it plain that he had discarded Free Trade principles and was prepared, in conjunction with the colonies,
each of them highly protectionist against the mother country,
to undertake a gigantic fiscal experiment that would increase
the cost of the necessaries of life. Mr. Balfour treated the
subject as one of future rather than of present interest, and
foiled sundry attempts to get it debated in the Commons.
A furious controversy began in the country immediately after
the speech of May, 1903. The Protectionists, whose spokes-

men in politics had been Mr. Henry Chaplin and Colonel Sir Howard Vincent, rallied to Mr. Chamberlain's support; the Free Traders, in the persons of distinguished Unionists and the leaders of the Liberal Party, applied themselves to a destructive analysis of his ideas. Meanwhile a struggle went on within the Cabinet because of Mr. Chamberlain's advocacy of a policy unacceptable to that body. Mr. Balfour took a course midway between the two groups, and succeeded in preventing a disruption until September, his own declarations in the meantime having been indeterminate, though showing a leaning towards a policy of fiscal retaliation upon protectionist Powers. On September 18th it was announced that Mr. Chamberlain, Lord George Hamilton and Mr. Ritchie had resigned; and correspondence between them and Mr. Balfour was published which showed that Mr. Chamberlain had left the Cabinet because of the exclusion of Preference from its programme, and in order to devote himself to the propagation of his views in the country.

Resignation of Mr. Chamberlain, Sept., 1903.

It appeared that Mr. Ritchie and Lord George Hamilton had resigned in ignorance of Mr. Chamberlain's resignation, of which they had not been informed by Mr. Balfour. Their departure was followed by that of Lord Balfour of Burleigh and Mr. Arthur Elliot, and the world wondered why the Duke of Devonshire remained. He also resigned on October 2nd, having in vain expected, in a public speech by Mr. Balfour, "an explicit declaration of adherence to Free Trade as the ordinary basis of our fiscal and commercial system and an equally explicit repudiation of the principle of Protection." Mr. Balfour wrote a reproachful letter to the Duke which emphasised the disruption of the Unionist Party. The Ministry was re-formed, Mr. Austen Chamberlain being transferred from the Post Office to the Chancellorship of the Exchequer, a promotion regarded as a sign of the sympathy of the new Cabinet with his father's programme; and Mr. Alfred Lyttelton became Secretary for the Colonies. This is not the place to record the strife within the Unionist Party. It must suffice to say that Mr. Chamberlain continued his propaganda until the summer of 1906, when he was stricken with an illness which has since prevented him from doing any platform work. Mr. Balfour devoted himself to preserving

Disruption of the Unionist Party.

a semblance of unity in his party, but, of course, without satisfying either the Unionist Free Traders or the Tariff Reformers and Protectionists—for while all Protectionists are Tariff Reformers, some Tariff Reformers, among them Mr. Balfour, repudiate Protection. He had, however, a Ministry wholly docile under his leadership, and, by foiling the efforts of the Opposition to have the controversy threshed out on the

Photo: Miss Murrell Marris.

THE RIGHT HON. JOSEPH CHAMBERLAIN, M.P.

floor of the House of Commons, he kept his Administration alive until the end of 1905.

The General Election of 1906. Then occurred the greatest electoral upheaval since the Reform Bill. The question of Free Trade *versus* Protection dominated all others during the General Election, though "Chinese slavery" in the Transvaal was denounced energetically on Liberal platforms. A turnover of votes was expected, but none foresaw its magnitude. Birmingham, alone among great cities, was faithful to Unionism and to the fiscal ideas Mr. Chamberlain had set forth; but the country as a whole swept them aside. Two hundred and fifteen Unionist seats were captured. Four hundred Liberals were returned—including twenty-four members supported by the Labour party—thirty Labour-Socialists forming an independent group, and eighty-three Nationalists: a total of five hundred and thirteen against a hundred and thirty-one Conservatives and twenty-six Liberal Unionists. There were startling surprises in the election, the chief being that Mr. Balfour was defeated in Manchester. A place in Parliament, however, was found for him by the retirement of one of the members for the City of London. The Liberal, Labour and Nationalist majority over the Unionists was 356; in the event of a defection of the Labourists and the Nationalists the Liberal majority over all parties would be 132. Even more noteworthy than the number of Liberals and Labourists was the number of men who had specialised in social questions and could speak with close and accurate knowledge. Authors and journalists appeared in Parliament on the Liberal side in unusual numbers, while the Labour group, which consisted wholly of specialists in the facts of industrialism, comprised a few men of high mental power who, either by pen or tongue, or both, commanded immense audiences in the country. For the first time the country had a Parliament in which the democracy was represented with adequacy by men who knew the life of the people from within. Except Mr. Chamberlain, soon to be stricken with illness, the sorely depleted Unionists had but one man of pre-eminent ability and influence—Mr. Balfour; though among the survivors of the disaster, and among those who found their way back to the House in bye-elections, were a few Parliamentarians of skill and experience. Mr. Balfour led this party with consummate skill. By sheer talent he regained his personal ascendency in a House of Commons which was at first disposed to treat him as a dethroned sovereign in politics; and by declining to commit himself to the policy of taxing foreign food imports he contrived that the fiscal question should remain one upon which there could be freedom of thought within the party. This attitude did not satisfy either section, and there

The Unionist Minority.

were intrigues against his leadership and a movement to drum
out those who would not subscribe to the new economics;
but Mr. Balfour was indispensable because of his over-
shadowing abilities, his unrivalled power of criticism, his
mastery of Parliamentary arts, the force and grace of his
oratory, the strength and subtlety of his character, the charm
of his personality.

Some Causes of the Victory. The enormous Liberal majority was due in no small
measure to Unionist defections at the polls. The party had
been split asunder by the propaganda of Protection, and
Unionists who found the reasoning of the Duke of Devonshire and Lord Goschen more convincing than that of the
exponents of the new Imperialism either abstained or voted
for the Liberal candidate in constituencies where the Unionist
was a Tariff Reformer. This the Unionist candidate usually
was, for many of the Conservative party outside the great
towns were still Protectionist at heart, and Mr. Chamberlain,
by a daring *coup*, had captured the Liberal Unionist organisation and was thus able, for the time being, to exclude Free
Traders from the list of officially approved candidates.

Growth of Socialist Thought. The main cause of the Liberal victory, however, was not
to be found in Unionist dissensions, nor even in the fear of
the populace that a Protectionist revival, masked by a movement for Imperial unity, would add to the cost of food and
give an added bitterness to the life of the poor; rather was it
to be found in the discontent of the masses of the people with
the smallness of their share in the ever-growing wealth of
the country. Great strikes in the coal and engineering trades
in the period under review, and countless minor strikes, had,
on the whole, failed to raise the wages of the industrial
classes. The net gain of these struggles was little more than
the passing of a Conciliation Act in 1896 and the setting up
of a standing Court of Arbitration by the Board of Trade—
measures which, however, have been helpful in averting labour
conflicts. Meanwhile, the cost of living has appreciated, and an
insufficiency of employment, accompanied by a degeneration
of its victims into the unemployable class, has been a chronic
evil. In these and other industrial and social circumstances
Socialists found ample material for incitement to new methods
of political action. For twenty years the trades unions had been

permeated by Socialist thought; new unions had arisen
which gave solidarity to vast classes of "unskilled" labour
—a misnomer this, for no bodily labour which is worth a
wage is in reality unskilled. All the unions, old and new, in
greater or less degree, had fallen under the influence of men
whose policy it was to form a party in Parliament strong
enough to use either Liberals or Unionists as instruments
for passing the legislation they desired, and whose pro-

WILLIAM MORRIS.
(From the portrait by G. F. Watts, R.A.)

gramme may be epitomised in a phrase—the diversion of
wealth from the pockets of the few to those of the many.
Outside the domain of the trades unions there also had been
carried on for twenty years a street-corner crusade against
the governing classes. New and disturbing views of capital
and labour, of the production and distribution of wealth, of
the principles underlying human relationships, of individual
rights and of the duties and responsibilities of the State—
views rigorously excluded from discussion in the party newspapers except for the purpose of derision—had been set forth

by a new order of street-preachers who derived their knowledge from Socialist literature and their inspiration from a passionate sympathy with the lot of the serfs of the industrial system.

William Morris. Nor were all these teachers untutored men. William Morris, scholar, poet, artist, whose life and pursuits set him high above the demagogues of his day, was typical of a group of thinkers who, by speech and pen, placed their intellects at the service of the democracy. Their teaching had this in common with that of the mob orators of the streets and open spaces: it was destructive alike of Liberalism and of Toryism as a means by which social change could be brought about without pressure from the democracy; and it was constructive in so far as it gave intellectual reality to the vision of a society in which both extreme wealth and extreme poverty should have no place. How far their influence told in producing this astounding General Election cannot precisely be determined; it is enough to point to the fact that the Labour party in the House of Commons numbered thirty Socialists. Nor has an Anti-Socialist League that has since been formed arrested the Socialist movement, as certain bye-elections have proved, though the Conservatives, both in municipal and in national politics, have found it a useful ally.

Sir H. Campbell-Bannerman's Administration, 1906–1908. Sir Henry Campbell-Bannerman had a Liberal majority strong enough to hold Irish Nationalists and Labour-Socialists alike in check. But he endeavoured to placate both groups. The development of his legislative policy and of a foreign policy directed to a reduction of armaments was arrested by illness, which compelled him to resign in April, 1908. He died within a few weeks. During his short term of office he had won the respect of the nation by the exhibition of gifts of higher quality than it had been the custom to credit him with, and among his intimates he was regarded with strong affection. His greatest political achievement had been the grant of self-government to the republics in South Africa. Next in importance—though of this the credit belongs largely to Mr. Asquith, who unfolded the scheme in his Budget statement for 1908—was an Old Age Pensions Act, granting a pension of five shillings a week to persons over seventy years of age who had not been in receipt of Poor Law relief. This great social reform had been advocated for nearly twenty

Old Age Pensions Act, 1908.

years by politicians of all parties, but the difficulties of
framing a contributory scheme had stood in the way of its
accomplishment by the Unionist Administrations. The
Liberals got rid of them by making their scheme non-
contributory, and by risking a cost which proved to be far
greater than was estimated. Another important measure was
Mr. Lloyd George's Patents Act, which compelled foreign
patentees to manufacture in this country patented articles
sold in this market. The effect was to oblige foreign firms
either to set up factories here or commission British
factories to manufacture for them. A very useful measure, **The**
eventually carried through in the autumn session of 1908 by **Children's Charter.**
Mr. Herbert Samuel, who has made a considerable Parlia-
mentary reputation, was a Children's Act, which became
known as the Children's Charter. It was aimed against
baby-farming, cruelty to children, and evil conditions of child
life among the disreputable classes, and it established
a system of children's courts for juvenile offenders.
Another salutary measure prohibited children under fourteen from entering or being served in licensed premises.
In other domestic legislation Sir Henry Campbell-Bannerman
was less fortunate, for the House of Lords destroyed an
Education Bill designed and carried through the House of
Commons by Mr. Birrell on lines desired by the Nonconformist
section of the party.

A novel legislative project discussed in the session of 1908 **Daylight Saving.**
was a Daylight Saving Bill promoted by Mr. Willett, who
proposed, by putting the clock forward in April and backward
in September, to move the usual hours of toil nearer sunrise,
and thus give the population more daylight for recreation
at the close of their work. A committee of the House of
Commons reported against the Bill.

When Mr. Asquith became Prime Minister in succession **Mr.**
to Sir Henry, Mr. Lloyd George succeeded him as Chancellor **Asquith's Adminis-**
of the Exchequer, Mr. Winston Churchill, who had been **tration, 1908.**
Under-Secretary for the Colonies, taking the Presidency of
the Board of Trade. With Sir Edward Grey at the Foreign
Office, Lord Morley at the India Office, and Lord Crewe as
Secretary for the Colonies, oversea affairs, whether foreign or
Imperial, were in safe hands. Mr. Haldane remained at the

War Office, Mr. Birrell became Chief Secretary to the Lord Lieutenant of Ireland, and eventually Mr. McKenna was appointed First Lord of the Admiralty and Mr. Runciman Minister for Education. On the formation of the Ministry in 1905 Mr. John Burns, formerly a working engineer and the leader of the men in a great strike of dock workers in 1887, had been made President of the Local Government Board, in which office he remained, to the dissatisfaction of the Socialists, from whom he had parted company. At the time Mr. Asquith became Premier Mr. Haldane had already contrived and carried through Parliament a scheme of army reorganisation under which the Volunteers and other auxiliary troops disappeared, and reappeared as a Territorial Army equipped in all respects as the Regular Army, of which it forms a part. This home defensive force now consists of over a quarter of a million men of all branches. No army reformer since Cardwell has done so great a work as Mr. Haldane, and the reorganisation of our land forces on a plan applicable to all parts of the Empire, and accepted by the self-governing Dominions, is one of the most notable constructive achievements of the Ministry. It is too early yet to say whether the scheme will give us a sufficiently numerous and well-trained army for oversea warfare and home defence in the event of foreign complications and an attempt at invasion of these islands. Lord Roberts and the advocates of compulsory service assert that it will not; but the scheme has met with so ready a response from the youth of the country that any danger there may have been of having to adopt conscription has for the time being passed. Under the influence of his Majesty, who gave an opportune lead in the formation of the voluntary County Associations, and of Mr. Balfour, political opposition to the new system has ceased, and all parties and classes are united in its support.

The Territorial Army.

The Navy

In naval affairs during the past quarter of a century there has been a revolution by the construction of gigantic vessels of a tonnage and destructive capacity undreamt of in other days, and the British fleet and the navies of other Powers are in process of rebuilding, mammoth vessels replacing those of a smaller type. Contemporaneously with this development and the enormous cost it entails, present and prospective, a satisfactory type of submarine vessel has been evolved, and has added a new complication to naval warfare. In its technical aspects, our naval strength, in relation to that of other Powers and possible combinations of Powers, varies so much from time to time that the reader would not be assisted if naval programmes were here reviewed; it must suffice to say that the fact which emerges from the heated and recurrent controversies in Parliament is that both the great political parties are agreed upon the obligation to maintain an un-challengeable supremacy at sea. In the summer of 1909 a vast fleet of all types, from submarines to "Dread-noughts," was assembled in the Thames—a unique and splendid spectacle designed to bring home to the mind of the people the reality of our defensive power at sea. A naval conference between the Home Government and representa-tives of the self-governing Dominions, later in the year, resulted in an agreement by which the colonies are to make provision for their sea-defence in co-ordination with the Imperial navy. The lines have thus been laid down by which these young and growing nations may, as wealth and popu-lation increase, create subsidiary fleets which will form part of a naval whole should Imperial interests in any quarter be menaced. The colonial warship or the colonial soldier will fit automatically into the Imperial fighting line ashore or afloat. That is the principle of defence which is to be worked out in detail in the organisation of land and sea forces throughout the Empire.

An attempt to reform the licensing system was one of Mr. Asquith's most ambitious measures of social reform. The Bill was contested fiercely in the Commons and in the country throughout the session of 1908, the controversy raging on the question whether it was equitable for the State to appropriate the monopoly value of the annual licence, which monopoly value the Government treated as national property. The Bill passed the Commons at all its stages by huge majorities. Lord Lansdowne, the Leader of the Opposition in the House of Lords, called a meeting of Unionist peers at Lansdowne House, and it was there decided that the Lords should throw out the measure. This was done after a somewhat perfunctory debate.

The Licensing Bill, 1908.

Not for the first time since 1906 was it proved that the Liberals were powerless to legislate, however large their majority might be, except on lines agreeable to Mr. Balfour and the Opposition reserves in the hereditary House. The Liberal outcry against the Lords was renewed, but Mr. Asquith judged that the time had not yet come for trying conclusions with the Upper House.

The Budget of 1909.

The prolonged session of 1909 was chiefly occupied with the Budget, introduced by Mr. Lloyd George in a four hours' speech. It proposed to levy additional taxes on land and on accumulations of wealth passing at death, and swingeing taxation on the liquor trade. Earlier in the session the Government had unfolded an enlarged naval programme, and the First Lord of the Admiralty and the Prime Minister had created serious apprehension by justifying their proposals on the ground of German naval activity and resources. This feeling had been accentuated by Mr. Balfour, who urged that the proposals were inadequate, demanded eight first-class battleships instead of the four the Government intended to lay down forthwith, and started an agitation in the country on this issue. Mr. Lloyd George found himself compelled to raise £16,000,000 more money by new taxation. In so far as this increase was due to naval expenditure the Opposition were precluded from criticism, except as to the means by which the money was to be raised; nor were they in a better position with regard to the money which had to be found for old-age pensions; for in shipbuilding they wished to do more than the Government thought necessary, and in the pension scheme there could be no turning back. The sixteen millions had to be raised somehow. Mr. Lloyd George's plan was to take three millions from the Sinking Fund and to raise the rest to the extent of one-half by taxing the rich and the other half by taxing the luxuries of the poor. By extra duties on spirits and tobacco he sought to accomplish the latter purpose, embodying in his taxation scheme some of the financial effects of the abortive Licensing Bill of the previous year. The rich he proposed to shear by a new and higher scale of death duties, by taxing motor cars, and by diverting into the Exchequer a proportion of the wealth that passed into private hands by the "unearned increment"

New Sources of Revenue.

of the value of land. The land taxes were three—£1 in
every £5 of the increment value of non-agricultural land in
the neighbourhood of towns, on sale, transfer, or death of
the owner; a tax of a halfpenny in the pound on the capital
value of undeveloped land; and a tax of £10 per £100 on
the falling-in of leases. There was also a tax of five per cent.

Photo: Reginald Haines, Southampton Row, W.C.

THE RIGHT HON. H. H. ASQUITH, M.P.

on mining royalties. By taxing the accretion of wealth
in land due to the growth of the community, and to that
demand for land which arises independently of any energy
or expenditure on the part of its owner, the Chancellor
was introducing a novel principle in taxation and opening
up new and permanent and limitless sources of revenue.
The case for Tariff Reform had in part rested on the
necessity for "broadening the basis of taxation," and pro-

viding new sources of customs revenue. Tariff Reformers had
declared that "Free Trade finance" was bankrupt, and that
the unavoidable necessity of raising money for the navy, for
old-age pensions, and for measures of "social reform" would
sooner or later compel Free Traders to set up a tariff. Mr.
Lloyd George met that contention by proposing to form deep
reservoirs of taxation out of the wealth that accrued to land
from general public causes—wealth which the community,
not the landowners, created. His argument was that, so far
from Free Trade finance being bankrupt, there were vast
taxable reserves to be drawn upon, and that the only alternative to the use of them was the setting up of a general tariff
taxing the necessaries of life of the poor and increasing the
cost of all commodities. On this issue the Government fought
the Budget; and in this respect the battle was essentially
one between Free Trade and Protection as rival methods of
financing the country.

Social Legislation. Simultaneously with the Budget further plans of social
legislation were brought forward and others promised, these,
with the Budget, apparently forming an electioneering manifesto, which the Government intended to round off by a comprehensive measure of electoral reform. Among the measures
was a Development Bill, providing, *inter alia*, for afforesta-
tion on a large scale; another setting up a system of labour
exchanges in the cities and towns; a third establishing a
system of wages boards with power to fix minimum rates
in a group of minor industries in which "sweating" has prevailed, and a fourth dealing with housing and the planning
of towns. A scheme of State-aided insurance against un-
employment and a reform of the Poor Law system were also
promised. Limits of space prevent pursuit of this theme;
we must be content if we have succeeded in suggesting to
the reader's mind that the emergence of the Labour and
Socialist party, the advent of the huge Liberal and Labour
majority in the Parliament of 1906, the rise of new men and
the invention and application of new principles of taxation,
have opened up an era of change in domestic politics which,
sooner or later, may have a far-reaching effect on the social
life of the country.

Among the elements of change is the revolt of many

women against their political and legal status and the *The Fem-*
economic conditions of their life.   This sex-rebellion has *inist Move-*
found expression in an organised movement for an exten- *ment.*
sion of the suffrage to women on the same terms as to
men.   It originated among women of the middle classes,
with a leaven of women of aristocratic birth, and was a
by-product of higher education; but it has spread through
all ranks of society, and the majority of its supporters are
now women who earn their bread in the professions and
in industry and commerce.   It has attracted to itself many
lawless spirits who have prejudiced the movement by harassing
Ministers, by disturbing public meetings, and by acts of
violence for which the worst offenders have been imprisoned.
But at the heart of the movement is a deep-seated discontent
with the economic position of woman in modern life and a
determination to use political machinery through the ballot-
box for its amelioration; and no review of the immediate past
would be complete which did not take note of this as a
disturbing element in affairs.

There still remain to be mentioned some important
measures of a social character for which the Parliament
elected in 1906 is responsible.   In 1908 was passed an *Miners'*
Act limiting the hours of work in mines to eight.   The *Hours.*
eight hours are hours actually spent in the mine, and
the ideal of an eight-hour day from bank to bank is not
yet realised by the miners' organisations.   A still more important social measure is the Small Holdings Act of 1907, *Small*
the principle of which is that the County Councils have power *Holdings.*
to acquire land and lease it to suitable applicants.   So
numerous have been the applications for land under this
measure that the demand has not been satisfied with sufficient
rapidity to satisfy the advocates of small holdings, and complaints have been made of obstructiveness on the part of
some County Councils, which are accused of being more or
less under the influence of landowners reluctant to part with
any portion of their property.   Under the pressure of the
Board of Agriculture, these complaints are being remedied.
The movement has the support of both political parties,
but the Unionist claim is that the small holder should be
the owner, not the occupier, of his plot, the argument being

that ownership alone gives a man the necessary incentive to put into the soil the skill and labour needful for economic success. Against this it is argued that, under a system of ownership, the strong would buy up the weak, and that the small holdings would thus be reconverted into great holdings.

Court of Criminal Appeal. Yet another measure of importance is an Act which came into operation in 1908 establishing a Court of Criminal Appeal. This closed a controversy which had long divided the legal profession and on which eminent judicial authorities held strong and irreconcilable convictions. It has worked well, and the mischief that was apprehended has not occurred. Appeals have not been numerous, and the decisions have been such as to confirm public confidence in the Criminal Courts and to establish the contention of those who urged that an appeal should be allowed where a *primâ facie* case for re-hearing could be alleged.

Statistical In so far as statistics afford a trustworthy measure of social progress, it may be worth while to supplement those given in Chapter XXIV. with a few totals. The Registrar-General's returns show a decline in the birth-rate, due in part to a tendency to defer marriage to later life, which has become noticeable among the middle classes, and in part to a disinclination to incur the responsibility of large families. In 1890 the birth-rate per thousand of the population of the United Kingdom was 29·2; in 1907 it was 26·0, there having been a gradual fall year by year. Improved sanitary conditions account for a similar decline in the death-rate, which in 1890 was 19·4 per thousand, falling to 15·4 in 1907. The population of England and Wales in 1908 was 35,348,780; that of Ireland was 4,364,226. The persons in receipt of Poor Law relief in England and Wales on January 1st, 1908, numbered 928,671, and the total expenditure for the year ending Michaelmas, 1907, was £14,222,603. Though there has been an actual increase in the number of paupers, the decline relative to population has continued. The Poor Law system has, however, been shown to be unsatisfactory. A Royal Commission, which sat for three years, issued in 1909 a series of reports containing adverse conclusions and constructive proposals for reform, upon which the Liberal Government pledged itself to legislate. As a result of the report of a minority of the Commissioners, an agitation was begun for the extinction of the existing Boards of Guardians.

Limits of space forbid the enumeration of many minor advantages which the better organisation of society has conferred upon the people, but mention should be made of the increased facilities of communication by letter throughout the British Empire. Thanks in large measure to the pertinacity of Mr. Henniker Heaton, a penny stamp will now carry a letter wherever the flag flies. Postal business of all kinds has enormously increased. Illiteracy has disappeared during the past quarter of a century. Elementary education has done its work in the sense of making a nation of letter-writers. In 1907 the number of letters posted was 2,863,900,000, an average of 64·8 for each person. Including postcards, newspapers, and parcels, the total handled by the Post Office was 4,972,070,000, or 112·5 per head of the population. It may be added incidentally, as evidence of thrift among the classes who do not keep a current banking account, that the number of depositors in the Post Office Savings Bank in 1907 was 10,692,555, and that the sum on deposit reached the enormous total of £157,500,077.

The acreage under wheat in the United Kingdom in 1907 was 1,666,017; there had been a continuous decline since the repeal of the Corn Laws. The population of the rural districts in England and Wales in 1901 was 7,469,488, or 23 per cent. of the whole, an unsatisfactory figure in relation to the increase of population, but one that may be arrested by the operation of the Small Holdings Act of 1907 and by the new policies that aim at the better utilisation of the land. The value of the imports of merchandise into the United Kingdom (exclusive of coin and bullion, £62,370,667) for the year ending September 30th, 1909, was £606,952,672, and of exports (exclusive of coin and bullion, £60,232,066), £458,064,654. Taking a period of years sufficient to cover the oscillations of trade, the growth of commerce, and therefore of national wealth, is astounding.

THE period covered by this chapter is notable for a vigorous **Religion.** prosecution of the campaign for the reconquest of England by

317—N.E

the Roman Catholic Church, an output of energy by the Established Church of England to recover lost ground in the cities and towns, and a movement of opinion within the Church of England and among various Nonconformist bodies along the lines of the democratic agitation for a larger share of the desirable things of life. The era in which we live is one in which no great class cares strongly for the ultimate problems of man's existence. Amid these conditions it is doubtful whether the churches have increased their influence. But the movement to disestablish and disendow the Church of England has made no appreciable progress. The Church in Wales has not yet been disestablished, although every member for the Principality is pledged to the policy. Nor have efforts of the Liberals to legislate in educational matters in a sense hostile to the Church met with success. The Established Church is now adapting her organisation to the needs of the time and is learning to make her appeal frankly to the democracy. That she must win over the democracy or perish as a political institution and decline as a religious force has become clearer to her leaders than it was a generation ago. But those leaders who have taken up the cry of the people for higher wages, shorter hours, better houses, more light and air in urban slums, and such changes in their environment as will add to their chances of happiness, have found the path of social reform hard to tread. On the one side they have had to encounter the popular prejudice which still regards the Church as the Church of the aristocracy and the prosperous classes, and, on the other, the fears of the rich lest they should incite the people to deeper discontent. Nevertheless there is a noticeable tendency towards an identification of the social teaching of the Church with the protests of the democracy against an economic system which condemns the majority to excessive labour for a meagre reward. The Pan-Anglican Congress, which was a gathering of clergy and laity from all parts of the Empire and from the United States—in the colonial days a part of the Diocese of London—was a remarkable demonstration of Anglican unity. Perhaps its chief result was to bring home to the mind of England the extent of the mission field in the oversea Dominions and in India and the protectorates.

The Church in Wales.

Pan-Anglican Conference, 1908.

In 1908 the Roman Catholic Church held a Eucharistic **Euchar-**
Congress in London—a series of services and meetings insti- **istic**
tuted in France in 1900 for the purpose of focussing attention **Congress,**
upon the significance and history of the Mass. The Holy **1908.**
Father was represented by his Eminence Cardinal Vincent
Vannutelli, the first Legate to tread English soil since the
Reformation, and the congress was attended by many bishops
and dignitaries from various parts of the world. The services
in the cathedral at Westminster—a noble addition to the architecture of London during the period under review—were of
a magnificence and solemnity such as England had not seen
for more than three centuries. It was intended at the culminating service at the cathedral to carry the Host in procession through the neighbouring streets, the edifice being
unable to accommodate more than a fraction of the Roman
Catholic multitude which thronged to London; but against
this there is still a technical prohibition in law, and as certain
Protestants remonstrated on this ground, and there was
reason to believe that there would be a disturbance, the
Government prohibited the carrying of the Host, and the procession took place without it. The Roman Catholic world
accepted the intervention of the Government with dignity
and calmness, but not without protest against the remaining
disabilities under which Catholics in England live.

Touching the numerous Nonconformist bodies, one of the **The**
facts to be put on record is the still closer identification of most **Noncon-**
of them with the Liberal party in politics, and the zeal with **formists.**
which many of their ministers have made the cause of Labour
their own. A "National Council of Evangelical Free Churches"
was formed in 1896, and has exercised considerable political
influence, especially on the education controversy in Parliament. Several of the Labour members in the Commons have
graduated in chapels and as local preachers; and, on the
religious side, the Labour movement has intimate associations
with Nonconformity—a fact significant of the relative failure
of the Established Church to produce workmen leaders of
the working classes. The period has been notable for the
unification of three of the smaller sections of Methodism—the
Bible Christians, the United Methodist Free Churches, and
the Methodist New Connexion—under the title of the United

Methodist Church, and by the union of the Free Church and the United Presbyterian Church under the style of the United Free Church of Scotland. Nor is the tendency to union among the Nonconformist bodies confined to this country. It is also characteristic of religious life in the colonies, especially in Canada. A feature of the mixed religious, social and political activity of the Nonconformist churches throughout the Empire is the Pleasant Sunday Afternoon movement—the "P.S.A.," as it is called. These afternoon gatherings, at which addresses are given on religious and social topics, have attracted to the chapels of the various denominations large numbers of men other than the regular frequenters of places of worship, and it is claimed for them that they have a high educative value in leavening democratic politics with Christian thought.

"Christian Science." Another feature of the period is the rise of what is called "Christian Science," a cult which originated in the United States. Its followers believe that disease is essentially imaginary, a mere dream of the mortal mind, and that it can be both prevented and cured by the "metaphysical mind"; and "churches" and other meeting-places have sprung up in almost every great city.

The Salvation Army. Mention must also be made of the rise of the "Salvation Army," the creation of Mr. William Booth, at first a Methodist evangelist in the East End of London. He gave his converts a military organisation, taking for himself the title of General. A man of very remarkable powers and personality, he acquired a large following among the poorest classes of Londoners, and extended his system first throughout these islands, and thereafter to many parts of the world. The principle upon which General Booth proceeds is that there can be no reformation of society without an entire change in the heart of the individual man or woman; his efforts are therefore directed first to the conversion of the outcasts of society and, second, to the organisation of means by which his converts can support themselves. The Church of England now has a similar organisation known as the Church Army, the founder and head of which is Prebendary Carlile.

IN literature the quarter of a century with which we **Literature** are here concerned has been marked, both in poetry and in fiction, by the production of works of great technical merit rather than by an efflorescence of genius. Poetry of high merit has been produced by Mr. William Watson, W. E. Henley (1849-1903), John Davidson (1859-1909), and others; but, though Mr. Alfred Austin was appointed Poet Laureate after Tennyson's death, no one has risen to carry on the succession of the great Victorian poets. Swinburne, the last of the race, survived until 1909, but the greater part of his fine tale of work belongs to an earlier period. The same may be said of George Meredith, who died in the same year. Like Browning, this writer had to wait for adequate recognition of his genius, but long before his death he was regarded by general consent as one of the first of Victorian novelists and a poet whose work has rich significance and high distinction. The long series of great novels which began with "The Ordeal of Richard Feverel" (1859) ended with "The Amazing Marriage" (1905). In the later ones his idiosyncrasies of style became more pronounced, but all of them scintillate with epigram and are charged with concentrated thought and deep feeling, and in all, too, there flickers the humour of true comedy. Mr. Rudyard Kipling, like Meredith, has divided himself between poetry and fiction, and has done brilliant work in both kinds. Mr. Thomas Hardy did not abandon fiction for poetry until he had added to his earlier novels "Tess of the d'Urbervilles" among other stories in which he strikes a note of pessimism and mordant irony. The works of Robert Louis Stevenson (1850-94), founder of the English Neo-Romantic School, showed, to the end, no falling-off, and "Catriona," published the year before his untimely death, takes high rank among his achievements. Mr. Rider Haggard, who started with much the same *motif* as "R.L.S.," at once showed himself the possessor of a very individual talent, and he has found local colour for his powerfully imaginative stories in divers lands and ages. Mr. J. M. Barrie's tales of lowly Scottish life, full of humour and fine feeling, have provoked imitation of no unworthy kind. Mr. S. R. Crockett began by following

Mr. Barrie's lead, but was not long in striking another vein and showing himself to be in the true romantic succession. But in recent English fiction there has been no very marked stream of tendency. A few writers showed a disposition to tread the path of naturalism, but French influence has made its mark upon English fiction in the form rather of realism—as in the novels of George Gissing

Photo: G. C. Beresford, Brompton Road.

J. M. BARRIE.

(1857-1903)—than of naturalism. Many novelists have found their material less in the primary passions than in the complexities of social life and the unsettlements of belief, though more daring flights have been essayed by Mr. H. G. Wells. Not a little of the best fiction of the period has been produced by women, and notably by Mrs. Humphry Ward, "Lucas Malet" (a daughter of Charles Kingsley), and "John Oliver Hobbes" (1867-1906). Foremost among works of biography

LITERATURE

are Mr. John (Viscount) Morley's authoritative Life of Gladstone, Mr. Winston Churchill's brilliant Life of his father,
and Lady Burne-Jones's beautiful Memoirs of her husband.

Photo: Pictorial Agency.
H. G. WELLS.

Much admirable critical and miscellaneous work has been done
by Walter Horatio Pater (1839-94), Sir Leslie Stephen (1832-
1904), Mr. Andrew Lang, Mr. Theodore Watts-Dunton, Dr.

The Drama. Stopford Brooke, Professor Saintsbury, John Churton Collins (1848-1908), and a host of other writers.

Among English playwrights there has been no dearth of talent. The later work of Sir A. W. Pinero, the plays of Oscar Wilde (1856-1900), of Mr. George Bernard Shaw and of Mr. J. M. Barrie gave new life to the English drama, and the tendency has seemed latterly to be towards the closer union of literature and the stage. Musical comedy, however, not the drama, has drawn the largest audiences and the most money, although in the 'nineties the plays of Ibsen enjoyed a considerable vogue. The Norwegian dramatist used the theatre as a means for the expression of a destructive analysis of modern social life, and his method strongly influenced our own playwrights, notably Mr. Shaw. The work of the Censorship under Mr. George Redford, as the executive officer of the Lord Chamberlain, led to friction from time to time with dramatic authors and managers, and in 1909 a Parliamentary Committee was appointed to investigate and report upon the system. The principal authors, actors and managers gave evidence, some in favour of the abolition of the Censorship, and others in favour of its modification.

Music. A DISTINCT change of taste, so far as certain forms of music are concerned, and a very rapid and gratifying development of knowledge and appreciation of good music, have marked the past twenty-five years. One or two of the old masters who were worshipped with intenseness during the mid-Victorian era have been superseded; oratorio, except for a few notable compositions, such as Elgar's *Dream of Gerontius* and *The Apostles*, written in recent years, has lost much of its hold; the continental school of composers, headed by Wagner and his successors—if successors they may be called —have gained an ever-widening public; orchestral music has advanced in public favour to a degree little dreamed of by composers in the past; orchestral organisations, containing skilled musicians worthy of the encomiums bestowed upon them by conductors from abroad, have sprung up, particularly in London, to a surprising extent; Sunday concerts, such as those controlled by the National Sunday League, organised indirectly to encourage the love of cheap, popular and good music, have met with well-merited success; and visiting musicians, drawn from all parts of the musical world by the magnet of British approval, have given to receptive and increasingly intelligent audiences the best products of the world's composers. The development, in fact, has been so amazingly fast that one wonders, not so much at the oft-quoted remark that "the British is not a musical nation," as that such a remark should ever have been made.

It may be said, indeed, that the gradual acceptance of Wagner and his epoch-making theories by the British musical public, after a critical onslaught rarely equalled in musical history, has been the most marked fact in the period under review. The very recent performances of the "Ring" in English, under the direction of Dr. Hans Richter—still a highly honoured name amongst contemporary orchestral leaders—testifies warmly to the present influence of Wagner upon all classes of music-lovers. It is hardly to be wondered at, therefore, that once having been drawn away by such a master-hand from the somewhat slavish devotion to classical forms which dominated composers fifty years ago, the creative minds in English music refuse to look back, except in a detached sense, to the old masters for guidance. A sort of revolutionary spirit has been shown and is now prevalent. Technical correctness has given way to inspiration, and a future of boundless possibilities seems to be opening up for the younger British school of composers. The more conservative of present-day musicians naturally look with some distrust upon the development of individuality and independence in the younger school, and properly condemn the violence and striving for noisy orchestral effects which is characteristic of its more "advanced" members. Just so long, however—and we need enter no further into the polemics of a burning discussion—as the public indubitably shows its appreciation for strong colour and emotion in music, just so long will the young composer, with all his excesses, thrive. The growing popularity of Richard Strauss, the most advanced of Germans in boisterous effects, with British audiences; the vogue, now waning, of Tchaikovsky, the celebrated Russian composer who, for a decade at least

General Tendencies.

exercised a considerable influence, especially in London, upon public taste; the present attention being paid to the most characteristic works of the young French school, and the increasing fondness for Scandinavian music, which, with the works of the Russian school, the esteemed leader of the London Queen's Hall Orchestra, Mr. Henry J. Wood, has so earnestly encouraged—all go to prove how greatly taste has altered, how exigent in its demand for novelty the public has become.

British music has reason for growth in such pleasant conditions. The demand for orchestral compositions is begetting a supply which, at the great provincial festivals, at "promenade" concerts, and even at the concerts of the conservative Philharmonic Society, now rapidly approaching the centenary of its fine career, need little fear comparison with continental work. In these conditions such excellent musicians as Sir Edward Elgar, H. Walford Davies, Granville Bantock, Joseph Holbrooke, Percy Pitt, Arthur Hervey—to mention a few names only—have prospered, and promise still further to develop.

Painting. By the death in rapid succession of Lord Leighton (1896), Sir John E. Millais (1896), and G. F. Watts (1904), the art of painting in England suffered almost irreparably. More severe than the loss of the men themselves was the removal of the force of their influence towards the development and encouragement of a truly national art. Under the direction of Leighton the Academy attained a higher position than it had done since its foundation: it became more eclectic in its membership, less conservative in its exhibitions. Individuality was encouraged, and men of exceptional talent were quickly absorbed into the Academic ranks. The personality and influence of the President were, indeed, the dominating factors of the art of the time.

Millais as a painter wielded even greater influence. Himself a fighter of convention in his early days, he was always ready to do all that lay within his power to broaden and strengthen the basis of English art.

One of the most interesting developments of later nineteenth

A HOPELESS DAWN, BY FRANK BRAMLEY, A.R.A.

(*National Gallery of British Art*)

The Newlyn School. century English art was the movement associated with the Cornish fishing village of Newlyn. Its principal object may be said to have been the attractive combination of homely British sentiment with French technique. The public success of the effort was undoubted, and was recognised by the election of its two leading exponents, Mr. Stanhope Forbes and Mr. Frank Bramley, to Associateships of the Royal Academy. The "School" had a vogue for a score or so of years, but it cannot now be accounted of importance.

French Influence. Its greater significance rather lay in the display of French influence upon our national art. Paris offered attractions as the teaching centre of the world which were unrivalled, and the influence of its *ateliers* was overwhelming. From thence came Mr. John Singer Sargent, the brilliant American portraitist whose style has made such a mark upon portraiture in England. From France, too, came the inspiration of Mr. George Clausen and Mr. H. H. La Thangue, the leading representatives of the *plein air* school of painting in England. The words of Millais that many of our artists "painted with a broken French accent" were, indeed, amply justified.

The Glasgow School. Another distinct movement in British art was that of the so-called Glasgow School. Confined entirely to Scottish painters, the "School" aimed at sincerity and seriousness in painting with the full display of individual idiosyncrasies. All more or less imbued with a love of Nature in her more sombre moods, the work of its exponents was generally remarkable for its quietude of tone and colour, a quality especially notable in the landscape section. Mr. Peppercorn, Mr. D. Y. Cameron, Mr. Austen Brown, Mr. A. K. Brown, Mr. J. Lavery and Mr. E. A. Hornel may be cited as leading members of the "School."

Landscape Painting. It is, perhaps, in landscape art that the national feeling now, as in the past, is more definitely expressed. The work of Mr. David Murray, Mr. Alfred East, Sir Ernest Waterlow, Mr. J. MacWhirter, David Farquharson (1839-1907), Mr. Adrian Stokes, Mr. Leslie Thomson, and Mr. Hughes-Stanton worthily upholds the reputation of the English School in this direction. In sea-painting Mr. Napier Hemy and Mr. W. L. Wyllie maintain the high standard set up by Henry Moore (1831-1895) and J. C. Hook (1819-1907).

Portraiture has assumed a preponderating position in British art quite apart from the work of Mr. Sargent and the meretricious strivings of his followers. The finest productions of Millais' later years were his portraits, and his presentation of Gladstone in the National Gallery was pronounced by no less a critic than Benjamin-Constant to be "the finest portrait of modern times." Watts expressed his individuality in his portraiture in the same degree as in his ideal works, and the magnificent series of paintings of his great contemporaries in the National Portrait Gallery testifies to his genius. The works of Sir William Orchardson and Sir George Reid, too, rank among the finest productions in recent portraiture, while those of Sir Luke Fildes, Sir H. Von Herkomer, Mr. J. J. Shannon—another talented American—Mr. George Henry, and Mr. A. S. Cope take high positions. Outside the ranks of the Academy Sir James Guthrie, Mr. John Lavery, Mr. William Nicholson, and Mr. W. Orpen have distinguished themselves by the force and originality of their work. **Portraiture.**

In art, as in many other directions, women workers steadily gained ground during the closing decade of the nineteenth century. Miss Eleanor Fortescue Brickdale, Mrs. Stanhope Forbes, Miss M. L. Gow, Miss Margaret Dicksee, Miss Lucy Kemp-Welch, and Mrs. Ernest Normand (Henrietta Rae) all produced work that was noteworthy for its strength and originality. **Women Painters.**

Due to the more general combination of architecture and sculpture, the position of the latter art has greatly advanced during the twenty-five years under review. Decorative sculpture has become a feature of our great buildings, whether of official or private enterprise, and a wider outlet has thus been provided for the work of the sculptor. In Mr. Alfred Gilbert England possessed one of the most talented sculptors of modern times, and in Sir George Frampton, too, we have a decorative sculptor of the highest order. Mr. Thomas Brock ranks as the foremost sculptor of the academic tradition, and his great National Memorial to Queen Victoria —impressive and dignified—is the finest work of its kind in our country. Among other men of note in this branch of art may be named Harry Bates (1850-1899), E. Onslow Ford **Sculpture.**

(1852-1901), Mr. Hamo Thornycroft, Mr. Goscombe John, Mr. Alfred Drury, and Mr. Bertram Mackennal.

Architecture.

London, during the past twenty-five years, has been undergoing a process of rebuilding, and stately new edifices have arisen in many main thoroughfares. Kensington, Whitehall, Piccadilly, Oxford Street, the Thames Embankment and the Strand, bear evidences of a change that is converting London into a city which would be unrecognisable by our forefathers who lived over their places of business and to whom palatial shops, vast hotels and huge blocks of flats were unknown. Since King Edward came to the throne improvements have been effected around Buckingham Palace which make it more worthy of a royal residence in the capital of an empire, and will give to State processions an outlet to Charing Cross through a noble archway. Whitehall has been vastly improved by the erection of a new War Office, and Parliament Street by the substitution of a stately block of Government offices for unattractive houses and shops. The Abbey and the Houses of Parliament have thus been opened up to the view from Whitehall, and the thoroughfare is now one of the finest in the world.

London Traffic Revolutionised.

ELECTRIC traction and mechanical methods of propulsion have revolutionised life in London by multiplying the means of communication and quickening the speed of transit. In the 'eighties the only choice of the traveller from east to west of the metropolis lay between the six-miles-an-hour omnibus or the cab and the scarcely quicker underground train, running in dark, dank tunnels, the atmosphere sulphur-laden, steaming, charged with smoke and dirt. In the use of electric power we were a decade behind many cities of Europe and the United States, and it was not until 1890 that the first electric railway was opened in London—the City and South London line, which goes under the Thames near London Bridge, and now runs from Clapham Common to Islington. In 1896 work was begun in tunnelling for a six-and-a-half-miles line from the Bank to Shepherd's Bush, and the railway was opened in 1900. It was a great relief to the traffic on the great trunk highway beneath which, for the

TRAVELLING FACILITIES 1039

greater part, it passes. Other "tubes" have been laid from Moorgate Street to Finsbury Park, from Finsbury Park to Hammersmith, from Charing Cross to Hampstead and Highgate, from Waterloo Station to the City, and from the Elephant and Castle by way of Baker Street to Edgware Road. In addition to these new facilities for cheap and rapid transit the original underground railways, the Metropolitan and the District lines, have been electrified, as has also been a section of the suburban service of the London, Brighton and South Coast line. Simultaneously with these changes nearly all the horse tramways have passed into the possession of the London County Council, and an electric system of traction has gradually been substituted. New electric tramway lines have been constructed by the Middlesex and Essex County Councils, and the western and south-western services of a private company have been electrified and now extend to Hounslow in the west and Hampton Court, Richmond and Tooting in the south-west. In the last mentioned suburb they link up with the service of the London County Council, whose trams now serve many suburbs in the counties of Surrey and Kent.

The Electric Tram.

Other road traffic has also undergone a remarkable change by the partial replacement of horse-drawn omnibuses by larger, more rapid and, unfortunately, much noisier vehicles propelled either by petrol engines, steam, or electric motors. Though a perfect type of mechanically propelled omnibus is not yet evolved, the total disappearance of the horse-drawn omnibus and cab from the streets of England is, in the judgment of experts, a certainty. Motor vehicles for commercial purposes have come into general use, for both light and heavy traffic, and are employed by the Post Office on long-distance routes which ten years ago were traversed by four-horse coaches, and special types of motor vehicles have been constructed for army purposes. Contemporaneously with these developments well-to-do persons who formerly kept horses and carriages have supplied themselves with motor cars of various types, and a gigantic new industry has arisen for the manufacture of these vehicles. A new sport is that of motor racing, and on the spacious track at Brooklands, in Surrey, speeds exceeding those of the fastest

Motors.

railway expresses have ceased to cause surprise. Indeed, many non-racing cars on the roads are capable of a rate of movement undreamt of thirty years ago. Successive Acts of Parliament have been passed, in the interests of public safety, regulating the use of these vehicles.

One social effect of this revolution in the means of long-distance travelling has been to open out new suburbs, and to revive the prosperity of the country inn and the provincial hotel. Yet another has been to rob the countryside of much of its quietness, to make the country roads in the neighbourhood of great cities places of dust and racket, and of danger to village children. Touching the development of new suburban areas in London, there should be noted here a hopeful change in the evolution of towns—a change as yet in its initiatory stage, but possibly destined to bring about immense improvement in the conditions of life for the industrial and middle classes. It has shown itself in two **Garden Cities.** forms: the creation in rural districts of new "garden cities," and the clearance of insanitary areas in old towns and provision for the extension of such towns on definite plans for the preservation of open spaces. A pioneer of the new type of industrial city, Mr. Ebenezer Howard, devoted himself to the formation of a Garden City Association, and a limited liability company was started to acquire an estate at Letchworth, near Hitchin, which is laid out in separate factory and residential areas. This was the first "garden city," and its success from various points of view seems to be assured. Other schemes on residential lines have been carried out in the western and north-western suburbs of London—Ealing and Golder's Green, at Bournville, outside Birmingham, and at Port Sunlight, near Liverpool. The Housing and Town Planning Bill referred to on an earlier page was in two parts, the first dealing with rehousing in existing congested areas, and the second with town-planning; and the underlying principle throughout was the compulsory institution of housing and town extension, or town-planning, schemes by the local authorities, on lines approved in each case by the Local Government Board. The measure was a tardy fruit of the Royal Commission on Housing, of which the King, when Prince of Wales, was Chairman.

An invention which has had a most beneficial effect **The Pneumatic Tyre.** upon the lives of many thousands of people of the middle and poorer classes, and has, indeed, made the motor industry itself possible, is the pneumatic rubber tyre, which reduced to a minimum the labour of pedalling a bicycle and brought into being a type of machine which women and children, as well as men, could ride with ease. Though the added dangers of the streets of London and other great cities, due in part to growing congestion of the traffic and the introduction of motors, have checked bicycle riding in towns, the use of the bicycle in the country has extended enormously. The machines are now made so cheaply that quite poor people can acquire them. The bicycle, in fact, far more than the railway, has put an end to the isolation of the village. The motor bicycle is the latest development of the machine, and a satisfactory and inexpensive type is now in course of evolution.

It is not improbable, however, that in the next generation **Aviation.** it will be as much a matter of course to enter a flying machine and journey at will through the air as it now is to step into a motor car or mount a cycle. Many minds in England, as in other countries, are now working with increasing success in the invention of dirigible airships. Count von Zeppelin, a German, was the first to achieve marked success with a manageable air-going craft, and M. Blériot, a French aviator, was the first to cross the English Channel in a monoplane. The English Government have appointed a committee of experts whose duty it is to watch developments in this science, in so far as they bear upon military and allied problems, and the War Office have an aeronautical branch at work constructing experimental machines. But the sovereignty of the air has yet to be won by man.

Further conquest has been made over time and distance **Wireless Telegraphy.** by the perfection of the telegraph. In 1897 Signor Marconi, an Italian electrician, patented a method of transmitting messages without wires. This was adopted by the British Admiralty in 1900, and every man-of-war and every ocean-going vessel of the principal shipping lines is now fitted with a wireless installation. The Marconi stations in the United Kingdom were acquired by the Post Office in 1909, under

318—N.E.

conditions which preclude the growth of any monopoly in wireless telegraphy. Nearly every mailship that crosses the Atlantic now has a daily bulletin of intelligence and can communicate news of its own to other vessels with similar installations or to the shore. A daily business is done by the Marconi Company in wireless messages across the Atlantic, and the conditions of naval warfare and of life at sea in other respects have been profoundly modified.

X-Rays.   A discovery of incalculable utility in surgery and medicine was made in 1895 by Dr. Röntgen, of Wurzburg, who found that the invisible or X-rays could be used to photograph the bones and other dense tissues of the body. Apparatus for this purpose was extensively employed by surgeons during the South African War, with great advantage in the location and extraction of bullets. The discovery is now in general use throughout the hospitals of the world, not only for diagnostic but also for curative purposes. The Finsen light must also be mentioned in this connection, and with it radium, both of them marvellous additions to the healing resources of the medical profession.

We must not pass on to the last section of this chapter without recording the fact that the University of London has been reorganised as a teaching, instead of being merely an examining, institution, and that since the year 1900 it has been installed in the Imperial Institute Buildings at South Kensington.

Explora-   KNOWLEDGE of the earth has been greatly advanced during
tion.   the past quarter of a century, not in the discovery of regions unknown to Western civilisation, for none remain to be revealed, but in filling in the details of areas imperfectly known. Science and diplomacy have worked together; the labours of the geographer and those of the treaty-maker are inextricably intertwined. The partition of Africa and the other political events outlined in this chapter have been accompanied by innumerable expeditions, in which nearly all European nations have shared, to the enrichment of geographical knowledge. Boundary disputes in South America and their arbitral settlement have perfected knowledge of the Andean chain and

the river systems of the southern portion of the New World. The increasing accessibility of Central Asia has been proved by daring explorations in regions that had lain hidden for ages from alien eyes. Dr. Sven Hedin and Dr. Stein have in this sphere done notable work in revealing mountain ranges and desert tracts into which no European had ventured. Alike in the Arctic and the Antarctic, there have been continuous efforts to complete the work of earlier adventurers into Polar solitudes. Nansen, Cook, Scott, Peary, and Shackleton are names that have to be added to the roll of honour in this branch of endeavour. Commander Peary, of the United States Navy, left Sydney, Cape Breton, in the steamer *Roosevelt*, in July, 1908, and reached the North Pole on April 6th of the following year, the news being made known to the world on September 6th from Indian Harbour, Labrador. Dr. Cook, who was beforehand with his intelligence by seven days, claimed that he had reached the Pole on April 21st, 1908. Mr. Ernest H. Shackleton, a lieutenant in the Royal Navy Reserve, conducted a British Antarctic expedition which left New Zealand in the *Nimrod* on New Year's Day, 1908, and on January 9th, 1909, reached, by overland travel with sledges, latitude 88° 23' South. At this point the party were compelled to return because of the exhaustion of their provisions. With the knowledge and experience now available, there seems to be no doubt that the South Pole will sooner or later be reached, as the North Pole has been, and the only question is whether the first man to succeed in returning from it will be an Englishman, an American, or a Frenchman.

INDEX

Abdul Hamid, 976, 980
Abdullah, Khalifa, 938 *seq.*
Aberdeen, Earl of, as Foreign Minister,
164, 165; his Ministry (1853), 348, 352
Abyssinia and the Soudan, 938
Abyssin'an War (1868), 522, 569, 909
Adams, ohn Couch, 246
Adullam. s (1866), 579
Æsthetic .)vement, 860
Afghanistan, exploration, 90; relations
with (1841), 163, 174; war of 1873,
570; war of 1878, 531, 532; Penjdeh,
541
Africa, East, and Central, 949
Africa, exploration of, 908—918
Africa, South, Kaffir wars, 174; Boer
war (1880), 571; Zulu war, 571 *seq.*
See also South African War
Africa, West, 945 *seq.*
African Steamship Company, 462
Agricultural labourers' unions, 820
Agriculture (1802—1832), 102—115; (1832
—1846), 290—297; (1846—1865), 468—
484; (1865—1885), 805—814; effect of
French war on, 106; distress after
1815, 112; machinery, 108, 477; (1865—
1885), 811—813; chemistry applied to,
262, 264, 292, 483, 484, 813; distress
(1832—1836), 290 *seq.*; increase in product, 297; prosperity (1836—1876),
292; (1862—1872), 475; improvements,
476, 477; list of prominent agriculturists, 480 note; foreign competi-
tion, 806; decline of, 809; depression
after 1879, 806 *seq.*, 814; in Scotland,
878 *seq.*; acreage under wheat (1907),
1025; authorities, 151, 518
Ainsworth, W. H., 227
Alabama claims, 357, 525
Alaska boundary dispute, settlement
of, 986
Alaska, the, 463
Albert, Prince. *See* Prince Consort
Alford, Dean, 668
Allingham, Mrs., paintings by, 611
Alma-Tadema, Sir L, 615 *seq.*
Almack's, 132
Alpine Club, work in topography, 924
Althorp, Lord, his dge' (1833), 152
America, explorat of, 918—920
Ampère, André Mari and electro-mag-
netism, 252; and telegraphy, 783
Anæsthetics introduced, 442
Anchor Line, 462
Anglo-American Commission, 984
Anglo-German Treaty of 1890, 950
Anglo-Japanese Alliance, 990—992
Anglo-Russian Treaty, 993
Anglo-Saxon, study of, 674 *seq.*
Aniline dyes, 713 *se*
Animism, 680
Antarctic exploration, 899, 900, 1043

Anthropology, study of, 680
Anti-Corn Law League, 308
Archæology, classical, 666
Architects *c.* 1846, 393
Architecture (1815—1840), 234—239;
domestic, in late 19th century, 634;
in London, 1038
Arctic exploration, 892 *seq.*, 1043
Armenian atrocities, 975 *seq.*
Armitage, E., 401
Armstrong guns, 574 *seq.*
Army, the (1815—1854), 166—174; (1854—
1865), 360—370; (1865—1885), 557—573;
retrenchment, 167; recruiting, 169;
condition of soldiers, 169—171;
liberty of worship introduced in
(1839), 171; punishments, 172; shooting, 172; weapons, 172; in Crimean
War, 360—368; in Persia and
China, 369; Indian Mutiny, 370;
Volunteer movement, 370; education in, 173, 560 *seq.*; camps,
562; barracks, 562; medical service, 445 *seq.*; abolition of purchase, 525, 560; Cardwell's reforms,
557 *seq.*; short service, 558; strength
of, in 1885 and 1895, 559; position of
Militia, 559; localised corps, 559;
territorial system, 559; linked battalions, 560; reserves, 559 *seq.*, 564;
Volunteers and Yeomanry, 564; care
for the soldier, 369, 562 *seq.*; withdrawal from colonies, 565; tactics
and weapons, 566; authorities, 933;
reorganisation by Mr. Haldane, 1018
Arnold, Dr. Thomas, on the Church, 31;
and the Broad Church movement,
190; scholarship of, 664 *seq.*
Arnold, Matthew, poems of, 381—383
Art (1846—1865), 397—413; (1865—1885),
608—618; decorative, in 19th century, 618—639; "popularising" of,
635; domestic, in 1885, 639. *See also*
Painting
Ashanti War (1873), 526, 570; (1895—1896),
945 *seq.*
Ashley, Lord. *See* Shaftesbury
Asia Minor, travel in, 904, 906, 907
Asquith, H. H., Administration of, 1017
Association of ideas, 413 *seq.*
Astronomy (1815—1846), 239—248; (1846—
1885), 686—696; authorities, 934
Atlantic Cable, 787
Austen, Jane, 47
Australia, communication with, 457, 465,
466; military help from, 566; ex-
ploration of, 920—924; recent rela-
tions with Great Britain, 929—931;
created into a Commonwealth, 1008
Austria, relations with, 344, 349, 352
Authorities: Astronomy, 934; Agricul-
ture (1802—1846), 151; (1846—1885),

PRINTED BY CASSELL AND COMPANY, LIMITED, LA BELLE SAUVAGE, LONDON, E.C.